Himmler's Auxiliaries

· ·

VALDIS O. LUMANS

• •

Himmler's Auxiliaries

THE VOLKSDEUTSCHE MITTELSTELLE

AND THE GERMAN NATIONAL MINORITIES

OF EUROPE, 1933 – 1945

• •

THE UNIVERSITY OF NORTH CAROLINA PRESS

CHAPEL HILL AND LONDON

Library of Congress Cataloging-in-Publication Data

Lumans, Valdis O.

Himmler's auxiliaries : the Volksdeutsche Mittelstelle and the German national minorities of Europe, 1933–1945 / by Valdis O. Lumans.

    p. cm.

Includes bibliographical references and index.

ISBN 0-8078-6564-8

1. Nationalsozialistische Deutsche Arbeiter-Partei. SS-Hauptamt Volksdeutsche Mittelstelle. 2. Germans—Europe—History—20th century. 3. Germany—Population policy—History—20th century. 4. World War, 1939–1945—Evacuation of civilians. 5. National socialism. I. Title.

DD253.3.S68L86 1993   92-24080

369'.33104'09041—dc20   CIP

97 96 95 94 93   5 4 3 2 1

TO PATTY, ALEX, AND CHRISTINE

CONTENTS

• •

A C K N O W L E D G M E N T S

• •

I would like to express my gratitude to the many individuals at the following libraries and document repositories for their invaluable assistance: National Archives, Washington, D.C.; Bundesarchiv, Koblenz; Institut für Zeitgeschichte, Munich; Politisches Archiv, Auswärtiges Amt, Bonn; Berlin Document Center, Berlin; and the interlibrary loan staff of the Wilson Library at the University of North Carolina, Chapel Hill. I would also like to note the two faculty-exchange grants provided by the University of South Carolina, which helped me prepare this work for publication. My appreciation also goes to two colleagues, Paul Cimbala and Bob Botsch, whose advice, encouragement, and "PC" skills guided me to completion. I especially would like to acknowledge Gerhard L. Weinberg for reminding me over the years of my duty to get my study into print.

ABBREVIATIONS

• •

The following abbreviations are used in the text. For source abbreviations used in the notes, see page 263.

ADEuRST	Amtliche Deutsche Ein- und Rückwandererstelle
AO	Auslands-Organisation der NSDAP
APA	Aussenpolitisches Amt
BDO	Bund Deutscher Osten
BfE	Beratungsstelle für Einwanderer
DA	Deutsche Akademie
DAI	Deutsche Auslands-Institut
DNSAP	Dansk National Socialistik Arbejder Partiet
DP	Deutsche Partei
DUT	Deutsche Umsiedlungs-Treuhandgesellschaft
DVL	Deutsche Volksliste
DVR	Deutsche Volksgruppe in Rumänien
EWZ	Einwandererzentralstelle
GAB	German American Bund
HSSPF	Höhere SS- und Polizeiführer
JDP	Jungdeutsche Partei
KP	Karpathendeutsche Partei
KZ	Konzentrationslager
NSDAP	National Sozialistisches Deutsches Arbeiters Partei
RFSS	Reichsführer SS
RKFDV	Reichskommissar für die Festigung deutschen Volkstums
RSHA	Reichssicherheitshauptamt
RuSHA	Rasse und Siedlungs-Hauptamt
SA	Sturmabteilung
SD	Sicherheitsdienst
SDKB	Schwäbisch-Deutsche Kulturbund
SdP	Sudetendeutsche Partei
SHB	Schleswig-Holstein Bund
Sipo-SD	Sicherheitspolizei-Sicherheitsdienst

SS	Schutzstaffel
UDV	Ungarländischer Deutscher Volksbildungsverein
UTAG	Umsiedlungs-Treuhand Aktien Gesellschaft
VDA	Volksbund (Verein) für das Deutschtum im Ausland
VDU	Volksbund der Deutschen in Ungarn
VoMi	Volksdeutsche Mittelstelle
VR	Volksdeutscher Rat

Himmler's Auxiliaries

. . . .

Map 1. North Central Europe

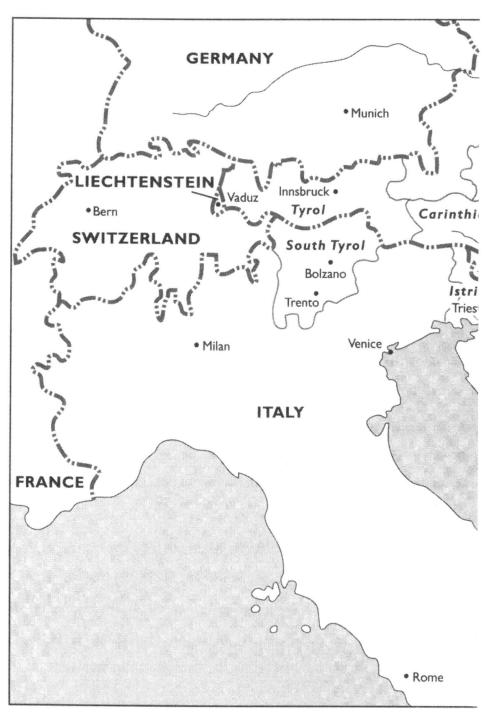

Map 2. South Central Europe

Map 3. Southeastern Europe

• •

As this book is going to print, events of enormous historical significance are sweeping Europe. One of the consequences of these developments is the reemergence of a phenomenon, nationalism, which since 1945 has more or less lain dormant. As postwar Europe split into two rival blocs, the respective members set aside historic differences in the interest of unity and security. Traditional national and ethnic rivalries either receded in importance as they gave way to efforts at integration, as was the case in the West, or were forcibly repressed, as in the case of the East. Nationalism had become an anachronism, relegated to the dustbin of recent history. Few regarded it as a vital force in a modern Europe, and few would have anticipated its resurgence.

But the East European revolutions, the reunification of Germany, and the disintegration of the Soviet Union have revived this dormant force. These developments have liberated and given free play to countless urges, including those based on ethnicity and national distinctions. Old ethnic animosities, especially in the east, repressed by Soviet force and ignored by Marxist ideology since 1945, have reappeared. Hungarians and Rumanians are resuming their ancient rivalry; Slovaks are questioning their relationship with the Czechs; Croats and Serbs have returned to the bloodletting of the war years. Over this arena of ethnic conflict and rivalries looms another historic presence, until recently laid low by the outcome of World War II but resurrected and magnified by the reunification of the two Germanies—a powerful, unified Germany in central Europe.

German reunification, occurring concurrently with the tumultuous changes in eastern Europe, raises once more the most important nationality question in central and eastern Europe in the twentieth century—what to do with the region's Germans, and what role they should play in the region. It also brings up the question of former as well as future relationships between Germany and eastern Europe. In a new relationship, past experiences will play a decisive role. Historically the contact between the peoples of eastern Europe and the Germans has been mixed, at times amicable and at other times hostile. More recent, twentieth-century, pre-1945 relations, however, can generally be characterized as an overbearing, nationalistic Germany trying to impose its dominance over its neighbors, through both economic control and direct rule resulting from aggressive expansionism.

The most recent effort to establish dominance was Hitler's drive to conquer this region as part of the *Lebensraum*—additional living space for the German people—needed for building a new, German-dominated racial order in Europe. As the peoples and states of eastern Europe reconsider their relations with the new, unified Germany, the memories of their experiences with Hitler's Germany loom large. As Czechs and Slovaks attempt to work out a viable partnership, the Czechs no doubt recall how the Third Reich had dismantled Czechoslovakia and then sponsored a separate Slovak state. The Serbs, as they resist the breakup of Yugoslavia and the granting of Croat independence, remember the German role in doing just that in World War II. The Croats also remember Germany's part, and it is no wonder they have courted German recognition for their separatism. As for the Poles, who benefited territorially at the expense of a defeated Germany, they are anxious about possible German demands for a frontier revision now that a guarantor of their postwar border, the Soviet Union, is gone and a more powerful, reunified Germany has arisen. After all, a resurgent Nazi Germany revised the post–World War I borders, which had been drawn favorably for Poland. And the Hungarians and Rumanians, as they renew their national disputes, no doubt recall how Germany forcefully imposed its mediation into their wartime disagreements. These and other memories will help determine the relationship between the new Germany and eastern Europe.

To better understand the relationship between Hitler's Third Reich and eastern Europe as a key to evaluating the course of present and future relations in the region, we need to examine the different dimensions of that earlier relationship. One dimension will be the focus of this study, the role of ethnic Germans, *Volksdeutsche*—as distinct from *Reichsdeutsche*, or Reich citizens—in the relationship between Hitler's Germany and the states and peoples of eastern Europe. An estimated 10 million *Volksdeutsche* lived throughout Europe, including all of the states of eastern Europe, as members of German national minorities and citizens of non-German states. They not only became vital considerations in the formal relations between the Reich and these states but also were important players in the day-to-day intercourse of the peoples of the region. They were participants—sometimes active, at times passive—in many of this area's nationality disputes and controversies. Understanding their wartime roles, experiences, and ultimate fates helps one comprehend the power of nationalism in the region as well as German–eastern European relations, both past and present.

This study will examine the German minorities within the context of Hitler's foreign policy as well as the context of the ideas, purposes, and policies of the man most directly responsible for determining their fate during this period, Heinrich Himmler, the Reichsführer SS (RFSS). After Hitler's appointment as Reich chancellor in January 1933, his Nazi cronies seized as rewards for loyalty and perseverance whatever spoils they could in the way of positions and titles. In this scramble for power, Heinrich Himmler was ultimately the most successful. With Hitler's blessings, he accumulated so many positions within both party and state that in time he emerged as the second most powerful man in the Third Reich.

Himmler's rise to prominence began in 1929, when Hitler appointed him Reichsführer SS, chief of the Schutzstaffel (SS), a special, elite party formation initially serving the Führer as a security force. After 1933, relying on the SS as a political base, Himmler collected other positions of power and staked out new areas of responsibility for the SS, which in turn created additional opportunities and strengthened his hand in the competition with fellow Nazis. In the process he became chief warden of the concentration camps and commander of Reich security—including chief of all German police. With the creation of special armed units within the SS, which eventually became the Waffen SS, he also challenged the exclusive right of the Wehrmacht, the official Reich military, to be the bearer of arms in the Third Reich. Each new position for Himmler, each new responsibility for the SS, enhanced his authority and helped him pursue even more titles and power.

But power was not an end in itself for Himmler. The titles and posts served a greater purpose—the creation of a new racial order, a new Europe, rebuilt on racial principles and under the leadership of an invigorated German nation and its Führer. The opportunity to realize his dreams came with the beginning of war in 1939, when Hitler, in order to eliminate points of friction in his partnership with the leader of the Soviet Union, Josef Stalin, decided to resettle *Volksdeutsche* from those parts of eastern Europe destined to fall to the Soviets according to the Nazi-Soviet Friendship and Non-Aggression Treaty of August 1939. Hitler charged Himmler with responsibility for the resettlement and allowed him to assume the lofty title of Reichskommissar für die Festigung deutschen Volkstums (RKFDV), translated as the Reich Commissioner for the Strengthening of Germandom. Whereas Hitler and most observers regarded the resettlement primarily as a matter of diplomatic necessity, Himmler considered it a chance to begin the construction of the new racial order.

In fulfilling his commission as RKFDV, and in launching the construction of the new order, Himmler relied on the SS as well as other institutions and organizations, such as the concentration camps and the police, which had become part of the wider SS system. He also utilized and exploited for his purposes groups and organizations from outside the formal SS system, among them the Volksdeutsche Mittelstelle (VoMi), which translates as the Ethnic German Liaison Office, and the *Volksdeutsche* themselves. These two entities, VoMi and the German national minorities, as Himmler's auxiliaries, will be the major subjects of this study. They will be considered together, within the context of the purposes and goals of the SS—as defined by Heinrich Himmler—and more broadly, within the context of the Third Reich's ideological and political imperatives, especially those of Hitler's foreign policy.

VoMi was a Nazi party organ founded in 1935 to centralize and coordinate all organizations and activities in the Reich dealing with the *Volksdeutsche*. Himmler gradually drew VoMi into the SS sphere through the calculated manipulation and placement of SS personnel in its leadership positions. Although he never formally incorporated it into the SS, with time it functioned as part of the SS, and contemporaries accepted it for all practical purposes as an SS organ. What interested Himmler in VoMi was its unique position as the primary intermediary between the Reich and the 10 million *Volksdeutsche* of Europe, a number comparable to the population of a medium-sized European state. Not only were these people a reservoir of political power, awaiting the claim of some ambitious Nazi, but they also could serve as a source of foreign intelligence for Himmler's rapidly developing security services. Eventually they would provide him with a pool of manpower for the Waffen SS, and with the start of the resettlement program, they became for him the vital element in building the new order— providing the racially pure German infusion needed to Germanize the conquered territories.

Examining VoMi and its dealings with the minorities provides insights into several significant historical issues. Regarding the Third Reich, this study takes yet another look at the nature of Hitler's system. Reviewing the struggle over who or what agency would control the *Volksdeutsche* reconfirms that the Third Reich was indeed a chaotic mix of overlapping jurisdictions and competing authorities. Hitler appears as the ultimate arbiter who preferred to let his lieutenants quarrel while he himself was preoccupied with his favorite pastimes, foreign affairs and, as of September 1939, waging war. From time to time, when their disputes required adjudication, he descended to settle the matter. Out of this administrative and jurisdictional morass Himmler and his SS emerged as the most effective and successful political force in Hitler's Reich.

A careful examination of the process by which Himmler drew VoMi into the SS system—first as an auxiliary and eventually as a de facto member— touches on several issues related to the SS and provides insights into its nature, purposes, and functioning. First, it reflects on Himmler's ability to compete successfully with other leading Nazis in the internecine power struggle. It also reveals quarrels within the SS. Different individuals and units, in pursuit of their own interests, clashed with one another, thereby tainting the conventional image of the SS as an organization of complete harmony and obedience. And a closer look at the personnel staffing VoMi contributes to a better understanding not only of the nature and purposes of the SS but also of the motivation and character of its individual members.

Reviewing VoMi's functions and purposes, specifically its role in the RKFDV project, also offers a glimpse into a neglected aspect of implementing the Nazi racial ideology. Rather than dealing with people deemed racially inferior, with non-Germans, and with the so-called enemies of the Reich—as did most other SS units—VoMi was mostly preoccupied with the German side of the Nazi racial equation, specifically the *Volksdeutsche*. However, although its part in building the new order was limited mostly to Germans, and although many of its activities could be regarded as social work, VoMi nevertheless pursued the ultimate goal of creating the new racial order, a goal it shared with other SS interests and units, including those responsible for the concentration camps and the extermination of non-Germans, in particular the Jews.

This is the first comprehensive study of the Volksdeutsche Mittelstelle, an organization vital in determining the wartime experiences of the *Volksdeutsche*. One reason for the neglect of this important Nazi office as a subject for historical research has been the wartime destruction of its archives by bombing. The lack of a consolidated, core collection of documents has discouraged some scholars from tackling VoMi as the focus of a research project. Three works, however, have dealt in considerable depth with certain aspects and activities of this organization. Hans-Adolf Jacobsen, in *Nationalsozialistische Aussenpolitik, 1933–1938*, presents an excellent, extensive study of the structure and functioning of the Nazi foreign policy apparatus, including those interests—among them VoMi— involved with the *Volksdeutsche*. His work is especially valuable for its coverage of the prewar activities related to the *Volksdeutsche* and the founding of VoMi. But since VoMi's activities went beyond the minorities in scope, and in time extended into the war years, Jacobsen's discussion of VoMi—although valuable—is incomplete.

Robert L. Koehl's *RKFDV: German Resettlement and Population Policy, 1939–1945; A History of the Reich Commission for the Strengthening of Germandom* covers VoMi's role and activities as a part of Himmler's RKFDV system. Koehl has updated this work and deals with the RKFDV as well as VoMi in a comprehensive study of the SS, *The Black Corps: The Structure and Power Struggles of the Nazi SS*. But the focus of both studies, as far as VoMi is concerned, is mostly limited to its place in the RKFDV system and its resettlement responsibilities. Koehl's works, valuable also for placing the *Volksdeutsche* within the context of the SS's racial ideology and practices, neglect VoMi's non-RKFDV activities with the minorities.

As for Himmler's other "auxiliary," the German minorities and their constituent *Volksdeutsche*, my study examines them within the scope of Hitler's foreign policy and of Himmler's dual efforts to establish the SS as the preeminent force in the Third Reich and to build the new racial order. Limited in scope, this study is not intended to be the definitive history of Europe's German minorities during the Nazi years. It does not examine in depth all aspects of their wartime experiences. But since it deals with every sizable German minority group in Europe and covers the period from 1933 through 1945, it is the broadest and most comprehensive treatment of the subject to date. Because of the language barrier—the impossibility of any one person mastering the languages of all the peoples in whose midst the *Volksdeutsche* lived—and because of the limited access in the host states to sources and documents related to the various German minority groups, it is doubtful that any one will ever produce a complete study, adequately covering every aspect of the *Volksdeutsche* experiences during the war years.

Studies of individual groups, such as Ronald M. Smelser's *The Sudeten Problem, 1933–1938: Volkstumspolitik and the Formulation of Nazi Foreign Policy* and Geza C. Paikert's *The Danube Swabians: German Populations in Hungary, Rumania, and Yugoslavia and Hitler's Impact on Their Patterns*, will therefore remain the norm. One exceptional and outstanding effort is that of Anthony Komjathy and Rebecca Stockwell, *German Minorities and the Third Reich: Ethnic Germans of East Central Europe between the Wars*, which thoroughly covers several minority groups. But as the title indicates, it is limited both geographically and in time.

My study will focus on the relations of the individual minority groups to the Third Reich, relations maintained and directed by VoMi and the SS, beginning in 1933 and following through to the end of the war. Among the issues included will be the individual roles of the minorities in Hitler's plans, determined initially by diplomatic and later by military necessity. Closely related is the question of whether the *Volksdeutsche* served the Reich as willing accomplices, as "Fifth Columns," or were instead Nazi victims themselves, caught up in tragic circumstances. Another topic for consideration is the process of "nazification," by which the *Volksdeutsche* were converted to National Socialism.

As VoMi extended its control over the minorities, and as Himmler gradually imposed his influence over this organization, the *Volksdeutsche* of Europe were also drawn into the SS net as auxiliaries, primarily as manpower for the growing Waffen SS and as the human building blocks for the new order. This study will pay particularly close attention to these two aspects of the *Volksdeutsche* experience. It would be VoMi's duty to sort out and balance different SS demands on the *Volksdeutsche*. In the process its leadership would become embroiled in disputes with the most powerful SS authorities, men such as chief Waffen SS recruiter Gottlob Berger and the head of the SS security apparatus, Reinhard Heydrich, over which SS interests had the highest priority.

One other important issue arising when examining the relationship between the minorities and the SS is their role in the implementation of the Nazi racial ideology. Although for Hitler the *Volksdeutsche* were primarily a foreign policy matter, for Himmler and the SS they also assumed ideological significance. As they were resettled from abroad to the Reich and its conquered territories, or as they were elevated as a privileged elite in their homelands during the war years, their experiences, and correspondingly those of non-Germans, dramatically illustrated the inherent connection between the two Nazi-defined classes of humanity, the ruling *Herrenvolk* and the "subhuman" *Untermensch*. As VoMi promoted the well-being of the *Volksdeutsche* as *Herrenvolk* and elevated them to a leading place in the new order, other units of the SS dealt with the non-German *Untermensch*, subjugating and even exterminating them. But both types of SS activities, VoMi's essentially welfare actions and the other units' atrocities against non-Germans, served Himmler's ultimate goal of building the new order and Germanizing the *Lebensraum*. Both activities would also affect subsequent German relations with the non-German peoples of Europe and would become part of the collective memory that will help determine the future of that relationship.

• •

CHAPTER ONE

Himmler and the *Volksdeutsche*

• •

HIMMLER

Near an iron trestle bridge, small groups of uniformed Germans stood waiting in the snow. Their field-gray overcoats harmonized with the low, overcast January sky. Halfway across the bridge spanning the frozen San River, near the ancient Polish town of Przemysl, was a figure dressed in brown and wearing a peaked cap with a small red star, marking him as a soldier in the Soviet Red Army and, at least for the time being, as an ally of the Germans. At the far end of the bridge stood a few other brown forms. These allies in gray and brown occasionally glanced at each other but otherwise displayed no signs of comradeship.

Four months earlier, in September 1939, Polish forces retreating from the German blitzkrieg had fled eastward across the San River, only to encounter a Red Army offensive from the opposite direction. Once the rout of the Poles was complete, the German and Soviet authorities decided on a final line of demarcation between their shares of Poland, using the San River as a section of the boundary. The bridge at Przemysl became a principal link between the Nazi and the Soviet conquerors.

At last the moment everyone had been waiting for had arrived. The gray coats jostled and scurried into positions prescribed by rank and protocol. Attention turned toward the Russian end of the bridge. Framed by its superstructure, there appeared, as from a time machine, a plodding horse hitched to a covered wagon, which was followed by another, and then another. These wagons, laden with every sort of imaginable baggage, from pots and pans to farming tools, were centuries and worlds apart from the tanks and dive bombers in whose wake the Germans had arrived on the banks of the San. As the lead wagon drew closer, one could make out the driver, a bearded, peasant-like character, bundled in a pile of blankets and furs. Thanks to the photographers present, this rustic fellow would soon appear in Reich newspapers and journals, alongside ads for the Dresdner Bank, Siemens electrical equipment, and Bayer aspirin.

Although contrasts dominated this scene, the new arrival and his welcomers had a few things in common. Prominently displayed on his wagon was a swastika, the same runic symbol decorating the uniforms of the waiting entourage. Another similarity was soon disclosed, language. From under the peasant's beard came a gruff "Unser Vater hat uns gerufen! Wir sind gekommen, nun sind wir da!!"[1] Some of the welcoming party were astonished to hear recognizable German coming from this strange character. But all, including a short, bespectacled man with a bit of a mustache—who was obviously the preeminent figure at this gathering—were delighted.

The prominent figure was none other than Heinrich Himmler, the Reichsführer SS who, as head of the Nazi Schutzstaffel (SS), chief of all German police, supreme warden of the concentration camp network, and commander of the rapidly expanding Waffen SS, was well on his way to becoming the second most powerful man in the Third Reich. In addition, by the time of this January 1940 rendezvous, Himmler had established himself the leading Reich authority in all racial matters and in the affairs of Europe's *Volksdeutsche*, ethnic Germans living outside the Reich as citizens of foreign states. It was in this latter capacity, specifically as Reichskommisar für die Festigung deutschen Volkstums (RKFDV), or Reich Commissioner for the Strengthening of Germandom, that Himmler had traveled to Przemysl from Berlin by way of Warsaw, Lublin, and Cracow to greet the arriving wagons.[2]

As for the driver of the lead wagon, he was one of some 10 million *Volksdeutsche* living in the non-German states of Europe as members of national minorities. This ethnic German, along with the drivers and passengers of the wagons following his, came from Volhynia, in eastern Poland. For reasons to be discussed later, in late September 1939 Hitler had decided to remove all Germans from those parts of eastern Europe he had conceded to the Soviet Union in the Nazi-Soviet Treaty of 23 August 1939. Since Volhynia lay in the Soviet sphere, the wagon driver, his family, neighbors, and anyone else claiming German status had seized the opportunity to resettle. Responsible for their resettlement was the Reichsführer SS. The Przemysl encounter with Himmler was a step on the peasant's way to a final relocation, either inside the Reich or, more likely, somewhere in its recently conquered territories.

The Volhynian resettlement was not the first, nor would it be the last, reshuffling of *Volksdeutsche*. But for Himmler, an incorrigible romantic with a penchant for histrionics and dramatic symbolism, the arrival of the Volhynian caravan was a significant occasion. He had staged the "homecoming" ceremonies as the symbolic culmination of two developments, both of great personal importance. First, the arrival of the wagons marked the realization of his personal worldview, one based on race and focused on the creation of a new, Germanic racial order. Second, it underscored his successful quest to become the foremost Reich authority in racial matters and to establish his organization, the Schutzstaffel, as the racial vanguard of National Socialism. This success helped secure his status as the second most powerful figure in the Third Reich and contributed to establishing the SS as the most formidable political force in the new Germany.

As one examines the first development, Himmler's ideological evolution, it is clear that fundamental to his views was the concept of *Volk*, the essential ingredient in Nazi racial doctrines. For once one distills the disparate collection of ideas, theories, and prejudices that constitute the Nazi worldview into a single principle, one is left with an obsessive preoccupation with the spiritual and biological welfare of the German *Volk*. In the minds of Nazi racists such as Himmler, the *Volk*, which has no direct English equivalent and translates best as people, or nation, was an indivisible, living organism composed of its individual members. All Germans, whether living within the Reich or abroad, belonged to this organic *Volk* body. Thus, to the true *völkisch* believer, such as Heinrich Himmler, the *Volksdeutsche* of Volhynia were as much a part of the *Volk* as any Reich German. Their arrival at Przemysl was a "homecoming" truly worth celebrating.

Although initially the *Volk* was a cultural concept, defined by criteria such as German language and heritage, for the Nazis it was racially determined. One could only be born into it, and by virtue of this biological fact, one was permanently bound to it. No artificial divisions, such as state frontiers, could divide the *Volk*. Another tenet essential to the *völkisch* idea was a proper environment—an idealized, preindustrial German countryside, a simple, rural setting close to the soil and far from the complex, modern, urbanized world. The *völkisch* faithful eulogized the peasant farmer as the source of regeneration and strength. In his early, developmental years, Heinrich Himmler had become an ardent believer in this *völkisch* ideal and incorporated it as a basic component in his personal philosophy.

Another element in Himmler's worldview was the conviction that all of humankind belonged to one of two racial categories, the *Herrenvolk*, the ruling people, and the *Untermensch*, or "subhumans." The *Herrenvolk*—which included Germans, along with other Germanic peoples such as Scandinavians—by virtue of their racial superiority were predisposed to rule, whereas the supposedly racially inferior *Untermensch* were fit either for servitude or extermination. But the *Herrenvolk* were not automatically guaranteed the superior position. Preordained conflict would determine a victor. Himmler postulated that "as long as men live on earth, there would always be a struggle between *Menschen* and *Untermenschen*."[3] And in order for the *Herrenvolk* to prevail, they would diligently have to protect and enhance their racial purity, by weeding out the inferior racial elements from the *Volk* while promoting the reproductive capacity of its higher quality members.

In translating this fantasy into real life, Himmler concluded that to promote the valuable racial component, the *Herrenvolk* would have to eradicate other races, in particular the Jews—in his mind the ultimate *Untermensch*. Correspondingly, the valuable German elements should be nurtured, by practicing total racial segregation within the main *Volk* body as well as by searching out and returning to the *Volk* all German blood living among alien peoples.[4] The Volhynian *Volksdeutsche* whom Himmler greeted at Przemysl were among the earliest to be salvaged for the racial good of the *Volk*.

Long before Przemysl, Himmler had systematically institutionalized his *völkisch* racial ideas in the SS. Under his leadership, which he assumed in 1929, the SS evolved as an elite order dedicated to promoting these racial principles. In this effort the SS eventually dealt with both the *Herrenvolk* and the *Untermensch*. It promoted the biological welfare of the German *Volk* while at the same time eliminating the allegedly harmful influences from the *Volk* body. In this purpose Himmler enjoyed the support of the Führer, who once had predicted that within a hundred years all of the German elites would be the progeny of the SS, since only the SS practiced proper racial selection.[5] It was also with the Führer's blessings that Himmler and the SS assumed the lead in working toward the ultimate goal of Nazi Germany, the building of a new European racial order, for which a racially pure German *Volk* would provide the nucleus. And it was because of this purpose of constructing the new order that the paths of the Reichsführer SS and the Volhynian peasant crossed at Przemysl. In Himmler's vision this peasant was to be one of the human building blocks for the new order. He and others would replace the *Untermensch* presently living in the conquered territories and would thereby help Germanize these lands.

By the winter of 1939–40, following the military victory over Poland, Himmler felt secure enough about his own political position within the Third Reich to begin building the new order. Indeed, his greeting of the Volhynian Germans at Przemysl might be considered a public curtain-raising for the project. The conclusion of this resettlement appeared to him an ideal occasion to provide the German public with a glimpse into the future. The rule of the *Herrenvolk* was at hand. By the tens of thousands the primitive peasantry, which the *völkisch*-minded had for so long romanticized, were arriving in the Reich and its conquered territories in trains, trucks, ships, and wagons. Although conspicuous anachronisms in the most industrialized and technologically advanced nation in Europe, they personified the simple preindustrial rural life the Nazis glorified. They also provided evidence of racial selection and purity. Surely from their beaming faces, which would soon appear in Reich journals and newspapers, one could surmise that the resettlers' racial vigilance and ties to the soil had paid off in spiritual and physical health. For Himmler, these peasants were a prototype of the generations of Germans to come.

• • THE *VOLKSDEUTSCHE*

Just as Himmler's ideological evolution and his rise to prominence in the Third Reich—more specifically, to his position as supreme authority in racial and *Volksdeutsche* matters—prepared his way to Przemysl, certain other developments had set the Volhynian peasant and his comrades on the road to this meeting. One was the changing image of the *Volksdeutsche* in the eyes of many Reich Germans. Another was their improving rank as a priority in the official concerns and policies of the new German Reich.

Europe's post–World War I German minorities, consisting of some 10 million *Volksdeutsche*, resulted from recent as well as more distant developments. Some minorities, such as the Baltic Germans of Estonia and Latvia and the Transylvania Saxons of Rumania, were the products of medieval conquests and colonization. Others, including the Volga Germans of Russia and the Swabians of the central Danube region, settled among non-Germans as recently as the eighteenth century. The drawing of modern state boundaries had also created German minorities, as statesmen and monarchs altered frontiers, traded lands at conference tables, and won or lost them on battlefields with no thought given to the nationalities of the inhabitants. As a result, by the beginning of the twentieth century, Europe, in particular central and eastern Europe, contained an inextricable mixture of nationalities, including the millions of *Volksdeutsche* living apart from the main body of Germans occupying the area formally known as Germany. The outcome of World War I exacerbated the nationality problem as Germans residing in territories taken from the German and Austrian empires joined those already living in non-German states.

Indeed, in the postwar period more Germans than any other Europeans lived as members of national minorities. One source estimated that in 1935, approximately 95,000,000 Germans inhabited the world. Of these, most resided in states with German majorities: 65,000,000 lived in the Reich; 6,500,000 in Austria; 2,950,000 in Switzerland; 400,000 in Danzig; 285,000 in Luxemburg; and another 10,000 in Liechtenstein.[6] Nearly 10,000,000 others, however, lived as members of national minorities. They included the *Volksdeutsche* of Czechoslovakia, 3,318,445; Poland, 1,190,000; Lithuania-Memelland, 100,000; Alsace-Lorraine, 1,500,000; Belgium, 70,000; Denmark, 30,000–40,000; Italy, over 200,000; Yugoslavia, 700,000; Hungary, 500,000; Rumania, 750,000; the Soviet Union, 1,240,000; and Latvia and Estonia, 80,000.[7]

In reference to the German minorities in the immediate postwar era, the term *Minderheit*, or minority, was most commonly used. It referred to all Germans residing within a state, for example, the minority in Poland. But this numerically defined term ignored the diversity of *Volksdeutsche* living within one state, and for many Germans it did not have enough of a *völkisch* ring. Therefore, as interest in the *Volksdeutsche* grew, this term gave way to another, *Volksgruppe*, which not only recognized the diversity of the Germans within a state but also appealed to rising *völkisch* sentiments. In common usage, the term *Volksgruppe* came to refer to a German minority within a state. But properly speaking, it more accurately referred to subgroups within each minority, each with its own political interests, social composition, and particular course of historical development. For instance, the minority in Poland consisted of six distinct groups of *Volksdeutsche*, or *Volksgruppen*.

In all, there were four categories of *Volksgruppen*, and several could compose one minority. The first consisted of those German communities located in territories separated from the Reich as a result of the postwar settlement. It included the Germans of North Schleswig in Denmark; the Memelland in Lithuania; Posen, West Prussia, Upper Silesia, and parts of East Prussia in Poland; the Hültschinerland in Czechoslovakia; Eupen-Malmédy in Belgium; Alsace and Lorraine in France; and Danzig. Another postwar loss, the Saar, was returned to Germany in 1935.

The second category included the Germans of the defunct Habsburg Empire, excluding those living in the reconstituted, predominantly German Austrian Republic. These were the Sudeten and Carpathian Germans of Czechoslovakia; the South Tyroleans and Kanaltalers of Italy; the Galician Germans in Poland; the Transylvania Saxons, Danube Swabians, and the Bukovina Germans of Rumania; the Swabians of Yugoslavia, along with former Austrians living in annexed parts of Carinthia, Carniola, and Styria; and the *Volksdeutsche* of Hungary.

The third group consisted of Germans who had never belonged either to the German Empire or the Habsburg crown. They included the Baltic Germans of Estonia and Latvia; the Lithuanian Germans; the *Volksdeutsche* of formerly Russian Poland; the scattered communities of the Soviet Union; and the numerous splinter groups dispersed throughout non-Habsburg southeastern Europe. The fourth category consisted of Germans living overseas, outside of Europe— the *Übersee* Germans.

Although many Germans had lived outside the Reich before the war, and although their existence had attracted the attention of some Reich Germans, in the postwar period, bitterness over the Reich's defeat and the real and imagined injustices of the settlement—including the forced separation of millions more Germans from the Reich and Austria—stimulated unprecedented Reich interest in all *Volksdeutsche*, of both older and more recent origin. Groups such as the Baltic Germans, who had never belonged to the Reich or Austria, benefited from the upsurge of interest in the recently separated Reich and Austrian Germans, the focus of irredentist and revisionist propaganda. Distinctions between the minority groups blurred in a growing number of Reich German hearts.

The new Weimar government, however, officially maintained the distinctions and formulated its policies toward the German minorities at least partly in view of their different origins. Furthermore, since the republic's foreign policy dictated its minorities policy, the latter was cautious and reserved, not actively supportive. Although Weimar statesmen sought ultimate revision of the Versailles settlement, initially they pursued the preliminary goal of reintegrating the Reich into the European state system, an effort that flagrant support for the minorities—which would be perceived as interference in the affairs of sovereign, foreign states—could undermine. Thus, in defending and promoting the interests of the minorities, the Weimar government mostly relied on the League of Nations minority protection system, a series of treaties and declarations of good intentions guaranteeing minority rights. By working through the League on minority issues, the Weimar government displayed a willingness to cooperate, an approach consistent with its overall foreign policy of fulfillment.

Because of increasing public awareness and the rising clamor about the plight of the minorities, it was difficult for Weimar statesmen to remain passive. Indeed, even though they openly advocated moral support and intercession at Geneva as the most appropriate and effective aid the Reich could provide the minorities, in fact, unseen to the public eye, Reich assistance was more substantive.[8] The most valuable aid was financial, for which the primary provider was the Deutsche Stiftung. Created in the early 1920s and funded by the Reich Foreign Ministry and the Prussian Ministry of the Interior, the organization supported Germans living in lands split off from Prussia. The Stiftung financed cultural activities, maintained German schools, and paid pensions to retired Reich officials living outside the Reich.[9] Another official but unpublicized financial source was Ossa, Vermittlungs- und Handelsgesellschaft mbH, later called Vereinigte Finanzkontore, which provided credit for *Volksdeutsche* businesses, industry, and agriculture.[10]

Despite good intentions and limited success, Weimar policy toward the minorities evoked mostly criticism, both from the *Volksdeutsche* abroad and their patrons inside the Reich. From the critics' perspective, the government's efforts alleviated some difficulties and solved some incidental problems but did little to alter the status of the minorities. They saw compliance with the democratic principles of majority rule and reliance on the League's minority protection system as resignedly accepting minority status for the *Volksdeutsche*.

A flood of literature lamenting the loss of German land and *Volk* reinforced demands for a more active approach to the minority issue. Countless books and pamphlets publicized the allegedly wretched existence of the *Volksdeutsche* and bemoaned the injustice of the territorial settlements. *Völkisch* writers bombarded the public with slogans such as "*Volksdienst ist Gottesdienst*."[11] According to them, the Germans living outside Germany remained full members of the *Volk*, in which—contrary to Weimar's official policies differentiating between former Reich citizens and other *Volksdeutsche*—all Germans were of equal value.

Aiding the cause of the *Volksdeutsche* were numerous private organizations and interest groups. The most important was the Verein für das Deutschtum im Ausland (VDA). Its purpose was to maintain and strengthen the culture of the German communities outside the Reich, especially by financing and staffing their German schools. During the Weimar years the VDA cooperated closely with the government in distributing both private and state funds, such as those of the Deutsche Stiftung.[12] These essentially cultural activities were collectively called *Volkstumsarbeit*, or work for maintaining the *Volkstum*, the Germanness of the *Volksdeutsche*. Indeed, the entire range of activities supporting and nurturing the minorities, not only culturally but also politically, was commonly referred to as the "*Volkstum* field."

Another type of Reich establishment engaged in *Volksdeutsche* matters was the research institute. Financed by private funds as well as government subsidies and grants, these think tanks brought together academicians and experts from various areas of *Volkstum* studies. They served not only as research institutes, archives, and libraries but also as centers of *Volkstumspolitik* (the politics of "Germanness") and intrigue. They frequently associated themselves with prominent and influential patrons. The foremost of these institutes were the Deutsche Auslands-Institut (DAI) in Stuttgart and the Deutsche Akademie (DA) in Munich, which was closely associated with the renowned geopolitician Karl Haushofer.

The proliferation inside the Reich of organizations and individuals supporting the *Volksdeutsche* cause led to duplication, inefficiency, and confusion. The Weimar government made several attempts to bring some order out of this chaos, but with little success. Conditions abroad, within the minorities, were no better. Each minority was rent with factionalism and dissension, and hardly any had developed a single policy defining their relationship with either the Reich or their own state. *Volksdeutsche* factions sought patrons in the Reich, and Reich interests competed for clients within the minorities. Consequently, intrigues and bickering plagued the *Volkstum* field during the Weimar period.

In the immediate postwar years, the need for *völkisch* unity was not yet urgent as most European states, in particular the new ones, caught up in the euphoria of nation building, mostly abided by their commitments to preserve minority rights. But when national independence failed to meet lofty expectations for improving the lot of the previously repressed majority nationalities, many regimes, under pressure from chauvinistic segments of the public, began imposing cultural assimilation on their minority nationalities. Measures such as curtailing the autonomy of minority schools, suppressing the use of nonmajority languages in official business, and even forcibly changing family names to majority language equivalents became the order of the day.

Efforts to coerce national minorities into the mainstream of national life also affected their economic being. The primary threat to several German minorities was land reform. Usually reform broke up all large landholdings, not just German property. But in states where a high proportion of large landowners were Germans, such as the Baltic States and Czechoslovakia, agrarian reform struck at a minority's economic foundation. Even in states where land reform was not as severe, as in Poland, or where it was nonexistent, as in Denmark, the authorities nevertheless pressured German landowners to sell out to majority nationality farmers, thereby eroding the German hold on the countryside. Only financial support from the Reich, through agencies such as Ossa, enabled many German farmers to retain their land. Likewise this support protected countless German businessmen and industries from official, as well as popular, ethnically based discrimination.

As official policy abroad became more intolerant, and as the non-German authorities became less inclined to respect minority rights, relations between the German minorities and their host states deteriorated. Consequently, by the late 1920s, *völkisch* unity had become more urgent, and the *Volksdeutsche* increasingly looked for relief beyond their own resources to the Reich. In response, demands for greater official concern on behalf of the minorities grew more vocal in the Reich.

In many states, the European-wide economic depression of the early 1930s exacerbated the swelling animosity toward *Volksdeutsche*, who often appeared to be weathering the crisis better than the rest of the nation. The general atmosphere of ethnic distrust intensified, and the gap between the *Volksdeutsche* and their fellow non-German citizens widened. As the situation worsened, an increasing number of *Volksdeutsche* began paying closer attention to a movement inside the Reich, one that seemed to offer hope for a new approach to the issue of minorities—National Socialism. Meanwhile, neighboring states watched the rise of this same movement with trepidation. With popular anti-German feelings mounting, these governments, fearing the spread of revanchist National Socialism within their German minorities, further limited minority rights and activities.

As National Socialism gained popularity in the Reich, pro-Nazi sympathies became more pronounced among the *Volksdeutsche*, some of whom founded local Nazi cells. Many other activists, aroused by developments in the Reich but not entirely seduced by National Socialism, supported another movement, informally known as the *Erneuerungsbewegung*, the movement of regeneration.

Although it shared many features and ideas with National Socialism, including a *völkisch* base, the *Erneuerungsbewegung* had indigenous roots abroad and was not a Reich export. Like National Socialism, it appealed especially to younger *Volksdeutsche*, who challenged their leaders to take firmer, less compromising stands against their state governments. Indeed, in the early 1930s it enjoyed far more support and influence within the minorities than did National Socialism. One must keep in mind throughout that neither National Socialism nor even the *Erneuerungsbewegung* appealed to all *Volksdeutsche*. Considerable numbers professed more liberal, even socialist, political doctrines and remained loyal to their states. There was also, as in most polities, a relatively indifferent, apolitical mass in the center, a *Volksdeutsche* "silent majority," which left politics to the leadership and the activists and accepted the political flow passively, wherever it might take them.

In the long run, however, National Socialism wielded the most influence among the *Volksdeutsche*. Rather than swallowing National Socialism whole, individual *Volksdeutsche*, like Reich Germans, more often than not found certain aspects of it to their liking. The single element in National Socialism most appealing to them was revisionism, Hitler's avowal to destroy the postwar settlement, which many of them held responsible for their continued minority status.

Another attractive feature of National Socialism was its *völkisch* nature, especially since the *Volksdeutsche* based their efforts to maintain ethnic identity and exclusivity on the premise of the indivisibility of the *Volk*. In the midst of alien peoples, they had adhered to this principle for generations, faithfully nurturing their language and culture. Furthermore, the Nazi racial doctrine, which regarded the mixing of races as the most reprehensible violation of the *Volk*, seemed to justify what they had been practicing for generations. And Nazi panegyrics lauding the historic German role in the East as an outpost of civilization and a barrier against barbaric Asiatic intrusions revitalized their sense of mission and strengthened their resolve to maintain their ethnic distinction.[13] Most *Volksdeutsche* could also appreciate the antimodern bias of National Socialism. Particularly distasteful to many were the political manifestations of modernism—political liberalism and democracy. After all, liberal democracy was of little use to a numerical minority, since majority rule and national self-determination relegated them to perpetual minority status. Besides, pluralistic, parliamentary rule seemed to promote divisiveness rather than *völkisch* unity.

Many *Volksdeutsche* were also quite comfortable with the antiindustrial and antiurban biases of National Socialism. Since the vast majority were small farmers, the glorification of peasants and their ties to the soil was very attractive. In fact, the Nazi obsession with the peasantry and the soil was better attuned to the mostly rural *Volksdeutsche* than to the predominantly urban Reich Germans. Whereas the Reich had a shortage of primitive, unspoiled peasants who could serve as a source of spiritual and biological rejuvenation, the minorities had plenty of this commodity, as demonstrated by the Volhynian resettlers. Even urban *Volksdeusche*, engaged mostly as merchants, professionals, tradesmen, and bureaucrats, in general were not closely associated with the "evils" of modern industrialization. With the exception of those living in the industrial areas of Czechoslovakia and Poland, relatively few *Volksdeutsche* were employed in industry, either in management or as workers.

Nazi economic ideas also looked good to many *Volksdeutsche*. The emphasis on *völkisch* cooperation as an alternative to capitalist competition was already manifest in the agricultural cooperative movements popular with many *Volksdeutsche* farmers. German farmers, particularly in Yugoslavia, Rumania, and Denmark, experienced the success that economic cooperation based on *völkisch* unity could bring. *Volksdeutsche* in other sectors of the economy, in the trades and professions, also organized themselves according to the common denominator of Germanness.[14] They knew that by banding together, they could more easily overcome discrimination, whether public or official.

The Nazi racial antipathy toward non-German nationalities was also well received among the *Volksdeutsche*. Although the racial dimension was new, anti-Semitic as well as anti-Slavic prejudices were not. Many of the *Volksdeutsche* of eastern Europe, particularly those living in the "Jewish Pale" of southern Russia, eastern Poland, and northern Rumania, were probably more anti-Semitic than the average Reich German. *Volksdeutsche* farmers traditionally regarded Jewish middlemen as their exploiters. Although *Volksdeutsche* anti-Semitism was culturally or even economically founded, there was little reluctance to accept it in the new, racial terms. Anti-Slavism also assumed a more virulent form when presented as racist rhetoric. Another theme prominent in the collective *Volksdeutsche* mentality was anticommunism. Many *Volksdeutsche*, particularly in the Baltic States, Poland, Hungary, and of course the Soviet Union, had experienced bolshevism firsthand and had consequently developed a passionate anticommunism.

Overall, National Socialism appealed to the same types of people and for many of the same reasons within the minorities abroad as it did in the Reich. One might cautiously conclude that National Socialism was even more attractive to the average *Volksdeutscher* than to his Reich counterpart. In testimony to the popularity of Nazism among the *Volksdeutsche*, countless *völkisch* writers heaped lavish praise on the movement, lauding it as a source of regeneration for the *Volksgruppen*.[15] One enthusiast commemorated 30 January 1933, the day Hitler assumed the Reich chancellorship, as the day the *Volk* finally assumed its rightful, preeminent place in all Reich activities and considerations. He also boasted that Strassburg was not a French city but was a German city in France and that Eger, Reichenberg, and Troppau were not Czech cities but were German cities in Czechoslovakia.[16]

Although most *Volksdeutsche* activists and publicists enthusiastically welcomed the new regime, the leading Nazis did not always respond in kind. Contrary to their unceasing talk of the sacred, inviolable ties of the *Volk*, some of the most prominent Nazis, once in power, were not uniformly brotherly. The worst offender was Hitler himself. Since he was an Austrian, and by some definitions a *Volksdeutscher*, one might presume him sympathetic, but this was not always the case. His opinions were not always favorable. Indeed, they were often ambivalent and contradictory, as his feelings toward the Baltic Germans illustrated. At times he praised them for their historic accomplishments and credited them for creating and ruling the Russian state.[17] But at other times he expressed impatience with their arrogance and their talk of titles and former glories.[18]

A few leading Nazis were, however, quite partial to the *Volksdeutsche*. Rudolf Hess, deputy Führer and head of the Nazi party structure, had been born in Egypt and sympathized with their cause. Another notable Nazi interested in these people was a Baltic German from Estonia, Alfred Rosenberg, who was regarded by some—especially himself— to be the authoritative party ideologue. And then there was Heinrich Himmler, who took all *völkisch* matters seriously. Although he had very little to do with *Volksdeutsche* before the mid-1930s, and although hardly any evidence reveals his early attitude toward them, one may safely presume that in his *völkisch* mind, the *Volksdeutsche* were no more or no less a part of the *Volk* than were Reich Germans.[19] And by the time of the Przemysl homecoming, few in the Third Reich could match his interest in, or authority over, the *Volksdeutsche*.

CHAPTER TWO

Founding the

Volksdeutsche Mittelstelle

The ceremonies at Przemysl also commemorated Himmler's successful quest to become the preeminent Reich authority in all *Volksdeutsche* matters. Before his encounter with the Volhynian *Volksdeutsche* and before enlisting them as auxiliaries to serve SS purposes, he had already extended his personal authority over them. An important early step in this process was centralizing control over the myriad of groups and individuals inside the Reich promoting the *Volksdeutsche* cause. Himmler did not initiate the process but rather discovered it in progress and directed it to its conclusion and to his advantage. His principal instrument in this effort was an office from outside the SS, a Nazi party organ, the Volksdeutsche Mittelstelle (VoMi), translated as the Ethnic German Liaison Office. Several of its high-ranking officials shared with Himmler the shivering wait in the snow at Przemysl. They also had in common the same gray SS uniforms as the Reichsführer SS.

THE *GLEICHSCHALTUNG*

Most Germans interested in *Volksdeutsche* matters welcomed the Nazi assumption of power in January 1933. Frustrated with the personal rivalries, the duplication of efforts, and the jurisdictional disputes plaguing the *Volkstum* field, they expected the new regime to take immediate, firm control. But the first steps the Nazis took only made things worse. Since few Nazis had taken an active interest in the *Volksdeutsche* before 1933, this field presented new opportunities for Hitler's ambitious colleagues—especially for those interested in racial and *völkisch* matters and foreign affairs. As several of them began staking their claims, the *Volkstum* arena reflected the general condition of the Third Reich, an organizational nightmare of jealous personal rivalries, overlapping authorities, and duplication of labor and resources.

At the Reich level, Hitler contributed directly to the confusion by breaking down institutional structures, ignoring established procedures for running the state, and in general personalizing the system. He also condoned the encroachment of the party on the prerogatives of the state. After all, the Nazi faithful, who fancied themselves experts in some favorite field, expected to receive appropriate posts as reward for their years of struggle. Since there simply were not enough positions to go around, Hitler readily approved the creation of new ones without much concern for the consequences.

As the ultimate mediator, Hitler tolerated the anarchy he helped create, especially in areas that held little interest for him. In his dual capacity as Führer and Reich chancellor, he towered above the disputes, aware that his subordinates depended on him to settle their differences. He applied this same approach to minority matters, attending to this area only when it became absolutely necessary. He distanced himself from its quarrels and avoided associating himself with any individual or group, even declining the numerous honorary titles and chairmanships offered him by various organizations.[1] He probably would have preferred to ignore the minority issue altogether, but one of his most publicized themes had been his concern for the unity of the *Volk*. After all, he had enticed many followers with promises to revise the Versailles settlement and solve the problem of German minorities.

The minority issue forced itself on Hitler. The success of National Socialism had aroused activists among the *Volksdeutsche*, whose enthusiasm frequently led to unpleasant incidents abroad with the potential to complicate or even upset Hitler's foreign policy plans. Therefore, not only was it politically expedient at home to take action in this area, but the unmanaged situation abroad, if allowed to continue, could adversely affect his favorite domain, foreign policy. Strict control over the *Volksdeutsche* as well as over their sympathizers inside the Reich became imperative. In the prewar years it was political expediency, not *völkisch* concerns, that guided Hitler's actions regarding the minorities.

Extending Nazi control over *Volkstum* activities became part of the *Gleichschaltung*, the coordination process adapting all German institutions and organizations to National Socialism. It proceeded as both a redirection of purposes toward Nazi ends and as personnel changes placing Nazis or Nazi sympathizers in leadership positions. Nazis staking claims in *Volkstum* matters had to tread cautiously. Not only were they touching on diplomatically sensitive matters, closely scrutinized by foreign governments for outside interference with their citizens, but they were also mixing in the factional arena of minority politics. Although within the minorities some individuals advocated National Socialism and openly courted Nazi patronage, the established leaders, who controlled the local minority organizations and enjoyed the confidence of the majority of the *Volksdeutsche*, usually maintained close ties to the so-called traditionalists in the Reich—non-Nazi, *völkisch*-minded conservatives. To make headway with the minorities, interested Nazis at least initially had to find some grounds for accommodation with the traditionalists at home and the established leaders abroad.[2]

As for the "traditionalist" *Volkstum* leaders, facing the prospects of inevitable coordination of their organizations, some initiated their own *Gleichschaltung*. They hoped to preclude, or at least temporize, a Nazi-directed effort. The Verein für das Deutschtum im Ausland, the foremost Reich organization promoting the cause of the minorities abroad, tried to ingratiate itself with the new regime by altering its leadership and promoting a more activist image. The subsequent fate of the VDA and the events surrounding its eventual loss of independence offer not only insights into the politics of the *Volkstum* field but also a microcosmic view of a larger development occurring during the *Gleichschaltung*—the shifting relationship between the Nazis and the conservative nationalists, from a partnership to complete Nazi dominance.

The VDA changed its name to the more *völkisch*-sounding Volksbund für das Deutschtum im Ausland, discarded its democratic procedures, and then reached into its activist ranks to select the conservative, non-Nazi *Volkstumskämpfer* (veteran of the *Volksdeutsche* struggle abroad) Hans Steinacher as its new leader.[3] Steinacher and most of the VDA leadership were amenable to compromise with the Nazis and perceived little difference between their own principal goal and that of the Nazis—the welfare of the German *Volk*. Since little but style and methods differed, or so thought the VDA people, they, like many conservatives and nationalists during the first years of Nazi rule, expected the responsibility of office to moderate the Nazis. In return for its obsequious compliance, the VDA received a stamp of approval from Deputy Führer Rudolf Hess, whom Hitler, shortly after coming to power, appointed the foremost Reich authority in the affairs of *Auslandsdeutsche*—all Germans living abroad, Reich Germans as well as *Volksdeutsche*.[4] At least for the time being, the VDA had evaded coordination.

Despite having reached what appeared to be a favorable arrangement for the VDA, Steinacher was dismayed that Hitler seemed to care nothing for the VDA nor even much more for the *Volksdeutsche*.[5] He was not far from wrong. Hitler's primary interest in the *Volksdeutsche* was to control them in order to keep them from complicating his foreign policy. As for the VDA, for the time being its autonomy served him well. His apparent reluctance to interfere in its activities abroad—essentially cultural, and tolerated by most states—demonstrated to anxious foreign governments the Reich's reserve on the minority issue. It seemed that Hitler's policy toward the minorities was not appreciably different from that of the Weimar government. In addition, by allowing the VDA to continue its activities without ostensible interference from either party or state, Hitler was faithfully honoring his partnership with the non-Nazi conservatives and nationalists, who initially supported his regime wholeheartedly.

While the VDA was coordinating itself, other nonparty interests were trying to reorder and centralize *Volkstum* affairs. As of 1933, however, any hope for success lay with the party, that is, with Hess. Hess was at first indifferent to the effort, but in September 1933, with some prodding from Karl Haushofer, his former professor and head of the Deutsche Akademie, he consented to the creation of the Volksdeutscher Rat (VR), a coordinating body consisting of representatives of various *Volkstum* organizations. Since the VR received no enforcement authority, it was doomed from the start.[6] Even with Hess's backing, the mostly non-Nazi, conservative VR leadership did not have sufficient clout to force its will on powerful Nazis encroaching on this field.

The impotence of the VR, indeed of the traditionalists on the whole, soon became evident in a struggle over the VDA. With the self-imposed alterations barely in place, several Nazis launched forays against the VDA. The most serious attack came from the party's foreign affairs system, in particular the Auslands-Organisation der NSDAP (AO). The AO served as the liaison organization between the Nazi party and Reich citizens living abroad and was deeply involved in those clandestine, subversive activities attributed to "fifth columns." Although its director, Wilhelm Bohle, denied all charges of illegalities, its activities went beyond sponsoring beer evenings and celebrating Oktoberfests. It emerged as a center for foreign espionage and the export of Nazi influence.[7] The AO publicly insisted that its activities were limited to Reich Germans and had nothing to do with German citizens of other states—the *Volksdeutsche*. But for his own purposes, Bohle interpreted the ambiguous term *Auslandsdeutsche* to include *Volksdeutsche* as well as Reich Germans.[8]

Another assailant was Alfred Rosenberg and his Aussenpolitisches Amt (APA), an office within the NSDAP whose purpose was to help the Foreign Ministry formulate foreign policy.[9] Rosenberg, a *Volksdeutscher* from Estonia, not only fancied himself the party's master ideologue but also had set his sights on the Foreign Ministry. When it became clear that Hitler would by-pass him for the ministerial post, he settled for creating the APA, which seemed to guarantee him a place in making foreign policy. By virtue of his proclaimed expertise in foreign affairs and his *Volksdeutsche* background, Rosenberg also tendered a claim to authority in *Volkstum* matters.

Yet another rival was Joachim von Ribbentrop, who was to become Reich foreign minister in 1938. Ribbentrop based his claim on his self-styled expertise in foreign affairs, which he had acquired as an international wine and spirits merchant. His qualifications were his international business and social contacts, his command of both French and English, and his cosmopolitan demeanor, which impressed the provincial Adolf Hitler. Above all, Ribbentrop had the knack for espousing Hitler's foreign policy principles as his own, thereby leaving the Führer with the impression that the two saw eye to eye on many foreign issues.[10]

Ribbentrop gradually displaced Rosenberg as Hitler's principal foreign policy adviser, or rather, echo. Hitler first appointed Ribbentrop a special armaments expert and then in November 1934 assigned him to Hess's staff as Beauftragter für Aussenpolitische Fragen im Stab des Stellvertreters des Führers (Plenipotentiary for Foreign Policy Questions on the Staff of the Deputy Führer). Then in June 1935 Hitler named him special ambassador at large, under the nominal authority of the foreign minister. With his accumulation of both NSDAP and Reich titles, Ribbentrop organized his own office, the Dienststelle Ribbentrop, located across the street from the Foreign Ministry.[11] The Dienststelle combined party and state functions and exemplified the numerous quasi-state, semiparty offices so common in the Third Reich. Its ambiguous nature facilitated Ribbentrop's meddling in all areas of foreign affairs, including minority matters.

The claimants to turf in *Volkstum* affairs formed alliances. It would be through one of these that Heinrich Himmler became involved in *Volksdeutsche* affairs. One of the most important of these partnerships was between Ribbentrop, the ambitious, self-proclaimed foreign policy expert, and Himmler, chief of the SS. Without his own constituency in the NSDAP, Ribbentrop allied himself with a powerful force that could support him against Nazi rivals such as Bohle and Rosenberg. After Ribbentrop became foreign minister, Himmler exacted a price for his support in the way of increased SS influence within the Foreign Ministry. Ribbentrop complied by encouraging, even pressuring, his subordinates to join the SS. Himmler thereby gained entry for the SS into the exclusive enclave of the Foreign Ministry. It was prestigious for the SS to have many of the Reich's highest diplomats dressed in its black uniforms.[12]

The Himmler and Ribbentrop alliance first emerged as a force to be reckoned with in a quarrel with the AO chief, Bohle. When Bohle turned a covetous eye toward the VDA, claiming that his commission to deal with *Auslandsdeutsche* extended to *Volksdeutsche*, Ribbentrop, although not particularly interested in the *Volksdeutsche* or in defending the VDA, perceived a threat to his authority in the area of foreign policy and challenged Bohle. Bohle was not the only Nazi who found the VDA attractive. Several others, including Rosenberg, sought to appropriate its authority and influence for themselves. Especially lucrative were the funds it controlled for *Volksdeutsche* cultural programs.[13]

Hess, nominally the supreme authority in this matter, vacillated between allowing the VDA to continue in its independent ways and placing it under Nazi control. Eventually he came down on the side of the party and the AO. Above all he needed to strengthen his position within the NSDAP, for he could already perceive the presence of Martin Bormann as a rival. Siding with the VDA and its conservative supporters against the AO could only weaken his position within the party. Consequently, in October 1934, he appointed Bohle as the liaison man between his staff and the VR, thus making the AO chief next in the chain of command in *Volksdeutsche* matters and thereby superior over the VR and the VDA.[14]

But Bohle's ascendancy was short-lived. His authority over all *Auslandsdeutsche*—as chief of the AO and as the party's liaison with the VR—evoked the jealousy of others, including Ribbentrop, one of the few Nazis with a seat on the board of directors of the VR. Ribbentrop resented Bohle's growing influence in foreign affairs, an area he regarded as his own bailiwick.[15] Of special significance is the fact that Ribbentrop's entry into the fray indirectly brought in another combatant, his friend and ally Himmler. Although it appears that Himmler played no active role in the early stages of this contest, it undoubtedly whetted his appetite for *Volkstum* affairs and turned his thoughts to future possibilities.

Ribbentrop, in league with Haushofer, convinced Hess that Bohle had to be curbed, and in mid-July 1935 the deputy Führer ordered the AO to limit its activities to Reich Germans residing abroad and non-European *Volksdeutsche*, with the exception of American Germans. The latter, along with European *Volksdeutsche*, would be the responsibility of the VDA and the scarcely breathing VR. Hess also expressed his intention to create a new party liaison post for *Volksdeutsche* matters, which he did sometime in October. He chose as its director Otto von Kursell, who possessed two crucial qualifications: influential connections within both the NSDAP and the *Volkstum* movement.[16] Also significant was Kursell's membership in the SS.

• • THE BÜRO KURSELL

Kursell's office was at first referred to as the Volksdeutsche Parteidienststelle, but with time it was simply called the Büro Kursell. As early as March 1936 it was occasionally referred to as the Volksdeutsche Mittelstelle.[17] Its most important feature was its status as a party office. Although the Büro was charged with coordinating all activities related to the *Volksdeutsche*, Kursell did not overestimate his authority, nor did he have unreal expectations and ambitions. He limited his activities to *Volkstumsarbeit* and tried to avoid party squabbles. He maintained good relations with Ribbentrop and Hess on the party side, with the ministries on the state side, and with the minorities themselves as he attempted to unify their feuding factions and form legitimate centers of authority for the Reich to recognize. His office also worked closely with Ossa and the Deutsche Stiftung in the economic affairs of the minorities. Above all, the Büro was to avoid even a hint of Reich involvement in the internal affairs of foreign states.[18]

Kursell's authority also extended to *Volkstum* organizations inside the Reich, in particular the VDA. Although he protected the VDA from party interference, there could be no doubt that he regarded Nazi interests as supreme and those of the *Volkstum* organizations, or even the *Volksdeutsche*, as incidental. For instance, at a meeting in March 1936, Kursell decided not to bail out a financially strapped *Volksdeutsche* newspaper because its editorial stance was not sympathetic enough with National Socialism.[19] He set a precedent, making funding of *Volkstumsarbeit* conditional on a positive attitude toward National Socialism. In short, through this new post, Kursell continued the *Gleichschaltung* at home and initiated the "Nazification" of the minorities abroad.

And perhaps most important, Kursell's appointment facilitated Himmler's entry into the *Volkstum* arena. Himmler, accustomed to seizing every chance to enhance his own standing within the Third Reich, exploited Kursell's membership in the SS to his own advantage. At some point it must have occurred to Himmler that the Büro, directed by an SS subordinate, could become a channel of influence to the minorities. It is impossible to ascertain exactly when and precisely why Himmler decided to step into the *Volkstum* arena, but several considerations must have played a part in his decision.

Himmler's most important consideration was probably political. Extending his authority over the estimated 10 million *Volksdeutsche* of Europe—equivalent in number to the population of a medium-sized European state—would strengthen his position within the Reich. They would provide him another power base, to go along with the SS, the Reich security system, the growing concentration camp network, and the developing armed SS units, the future Waffen SS.

The *Volksdeutsche* could also serve Himmler in two other ways, as sources of foreign intelligence for the SS security system and as manpower for the armed SS units. Responsible for enlightening Himmler on using the *Volksdeutsche* as a source of foreign intelligence was his dynamic and powerful subordinate Reinhard Heydrich, whom many contemporaries considered the real force within the SS.[20] Heydrich had already convinced Himmler of the importance of the Sicherheitsdienst (SD) as a foreign intelligence operation that could project SS influence abroad. The *Volksdeutsche*, many of whom were eager to serve the Reich, could be enlisted for this cause.[21]

The second consideration, utilizing the *Volksdeutsche* as manpower for the future Waffen SS, was not a compelling reason in the prewar years, since voluntary Reich enlistments more than filled its needs. But with the outbreak of war, the Waffen SS needed numbers of recruits far beyond the quotas of Reich Germans the Wehrmacht allotted it. Nonetheless, perhaps as early as 1935, Himmler, although not yet actively looking for alternative sources of manpower, may have struck on the idea that he could recruit these people, who, as citizens of other countries, did not come under the authority of the Wehrmacht.

One final consideration that probably occurred to Himmler was ideological. Although as early as 1935 Himmler could not have foreseen his meeting with the Volhynian resettlers at Przemysl, he very well may have recognized the *Volksdeutsche* as a valuable source of racial "material" for building the new order. The vision of Germanic peasant soldiers colonizing the East under a feudal-like knightly order had been floating around in his mind for some time. But what this vision lacked was a link between his real power, that of the police and the SS, and these *völkisch* fantasies. Somehow it must have dawned on him that the function of the SS and the police of protecting the party, state, and *Volk* could be broadened to nurturing the racial well-being of the *Volk*, including the *Volksdeutsche*. Perhaps it was Heydrich again who planted this link between ideology and power in Himmler's mind. Regardless of the exact considerations motivating Himmler, the fact was that by the mid-1930s, his interest in the *Volksdeutsche* was being stoked.

In his drive to increase his personal power, Himmler encountered considerable opposition. One steadfast opponent was Rosenberg, who resented SS primacy in racial matters and saw Himmler as an inter-loper in *Volkstum* affairs. But a far greater threat to Himmler was the jealousy of Nazis with power rooted in the NSDAP, above all the *Altkämpfer*, old Nazis who had struggled alongside Hitler since the early days of the movement. They envied Himmler's meteoric rise and the Führer's apparent blessings to his accumulation of posts and titles. Among the most resentful were the *Gauleiters*, the regional leaders of the NSDAP. Directly responsible to the Führer, not to the central party apparatus, they took umbrage at the SS intruding on their local authority through the regional SS divisions, the *Oberabschnitte*. Gauleiter Albert Forster of Danzig was fond of pricking Himmler with barbs such as, "If I looked like Himmler, I wouldn't talk about race."[22]

Himmler waited for a propitious moment to make his entry onto the *Volkstum* field, and Hess's appointment of SS man Kursell to head the new Volkstumsbüro provided the opportunity. Whereas previously an assault on this area of activity meant an incursion into an amorphous mass with no focal point, Kursell's office presented a clear target for attack. Furthermore, Himmler could exploit his superior SS rank over Kursell. Although he had no right to interfere with Kursell's office, whose authority came from Hess, as Kursell's SS superior, Himmler nevertheless pressured Kursell to act according to the interests of the SS. Kursell, however, refused to cooperate. An old party loyalist, he had accepted only an honorary membership in the SS and therefore felt no great compulsion to follow Himmler's bidding. But the Reichs-führer SS would not tolerate insubordination from any underling, irrespective of the nature of his membership. When Kursell spurned Himmler's advances, Himmler set events in motion that resulted in Kursell's expulsion from the SS and removal from his post.

Matters came to a head between Himmler and Kursell in late 1936 in a disagreement over the Sudeten Germans of Czechoslovakia. Himmler supported a faction that had ties with the SD, whereas Kursell sided with the main organization under Konrad Henlein.[23] Kursell turned to his immediate superior Hess for support, but by this time Hess, even if he were so inclined, was already powerless to deter the SS. Karl Haushofer tried to intercede on Kursell's behalf and in early December met with Himmler's adjutant Karl Wolff to discuss the situation. Wolff informed him that Himmler had already proposed a plan to Hess, according to which an SS man would replace Steinacher as head of the VDA, and Kursell's post would go to a Gestapo man.[24]

Haushofer, distressed by his talk with Wolff and hoping for a more favorable decision from higher up, pleaded with Hess to turn to Ribbentrop and together take this matter to the Führer.[25] Haushofer's entreaty had little effect, for in mid-December Himmler summoned Kursell to his headquarters on Prinz Albrechtsstrasse, and in the presence of Wolff and Ribbentrop, he demanded Kursell's resignation from the SS. He accused Kursell of activities threatening the security of the Reich. Kursell's fate was sealed. Himmler expelled him from the SS, and during the first week of January 1937 Hess, who apparently was taking Himmler's cue in this affair, relieved Kursell of his post at the Büro, which by then was referred to as the Volksdeutsche Mittelstelle. Franz Wehofsich, one of Kursell's associates and a recent SS initiate, assumed the temporary direction of VoMi.[26]

Kursell's expulsion from the SS and his firing as chief of VoMi demonstrated how Himmler could use the SS membership of certain well-placed individuals to extend his influence and power. He did not need direct jurisdiction over an organization or office to have his way with it. Insertion of SS personnel sufficed. A loyal SS man would obey Himmler, and as Kursell's case demonstrated, a disloyal one would be defrocked of his black uniform, an increasingly desirable addition to any Berlin wardrobe. Dismissal from the SS carried with it a stigma that, for anyone but the highest of the Nazi faithful, could derail a promising career or lead to even more serious consequences.

• • ARRIVAL OF WERNER LORENZ

With Himmler in the background, Hess replaced one "black uniform" with another. Several days before firing Kursell, on 1 January 1937, Hess had already selected Himmler's recommendation, SS Obergruppenführer (lieutenant general) Werner Lorenz, as the new leader of the Volksdeutsche Mittelstelle. Hess understood that to achieve lasting harmony in the *Volkstum* field, to complete the *Gleichschaltung*, and to get in step with the political realities of Third Reich infighting, he would have to secure the cooperation and participation of the SS. Once Himmler's interest was whetted, he could not be denied his share.

In a letter to Foreign Minister Constantin von Neurath, Hess explained that he had removed Kursell and had charged Lorenz with responsibility for directing *Volkstumsarbeit*. Although organizationally Lorenz would be subordinated to Ribbentrop in the latter's capacity as the foreign affairs expert on Hess's staff—a concession to Ribbentrop's claim to a share in *Volkstum* affairs—Hess retained ultimate authority over VoMi and delegated to Lorenz the authority the Führer had granted him. Hess concluded the letter by requesting Neurath's cooperation for what he called the Büro Lorenz. Hess made no mention of Himmler's role in this affair except to say that the Reichsführer SS had given Lorenz a leave of absence from his former SS command.[27]

Shortly after Himmler kicked Kursell out of the SS and Hess named Lorenz as his replacement at VoMi, Ribbentrop summoned Kursell to his home for the official transfer of office. Lorenz's presence made an already unpleasant situation worse. When Ribbentrop informed Kursell of the transfer of authority, the latter facetiously replied that he had nothing to transfer because all authority had already been stripped from him. From this meeting, Kursell surmised that Lorenz knew nothing of *Volkstumspolitik* and showed little enthusiasm for the new post.[28]

On 1 February, Ribbentrop, in his capacity as Hess's deputy, convened some forty representatives of various *Volkstum* organizations, Nazi dignitaries, and state officials to announce the personnel changes and new guidelines for *Volkstum* activities. He informed them that VoMi would henceforth supervise all activities related to the *Volksdeutsche*. Among its duties would be promoting National Socialism. Another vital task was to eliminate the factious quarreling obstructing *völkisch* unity. Ribbentrop emphatically stressed the Führer's wish that *Volkstum* activities abroad must in no way interfere with the pursuit of Reich foreign policy. Therefore, VoMi must take special care that no "threads" appeared to connect the Reich to individuals and organizations in foreign countries. He then instructed both party and state offices to deal with the minorities exclusively through Lorenz and his office. The VDA and all other private organizations could no longer work directly with the *Volksdeutsche* but only through VoMi.[29]

Ribbentrop then introduced the new leader of the Volksdeutsche Mittelstelle. When Lorenz stepped up to the rostrum, he impressed on the audience the fact that the Führer had personally commissioned him with directing the office, a claim that undoubtedly raised a few eyebrows and perked up the dozing. It is unknown whether Lorenz had enjoyed the privilege of a personal audience with Hitler, but his superiors in this matter—Hess, Ribbentrop, and Himmler—most certainly had taken this matter to the highest authority. Lorenz confessed that he knew very little about *Volksdeutsche* affairs and made no pretense of expertise in this field. He was aware of problems and hoped that with the cooperation of those assembled, these could be overcome.[30] In general, the new boss did not leave a very favorable impression.

Kursell's removal was a victory for the SS and enabled Himmler to extend his influence to *Volksdeutsche* affairs, a move that some contemporaries as well as later observers have described as a step toward the "radicalization" of *Volkstumsarbeit* and *Volkstumspolitik*.[31] If by *radicalization* is meant a radical departure from previous policies and nature of activities, then not until the war years and the advent of the resettlement program can one speak of radicalization. Prewar SS policy in *Volkstum* affairs, at least as pursued by VoMi under Lorenz's leadership, aimed to moderate rather than stimulate activism among the *Volksdeutsche*. It was geared toward reconciling feuding factions both inside the Reich and abroad, and it differed from the policies of predecessors mostly by virtue of its success. Granted, the methods Lorenz used, as will be demonstrated in following chapters, were firmer, at times even ruthless, but the goals remained fundamentally the same. Another significant difference was that the new leadership commanded sufficient authority inside the Reich to enforce its will.

Even subsequent personnel changes were not thorough enough to warrant the term *radical*. Several workers in Kursell's office agreed to remain and to continue working under the new leadership. Although willingness to cooperate with the new leadership has been attributed to the ignorance of the so-called moderates as to the intentions of the SS,[32] one may argue that the moderates were well aware of SS intentions and were in complete agreement. Many of them longed for an end to the chronic dissension and disunity and were willing to surrender their independence for the sake of harmony. They disagreed only over who should restore order and to whom independence should be surrendered.

• •

Preresettlement VoMi

• •

VOMI, PARTY, AND STATE

For the Volksdeutsche Mittelstelle, as for all organizations in the Third Reich, Adolf Hitler was the ultimate authority. As Führer, he was the leader of the NSDAP and the "movement." As Reich chancellor, he was the head of the government and all its ministries and agencies. Originating at a common source, his authority filtered down through two channels, the Nazi party and the state. Although neither he nor his subordinates always respected the distinction between party and state, at times he found it useful. The state provided a counterbalance to the party. Within the party, certain individuals had built up personal power bases and thereby enjoyed some independent authority, whereas the Nazis whom Hitler had appointed to Reich posts held tenure solely by virtue of his goodwill.

For most Third Reich organizations, the nature of their authority was clear—either state or party. VoMi's status, however, was ambiguous, since its authority, as Hitler had charged, was both state and party. As discussed in the preceding chapter, Hitler first approached the *Volksdeutsche* issue through Deputy Führer Hess, whose authority was that of the NSDAP. Thus VoMi, created under Hess's auspices, received its original commission from the party, and as property, it was the responsibility of the NSDAP treasurer, (Reichsschatzmeister)

Franz Xavier Schwarz, who was also its paymaster. Although state funds subsidized many of VoMi's activities, the NSDAP covered its operating expenses and paid its salaries.[1]

Until 2 July 1938, VoMi's authority remained exclusively party, but on that date Hitler granted it state authority as well. He assigned to it responsibility for all Reich, party, and private organizations dealing with *Volkstum* and *Grenzland* (borderland) questions. He also charged it with the distribution of all funds, including state money, designated for the *Volksdeutsche* and their activities. All decisions regarding these allocations had to include VoMi.[2] In charging VoMi with official state tasks, Hitler not only was expanding its powers but also was confusing the source of its authority. Did it originate with the state or the party? The personal union of other state and party offices under VoMi's two immediate superiors, Ribbentrop and Hess, further clouded the issue. One VoMi official incorrectly testified that the connection between Hess and VoMi was based not on Hess's party post of deputy Führer but rather on his state title of Reich Minister without Portfolio.[3] Lorenz himself carelessly alluded to Ribbentrop as his superior, not as foreign policy adviser on Hess's staff but as foreign minister.[4] The fact is that even though VoMi enjoyed Reich authority, in the prewar years it remained organizationally within the Nazi party, under the immediate authority of Rudolf Hess as deputy Führer.

• • LEADERSHIP

Even though prewar VoMi was a Nazi party organ, the growing influence of the SS within it increasingly led many to regard it as an SS organization. Before 1939, VoMi's association with the SS was based primarily on the SS membership of its leaders: Werner Lorenz; his chief of staff, Hermann Behrends; and his adjutant, Walter Ellermeier. All three were loyal, dedicated career SS officers.

SS Obergruppenführer Werner Lorenz by most accounts was a good fellow, hardly a typical SS man, and the least "radical" of the higher SS leaders.[5] He was born the son of a farmer in Grünhof bei Stolp, Kreis Stolp, Pomerania, on 2 October 1891. Apparently the family did not belong to the landed nobility, even though it did have a coat of arms, a copy of which Lorenz proudly donated to decorate the halls of Himmler's SS castle at Wewelsburg. As a youth, Lorenz trained for a career as an army officer in the elite Kadettenkorps, the incubator for future members of the Prussian officer corps. In October 1912 he entered the Second Battery, First Field Artillery Regiment, of Prince August of Prussia and the following spring became a *Fahnenjunker* (officer candidate) in the Fourth Mounted Rifles Regiment. With the outbreak of war in August 1914, Lorenz was assigned to another mounted regiment, in whose service he won the Iron Cross, Second Class. By the end of the war, he had served in several other capacities—including a stint as a staff officer—had attained the rank of Oberleutnant, and had earned the Iron Cross, First Class, and the Ehrenkreuz. His unit was not demobilized immediately after the armistice, and it rode on as part of the Grenzschutz Freikorps in the border war against the Poles. Lorenz remained with this unit until March 1920, when it was finally disbanded.[6]

Lorenz had intended to pursue a military career, but for unknown reasons he did not remain with the army after leaving the Freikorps. One may speculate that the Versailles limitations on the size of the German army brought an end to his military career, forcing him to seek a civilian livelihood. Many other veterans finding themselves in similar circumstances failed to adapt to civilian life and eventually joined one of the many paramilitary organizations abounding in postwar Germany. But Lorenz was more fortunate. While still with the Grenzschutz, the dashing young cavalry officer had married Charlotte Ventski, a very rich socialite from Graudenz, a city on the Vistula, located in the part of West Prussia incorporated into the new state of Poland. His newly acquired wealth and social connections enabled him to lease an estate, Mariensee, in the territory of the Free City of Danzig, and to purchase a sawmill, a grinding mill, and a distillery. Here the Lorenzes established their home, where their two daughters, Rosemarie and Jutta, were born. They also maintained ties with Graudenz, the birthplace in 1928 of their son, Joachim-Werner.[7]

Hermann Rauschning, a prominent figure in Danzig politics, described Lorenz as a "sort of amateur farmer" whose financial returns from farming were meager.[8] Apparently Frau Lorenz's fortune was substantial enough to compensate for Werner's shortcomings as a farmer, since the Lorenzes managed to send their two daughters to finishing schools in England. Countess Waldeck, an international socialite of the day, raved about the Lorenz girls as "roaring, long-legged beauties . . . favorites with the Reichskanzler and outstanding debutantes of all German-dominated Europe, these beautiful, spoiled kids."[9]

Most of Lorenz's acquaintances held favorable opinions of him. Countess Waldeck described him as elegant and handsome, a "good-looking, middle-aged man with a peculiar habit of nervously turning his neck that was reminiscent of the Duke of Windsor in pre-Simpson days."[10] Rauschning considered him an "innocent bon vivant, fond of joke and of wine and women," and held his Prussian cadet and officer background in the highest regard.[11] Erhard Milch, former inspector general of the Luftwaffe, had known Lorenz since World War I and regarded him as one of the "outstanding adherents to the old conception of officer—decent, concerned, objective and just."[12] Georg Skowronski, an anti-Nazi witness at Lorenz's postwar trial, said that Lorenz was "a gentleman to the last, which could not be said of most other leading Nazis."[13] One detractor, however, was Hans Steinacher, who loathed everything to do with VoMi, including its leader. He considered Lorenz an ignoramus, as well as deceitful, untruthful, and arrogant. According to Steinacher, the Prussian officer Lorenz could only order others about; for Lorenz the Nazi, his ends justified his means.[14]

Frustrated in his ambitions of becoming a career army officer, unsuccessful at farming, Lorenz sought new interests and in 1929 became involved with the NSDAP in Danzig. Gauleiter Albert Forster introduced him to Himmler, who in 1930 began to court Lorenz to help with developing the Danzig SS, which at that time consisted of only twenty men. Lorenz eventually agreed and on 1 December 1930 joined both the SS and the NSDAP. He later claimed having little knowledge about the SS when he enlisted and justified his entry as an opportunity to fight corruption, to build a new *Volksgemeinschaft* (community of the Volk), and to educate and lead young men in the ways of honor, excellence, and a stable family life.[15] He failed to mention the opportunities the SS offered for pursuing a career similar to the military one that circumstances had forced him to abandon.

Although Lorenz later denied it, his advancement in the SS was rapid. Entering the SS in December 1930, he received the rank of SS Sturmbannführer (major) the following March, at which time he was assigned to Königsberg, the center for directing many Nazi activities in Danzig, including those of the SS. In July 1931, he was promoted to SS Standartenführer (colonel), and in November he was placed in command of the Königsberg SS. In July 1933, Lorenz attained the rank of SS Brigadeführer (brigadier general); by December he had reached the rank of SS Gruppenführer (major general); and in November 1936, he acquired the rank of SS Obergruppenführer (lieutenant general), the highest rank he would earn with the Allgemeine SS (the general SS, as distinct from the Waffen SS).[16]

Lorenz's SS activities in Danzig and Königsberg brought him into contact with the highest Nazis in the area, including Forster of Danzig; Arthur Greiser, the future Gauleiter of Warthegau; and Erich Koch, the powerful Gauleiter of East Prussia. Koch even offered him the post of police president in Königsberg, but Lorenz declined in order to remain at the head of his SS troops, which he built up to a formidable force of 8,000 men.[17] In February 1934, Himmler reassigned Lorenz to "Red Hamburg," a particularly anti-Nazi city, just in time for the Röhm purge. Lorenz's exact role in this event remains a mystery, but as early as 1933, Himmler had confided in him that the situation with the Sturmabteilung (SA) had become intolerable and that a sharp pruning of the party had become necessary. Lorenz later insisted that he arrived at his new post while the purge was in progress, implying that he played no part in these events. But records reveal that he arrived four months before the purge, giving him sufficient time to organize "the pruning" in Hamburg.[18]

Although Lorenz served the SS loyally and successfully, all was not well between him and Himmler. One of the earliest instances of friction occurred during the Röhm purge, when Lorenz interceded on behalf of two prominent Hamburgers arrested by the Gestapo. He and the local Gauleiter flew to Berlin to plead their case directly to Himmler, who informed them that the matter did not concern them.[19] Although Lorenz eventually won the release, this incident no doubt sowed some seeds of discord.

Adding to the friction was a difference of opinion over religious affiliation. Contrary to Himmler's preferences and the official anti-Christian position of the SS, Lorenz insisted on confirming his children in the Evangelical Church. And when the Reichsführer SS insisted that all SS men forsake Christianity and accept the status of *Gottgläubig*, whereby one renounced Christianity but still confessed a fundamental belief in a god, Lorenz balked. Although he accepted the status for himself, he argued with Himmler against ordering his men to do likewise. On this issue, Heydrich admonished Lorenz for his contrariness and berated him for being too middle class (*bürgerlich*). The SS also pressured Lorenz to send his son to a Nazi educational institution rather than to a private school, but here too the SS failed.[20]

Lorenz probably exaggerated the rift between himself and Himmler, especially so after the war, when many SS men sought to distance themselves from their former boss. After all, if the schism between the two was as wide as Lorenz claimed, Himmler would not have appointed him to a post so crucial for expanding SS authority. Besides, Lorenz's high standing in the SS belies any serious differences. Command of an Oberabschnitt was a very important SS duty, especially before the November 1937 creation of the position of Higher SS and Police Leader (Höhere SS-und Polizeiführer or HSSPF) as the primary regional SS authority. Another indicator of his importance was his SS rank. Lorenz outranked not only numerous Nazi party notables, including Ribbentrop, Bormann, and Lammers, but also many of the most notorious SS personalities. In a November 1944 listing of SS ranks, Lorenz was the fifteenth-ranking SS officer.[21]

Differences with Himmler aside, Lorenz was an excellent choice for chief of VoMi, at least Himmler's adjutant, Karl Wolff, thought so. According to Wolff, Himmler chose Lorenz for the post because it was basically a liaison position, an intermediary connecting the NSDAP, the SS, the *Volkstum* organizations in the Reich, the minorities, the Reich ministries, and even in some cases officials of foreign governments. Someone with social *savoir faire* was needed. The colorless, provincial Himmler did not have the inclination, the time, or the knack for the social life that the post demanded. Lorenz, on the other hand, a charming personality who felt at home in the highest social echelons, was a perfect representative of the SS. His SS record confirmed that he could also provide the firm leadership VoMi required.[22]

Lorenz lacked, however, one obvious qualification for the post, experience in *Volksdeutsche* matters. Steinacher, for one, deplored the fact that the new head of VoMi, the most important Reich office dealing in *Volkstum* affairs, knew nothing about *Volkstumsarbeit* except what he had seen from the limited perspective of a *Volksdeutscher* from the Polish Corridor. The only interest Lorenz had in *Volkstumsarbeit*, complained the head of the VDA, was to collect the Reich subsidies coming to him as a *Volksdeutsche* landowner.[23] Steinacher's disapproval aside, Lorenz, a conservative nationalist and former officer, won approval from many others active in the field. He possessed qualities valued by men such as Karl Haushofer and indeed by Steinacher himself—if these attributes had belonged to anyone else but the SS leader of VoMi.[24]

But rather than expertise in *Volkstum* affairs, Lorenz's position demanded a mediator and, above all, someone capable of commanding authority. Previous efforts at centralizing *Volkstum* activities had failed for relying too much on men well versed in these matters but not wielding effective authority. Lorenz had demonstrated his mettle in building up the Danzig and East Prussian SS while managing to get along reasonably well with regional Nazi potentates such as Greiser, Koch, and Forster. He was also popular with other highly placed Nazis and occupied some non-SS party posts. While in Hamburg, he was the Nazi representative in the Hamburg Council of State, served one term as a Nazi member of the Prussian Landtag, and after the dissolution of the Landtag until the end of the war, was a member of the moribund Reichstag. Perhaps the post best suited for Lorenz was that of Gau Jägermeister (hunting master) for Hamburg. In this capacity, he was subordinate to the Reich Jägermeister, Hermann Göring, the leading playboy of the Third Reich.[25] Hunting was a passion with Lorenz, who received several reminders that the personal use of official vehicles for hunting was prohibited.[26]

With his many connections and the backing of the SS for support, Lorenz proceeded to reconcile the *Volkstum* factions, centralize and coordinate *Volkstumsarbeit*, and complete the *Gleichschaltung*. In these efforts he enjoyed Himmler's confidence—any differences aside. But Himmler's blessings were not enough. Looming over all SS affairs was Reinhard Heydrich and his SD. If indeed Heydrich was the real force within the SS system, as some have asserted, then one could expect a link between VoMi and the SD. Just such a connection was Dr. Hermann Behrends, Heydrich's protégé. Himmler had assured Lorenz that he would not be burdened with administrative details in his new post, nor would he need *Volkstum* expertise. For these purposes, Himmler would provide him with a chief of staff—Behrends.[27]

Hermann Behrends was born the son of an innkeeper in Rüstingen, Oldenburg, on 11 May 1907. He studied law at Marburg University, but having earned his doctorate in December 1931, he found himself one of a legion of well-educated young people in an economically depressed Germany without suitable employment. Seeking a way out of his dilemma, in January 1932 he joined the NSDAP and the following month enlisted with the SS, presumably out of ambition and careerism but perhaps also a touch of idealism.[28] Too young to have served in the war, Behrends had no military experience, but with the SS he quickly earned noncommissioned officer rank. Heydrich, who at the time was assembling an entourage of bright, educated, capable young men, discovered Behrends and asked Himmler to transfer him to the SD.[29] Heydrich disdained what he considered the rowdy, brawling SA types and sought to nurture a cadre of future leaders who excelled in every respect—physically, intellectually, and ideologically. Evidently Behrends, with Nordic looks and a worthless doctorate, fit Heydrich's specifications perfectly.

Behrends viewed Heydrich's offer as a career opportunity and accepted a post in the Gestapo. He eventually commanded the most notorious section of the SD: Amt II in the SD Main Office, known as Inland, the section dealing with Jews, churches, and other designated enemies of the Third Reich. One of his subordinates in 1934–35 was the infamous Adolf Eichmann. Behrends, who became Heydrich's intimate confidant, was deeply implicated in the 30 June 1934 purge of the SA.[30] He served in his SD position until his assignment as Lorenz's chief of staff. Even after his arrival at VoMi, he remained on the rolls of the SD. Behrends was the first of several dynamic and capable SD men who at one time or another served with VoMi. His SS career was not limited to the SD and VoMi. He later distinguished himself with the Waffen SS and ultimately held the prominent post of HSSPF for Serbia, where he commanded counterinsurgency operations against the Yugoslav partisans.[31]

Behrends was consumed by ambition, for which he was renowned and resented. In December 1942, for instance, not long after his patron, Heydrich, was assassinated and thus removed from the SS scene, Himmler urged Lorenz to curb Behrends's ambitions for his own good. Behrends, without his protector, defended himself as an SS man who placed duty ahead of any personal ambition.[32] Nevertheless, his reputation stuck, and at Lorenz's postwar trial, the defense insisted that Behrends's zeal and ambition were responsible for many of the crimes charged to Lorenz and VoMi.[33]

A third figure, Lorenz's adjutant, Walter Ellermeier, must be included with the leadership. He was Lorenz's closest colleague and, along with his boss and Behrends, was one of only three career SS men in prewar VoMi. Ellermeier was born on 12 July 1906 in Berlin-

Schöneberg. Like Behrends, he had been too young to fight in the war, but he was not too young to join the Freikorps Wiking in 1923. From then on, he belonged to one paramilitary group or another, a preoccupation that left him little time to pursue a productive profession. He did, however, attend a business school and briefly interrupted his paramilitary career to try his hand at a white-collar bank job. Bored by such mundane pursuits, Ellermeier joined the Stahlhelm in 1927 and was back in uniform. In 1930 he enlisted with the NSDAP and the SA, where he distinguished himself driving SA trucks around the Brandenburg countryside. In 1932, for some unknown reason, he left the SA and enlisted with the SS. His transfer occurred two years before the beginning of the SA demise in 1934, and therefore it was not simply a matter of abandoning a sinking ship. Perhaps Ellermeier already perceived the SS as the elite Nazi vanguard of the future.[34]

Within one year after entering the SS, Ellermeier earned officer rank and by December 1933 commanded the 13th Motorized SS Standarte in Pomerania. Apparently he had discovered his calling. He shortly caught the eye of his Oberabschnitt leader, Werner Lorenz, an automobile enthusiast himself. When Lorenz transferred to Hamburg, Ellermeier accompanied him as his personal adjutant. Lorenz, who thought very highly of his adjutant and regarded Ellermeier as his closest and most reliable comrade, brought his adjutant along to Berlin to help him command VoMi.[35] Although Behrends was the chief of staff and thereby Lorenz's official deputy, Ellermeier was closer to the VoMi leader. When Himmler charged VoMi with responsibility for the resettlement, Lorenz appointed Ellermeier director.

Ellermeier's SS career, although successful, did not equal that of his associate Behrends. Even though he reached the rank of SS Oberführer (senior colonel) in June 1944, he never established an independent standing for himself, as did Behrends. Except for tours of duty with the Waffen SS, including assignments with the Division Wiking and the elite SS Leibstandarte Adolf Hitler, his entire career was associated with Lorenz.[36] Ellermeier does not seem to have been driven by the compelling ambition of Behrends and other more dynamic SS colleagues. His SS loyalties focused on Lorenz's friendship rather than on ideology or careerism.

These three career SS men—Lorenz, Behrends, and Ellermeier—provided VoMi with invigorated leadership. Their presence ensured the SS increased influence in, if not yet total control over, *Volksdeutsche* affairs. As one later observer has noted, Himmler wanted to demonstrate that henceforth *Volksdeutsche* matters would be handled more energetically. The authority of the revamped VoMi would rest on the "black uniforms" of the SS rather than on the experience of a few so-called *Volkstum* experts.[37]

But one must keep in mind that although SS influence became dominant in VoMi, before 1939 its SS connection remained exclusively personal, and absolutely no organizational or institutional connections existed. In the preresettlement era, VoMi was neither an SS main office (*Hauptamt*) nor an Allgemeine SS unit of any sort. Internal, even confidential, lists of SS offices and units in the pre-1939 period mention no Volksdeutsche Mittelstelle. If VoMi had been a part of the SS, it surely would have appeared on these lists. Lorenz's personal position as an SS Obergruppenführer, however, was not overlooked. SS routing lists noted him as a recipient of SS orders and notices.[38]

Himmler reinforced Lorenz's position as an SS Führer assigned to a non-SS post by awarding him on 10 January 1938 the same authority in SS disciplinary and promotion matters granted the highest SS regional commanders, the SS Oberabschnittsführer.[39] Lorenz's authority extended over all SS men working at VoMi and in Ribbentrop's party offices. It is not known whether the practice of granting such authority was common, but it clearly demonstrated that even though VoMi was not an SS organ, and remained a party office under Ribbentrop and Hess, the man at its head was a genuine SS Führer with full SS authority. Lorenz was not just another honorary SS officer adding to the black-uniformed population of Berlin. Himmler had not yet tendered formal claims to VoMi as SS property, but he had underscored the fact that the SS had a special interest in it and in its activities.

• • PERSONNEL

An examination of VoMi's personnel not only provides insights into this organization and its activities but also illuminates certain issues and questions related to the nature, functioning, and composition of the SS. For the prewar years, VoMi's personnel fall into four groups: the staff at the Berlin headquarters; its regional representatives inside the Reich, the Gaubeauftragten; the liaison men maintaining confidential ties between VoMi and the minorities; and the officials and employees of various offices and organizations that over a period of time came under VoMi's direct control.

Of the four groups, the headquarters staff in Berlin, located at 64 Unter den Linden, was the most important. Lorenz began operations with a relatively modest staff of some twenty workers. As VoMi's responsibilities grew, more people were added, but before the resettlement, the headquarters never employed more than thirty people. VoMi obtained its personnel from diverse sources. Some, such as Gunther Stier, had worked for Kursell and continued serving under the new leadership. Franz Wehofsich and Georg Stahmer had been associated with Ribbentrop. The majority, however, were newly employed, arriving in the first half of 1937. Some came from other NSDAP offices, but most were from organizations already involved in *Volkstum* activities.[40]

The striking feature of the prewar headquarters staff is that only the three leaders—Lorenz, Behrends, and Ellermeier—came directly from within the SS system. Most others had not belonged to the SS before their employment at VoMi. Of known VoMi officials, only Franz Wehofsich belonged to the SS before joining VoMi.[41] The rest voluntarily enrolled only after their arrival. It should be noted that since enlistment in the nonmilitary Allgemeine SS was voluntary, it was possible, but not common, to avoid joining the SS while employed at VoMi. Lothar Heller and Adolf Puls, both department heads during the war years, did not enlist in the SS until 1944.[42] Voluntarism, however, did not preclude the use of coercion. If honorary SS officers such as Ribbentrop pressured their subordinates to enlist with the SS, one may expect an SS careerist like Lorenz to do no less. Indeed, Heinrich Lohl, VoMi's financial administrator, testified after the war that "civilians" working for VoMi had little choice in the matter of enlisting.[43] Available evidence, however, does not reflect any opposition or even reluctance toward joining the SS—perhaps with the exceptions of Heller and Puls, whose reasons for not joining the SS until 1944 are not known.

Just as membership in the Allgemeine SS was voluntary, so was employment with VoMi. Only men already belonging to the SS could be ordered by the SS to serve at VoMi. As far as can be determined, only Lorenz and Behrends were commanded to their new posts. Not until wartime could the SS draft nonmembers to perform certain official, state tasks, and even then induction did not automatically bring with it SS membership.

Although most VoMi employees eventually joined the SS, very few seemed to fit the stereotype of the young, ruthless, ambitious careerist in the mold of Heydrich or Behrends. Of the prewar staff, only Franz Wehofsich and Hans-Jochen Kubitz might have fit this image, a conclusion based on their distinguished wartime service with the Waffen SS and as ranking, official Reich functionaries of one kind or another.[44] The fact that only the three top men at VoMi were genuine, career SS men invalidates—at least for the prewar, preresettlement period—the misconception that VoMi was staffed throughout with "radical" SS men inherently different from the traditional *Volkstum* activists such as Steinacher. Paul Minke, Franz Wehofsich, Gunther Stier, and Wilhelm Luig had been very active in *Volkstum* affairs before coming to VoMi. And at least one ran into trouble with the SD for being a "reactionary," a designation the SD applied to conservatives such as Steinacher. Over Lorenz's protests, Karl Henniger, VoMi's expert on southeastern Europe, was expelled from the SS for allegedly maintaining ties in Rumania and Yugoslavia with "reactionaries" and others disapproved by the SD. Before his expulsion and after his subsequent reinstatement, Henniger received nothing but praise from Lorenz and approval for his connections with the so-called reactionaries.[45]

A closer examination of the personnel also reveals that charges by Steinacher and others that incompetents and men inexperienced in *Volkstum* affairs staffed VoMi were unfounded. Granted, the leadership had little experience, but many of their immediate subordinates were veterans of the *Volkstumskampf*, with impressive credentials. Franz Wehofsich had been very active in Steinacher's own homeland of Carinthia and was intimate with leading figures of the *Volkstum* movement, including Haushofer, whom he addressed endearingly as "Onkel Karl."[46] Paul Minke had also fought for the cause in Austria, and Hans-Jochen Kubitz had been active in Poland. Several of these men, including Wilhelm Luig, deputy chief of staff to Behrends and the "number four" man at VoMi, had worked for the VDA before coming to VoMi.[47] Others, without experience in *Volkstum* affairs, were nevertheless qualified for their duties in finance or administration.

Another interesting generalization relates to the staff's education level. As a whole they were very well educated. At least five—Behrends, Luig, Wehofsich, Henniger, and Capra—had earned doctorates, and several others had studied at universities or other institutions of higher learning. Perhaps the observation that many SS men were would-be intellectuals who had failed to complete their studies was true for some, but the number of Ph.D.'s at VoMi contradicts that conclusion, at least for VoMi.[48] It does appear, however, that a number of SS men at VoMi had to settle for employment beneath their expectations and therefore may in fact have belonged in the ranks of "alienated" or "pauperized resentful intellectuals."[49]

A look at the personnel should also dispel the lingering misconception that SS men were innately a breed separate from the brawling ruffians of the SA. SS apologists have been fond of distinguishing between the SA rowdies and the supposedly idealistic, intellectually oriented SS men. But most SS men on VoMi's staff had belonged to the SA, including Ellermeier, Henniger, Kubitz, Minke, and Stier. The four latter men did not quit the SA until after they arrived at VoMi. Thus one may conclude that the differences between SS and SA men were not so great. The SA evidently had its share of idealists and intellectuals, and the SS probably accepted street brawlers.

This survey of VoMi's personnel sheds some light on yet another issue, the presence of the SD throughout the SS system, and its corollary, the influence of Heydrich. It appears that the SD connection at the headquarters before the outbreak of war was probably limited to Behrends and that SD influence was not as pervasive as elsewhere in the SS system. With one exception, no one else had anything in his background to suggest ties to the SD, the Gestapo, or any other SS security organ. However, because of the clandestine nature of the SD, some of the ties might not have been apparent. The activities of Horst Hoffmeyer suggest the existence of a covert SD connection. Hoffmeyer, a *Volksdeutscher* from Posen, was the paradigm of the Freikorps activist who followed an uninterrupted paramilitary career from the postwar Freikorps to the SS.[50] During this time, he performed some "special services" for the party, services that could not be revealed in his personnel records.[51] It is not certain exactly when Hoffmeyer began working for VoMi, but in March 1939 Lorenz noted that he had been serving as a special adviser to Behrends on eastern borderlands issues for some time. Although no documented evidence links Hoffmeyer directly to the SD, his secret activities and close ties with Behrends make the connection a strong possibility.[52] But even with the presence of Behrends, and Hoffmeyer's probable SD ties, the case of

Karl Henniger and his run-in with the SD indicates that by no means did VoMi acquiesce to become Heydrich's pliant tool.

Another conclusion regarding personnel is that before working for VoMi, no one, including its three leaders, had any experience or connection with any of those armed SS units that later became the Waffen SS. This is an important observation, since some experts on the Waffen SS have used the extent of personnel interchange between the armed SS and other SS units and offices as a measure of internal integration within the SS system.[53] In the postwar period, many former Waffen SS men claimed that they and their units had nothing to do with other branches of the SS, certainly not those responsible for the atrocities. The Waffen SS and its soldiers were separate from the rest of the SS, so the argument runs. Evidence of personnel transfers between the Waffen SS and other SS branches would, however, undermine that contention. Applying this litmus to VoMi, it is clear that although during the war years transfers between VoMi and the Waffen SS became common, before 1939 there was little, if any, exchange.

THE BERLIN HEADQUARTERS

Before VoMi's leaders could proceed with their tasks, they had to organize a staff and office to assist them. Kursell had initiated the process, but he had held his post briefly—a little over a year—and the functions of his office and the division of labor had not yet assumed the regularity of bureaucratic routine. It was left to Lorenz and his subordinates to organize the office according to their own needs.

The shape VoMi assumed as an organization reflected the compromises and agreements of men such as Hess, Himmler, and Ribbentrop regarding the direction a nazified *Volkstum* movement should follow. As they decided VoMi's functions and assigned to it new tasks, Lorenz and his associates molded it accordingly. As certain activities became routine, Chief of Staff Behrends created sections, *Referentent* or *Hauptreferenten*, to perform them. Included were an adjutant's office and personnel section, an administrative section in charge of finances, a legal section for minority rights, and Behrends's office. There may have been other functionally defined sections—probably one for supervising *Volksdeutsche* economies—but this is uncertain.[54]

Another routine responsibility was maintaining contacts between the Reich and the minorities. For this purpose, Behrends created five regional sections, the *Länder Referate*. Each would transact routine business with the *Volksdeutsche* living in a particular region. Sections were designated for *Osten-Nordosten*, which included Poland, the Baltic States, and Memelland; *Schweiz und Westen*, dealing with France, Belgium, Denmark, and the Netherlands; the *Südosten*, responsible for Austria, Czechoslovakia, and the South Tyrol; a Balkan section, which also included Rumania; and *Übersee*, which worked with *Volksdeutsche* outside Europe.[55] When some of the groups ceased to exist as minorities, either through annexations or resettlement, VoMi eliminated their sections, and when new states appeared, beginning with Slovakia in 1939, it created additional ones.

While the section chiefs performed the routine work, Lorenz and Behrends handled the most important, most sensitive business. Eventually a personal division of labor emerged between the two. Lorenz, with little time and even less desire for supervision and details, assumed the role of a high-level representative for VoMi and the *Volkstum* field. As such, his duties kept him away from his desk for months at a time. His subordinates estimated that he spent no more than half his time in Berlin. He managed, however, to find some time for his non-VoMi duties, including his favorite ones, those of the hunting master of Hamburg. As a result Behrends, whom some have regarded as the real force in VoMi, managed everyday operations.[56]

Although Behrends enjoyed considerable latitude in running the Berlin office, the assertion that he was VoMi's real director is disputable. The overestimation of his role as well as his reputation as the diabolical force behind Lorenz can be mostly attributed to the testimonies of Nuremberg witnesses at Lorenz's postwar trial, when VoMi officials—although not on trial themselves—sought to minimize their own and Lorenz's complicity in alleged criminal activities by laying blame on Behrends. The latter was then a prisoner in Yugoslavia and conveniently became the proverbial scapegoat for his former colleagues. In addition, Steinacher, whose papers have otherwise provided invaluable information about *Volkstum* matters and VoMi, vindictively attributed the worst to Behrends. The result has been a distortion of the relative importance of the individuals within the VoMi leadership: Behrends's role has been overestimated; Lorenz's has been undervalued; and Ellermeier's has been ignored. A more accurate scenario would portray Lorenz as the primary figure, representing VoMi and the *Volkstum* movement to the highest Reich and party authorities; Behrends as the chief administrator but not the dominant figure; and Ellermeier, although not as important as Behrends, as a significant figure nonetheless by virtue of his position as Lorenz's adjutant and closest confidant.

• • VOMI OUTSIDE BERLIN

The leadership and the headquarters staff was by no means all there was of VoMi. It extended beyond Berlin into the Gaus and across Reich frontiers. Learning from the experiences of their predecessors, who had commanded little support within the party structure, the new leaders anchored their organization firmly in the NSDAP, especially at the local Gau level. In October 1937, they persuaded Hess to consolidate the local representatives of all organizations under VoMi's jurisdiction with one official in each Gau. This person would supervise all local *Volkstum* activities.[57] Aware of the sensitivities of the Gauleiters to any interference in their domains, and in order to secure their good graces, Lorenz consulted the individual Gauleiters before appointing these new officials, the Gaubeauftragten.

With very few exceptions, Nazi faithful, preferably *Altkämpfer* rather than SS men, filled these posts. Fritz Hube, Gaubeauftragter for Pomerania, traced his activist record back to the Kapp Putsch of 1920 and was widely acknowledged as one of the most influential Nazis in Pomerania.[58] Heinz Kubelke, VoMi's man in Gau Niederdonau, had started his party career as a protégé of Erich Koch in East Prussia, had worked his way into Hess's confidence as a staff member of the "Brown House" in Munich, and after the Anschluss, had briefly served with Gauleiter Bürckel in Vienna.[59] Many of these people sooner or later obtained at least honorary SS membership, but in the prewar years they were mostly local Nazi notables with impressive credentials of party service, enjoying the confidence of their Gauleiters.

In addition to party service, the Beauftragten in the border Gaus, especially in the east and southeast, could also boast of their experience in the *Volkstumskampf*, since they were expected to understand the issues and become actively involved. For instance, after the Anschluss, Alois Maier-Kaibitsch, a veteran *Volkstumskämpfer* who had campaigned actively for the Carinthian plebiscite and later worked for the illegal Nazi movement in Austria, became VoMi's Beauftragter for Carinthia. He and others like him were in great demand by competing Reich and party offices. From his Klagenfurt office, Maier-Kaibitsch served not only VoMi but also other organizations, with such disparate interests as the VDA and its eternal nemesis the SD.[60] In newly annexed areas, VoMi often recruited men with experience in undercover activities, men who could also serve Himmler's security offices, in particular the SD. VoMi's representative in Styria, for example, was instructed to establish close ties to the local Gestapo.[61] Even though at headquarters VoMi's connection to the SD was limited, it appears that such ties increased proportionately with distance from Berlin.

The SD link became even more pronounced among a third type of VoMi associate, the Vertrauensleute, the liaison and contact men within the minorities. An important task of the Gaubeauftragten for the border Gaus was to keep in touch with the Vertrauensleute, who, during the prewar years, when all political contacts abroad were by necessity clandestine, were the crucial links between VoMi and the minorities. In establishing its network of contact men, VoMi frequently encountered the ubiquitous presence of the SD, which had either already weaved or was in the process of weaving its own net. The resulting relationship between VoMi and the SD abroad was paradoxical. Although they often enlisted the same people, such as Maier-Kaibitsch, at other times, as in the case of Karl Henniger, they were at odds and worked at cross purposes.

A final group of VoMi personnel includes those who worked for one or another of the organizations that VoMi brought under its control, such as the VDA; the Bund Deutscher Osten (BDO), a center for irredentist propaganda and agitation focusing on the eastern borderlands; and the NSDAP Flüchtlingshilfswerk, the party office responsible for political refugees. Although these people were not officially on VoMi's rolls, they indirectly came under its authority. Interchange of personnel between these organizations and VoMi became common practice. VoMi also appointed some of its officials to direct these organizations. For instance, Horst Hoffmeyer assumed leadership of the BDO, and Luig and Minke held high positions with the VDA.

Several of VoMi's most valuable and capable workers arrived by way of these subordinate organizations. As a rule, their political experience and *Volkstum* expertise were comparable to those of the headquarters staff. One such transfer was Friedrich-Wilhelm Altena, who

had served with the Flüchtlingshilfswerk and with the Beratungsstelle für Einwanderer (BfE), a welfare and advisory office for *Volksdeutsche* fleeing from Poland, Czechoslovakia, and other fronts of the
Volkstumskampf. His experience administering refugee camps brought
him to Lorenz's attention.[62] Another transfer was an Austrian, Hans
Hagen, who also arrived via the BfE, but with bookkeeping as his
forté.[63] Both Hagen and Altena fit very well into the general character-
ization of VoMi's second-level officialdom. Both had been active party
and SA members who joined the SS only after coming to VoMi. They,
like most other VoMi officials, were well qualified for their positions
at VoMi—Altena with his expertise in constructing and managing
camps, and Hagen with his accounting skills and past participation in
the *Volkstumskampf* in Austria.

• •

VoMi's Prewar Activities

• •

COMPLETING THE *GLEICHSCHALTUNG*

Having an SS officer of Werner Lorenz's stature directing the Volksdeutsche Mittelstelle was an important preliminary step in Himmler's campaign to extend his influence over the German minorities of Europe. By no means was this step an end goal. Much still remained to be done before Himmler could claim the *Volksdeutsche* as his exclusive auxiliaries and exploit them for SS purposes. Kursell and others had already initiated efforts to nazify the minorities, and the new leaders actively continued the effort. But nazification abroad required completing the *Gleichschaltung* at home.

In pursuit of this objective, Lorenz focused on securing direct VoMi control over the VDA, the most important *Volkstum* organization. He allowed it to continue its activities both at home and abroad as before, but under VoMi's guidance. At the outset he tried to work with the VDA leadership. For instance, he demonstrated how he could use his SS influence on behalf of the VDA when he warned Ernst Bohle that unless the AO ceased its attacks on the VDA, he would veto Bohle's promotion to SS Gruppenführer.[1] But VDA chief Steinacher, who had nothing but contempt for Lorenz, was unimpressed and doubted Lorenz's sincerity in protecting the VDA. Finding Steinacher unresponsive, Chief of Staff Behrends warned him that he could either get in step with the Nazi movement "or dig his own grave."[2]

Steinacher's removal became a matter of time. His eventual dismissal and replacement with someone more sympathetic to the Nazi cause previewed similar substitutions in the military and at the Foreign Ministry in early 1938. As the usefulness of the conservatives as collaborators ran its course, men such as Steinacher, Foreign Minister von Neurath, and War Minister Werner von Blomberg became expendable. Besides, VoMi employed several men, including Franz Wehofsich, Paul Minke, and Alois Maier-Kaibitsch, veterans of the *Volkstumskampf* as well as ardent Nazis, who could readily take over the VDA. Why tolerate Steinacher when these others were eager to serve the cause?

One of the more troubling consequences of the VDA controversy was the dissension it created within the minorities. The established leaderships, with a few exceptions, sided with Steinacher, whereas the younger elements and dissidents generally favored his removal.[3] And as the factions abroad chose sides, they threatened to complicate Hitler's favorite preoccupation, foreign policy. The Foreign Ministry, interested in maintaining harmony, demanded a resolution.[4] The immediate pretext for Steinacher's removal was the issue of the South Tyrol. When, in September 1937, Italian leader Benito Mussolini complained to Hermann Göring about the activities of the VDA among South Tyrolean *Volksdeutsche* and suggested that if allowed to continue, this involvement could impair Reich-Italian relations, Steinacher's fate was sealed.[5]

Hess relieved Steinacher on 19 October and appointed Behrends's deputy, Wilhelm Luig, as a temporary replacement.[6] Personnel changes throughout the VDA hierarchy followed. But the final act in its *Gleichschaltung* came several months later, with the 2 July 1938 Führer decree in which Hitler granted VoMi full authority in all matters pertaining to the *Volksdeutsche*, including total control over the VDA.[7]

Securing its hold over the VDA was VoMi's most important success at home, but not the only one. Concurrently VoMi also brought under its control the Bund Deutscher Osten (BDO).[8] Its leader, Theodor Oberlander, a Nazi closely associated with Steinacher and the VDA, had earned the enmity of powerful figures in East Prussia, including

Gauleiter Erich Koch. With the latter's complicity, Lorenz forced Oberlander from his post and then appointed Behrends head of the BDO, with Behrend's shadowy associate, Horst Hoffmeyer, directing its day-to-day operations.[9]

With the two most important *Volkstum* organizations, the VDA and the BDO, securely under VoMi's control, in February 1939 Hess instructed all NSDAP offices and individuals involved in any *Volkstum* activities to align themselves with one of the two. VoMi issued similar orders to all nonparty groups. Henceforth there would be no more independent *Volkstum* organizations. All cultural *Volkstumsarbeit* would come under the aegis of the VDA, whereas political matters, or *Volkstumspolitik*, would be the concern of the BDO.[10]

VoMi also targeted the research institutes. Before Lorenz's arrival, the two most prominent—the Deutsche Auslands-Institut (DAI) and the Deutsche Akademie—had already initiated their own, internal *Gleichschaltung*. But in the interest of complete control, VoMi imposed its rule over these think tanks. In early February 1937, Lorenz informed both that his jurisdiction extended to them as well.[11] He and Behrends traveled to Stuttgart to impress on DAI officials that they too would have to submit to VoMi's authority.[12] The Deutsche Akademie experienced a similar fate. Although allowed to maintain its nominal independence, it henceforth had to consult VoMi before pursuing any activities affecting foreign policy or involving substantial sums of money. An official at the Akademie later complained to its director, Karl Haushofer, that VoMi would not permit him to publish a calendar, *Aufbau des Reiches*, because it competed with the VDA calendar, *Deutsche in aller Welt*.[13] Apparently the men at VoMi decided that one calendar displaying photos of German castles, farmhouses, and blond maidens was enough. They were serious about eliminating the duplication, bickering, and general chaos endemic to the *Volkstum* field.

• • • **VOMI, PARTY, AND STATE**

The revamped Volksdeutsche Mittelstelle also had to deal with individuals and groups within the NSDAP. Even though VoMi was a party office, and even though its superior, Hess, as deputy Führer was head of its organization, his power outside the central offices of the "Brown House" in Munich was limited, especially in the Gaus, where he commanded almost no authority. Even his control over the central apparatus, which he shared with Franz Xavier Schwarz, the party treasurer, and Robert Ley, the party's Organisationsleiter, was not total. Therefore, his orders to the NSDAP to accept VoMi as the exclusive party authority in *Volksdeutsche* matters carried little weight. VoMi had to arrange separate understandings with virtually every NSDAP office, such as the Hitlerjugend, the Frauenschaft, and Ley's staff.[14]

The Gaus posed the greatest obstacles to complete authority. To secure the cooperation of the independent-minded Gauleiters, VoMi created the aforementioned liaison post of Gaubeauftragter. But the new position competed with the party's Gaugrenzlandsamt, responsible for *Volksdeutsche* business on the Gau level. In addition, the Dienststelle Ribbentrop had assigned its own agents to some of the border Gaus, as had the Interior Ministry and the VDA. Some Gaus had all of these offices, some only a few. In time the new VoMi posts simplified matters somewhat, since everyone, including most Gauleiters, agreed to consolidate this myriad of positions and functions under them.[15]

VoMi also had to make arrangements with Reich offices and ministries. Here too VoMi resorted to persuasion rather than coercion. Facilitating the process somewhat was the attitude of the Foreign Ministry, which had been in the forefront pushing for centralization. With a few incidental exceptions, relations between VoMi and the Wilhelmstrasse during the prewar years were cooperative. Indeed, after Ribbentrop became foreign minister in early 1938, the relationship became a family affair, nurtured and reinforced by the Ribbentrop and Himmler alliance. One must keep in mind, though, that neither VoMi nor Lorenz was organizationally connected with the ministry. The Ribbentrop link was based on his NSDAP positions, not his post as foreign minister.

After Ribbentrop became foreign minister, Lorenz briefly entertained the idea of holding a position at the ministry.[16] But Ribbentrop squelched the notion, insisting that all ties between the Reich and the minorities remain unofficial and confidential. He feared that a dual position for Lorenz as head of VoMi and as a functionary in the ministry would jeopardize the confidentiality. But another consideration—and perhaps more compelling in denying Lorenz a desk at the Wilhelmstrasse—was Ribbentrop's preference to keep any further party influence from creeping into his ministry. Lorenz's presence would have enhanced the influence of both Hess and Himmler. Although Ribbentrop was on good terms with both, there was a limit to his goodwill.[17]

In dealing with the Foreign Ministry, Lorenz and Behrends usually carried important matters there in person or sent one of their top subordinates. For more routine but politically sensitive business, VoMi turned to one of the permanent liaison offices Ribbentrop had set up for party affairs, either the Referat Partei or Referat Deutschland. For cultural matters they dealt with the Kulturabteilung, or one of the ministry's regional departments. To its missions in countries with large German minorities, the ministry attached Volkstumsreferenten, whose responsibility was to maintain clandestine contact with local VoMi liaison men as well as with the *Volksdeutsche* themselves. Other ministries in close, regular touch with VoMi were the Ministry of Finance and the Reich and Prussian Ministry of the Interior. Although these and others were inclined to cooperate with VoMi, they felt no obligation to submit to its authority.

Indeed, most Reich offices were uneasy about surrendering any official Reich authority to a party organ. In early 1938, several proposals arose for consolidating all official Reich activities related to the *Volksdeutsche* within one state agency, in competition with VoMi.[18] One such suggestion came from within the Foreign Ministry, proposing a Reichskommissar für Volkstumsfragen, who would have state authority and would assume many of VoMi's responsibilities.[19] Another, more compromising suggestion called for creating a Reichskommissariat, which, under Lorenz's command, could be brought into a personal union with VoMi. Ribbentrop toyed with the idea but rejected it, since this new Reich office would have encroached on his own turf.[20] The Nazi who would have gained most from this proposed dual office was Himmler, since any augmenting of Lorenz's influence increased his own. Although the idea of a commissar was shelved for the time being, it reappeared with the resettlement program in the form of the Reichskommisar für die Festigung deutschen Volkstums—a position Himmler appropriated for himself.

Hitler partly filled the gap in state authority with his decree of 2 July 1938, in which he explicitly granted state authority in *Volksdeutsche* matters to VoMi, a party office. He did not, however, grant it absolute powers over the ministries, since its authority was conditional on their consent.[21] VoMi wielded official Reich authority equal to, but not superior to, that of the ministries. Hitler had left the delineation of state authority in *Volkstum* matters ambiguous enough to ensure his position as the supreme arbiter among quarreling subordinates trying to sort things out.

VoMi also brought under its central authority certain functions and activities that were the responsibility of no single office, organization, or ministry. The most important of these was the financing of *Volkstumsarbeit*—the procurement, allocation, and distribution of financial aid for the minorities—a responsibility VoMi explicitly received in the Führer's decree of 2 July 1938. But even then its authority was not absolute. Hitler made VoMi's participation in any decisions on financing the minorities mandatory but did not grant it power of enforcement.

In their attempt to centralize the financial side of *Volkstumsarbeit*, Lorenz and Behrends approached their task with tactics similar to those used in coordinating the *Volkstum* organizations, imposing their own control over the principal agencies involved in financial activities. In early July 1938, in the wake of the Führer's decree, Behrends secured a seat on the board of directors of the Vereinigte Finanzkontore, the institution providing financial aid and credit for *Volksdeutsche* economic enterprises.[22] Then in March 1939 he joined the directory of the Deutsche Stiftung, the quasi-official institution subsidizing *Volksdeutsche* cultural activities abroad.[23] Behrends's positions with the two agencies did not, however, guarantee VoMi complete control in *Volksdeutsche* financial matters, since these agencies were not the sources of funds but were merely conveyors. The money originated with other offices of the state, party, and private sector, including the Foreign Ministry, the Interior Ministry, the Ministry of Finance, the Four Year Plan Office, and the Reich Currency Management Office.[24]

Despite their efforts, the VoMi leaders never got a firm grip on the financing problem. Because of the clandestine nature of most financial transactions involving the *Volksdeutsche*, complete supervision was impossible. Planned, regular expenditures caused few difficulties, but special expenditures not included in budget requests were impossible to regulate. Each ministry and agency had its own discretionary funds to meet emergency expenses, and tracking these payments was beyond VoMi's—indeed anyone's—supervisory capacities. It was not uncommon for two or more Reich offices to supply funds for the same purpose. As for VoMi, whether purchasing radios for the Germans in Hungary or building an athletic field in Poland, the organization faithfully consulted the Foreign Ministry on the political ramifications and the Finance Ministry on the financial aspects of the deal before taking action.[25]

VoMi's participation in these financial matters not only cut down on waste but also served other purposes, including political. Its control over funds became the most effective means to enforce its authority abroad. Although many minorities financed their own cultural activities, Reich subsidies often provided the margin of solvency. And as the *Volksdeutsche* became more dependent on the Reich, they had to accept whatever conditions VoMi placed on the contributions—above all, a pro-Nazi attitude and compliance with orders from Berlin. Lorenz and his associates were not, however, the first to attach political strings to the subsidies. Kursell had demanded correct political attitudes as prerequisites for Reich financial support, as had the VDA. VoMi officials discovered, however, that control over these subsidies was not always a foolproof means for enforcing political compliance. This approach usually brought the established, responsible leaders around to obedience, but it had little success with the more "radical" dissident factions, who were not responsible for the functioning of *Volksdeutsche* institutions.

Since financial control was not always effective, another tactic, political recognition, was often applied. The Führer's decree of July 1938 also granted VoMi the authority to designate and recognize the leadership of each minority and to prohibit any Reich, party, or private office from dealing with any other faction. Official recognition was vital, since the recognition of one group brought with it the political isolation and abandonment of all others. Although it did not guarantee success, political recognition, applied concurrently with financial pressure, made the latter more effective.

Centralized control over the subsidies also served financial and economic purposes, especially in helping to regulate the Reich's foreign exchange balance.[26] With the resumption of rearmament and the mobilization of Reich resources for the effort, Germany set out on a course of autarky. Austerity was the order of the day, and it was VoMi's responsibility to prune and budget the financial needs of *Volkstumsar-*

beit, both cultural and economic. Since most of VoMi's expenditures were abroad, it had to compete for increasingly scarce foreign exchange. This valuable commodity was needed to purchase strategic materials, and since cultural *Volkstumsarbeit* brought little in return but intangible political benefits and the gratitude of *Volksdeutsche* schoolchildren, it ranked low on the list of priorities for receiving foreign exchange. Nonetheless, VoMi's needs were not entirely ignored. Since the future of the minorities as distinct ethnic entities depended on the *Volksdeutsche* youth's retaining their German language and culture, it was vital that they be properly educated. Consequently, Vomi somehow always managed to find enough foreign exchange for supporting *Volksdeutsche* schools.

Since the schools were crucial in the *Volkstumskampf*, they frequently became a point of contention between the Reich and the host governments, some of which were openly hostile to the German schools in their states. They maintained close supervision of these schools and guarded against any foreign interference. As a result, VoMi's duties toward these schools were limited mostly to providing funds. It could do very little in the way of intervening on behalf of the *Volksdeutsche* on administrative or educational issues, such as curriculum. It could pressure *Volksdeutsche* teachers paid with Reich funds for greater conformity, but it had no authority over those salaried by the foreign states. Their regimes closely watched what was taught in the German schools, and pro-Nazi or too-völkisch-minded teachers were quickly removed. In general, even though VoMi spent considerable time and funds on these schools, in the prewar years it failed to assert total control over them.

The second most important *Volksdeutsche* cultural institution was the church. For many *Volksdeutsche* communities, the church was the center of social life, and in some instances, as in the case of the Transylvanian Saxons, it provided the only German education.[27] Since the churches contributed to keeping the minorities ethnically distinct, they too received Reich financial assistance. But VoMi paid relatively little attention to the distribution of church funds, leaving that duty to the Foreign Ministry, which supervised them scrupulously.

The VDA and Reich congregations contributed to *Volksdeutsche* churches, but their gifts were meager in comparison with the amounts provided by the Foreign Ministry, which maintained a special *Kulturfund* for the churches. Initially it paid Protestant congregations abroad through the Kirchliches Aussenamt of the German Evangelical church and paid Roman Catholic churches through the Reichsverband für das katholische Deutschtum.²⁸ When Ribbentrop became foreign minister, he insisted on having total control over these funds and in May 1938 eliminated both church organizations from the process. Henceforth, Reich diplomats decided who would receive the subsidies. They, not the church offices, paid church officials directly. Payments were predicated on the correct political attitudes of individual pastors, priests, and congregations.²⁹

With political strings attached to the subsidies, many *Volksdeutsche* churches were forced to cooperate with National Socialism. By no means, however, did all churches submit, nor did most of them even espouse National Socialism openly. But very few—in particular the Protestant ones—actively resisted. Overall, their contribution to the Nazi cause—and this was all VoMi expected from them in the prewar years—was to nurture the cultural exclusivity of the *Volksdeutsche*. As long as the *Volksdeutsche*, with the encouragement of their churches, maintained their Germanness, VoMi and others tended to their political care.³⁰

Another area of activity over which VoMi sought to extend control was the *Volksdeutsche* economy. Here too VoMi focused on Reich subsidies as leverage for enforcing its will. In this effort it concentrated first on the credit institution, the Vereinigte Finanzkontore. After Behrends joined its board of directors, he was in a position to manipulate the allocation of its funds to the minorities. VoMi could either grant or deny assistance to *Volksdeutsche* enterprises based on the same political considerations it applied to cultural activities.

Manipulating the strings to financial aid, VoMi brought the *Volksdeutsche* economies under its authority and supervised them in the interest of the Reich's economy. After 1936, the Reich goal of economic self-sufficiency required the mustering of all German economic resources, material as well as human. The *Volksdeutsche* could contribute to both, especially as a supplemental labor source. As Germany mobilized its economy and rearmed, its unemployment problem became one of labor shortage, especially in agriculture. Walther Darré, the Reich food minister, became quite concerned about the shortage of seasonal agricultural laborers, especially since racial considerations had become a factor in labor procurement abroad. When Hitler authorized the importation of 120,000 foreign agricultural workers,

Himmler, as head of Reich internal security and watchdog for racial purity, decreed that they could only be of Germanic origin. Undesirable "eastern elements," according to Himmler, once let loose among the Germans, could do irreparable racial harm.[31] Consequently, the Reich increasingly turned to the *Volksdeutsche* for additional, imported manpower. Furthermore, they provided a valuable economic link between the Reich and their homelands. In several East European lands, particularly Yugoslavia and Rumania, they were extremely productive contributors to local agriculture and wielded considerable influence in the economic orientation of their states.[32]

Completing the *Gleichschaltung* and supervising various *Volksdeutsche*-oriented tasks were not VoMi's only domestic duties. It also had its own *Volkstumsarbeit* to perform: refugee care. *Volksdeutsche* refugees had been fleeing to the Reich since the end of World War I, but the problem became more serious in the mid-1930s. *Volksdeutsche*, in trouble in their own states because of their pro-Nazi activities, arrived in the Reich in a steady stream. To assist these faithful, mostly from Poland, Czechoslovakia, and Austria, Hess established the NSDAP Flüchtlingshilfswerk, which coordinated the various Nazi agencies caring for them. Since so many of these refugees had been involved in espionage and other subversive activities, Himmler, as head of Reich internal security, eventually took over their care. In June 1938 he assigned responsibility for these homeless people to his SS subordinate, Lorenz.[33] Lorenz later organized the Beratungsstelle für Einwanderer (BfE) to replace the Flüchtlingshilfswerk. Through the BfE, VoMi operated five or six camps, which housed as many as 20,000 refugees during the prewar years. Eventually VoMi absorbed the BfE as a department.[34]

One additional domestic responsibility for VoMi was supervising non-German minorities residing in the Reich, a task assigned to it in the Führer's decree of July 1938. There is, however, no indication that VoMi ever fulfilled this duty. Its leadership had little interest in extending its authority beyond the *Volksdeutsche* and, probably on the suggestion of Himmler and Heydrich, agreed to pass this duty to the Reichsführer SS and internal security. In the highly personalized administration of the Third Reich, transfer of this responsibility to Himmler would have been a simple affair—as long as all parties involved consented. It appears that in this SS family affair, no one raised objections.

A final, significant act in the coordination process—as far as the *Volksdeutsche* were concerned—was the formal, legal establishment of these people as members of the *Volk*. The Nuremberg Laws of 1935 set legal precedents for future legislation by making race a legal principle and a prerequisite for membership in the *Volk*. But it was not until March 1939 that the Reich Ministry of the Interior officially defined the status of the *Volksdeutsche*. It stipulated that membership in the *Volk* (*Volkszugehörigkeit*) presupposed racial membership and that all Germans, Reich citizens as well as foreign citizens, were included.[35] This definition stopped just short of making the *Volksdeutsche* official Reich citizens. This was as far as the two men ultimately making decisions in *Volksdeutsche* matters—Hitler and Himmler—were willing to go at this time. Granting Reich citizenship to *Volksdeutsche* not only would have complicated the Reich's foreign relations and upset Hitler's foreign policy but also would have conflicted with Himmler's purposes. As future developments demonstrated, to utilize these people as SS auxiliaries, Himmler was willing to recognize them as members of the German *Volk* but not as Reich citizens.

• •

VoMi and the Minorities, I

The Southern and Eastern Borderlands

• •

THE MINORITIES AND HITLER'S FOREIGN POLICY

The *Gleichschaltung* of *Volkstum* activities in the Reich, as performed by Himmler's SS subordinates at VoMi, prepared the way for the nazification of the minorities abroad. As VoMi brought Reich organizations and individuals in line, it also guided the minorities onto the correct political path. Once converted to National Socialism, or at least to sympathy with the Nazi cause and to accepting Adolf Hitler as their Führer, the *Volksdeutsche* of Europe could be exploited in the interests of the Third Reich—or more specifically, as Himmler hoped, the interests of the SS.

Before the war, it was Hitler's foreign policy, above all else, that determined how the *Volksdeutsche* would be utilized. Ultimately his foreign policy aimed at creating a new European racial order. Although he proclaimed the revision of the postwar Versailles settlement as his primary foreign policy goal, his final objective went beyond the revision of borders to creating a new Europe, dominated by a racially pure Germany in which all Germans, Reich as well as *Volksdeutsche*, would be consolidated. Crucial to his scheme was acquiring *Lebensraum*, additional living space, where the German *Volk* could reestablish ancient ties to the soil and thrive for generations to come. In Hitler's view, *Lebensraum*, located primarily in eastern Europe and the Soviet Union, would be acquired through aggressive diplomacy and war.[1]

Since securing the *Lebensraum* would take time, Hitler pursued his ultimate goal in stages, each with its own immediate objectives, but each preparing the way toward the final goal. After initially following a relatively moderate and conciliatory foreign policy—in order to relieve the anxieties of nervous neighbor states—in 1936 Hitler moved into the next phase, more aggressively pursuing his expansionist goals.[2] As he progressed on this new course, the relative importance and roles of the states of central and eastern Europe in his master plan changed, and the services he expected of their respective German minorities were modified accordingly, always in consideration of his latest diplomatic needs.

Consequently, in the prewar years, Reich policy toward the minorities was attuned to Hitler's pragmatic, immediate foreign policy needs rather than the ultimate, ideological aim of building the new racial order. Although the premise that the *Volksdeutsche* were an integral part of the *Volk* remained fundamental to the Reich's interests, at this stage, ideology played a minimal role. Not until military conquests secured the essential *Lebensraum* did ideology assume a more prominent place in Hitler's plans for the *Volksdeutsche*—which, more precisely, would be Himmler's plans.

In the pursuit of his foreign policy aims, Hitler expected all Germans, including *Volksdeutsche*, to contribute. He demanded their allegiance. Many complied and, renouncing loyalties to their own states, placed themselves at his disposal. But in return, they expected Reich support for their revisionist ambitions, the most common being unification with the new Germany. For many of them, encouraged by Hitler's constant denunciation of the Versailles settlement, revision of existing boundaries held top priority. More than anything else, the prospect of ending their minority status attracted *Volksdeutsche* to the swastika.

Although millions of *Volksdeutsche* took Hitler's revisionist rhetoric seriously, many would eventually discover that his support was forthcoming only when their ambitions coincided with his immediate foreign policy goals. Even though their aspirations were in accord with his ultimate goal of building the new order, their aims did not always correspond to his short-term goals. For Hitler, revisionism was merely a means, and as a goal, it was only a short-range one to be compromised and abandoned as the needs of the moment dictated. Consequently, the Reich's policies toward the minorities often resulted in disbelief and disappointment. One of the most difficult tasks facing Lorenz and his associates at VoMi—who came aboard as Hitler was moving apace with his more aggressive policy—was to retain the loyalties and services of *Volksdeutsche* in the face of what many of them saw as a betrayal.

Because Hitler's foreign policy imperatives determined the Reich's policy toward the *Volksdeutsche*, following the latter became a balancing act, with VoMi trying to maintain a three-cornered relationship among the minorities, the host states, and the Reich. In this precarious effort, VoMi had to consider three factors. The first was the historic relationship between a minority and its host state. This was critical in determining the attitude of the host government toward the *Volksdeutsche*. VoMi could not control this variable, since it was beyond VoMi's power to overcome traditional prejudices so fundamental to the relationship. The second factor was the relationship between the Reich and the government of the host state. This factor, determined primarily by where a particular state fit into Hitler's short-term foreign policy schemes, also lay outside the range of VoMi's influence. Hitler personally determined the Reich's policy toward a certain state and seldom, if ever, solicited VoMi's advice.

VoMi was powerless to alter the first two factors, but it helped forge and maintain the third, the relationship between the Reich and a particular minority. Working within the parameters and constraints of Hitler's foreign policy, the men at VoMi enjoyed considerable latitude in constructing this relationship, which, before the war, focused on nazification. As promoted by VoMi, nazification meant bringing the *Volksdeutsche* around to accepting the leadership of the Führer and to realizing that they too, no less than Reich Germans, had obligations to the Third Reich. Once nazified, they would be charged at the appropriate time with their specific duties and responsibilities. Perhaps the most common demand VoMi made of the *Volksdeutsche* during the prewar years was discipline—not creating incidents abroad that could unexpectedly divert the course of Hitler's foreign policy. Another service was a more active one, performing as a "fifth column" by betraying their own state in the service of the Reich. Indeed, this latter role was the one contemporaries most frequently attributed to the German minorities.[3]

Although the "fifth column" label was commonly ascribed to the minorities, the services that *Volksdeutsche* rendered the Reich individually as well as collectively were varied and diverse. No single generalization adequately covers their roles and their relationships to the Reich. These complex and varying relationships can best be evaluated through individual examinations of each minority and its ties to both the Reich and its host state—the approach this study will follow in this and subsequent chapters. Deeply involved in establishing these relationships and in determining the roles of the minorities was the Volksdeutsche Mittelstelle. Its status as the primary intermediary between the Reich and the minorities continued to evolve as Hitler's foreign policy passed through its stages and as the Reich's relations with its neighbors changed accordingly.

It is impossible to order discussions of the individual minorities and their dealings with VoMi chronologically, since VoMi was involved with all of them simultaneously. But at times certain groups attracted greater attention as events related to them and their states came into prominence. Hitler's campaign of aggression dictated the sequence of events, as he dealt with the host states of the minorities one by one. Since the Austrian *Anschluss* was Hitler's first significant international step of aggression, the first *Volksdeutsche* to warrant discussion are the Germans of Austria.

• • • AUSTRIA

The 6 million Germans of Austria constituted a national majority, but since they were not Reich citizens, by some definitions they were *Volksdeutsche*. Therefore, the new leaders of VoMi inherited an interest in Austrian affairs, even though it was to be short-lived. The annexation of Austria (the *Anschluss*) in March 1938—one year after Lorenz assumed control at VoMi—terminated the status of Austrians as *Volksdeutsche*, and once they received Reich citizenship, VoMi had no further interest in them.

Before the *Anschluss*, VoMi played a minimal role in Austria, since initiative in Austrian affairs lay with the very highest Nazi circles. VoMi served only as an auxiliary and lent whatever assistance it could to advance the Nazi cause. It was well suited for this task because of several Austrian exiles employed on its staff.[4] One of its contributions was to gather information about the political situation through its network of contacts in the illegal Nazi underground.[5] After the *Anschluss*, VoMi established an office in Vienna under the leadership of Franz Wehofsich, who became responsible for all *Volksdeutsche* matters in the new Ostmark, as well as for all non-German residents. The Vienna office also became one of the primary contacts with *Volksdeutsche* living in two former Austrian territories, northern Yugoslavia and the South Tyrol.[6]

• • ITALY

The *Anschluss* raised the hopes of countless *Volksdeutsche* throughout Europe who concluded that Hitler was about to redeem his promises to rectify the other alleged injustices of the postwar settlement. Since excited *Volksdeutsche* could disturb the tranquility Hitler sought with the Reich's neighbors, it became VoMi's duty to calm them and to keep their expectations from rising any further. This, in essence, was VoMi's primary task with the *Volksdeutsche* living in the Italian South Tyrol.

The South Tyrol, before its post–World War I annexation by Italy, had belonged to the historic Austrian province of the Tyrol. As a reward for fighting on the winning side, Italy received the southern part of the province, south of the Brenner Pass. The southernmost annexed territory, the Trentino, was indisputably Italian in ethnic composition, but the northern part, the Alto Adige, which included the cities of Bolzano (Bozen) and Merano (Meran), was mostly German. In the 1920s, more than 210,000 of its 260,000 total population were Germans. Another postwar acquisition, with a German population of 5,600, was the Kanaltal, formerly belonging to the Austrian province of Carinthia, located at the junction of Italy, Austria, and Yugoslavia. Austria also surrendered to Italy Istria, with 12,700 Germans; Trieste, 11,856; Gorz-Gradiska, 4,486; and Dalmatia, 462.[7]

Italy's treatment of its national minorities was among the worst in Europe. The Italians had not fared as well as they had expected at the postwar conference tables, and they vented some of their frustrations by disregarding the rights of their new, non-Italian subjects. They refused to commit themselves to binding treaties or declarations guaranteeing minority rights. In their new territories, they relentlessly pursued a policy of de-Germanization. Italians replaced German officials and teachers, and German economic enterprises were singled out for bureaucratic harassment. Italian was also made the exclusive language for transacting official business. The process of Italianizing the land was not limited to the living: some local authorities exhumed German soldiers from Tyrolean cemeteries.[8]

When Lorenz arrived at VoMi, he presumed it was his duty to protect the interests of the South Tyroleans and win them over to National Socialism. In this effort, VoMi built up a network of contacts in the area, relying mostly on people already working for other Reich offices, such as the AO and the VDA.[9] The foremost enticement used in attracting these devoutly Roman Catholic, conservative, mostly peasant Tyroleans to the Nazi cause was the prospect of fulfilling their irredentist goal of reuniting the South Tyrol with Austria—and after the *Anschluss*, with the Reich.[10]

Before the *Anschluss*, rumors abounded in the South Tyrol that Mussolini had offered the region to Hitler as a gesture of goodwill. But it was Hitler who was prepared to make concessions, to compromise ideological principles, and to abandon revisionist claims in order to gain the duce's support for the merger. Mussolini's backing for the *Anschluss* was more important to Hitler than restoring the South Tyroleans to the *Volk* or rectifying the injustices they suffered under Italian rule. In consideration of these priorities, by mid-December 1937, VoMi had reversed its policy toward the South Tyroleans and tried to calm rather than incite them.

Restraint and moderation became the order of the day, but reversing VoMi's approach toward the South Tyroleans was difficult. After years of repressive Italian rule, they had no recognized, established leadership to which VoMi could award or deny recognition as a means of enforcing compliance. The lack of a recognized leadership made even communicating orders to the minority a next-to-impossible task. Furthermore, since the Tyrol had never belonged to Germany, the Reich provided few funds here, and therefore the threat of withholding payments made little difference. VoMi's only effective means for securing South Tyrolean loyalty had been revisionist propaganda, and once it reversed the appeal, VoMi lost much of its leverage.

The South Tyrol was a major issue when in May 1938, shortly after the *Anschluss*, a grateful Hitler—thankful for Mussolini's support for the annexation—visited in Rome. Afterward Ribbentrop, recently appointed Reich foreign minister, summoned Lorenz, Behrends, and several VDA officials to the Wilhelmstrasse to impress on them that continued Italian-German friendship was more important to the Reich than the interests of the South Tyroleans. The Reich would no longer recognize them as a formal *Volksgruppe* or regard them as an official Reich concern. He then sent Behrends to the region to identify the local leadership. Behrends was to set up a line of communication with the minority and summon its leaders to Berlin so that Hitler could impress on them, in person, the new facts of political life in their land.[11]

During the rest of 1938, VoMi tried to undo the propaganda work it had done so successfully. It even requested the Gestapo to intercept Tyrolean folk song records at the frontier, since these helped keep the revisionist issue alive.[12] Matters subsided somewhat until March 1939, when the final dissolution of Czechoslovakia not only rekindled South Tyrolean hopes but also planted new anxieties in Mussolini's mind about the intentions of his northern friend.

By early 1939, Hitler, aware of Mussolini's concerns, had decided that the only effective solution was resettlement. As Italian Foreign Minister Galeazzo Ciano observed, since men could not move mountains, the men would have to be relocated.[13] In fact, as early as January 1937, Göring had confided to the Reich ambassador in Rome, Ulrich von Hassell, that if relations with Italy demanded, the Reich was prepared to resettle the South Tyroleans.[14] Thus in March 1939, Hitler instructed the minority leadership—presumably through VoMi—to begin secret preparations for the relocation. When, in May, Mussolini urged Hitler to speed up the process, resettlement became official Reich policy not only for the South Tyrol but also for the Kanaltal and Grödnertal, located in northeastern Italy.[15]

The *Volksdeutsche* of Italy had no say in the matter. Their fate was decided without their assent. Some Tyroleans traveled to Berlin to plead against resettlement but received only evasive replies from the Foreign Ministry and VoMi.[16] On 7 July 1939, VoMi instructed all Reich and party offices to sever all remaining contacts with the South Tyroleans.[17] Resettlement, the details of which will be discussed later, ended the status of the South Tyroleans not only as a distinct ethnic group but also as an officially recognized national minority. According to the resettlement agreements, individuals had the option of resettling in the Reich or remaining in Italy and thereby renouncing their German status. Those opting for the latter would henceforth be recognized as Italians by both Reich and Italian authorities. The Reich surrendered all claims to them, and since they were no longer considered *Volksdeutsche*, VoMi's responsibility for them also ended.

The case of the South Tyroleans contradicts the generalization that all German minorities were "fifth columns" and offered themselves as pretexts for Nazi aggression. The South Tyroleans did not collaborate with the Reich against Italy, nor were they pliant tools of the Reich. They were passive, even disapproving, spectators to these events, as Hitler bypassed them and dealt with the Italians directly. Their revisionist interests were sacrificed in the interest of Italian-Reich friendship, a crucial element in Hitler's overall foreign policy scheme. As subsequent events unfolded, the common response of the Tyroleans to the resettlement was procrastination, not blind obedience to the Führer. Many, embittered by what they perceived as a betrayal, were unwilling to sacrifice their homes and homeland for the Nazi cause and, refusing to heed the call of the Führer, chose not to emigrate.

• • • CZECHOSLOVAKIA

The German minority that attracted the most worldwide attention following the *Anschluss* was that of Czechoslovakia. Its fate was decided concurrently with that of the South Tyroleans, but the result was notably different. The *Volksdeutsche* of Czechoslovakia, including the Sudeten Germans of Bohemia, Moravia, and Austrian Silesia, the Carpathian Germans of Slovakia and Ruthenia, and the former Reich Germans of the tiny Hültschin region, constituted not only the largest German minority in Europe but also the second-largest national group in the multinational state of Czechoslovakia. In 1930, out of a total population of just over 14,500,000, there were 7,349,039 Czechs, 3,318,445 Germans, 2,407,565 Slovaks, and some 1,500,000 people of other nationalities.[18]

More clearly than any other developments up to that point, events in Czechoslovakia demonstrated the aggressive nature of Hitler's foreign policy. Hitler's intentions for Czechoslovakia arose from his Austrian-bred conviction that Germans were the historic and rightful inhabitants and rulers of Bohemia and Moravia and that the creation of Czechoslovakia in 1918 violated this natural order. The country had to be destroyed. Members of the local German minority would lend a helping hand, both as an active fifth column and as passive pretexts for aggression. VoMi would be instrumental in nearly every step and at every level of the destruction.

At the founding of the new Czech and Slovak state, its leaders signed a treaty that guaranteed the rights of their national minorities. But unlike the governments of most other new states, which frequently failed to honor such commitments, the regime in Prague generally lived up to its promises and accorded its minorities, including the Germans, some of the most generous minority rights in Europe. In time, however, with the onset of the economic depression of the 1930s, the relatively good relationship between the national minorities and the Prague government deteriorated. Even though the Germans suffered no greater economic hardships than any other ethnic group in Czechoslovakia, they complained that Prague favored the Czechs.

The Germans of Czechoslovakia received some economic assistance from the Reich, but they mostly relied on their own resources to sustain their economic interests and maintain their cultural institutions and programs.[19] These economically and socially diverse people also protected their interests politically by organizing along a broad political spectrum, from their own indigenous Nazi movement on the extreme right to liberal, even socialist parties on the left.[20] By far the most important and most effective was Konrad Henlein's movement, which emphasized the *völkisch* unity of the Sudeten Germans as its guiding political principle.

Ideologically, Henlein's movement, formally founded on 1 October 1933 as the Sudetendeutsche Heimatfront (SHF), was closer to the conservative, *völkisch* tradition than to the radical racism of National Socialism. In the spring of 1935 Henlein renamed it the Sudetendeutsche Partei (SdP), and in the May national elections it won the largest popular vote of any single political party.[21] As a result, both the Prague government and the Reich had to recognize Henlein and his movement as the dominant political force among the country's Germans. At least for the time being, official Reich authorities, in particular the Foreign Ministry, abandoned the Sudeten Nazis led by Hans Krebs.[22] The immediate goal of the Sudeten German mainstream, as represented by Henlein, was German national autonomy. But there were also those who envisioned separation from Czechoslovakia and unification with the rest of the *Volk*.

By the time Lorenz arrived at VoMi in January 1937, the majority of Sudeten Germans faithfully followed Henlein, and it became VoMi's job to court the latter and win him over to the Reich's cause. As a secondary goal, VoMi sought a reconciliation between the Sudeten Nazis and Henlein. In pursuing both objectives, the SS men at VoMi realized for the first time that their efforts did not always serve all Reich interests, or even all SS interests. In courting Henlein, they antagonized Heydrich and the SD, who favored the Nazi dissidents around Krebs.

VoMi also discovered that it was hardly in a position to force Henlein into compliance. The economically independent Sudeten Germans did not rely on Reich subsidies, and therefore VoMi's control over the purse was not very effective with them. Furthermore, since Henlein and the SdP enjoyed a genuine, popular mandate as well as official status with the Prague government, VoMi could not exercise its power of granting or withholding political recognition. As a result, it had to employ the utmost tact and persuasion to get its way with Henlein.

It was the activities of the radical, pro-Nazi wing of the SdP in the summer of 1937 that interjected VoMi into Sudeten affairs. These dissidents were attracting an increasing number of disenchanted Sudeten Germans who resented Henlein's rising international stature and felt that he no longer adequately served Sudeten interests. In mid-June, VoMi ordered some of the renegades to Berlin, lectured them on the need for unity, and reaffirmed its support for Henlein—even though ideologically it would have preferred to support these pro-Nazis.[23]

The Foreign Ministry also became concerned that Henlein's travels abroad and his much publicized efforts to unify all German minorities in an international association might be viewed as a campaign directed from Berlin.[24] In late August, Lorenz met with Henlein and expressed his displeasure with the latter's international ambitions. Lorenz suggested that Henlein curtail his travels and limit his activities to the SdP.[25] Subsequent events demonstrated to Henlein the wisdom of following Lorenz's advice. Steinacher's firing, for one, sobered him to the changing political realities in the Reich. It was evident that conservatives in the Reich, with whom Henlein had associated, had become expendable politically and were unreliable as allies. And since the Foreign Ministry, which had staunchly supported him all along, also disapproved of his outside activities, Henlein was left with little Reich support. Lorenz perceived an opportunity to draw nearer to Henlein, and as a gesture of goodwill—even at the risk of incurring Heydrich's wrath—he cracked down on several of the anti-Henlein groups active inside the Reich.[26]

Lorenz's intercession impressed Henlein, who realized the wisdom of heeding VoMi's advice. In early December, the two met again to discuss the expulsion of some Nazi sympathizers from the SdP. Assuring Lorenz that he had regretted taking the step, Henlein insisted that it had been necessary in the interest of unity and discipline. Lorenz, for whom unity and peace within the minorities were paramount, endorsed the action—even though it was taken against Heydrich's favorites. Henlein had found in VoMi a new, influential patron. The price he paid for this patronage was heavy—increased Reich influence over the SdP and the subordination of Sudeten interests to the imperatives of the Führer's foreign policy. The Foreign Ministry was pleased with the new understanding, since bringing Henlein under VoMi's wing greatly reduced the potential for complications in the Reich's relations with Czechoslovakia.[27] As for VoMi, it secured its position as the primary intermediary between the Reich and Henlein's movement. As a result, in the critical events of 1938, which were about to unfold, Lorenz would be an important, active participant.

VoMi's relations with the Sudeten Germans went beyond meetings between Lorenz and Henlein. As the Sudeten issue gained in importance, Behrends created a permanent Sudetendeutsches Referat, which performed a wide range of services, from arranging training in the Reich for Sudeten schoolgirls to approving Reich itineraries for prominent Sudeten visitors.[28] It remained VoMi's duty to ensure that such activities, closely watched from Prague, would not lead to complications.

VoMi's involvement with the Sudeten Germans climaxed in 1938 with the crisis that eventually led to the destruction of Czechoslovakia and terminated the minority status of most of its *Volksdeutsche*. The Austrian *Anschluss* had raised the expectations of many Sudeten Germans, who hoped that their fate would run a similar course. But what the Sudeten Germans expected and desired made little difference, since the final word on their fate would come from the Führer himself. Hitler summoned Henlein and his colleague Karl Frank to Berlin and on 28 March, in the presence of Hess, Ribbentrop, and Lorenz, lectured them on the ramifications of the *Anschluss*. In vain they tried to persuade Hitler to take similar action in Czechoslovakia. He explained that even though his aim was to destroy Czechoslovakia, conditions were not yet right. He made no firm commitments but instructed Henlein to begin pressuring the Prague government with demands that it could not meet.[29]

Apparently Lorenz was only a passive observer at this meeting, but his presence nevertheless underscores his importance and complicity in these events. He was also present at a conference the next day at the Wilhelmstrasse. Here, to select Reich diplomats as well as the Sudeten German visitors, Ribbentrop summarized the Führer's words of the previous day. He repeated to Henlein and Frank the need to pressure the Prague government and instructed them to keep in touch with both the Reich representative in Prague, Ernst Eisenlohr, and Lorenz.[30]

As the Sudeten crisis unfolded, VoMi tried to help Henlein maintain order in the ranks of the SdP and restrained his opponents in the Reich. In Czechoslovakia, Sudeten activists had escalated their agitation, and from inside the Reich party, SS and SA agents were stoking rumors about an imminent German invasion of the Sudetenland, raising the level of excitement among the *Volksdeutsche*. Henlein, losing control, pleaded for VoMi's intervention.[31] In response, it sent to Prague one of its leading troubleshooters, Wilhelm Luig, to reassure Henlein of VoMi's support and to urge the SA, for one, to restrain its hotheads. Ribbentrop, supportive of these efforts, suggested that VoMi should send even more of its men into the troubled areas.[32] For the time being, calm was required, since escalating tensions could force Hitler to act prematurely.

While the officials at VoMi labored to keep a lid on the situation, Hitler decided that the time had come for action. On 21 April he ordered the military to prepare an operational plan, "Case Green," for the destruction of Czechoslovakia. Three days later Henlein submitted to the Prague government intentionally outrageous demands, known as the Karlsbad demands, calling for the creation of a virtual German state within the state. Then, on 20 May, having received the completed plans for "Case Green," Hitler began looking for the opportune moment to settle with Czechoslovakia. Although the "May Crisis" subsided, the Sudeten issue had assumed international proportions.

The crisis not only had attracted world attention but also had re-affirmed Hitler's determination to finish off Czechoslovakia. On May 30 he issued the directive for "Case Green," with the attack to begin no later than 1 October.[33] Since he ordered the attack without any further thought to resolving the Sudeten question, it is evident that the issue itself was not essential and served merely as a pretext for aggression. Whether Lorenz was privy to the full scope of Hitler's ultimate intentions is uncertain, but one may safely conclude that he was aware the Karlsbad demands were not the real issue and that the negotiations between the Sudeten Germans and the Czechs were meaningless. It is certainly clear that Henlein was not fully informed of Hitler's intentions and continued in the belief that the Sudeten issue was essential. Throughout the remainder of the crisis, Henlein kept Lorenz fully informed about his negotiations with the Prague government as well as about his contacts with sympathetic English visitors. Much of this information, however, served little purpose, since the highest levels at both VoMi and the Wilhelmstrasse were aware that the negotiations were a ruse.[34]

Throughout the summer the negotiations continued, and the SdP kept VoMi informed. In early September, President Edvard Beneš caught the Sudeten negotiators by surprise when he accepted almost all of Henlein's demands. But clashes between Czechs and Germans led to a suspension of the negotiations and ended the hopes of those who saw in them a chance for a peaceful solution. On 12 September, Hitler—intent on destroying Czechoslovakia—harangued the NSDAP rally at Nuremberg, denouncing the Czechs for their allegedly atrocious treatment of the Sudeten Germans. Two days later Behrends notified the Foreign Ministry that Henlein had broken off negotiations and had fled across the frontier into Bavaria. From a safe haven inside the Reich, Henlein demanded nothing less than the annexation of the Sudetenland to Germany.[35]

Hitler's tirade at Nuremberg further incited Sudeten German activists, who provoked Czechoslovakian authorities to declare martial law. In response to Hitler's orders for even more agitation and for sending more provocateurs into action, on 20 September Henlein instructed special units, trained and equipped in Germany, to create at least ten incidents each inside Czechoslovakia by the next morning.[36]

With Henlein's flight, it appears that VoMi's involvement in choreographing unrest in the Sudetenland ended. Hitler assumed personal direction of events and resorted to summit diplomacy. He met with British Prime Minister Neville Chamberlain at Berchtesgaden and later at Bad Godesberg. When he raised his demands after a compromise on Sudeten autonomy had been reached, Chamberlain, who had hoped to find a diplomatic solution to the Sudeten problem, despaired of a peaceful resolution. War seemed imminent. But in late September, Mussolini interceded and persuaded Hitler to give a negotiated settlement one more chance. The result was the infamous Munich conference, a summit of the four leaders of Germany, Italy, France, and Great Britain. The details of this meeting are beyond the scope of this study, but it is noteworthy that VoMi had no visible role in these proceedings. Neither did the Czechoslovakian government or the Sudeten Germans.

The conference was concluded with the Munich Pact of 29 September. It provided for the immediate Reich annexation of Czechoslovakia's western border regions, bringing the majority of the Sudeten Germans into the Reich. Although no one yet knew exactly when and how the final destruction would take place, it was widely presumed that what was left of the country could not survive for long. Despite Hitler's assurances that he was satisfied, and despite guarantees by England and France to defend the remnants of Czechoslovakia, its days were numbered. One Nazi zealot, overcome with emotion by the "freedom bells ringing in the Sudetenland," assured the *Volksdeutsche* remaining in Czechoslovakia that it would be only a matter of time before they too would join the *Volk*.[37]

The final unraveling began almost immediately. On 6 October 1938, following complicated negotiations and intrigues, Slovakia proclaimed autonomy, and three days later Ruthenia, the easternmost section of the country, gained autonomy and became the Carpatho-Ukraine. Covetous neighbors also nibbled at the carcass. The Hungarians claimed Slovakia and Ruthenia but for the time being settled for small strips of both. Poland, itself destined for destruction, participated in the pickings by seizing Teschen and a few bits of Slovakia. As these territories were transferred to other states, the status of their *Volksdeutsche* changed. Those residing in lands going to Germany received Reich citizenship, and at least for the majority of them, their expectations were met. Those transferred to Hungary or Poland, however, were grievously disappointed, since their minority status not only continued but also worsened. Hungary and Poland had among the poorest records in Europe in the treatment of their national minorities.

Until the final dissolution of Czechoslovakia, VoMi continued its duties toward the remaining *Volksdeutsche*. Lorenz suggested to both Hitler and Ribbentrop that a comprehensive agreement on minorities should be concluded with Prague.[38] As a result, on 7 November a conference convened at VoMi, attended by representatives of the Foreign Ministry, the Ministry of the Interior, the OKW, the Education Ministry, and the Reichsführer SS. The Foreign Ministry pushed for a treaty, but Behrends, presiding over the meeting, opposed the idea on grounds that the Reich must not be bound by any reciprocal obligations to Czechoslovakia. He preferred instead an exchange of declarations that would bind the Czechs but not necessarily the Reich. Behrends's position prevailed and was presented to the foreign minister and the Führer for approval.[39]

Prague accepted virtually everything Berlin proposed and not only committed itself to minority protection but also offered to create a ministerial post for the *Volksdeutsche*. However, conciliation was not on Hitler's mind. The Reich orchestrated more incidents, providing the pretext for the final dissolution of Czechoslovakia. On 12 March 1939, presumably on orders from the very top, Behrends instructed contacts inside Czechoslovakia to arrange further provocations.[40] As expected, these resulted in violent incidents, and two days later Ribbentrop sent an angry protest to Prague, blaming the Czechs for the unrest and demanding a delegation to be sent to Berlin to discuss the situation.[41]

After arriving in Berlin, the Czechoslovakian president, Emil Hácha, and the foreign minister, František Chvalkovsky, met with Hitler in the early morning of 15 March. Under the most severe threats from Hitler and his military advisers, Hacha agreed to place Bohemia and Moravia under Reich "protection." Later that day German troops invaded the country, and on 16 March, Bohemia and Moravia became the "Protectorate," completely under German subjugation. Its *Volksdeutsche* became Reich citizens. Although not all Sudeten Germans had participated in the destruction of the state, many had. And since their leadership—with an electoral mandate from a majority of *Volksdeutsche*—had played a crucial part, collective Sudeten German involvement in these events can justifiably be characterized as that of a fifth column.

With the declaration of Slovak autonomy on 6 October 1938, VoMi turned its attention to the Carpathian Germans of Slovakia, who, during the Sudeten crisis, for the most part had been ignored. Their fate, as unfolding events would demonstrate, would not be tied to that of the Sudetenlanders. Their subsequent experiences—so different from those of the Sudeten Germans, for years fellow residents in the same state—illustrate the fallacy of drawing broad generalizations about the collective experiences and relationships of all *Volksdeutsche* with the Third Reich.[42]

In 1929 the estimated 130,000 Carpathian Germans of Slovakia and Ruthenia, lands formerly belonging to the Hungarian half of the Habsburg Empire, organized the Karpathendeutsche Partei (KP). After lengthy negotiations in November 1933 its leader, Franz Karmasin, affiliated the KP with Henlein's movement. In October 1937 this affiliation was reinforced when Henlein named Karmasin his deputy in Slovakia, and in return Karmasin brought the KP under Henlein's authority.[43] The Carpathian Germans had hoped their association with Henlein's movement would advance their cause, but instead it only complicated matters. Many came to resent Henlein's notoriety and felt that their interests were being neglected and had become secondary to those of the Sudeten Germans.[44]

In May 1938, at the height of the first Sudeten crisis, Karmasin, feeling ignored and frustrated, traveled to Berlin and pleaded at the Wilhelmstrasse to include Slovakia in any demands for territorial or political concessions from Prague. The diplomats admonished Karmasin for his impertinence and referred him to VoMi. Here he was again chastised for speaking out of place and not going through prescribed channels, that is, for not going to VoMi first. Besides, VoMi was too busy to give him a serious hearing. At the time it was preoccupied with pressing problems within other minorities and was monitoring the Sudeten crisis. Rebuffed by both the Foreign Ministry and VoMi, Karmasin took his case to the SD, which was willing to listen and to exploit Carpathian German discontent to secure its own influence within this group. Only then did VoMi pay attention; in cooperation with the SD, it established a liaison office in Berlin for the miffed Karmasin.[45]

Following the Munich conference and the declaration of Slovak autonomy, VoMi addressed the future relationship between the Reich and the remaining Germans of Czechoslovakia, including those of Slovakia. It instructed Karmasin to reorganize his minority and to nazify it further. To help with the process, VoMi would dispatch Herbert Kier to Bratislava to serve as a permanent liaison with the group.[46] As its involvement with this minority grew, VoMi became, in league with the SD, one of the most influential Reich authorities in Slovakia. The chief diplomat in Bratislava, Ernst Druffel, often complained about VoMi's interference and naively suggested that its authority should be curtailed.[47] But VoMi was not about to abdicate its prerogatives just as the Carpathian Germans were becoming one of the principal issues of mutual concern for the Reich and Slovakia.

The Slovaks, accomplices in the final demise of Czechoslovakia, reaped dividends in the form of independence, but independence only exacerbated a remaining problem—what to do with the Carpathian Germans. Before the final dismantlement, as early as 12 February 1939, Vojtech Tuka, the leader of the Slovak fascistlike Hlinka Guard, had traveled to Berlin for a personal audience with Hitler and Ribbentrop. At this meeting he agreed to cooperate in the final destruction. Karmasin also attended but evidently played no prominent role.[48] Further negotiations took place in early March. As a result, on 14 March, after last-minute conversations between Hitler and Slovak Minister Josef Tiso, and after a rubber-stamp approval from the Slovak diet, Slovakia gained independence. A treaty of protection between Slovakia and Germany followed, according to which Slovakia became Hitler's first client state.

The Carpathian Germans, excluded from playing any significant role in the events leading up to Slovak independence, reluctantly resigned themselves to remaining a national minority indefinitely. Two days after the declaration of independence, Karmasin wrote to Henlein, contrasting the joy among the Germans of Bohemia and Moravia with the dejection of the *Volksdeutsche* of Slovakia. But despite their great disappointment, Karmasin added, they were prepared to accept the role the Führer assigned to them.[49] As they would find out, it was the Führer's wish that they remain a national minority throughout the war years.

After the destruction of Czechoslovakia, Hitler turned his sights toward the Lithuanian city of Memel (Klaipeda) and its environs, the
Memelland. Until the Lithuanian seizure of this territory from Germany shortly after the end of World War I, the estimated 60,000
Germans living there had been Prussians and were quite distinct from
the 30,000–40,000 *Volksdeutsche* who inhabited the rest of Lithuania
and who were former subjects of the Russian czar. Although some of
the latter were urban folk, the majority farmed the countryside south-
west of Kaunas, near the East Prussian border, where their ancestors
had settled several generations earlier.[50] Neither the Memellanders
nor the *Volksdeutsche* in the interior were Baltic Germans, a term
exclusively reserved for the *Volksdeutsche* of Estonia and Latvia.

The Reich's relations with the two *Volksgruppen* constituting the
German minority in Lithuania differed greatly, not only because of its
special interest in the Memellanders as former Reich subjects but also
because of the different degrees of intercourse the Lithuanians allowed the two groups with Germany. On the basis of the Memelland
Statute of May 1924—which legitimized Memel as an autonomous
region within Lithuania—the Lithuanians recognized the Memel Germans as a distinct group with special status and guaranteed them
unlimited access to the Reich. As for the Germans of the interior, their
access to the Reich was restricted. Nevertheless, during the early years
of statehood, the Lithuanians treated the interior *Volksdeutsche* well. As
simple peasants owning only moderate amounts of land, they entertained no lofty aspirations for special status and no notions of cultural
superiority. They posed no threat to Lithuania.[51]

Relations between the Germans in the interior and the Lithuanians
worsened in 1926, when a coup brought Antonas Smetona to power.
This fervent nationalist introduced chauvinistic measures such as the
Lithuanization of family names. During the 1930s, Lithuanian nationalism intensified. As far as the Germans were concerned, it peaked
in 1935 when the regime dissolved their main political organ, the
Deutsche Partei Litauens, and curtailed the activities of their cultural
organization, the Kulturverband der Deutschen in Litauen. By 1936
the VDA considered Lithuania one of the most difficult lands in which
to pursue its activities.[52]

The Memellanders were not entirely isolated from the upsurge of

Lithuanian nationalism, but the autonomy statute shielded them from the most onerous measures. Furthermore, a growing National Socialist movement in the Memelland countered Lithuanian nationalism with a no-less-virulent German nationalism. Two rival Nazi groups surfaced in 1933, the Christlich-Soziale Arbeitsgemeinschaft, with connections to Hess, and the Sozialistische Volksgemeinschaft, under the leadership of Dr. Ernst Neumann, with ties to the most formidable Nazi in the northeast, Gauleiter Koch of East Prussia.[53] When Lorenz assumed command at VoMi, the Nazi movement in the Memelland was well developed but fragmented. VoMi's mission was not to nazify this *Volksgruppe* but rather to impose VoMi authority and to reconcile the feuding factions.

Another one of VoMi's tasks here was to discourage emigration to the Reich. Many Memellanders, tired of political conflict, tried to leave, but it was Reich policy to discourage emigration from disputed areas. Emigration would reduce the German population and thereby weaken Reich claims to these lands. VoMi also was involved in the distribution of Reich funds among these people.[54] These subsidies aroused the envy of Gauleiter Koch, who was eager to divert them through his own offices in Königsberg. VoMi and the Foreign Ministry forestalled Koch's efforts and in March 1938 turned to Hess. Hess confirmed VoMi's supremacy in this matter, and Koch backed down, but only for the time being.[55]

After the *Anschluss* and with the escalation of the Sudeten crisis in the spring of 1938, Memelland activists became more strident in their demands for a quick solution to the Memel issue—meaning reannexation. Hitler, busy with Czechoslovakia, pushed the issue to the back burner and left VoMi and the diplomats to monitor the situation. In July 1938, VoMi summoned Ernst Neumann, the official leader of the *Volksgruppe*, to Berlin to impress on him the need to maintain stricter discipline over the "hotheads." But Neumann found stifling the activists a difficult task, especially after the Munich conference, since it appeared that revisionist demands elsewhere were being met. In an effort to deflate their heightened expectations, the Foreign Ministry and VoMi advised the Memellanders to heed Hitler's public assurances that the Sudetenland was his final demand.[56]

The Lithuanian authorities reacted to the developments in Czechoslovakia with appeasement. In late October they restored several German organizations that had been proscribed years earlier and lifted the state of martial law that had been imposed to quell unrest. But despite these gestures of goodwill and Neumann's efforts to quiet the agitation, *"Ein Volk, Ein Reich, Ein Führer!"* resonated through the streets of Memel. VoMi officials even feared that reckless activists might attempt some sort of uprising and concluded that only the express orders of the Führer could restore calm.[57]

In early December, VoMi again ordered Neumann to Berlin for consultations, this time to the Wilhelmstrasse to meet with Ribbentrop, Lorenz, and Behrends. Ribbentrop promised to raise the issue of annexation with the Führer, for nothing could be done without his consent. Neumann was instructed to maintain order and to see that the upcoming Memel Landtag elections, scheduled for 11 December, proceeded without disruption.[58] On election day, the Memel electorate overwhelmingly endorsed all Nazi candidates, a mandate that could only be interpreted as a vote for reannexation. Berlin again summoned Neumann, this time for a brief meeting on 2 January 1939 with Hitler, who, in the presence of Ribbentrop, assured Neumann that the issue of the Memelland would shortly be resolved. After this interview, Lorenz instructed Neumann to keep in close touch with the Reich legation in Memel and assigned a SD man from Tilsit as a contact between Neumann and the Reich.[59] Having established communications with the Memelland, VoMi stood ready to execute all orders from above.

But the obstreperous Gauleiter Koch almost derailed the process. In early February, without any instructions or approval from above, he informed Neumann that the time had come for resolving the Memel question and that Neumann was to follow his orders. He even threatened to shoot Neumann if he disobeyed. When news of Koch's behavior reached Lorenz, the furious SS Obergruppenführer turned to Hess and demanded that Koch be reprimanded for his outrageous actions. Lorenz's protest brought fleeting results, for although Koch assured Neumann that the party would refrain from any further interference, less than one week before the final resolution of the Memelland issue, he was at it again, ordering Neumann to Königsberg. This time the wary Neumann turned to the Foreign Ministry for advice. The ministry as well as VoMi instructed Neumann to stay out of Koch's reach, for undoubtedly Koch was contemplating using him to precipitate matters in the Memelland.[60] The Reich's diplomats were engaged in sensitive negotiations with the Lithuanians over its transfer and feared that any disturbances might upset the process.

VoMi managed to deter Koch and prevented him and other hotheads from disrupting the diplomatic process that resulted in the peaceful reannexation of the Memelland to the Reich on 23 March 1939. Although the Lithuanians regretted having to cede the valuable shoreline and port city to Germany, they were relieved to be rid of the troublesome minority and thankful that Hitler's demands and intentions for Lithuania went no further. Hitler seemed satisfied with the territorial revision and did not exploit *Volksdeutsche* grievances as a pretext to destroy the country, as he had in Czechoslovakia and would soon in neighboring Poland. Most Memellanders were elated. The annexation brought them Reich citizenship and concluded their minority status. This was one instance where revisionism coincided with Hitler's immediate foreign policy goals.

As for the rest of Lithuania's *Volksdeutsche*, they would remain a national minority. Whereas VoMi no longer had any responsibility for the Memellanders, it retained an interest in the Germans living in the interior. Its duties toward them, however, were limited to keeping them quiet and preventing them from disturbing the Reich's future relations with Lithuania. After the cession of the Memelland, which eliminated the only serious point of friction between Germany and Lithuania, Hitler was interested simply in maintaining Lithuanian neutrality. VoMi recognized Oskar von Reichardt of Kaunas as the leader of the remaining minority. He had the unenviable duty of quieting his constituents, now aroused by the events in the Memelland. The Foreign Ministry agreed with VoMi that Reich contacts with them should be kept to a minimum.[61] It was not until 1940 and the resettlement of these Germans that VoMi would become actively involved in Lithuania again.

• • POLAND

After the annexation of the Memelland, Hitler turned his attention toward Poland and its estimated 1,200,000 *Volksdeutsche*, constituting the most diverse of all German minorities. It consisted of six distinct *Volksgruppen*, each with its own peculiar character and separate course of historical development. By far the most important to the Reich was the group residing in the formerly Prussian lands of Poznan-Pomorze (Posen-Pommerellen). In 1931 this territory contained 2,875,781 Poles and 298,480 Germans. It consisted of nearly the entire province of Posen and most of West Prussia, along with smaller pieces of East Prussia, Pomerania, Lower Silesia, and Brandenburg. The second most important group to the Reich was that of Upper Silesia, a territory awarded to Poland as a result of a 1921 plebiscite. Polish sources claim that in 1931, 1,195,635 Poles and only 90,545 Germans lived there. Some German sources insist there were as many as 300,000 Germans in the region.[62]

Two *Volksgruppen* consisted of former subjects of the Russian czar: the Germans of former Congress Poland—the Polish heartland centered on Warsaw—and those of Volhynia in eastern Poland. The largest concentration of these former czarist subjects lived in the industrial city of Lodz. Although it is impossible to determine precisely the number of Germans living in formerly Russian territories, one reliable source counted 311,574 Germans in Congress Poland in 1931, and another estimated 48,000 for Volhynia.[63]

Large numbers of Germans lived in two former Habsburg lands. The Polish share of partitioned Teschen, the eastern part of Austrian Silesia, contained some 40,000 Germans, and the former Austrian crownland of Galicia had between 40,000 and 60,000.[64] Another Reich loss was the overwhelmingly German city of Danzig, with its 400,000 inhabitants. It had a peculiar status, a "free city" under League of Nations administration but within the Polish customs area and represented by Poland diplomatically.[65]

In the immediate postwar period, the historic German-Pole struggle that had begun with the *Drang Nach Osten* of the Middle Ages resumed throughout the disputed border areas. When hostilities ceased, passions—once aroused—did not subside easily. Propaganda generated by Reich organizations such as the BDO perpetuated national hatred and sustained the belief among Poland's Germans that they and their ancestors had built the cities and tilled the fields of this region and that therefore the land was rightfully theirs.

Complaints about the injustices that Poland's Germans allegedly suffered at the hands of the Poles were not entirely unfounded. Poles were no less determined in asserting their control over the disputed lands than Germans were in retaining their claims. Even though

Poland had signed a minority protection treaty as a precondition for national independence, and the Polish constitution guaranteed its national minorities certain rights, Polish authorities frequently violated the rights of their German citizens. Poland had one of the poorest records in all eastern Europe in respecting minority rights.

As a result of official measures as well as public prejudices, Germans were often singled out for discrimination. Many were removed from administrative posts, a large number of German schools were closed, and Polish was declared the sole language for all official business. Although the Poles extended the right of military service to Germans, young Germans did not consider this a privilege. Rather than serving, many deserted to the Reich.[66] The authorities, however, did not view this practice with alarm and even encouraged German flight, hoping to reduce the German portion of the population and thereby strengthen Polish claims to the land. Neither the Weimar government nor the Third Reich accepted the eastern territorial settlement as permanent. Both helped maintain the indigenous German landowning population as a basis for legitimizing German claims. The measure most threatening to the German position in Poland was the land reform of 1925, which dispossessed many German landowners and redistributed confiscated land to Poles. It should be kept in mind, however, that by accepting the legitimacy of the Polish state, one could lighten or even escape any burdens resulting from one's German nationality.

In response to these Polonizing efforts, the *Volksdeutsche* of Poland, although receiving some Reich help, relied heavily on their own resources. Through their cultural, economic, and political organizations they sought to preserve their national identity. Although relatively successful in their cultural and economic endeavors, they mostly failed in their early efforts at political organization and unity. Differences in the levels of political experience between the former Prussians in the west and erstwhile Russian and Austrian subjects in the east impeded unity. Whereas the more advanced Prussians managed to organize, the less experienced Germans in eastern and central Poland failed. Early attempts at political organization, both east and west, were doomed as the Poles first restricted and finally disallowed all German political movements. Forced underground, some groups continued illegal, clandestine political activities. After the Poles eased their restrictions in 1934, the Deutsche Vereinigung emerged as the principal political association for the Germans of western Poland, and the Rat der Deutschen in Polen became the official organ representing all Germans,[67] recognized by both Berlin and Warsaw.

The leaders of these two organizations were mostly conservative, *völkisch*-minded nationalists, allied inside the Reich with the likes of Hans Steinacher. But in the 1920s a more activist movement, under Rudolf Wiesner, had arisen in Bielsko-Biala, considered the most German city in Poland. It eventually caught on and enjoyed its greatest popularity in Upper Silesia. In 1931 it became the Jungdeutsche Partei (JDP) and began spreading its activist message to all the *Volksdeutsche* of Poland.[68]

By the time Hitler came to power, the JDP was challenging the two established organizations for the leadership of the minority. Steinacher and Kursell tried to reconcile the factions but failed. When Lorenz took over VoMi, he and his associates inherited the chore of unifying the minority and preparing it to serve the Third Reich. An additional task was to support these Germans in their ongoing struggle against the Polish authorities. Maintaining an economically sound, culturally distinct, and politically unified minority was VoMi's goal in Poland.

The challenge was formidable. VoMi had to bring together not only competing organizations but also six distinct *Volksgruppen*. Furthermore, the factions had secured patrons in the Reich to support their respective causes and were reluctant to compromise. The traditional groups were associated with the VDA, the Foreign Ministry, and the two main financial sources, the Deutsche Stiftung and the Finanzkontore. The JDP, on the other hand, found patrons in the NSDAP, in particular the AO and the eastern Gauleiters.[69] In April 1937, VoMi invited the leaders of nine organizations and factions to Berlin for a conference. They agreed to form a provisional, unified minority leadership and promised to cooperate in finding a final solution to the organizational problem.

Meanwhile the Foreign Ministry was negotiating with Warsaw for a new agreement on national minorities. Although the Poles had eased their restrictions on *Volksdeutsche* political activities, they persisted with efforts to Polonize the country, thereby evoking loud protests from the local Germans. The Wilhelmstrasse had hoped for a treaty, but in early November 1937 it settled for a joint declaration that committed both Germany and Poland to treating their national minorities correctly.[70] Despite their profession of good intentions, the Poles continued with

Polonization efforts. *Völkisch* unity became even more crucial for the minority.

By the spring of 1938, however, the unity achieved the preceding year had already broken down, and the factions were quarreling again. Lorenz lost his patience with the bickering and settled the matter the SS way, by ordering unity. The Foreign Ministry tried to dissuade Lorenz from the firm approach and argued that only unification founded on consensus and compromise could last. By August, after several more efforts, Lorenz had managed to bring the factions together in a loose confederation.[71] But it was circumstances, more than Lorenz's prodding, that compelled them to cooperate. The Poles, anxious over the alarming events in neighboring Czechoslovakia, rather than appease the Reich by making concessions to the minority, came down even harder on all German activities. And the *Volksdeutsche*, in the face of an invigorated anti-German campaign, at last set aside their disputes to present a unified front.

Although the Polish government assured the Reich that it would respect the minority rights declaration of November 1937 and expressed its desire to solve the minority issue,[72] changing circumstances made resolving the problem even more difficult. Not only had the Sudeten crisis excited the *Volksdeutsche* of Poland, but it had also added to their numbers. Poland seized from Czechoslovakia parts of Teschen and a few other areas containing Germans. These *Volksdeutsche* had expected annexation to the Reich, but to their chagrin they found themselves transferred to Poland, a country whose record of minority treatment was far worse than Czechoslovakia's. In the newly acquired areas, the Poles closed many German schools, fired German civil servants and officials, and forced some *Volksdeutsche* to flee to the Reich. VoMi estimated that by November more than 5,000 had crossed the borders and were housed in VoMi refugee camps.[73]

Lorenz raised the Teschen situation with Ribbentrop and suggested that he take the matter to the Führer. He wanted Hitler to communicate to Warsaw a concern for the transferred *Volksdeutsche* and to insist on guarantees for their safety. Lorenz also asked the foreign minister to ascertain Hitler's plans for Poland so that VoMi could follow the proper course.[74] Lorenz then approached Karl Haushofer, hoping that the professor might also intercede with the Führer. Haushofer did, during a social visit to Hess's home in Munich. When he informed Hitler of the deteriorating situation in Poland, Hitler replied that he "did not intend to tolerate the attitude of our eastern neighbor toward the *Volksgenossen* any longer."[75]

Although the German side viewed Polish actions against the *Volksdeutsche* as outrageous, these measures were not entirely unwarranted. The JDP, for instance, went out of its way to provoke the Poles and incite the *Volksdeutsche*. Meanwhile Reich military intelligence was actively recruiting *Volksdeutsche* informers for its spy network, and as early as October 1938, SD agents were secretly organizing armed Selbstschutz units for eventual service to the Reich's cause.[76] As for VoMi, it tried to maintain some control over the minority, in particular over the activists, whose irresponsible actions could disrupt Hitler's sensitive operations in neighboring Czechoslovakia.

At this time, few people outside Hitler's most trusted circle of confidants were aware of his real intentions regarding Poland. As in the case of Czechoslovakia, neither the minority issue nor a negotiated settlement of territorial claims interested him. He was determined to destroy Poland by force. Poland was to become a vital part of the new *Lebensraum*, and as far as Hitler was concerned, war was the preferable means to acquire the new living space.

In early February 1939, probably unaware of Hitler's ultimate goals for Poland, lower-level Reich diplomats were planning a series of meetings with the Poles to discuss the minority issue. The VoMi leadership, also apparently in the dark on Hitler's intentions, felt entitled to participate in these negotiations. But since VoMi was a party office, the Foreign Ministry advised against such involvement. Lorenz and Behrends finally deferred to the wishes of the diplomats and agreed that as long as VoMi had a part in deciding the agenda and was consulted before any important decisions were made, they would be satisfied.[77]

Conversations with the Poles were held on two levels, between foreign ministers as well as between lower-level diplomats, but achieved no significant results. It is highly likely that Hitler had instructed Ribbentrop that there should be no negotiated agreement. At the same time, the Poles kept pressure on the minority. In response, both VoMi and the Foreign Ministry continued to provide material and moral support to the minority.[78] The subordinates involved in these activities were probably ignorant of the fateful decisions already made at the top regarding Poland and its German minority. Earlier, on 11 April, the Führer had issued "Case White," the operation plan for the attack on

Poland. All subsequent efforts, those serving diplomatic purposes as well as those relieving the plight of the *Volksdeutsche*, addressed only immediate needs and contributed nothing to a real solution of the problem.

The exact extent of VoMi's prior knowledge of the events of September 1939 is uncertain, but eventually Lorenz and Behrends were privileged to at least some of the most sensitive information. One source was Horst Hoffmeyer, head of the BDO and Behrends's associate, who was active inside Poland with secret preparations for the assault. During the critical August days, VoMi's prime responsibility was to keep the *Volksdeutsche* under control, preventing some unexpected incident from disrupting Hitler's scheme. One such potentially disruptive incident was the unsolicited offer by Rudolf Wiesner, head of the JDP, to serve as another Henlein. Only one week before the 1 September attack, Wiesner indicated from Danzig his willingness to mediate between the Reich and Poland. Lorenz, who by then was at least aware that Hitler was avoiding a negotiated settlement, immediately ordered Wiesner to Berlin. He wanted him out of the way before the Poles or anyone else learned of his offer to mediate. Hitler was already having a difficult enough time evading the high-level efforts of European statesmen to pin him down on negotiations. But Gauleiter Forster of Danzig, hoping for a greater share in directing events, defied Lorenz and told Wiesner to remain in Danzig. Lorenz repeated his summons and added that Hitler had no intention of solving the Polish question along "national lines," as had been the case in Czechoslovakia. Wiesner's offer to play Henlein's role was not appreciated.[79] Apparently Wiesner heeded Lorenz's warnings. There was no new Henlein, and there was no negotiated settlement.

The German attack on Poland on 1 September 1939 started World War II in Europe. It also initiated the process that eventually would lead to the demise of the historic German presence in this part of Europe. Although the suffering the *Volksdeutsche* of Poland endured during the hostilities paled in comparison with that inflicted on the Poles, many nevertheless fell as victims—those caught directly in the battle zones as well as those who became targets of violence and terror at the hands of desperate and vengeful Poles.[80] But once the fighting subsided, it appeared that *Volksdeutsche* persistence and their compliance with VoMi's policy of maintaining their presence in Poland had paid off. They could reassert—if they wished, and if they proved to be true Germans in spirit as well as blood—their interrupted dominance. With the direct annexation of the Corridor, Danzig, and western Poland, the Germans residing there received Reich citizenship. So did those living in central Poland, which was to become the political oddity called the General Government. As these people accepted citizenship, they concluded their *Volksdeutsche* status, and VoMi's involvement with them ended.

Volksdeutsche living farther east, in Volhynia and eastern Galicia, areas falling within the Soviet sphere of interest, would have to wait longer for their reunification with the *Volk*. In the early fall of 1939, the Volhynian peasants still had no idea that their paths would soon cross with that of the Reichsführer SS at Przemysl. But shortly the decision would be made to resettle them to the annexed regions. It would be VoMi's responsibility first to persuade the Volhynian peasants to heed the Führer's call and then to carry out the evacuation. Once relocated, these *Volksdeutsche*, if found politically reliable and racially sound, would also receive Reich citizenship.

• •

VoMi and the Minorities, II

The Baltic, the Southeast, the West,

and the Soviet Union

• •

With the exception of the South Tyroleans and the Carpathian Germans, the *Volksdeutsche* discussed so far achieved their principal revisionist goals of unifying their homelands with the Reich and joining the main body of the *Volk* as Reich citizens. Hitler's expansive foreign policy happened to coincide with their revisionist expectations. But with a few exceptions, for the rest of Europe's *Volksdeutsche*—those living in the Baltic States, southeastern Europe, the west, and the Soviet Union—their hopes for some sort of unification with the Reich did not materialize, either in the prewar period or even during the war years. Hitler's short-range goals did not correspond with their wishes. And his ultimate, long-range objectives, although envisioning the eventual unification of all Germans in the new order, did not conform to the revisionism they had in mind.

ESTONIA

Shortly after the destruction of Poland, the Baltic Germans of Estonia and Latvia came into prominence. Their ancestors, German crusaders and Hansa merchants, had conquered the area in the thirteenth century and had created a feudal society in which they were the masters, and the native Letts and Estonians served them. Through their ownership of the land and monopoly over trade, they came to dominate the social, economic, and political life of the region, even through subsequent periods of Polish, Swedish, and Russian rule. Regardless of the nationality of their sovereigns, the aristocratic Baltic Germans, entrenched in their privileged positions, maintained steadfast loyalty. Before the twentieth century, neither German nationalism nor the *völkisch* idea stirred them. And in World War I they dutifully fought in the czar's armies against the Reich. Only after the deposing of the czar in the Russian Revolution did they switch their allegiances to the *Volk*.

Beginning with the Revolution and into the immediate postwar years, the Baltic Germans, determined to hold on to their privileged way of life, pursued a three-cornered battle against both the Bolsheviks and the Baltic nationals. Eventually they realized that theirs was a lost cause and either resigned themselves to living in the new states of Latvia and Estonia or emigrated. Whereas before the war an estimated 160,000 Germans lived in the region, after the war only some 60,000 remained in Latvia and another 20,000 in Estonia.[1]

The Baltic Germans of Estonia, a new state created from the former Russian provinces of Estland and northern Livonia, had to adjust to new circumstances, especially after the October 1919 land reform, which, in redistributing land to Estonian peasants, terminated their social, economic, and political dominance. Although Estonia did not sign a binding treaty, in September 1923 it declared to the League of Nations its intention to respect minority rights. In 1925 the government allowed all national minorities, including the Germans, cultural self-administration. It recognized the Kulturselbstverwaltung as the official organ for administering German schools and other cultural institutions.[2] In the economy, military, and even government service, *Volksdeutsche* encountered less ethnic discrimination in Estonia than most anywhere else in Europe.

The relatively harmonious relationship between the Estonians and their national minorities deteriorated with the economic hard times of the early 1930s. Blatant anti-German measures such as economic boycotts and the dismissal of Germans from jobs were few, but it did become more difficult for young Germans to find suitable employment. In 1934 the increasingly authoritarian regime disbanded political parties as well as all politically oriented national minority organizations. It also restricted the use of minority languages in official transactions and initiated a campaign of Estonianization, changing names of towns, cities, streets, and even surnames to sound more Estonian.

The authorities did not, however, restrict contacts with the Reich. The Germans of Estonia could still travel freely to Germany, and Reich Germans could visit Estonia. Nazis from the Reich exploited this liberality to recruit Estonian Germans for National Socialism. Among those offices engaged in this practice was VoMi, which made inroads into the minority through the Kulturselbstverwaltung and its other cultural, political, economic, and welfare organizations.[3]

As elsewhere, it was VoMi's responsibility to bring the minority under control and prepare it for a role in Hitler's foreign policy schemes. Its assignment was determined by Estonia's part in his plans, which in the prewar years was that of a sympathetic neutral. Estonia was an important trade partner, and as long as its strategic location was not threatened, and the Estonians themselves did not compromise their own security, Germany had no reason to disrupt its internal order or raise any demands. Indeed, Nazi racists were favorably disposed toward Estonians, whom they regarded as predominantly Nordic. In view of these considerations, VoMi expected Estonia's Baltic Germans to remain passive and orderly, and only if circumstances demanded would it call on them to play a more active role.

VoMi found several willing collaborators among these Germans, but the official, government-recognized leader, Baron Wilhelm von Wrangell, head of the Kulturselbstverwaltung, was not inclined to cooperate. Lorenz at first tried to charm him into submitting to VoMi's authority and accepting its people into the leadership. When this approach failed to budge the baron, Lorenz ordered him to include VoMi's choices in the leadership in the spirit of "National Socialist comradeship." Only when Lorenz threatened to hand over control of Reich subsidies to VoMi's clients did Wrangell, aware that control of these funds determined the real authority within the minority, accept the Nazi sympathizers.[4]

By mid-1938, having secured its hold over the minority leadership, VoMi appealed to the rank and file by suggesting a return to the good old days of German dominance. It resorted to revisionism as a means to win them to the Nazi cause. But once the minority was converted and aroused by the prospects of regaining their lost supremacy, their enthusiasm was difficult to control. Following the *Anschluss* and the events in Czechoslovakia, activists in Estonia loudly proclaimed their commitment to the Nazi cause and openly aired their expectations for a German occupation of Estonia. Rumors of war circulated, and the Estonian people, heretofore positively inclined toward Germany, started to turn anti-German.[5]

Since the behavior of the activists endangered Reich-Estonian relations, VoMi tried to dampen their enthusiasm, stressing that Hitler had no intention of dealing with Estonia as he had with Austria and Czechoslovakia.[6] This approach had little success. While some VoMi officials were trying to throttle the hotheads, others were disseminating inflammatory propaganda to help in the illegal recruitment of young Germans for the armed branch of the SS, soon to become the Waffen SS.[7] These counterproductive activities illustrate the varied, and at times conflicting, interests VoMi served and tried to balance, including SS interests, other Reich interests, and those of the *Volksdeutsche*.

VoMi managed to keep the situation in check until the fall of 1939, when, to preserve his alliance with Stalin, Hitler decided to remove the *Volksdeutsche* from Estonia and Latvia, both designated to fall to the Soviet sphere of interest according to the treaty of August 1939. As they were resettled in the Reich and its conquered territories, Estonia's Germans achieved their revisionist goal of unification with the rest of the *Volk*, but not as they had expected, by way of a Reich takeover of their homeland. Their interests and Hitler's foreign policy goals clashed, and the latter always held precedence.

› • • LATVIA

The collective experience and fate of the 60,000 Baltic Germans living in Latvia—created from the former Russian provinces of Courland and Livonia—essentially duplicated that of Estonia's *Volksdeutsche*. After fighting against both the Latvian nationals and the Bolsheviks, the Germans lost their dominant position when the issue was decided in favor of Latvian independence. Radical land reform added the finishing touch. Divested of their land, many Baltic Germans either emigrated to the Reich or moved to the cities, especially Riga, Jelgava (Mitau), and Liepāja (Libau). Latvian legislation struck down what was left of German privileges by disbanding the guilds and the corporation of the nobility, the *Ritterschaft*.

At first the Latvians granted very generous cultural rights to their national minorities. Although Latvia did not sign a minority protection treaty, it declared to the League of Nations that it would abide by certain principles. Provisions in the Latvian constitution reinforced the declaration and guaranteed the rights of minorities. All nationalities could operate their own schools and churches, and the Baltic Germans even had their own institution of higher learning, the venerable Herder Institute. The Germans were free to maintain cultural ties with the Reich, and the VDA could function in Latvia as long as it limited its activities to cultural matters. In the political area the Germans were assured six seats in the Latvian parliament, as well as an office in the education ministry. Their official organ, recognized as such by the Latvian authorities, was the Deutsch-baltische Volksgemeinschaft.[8]

Except for the issues of agrarian reform and compensation, relations between the Latvians and the Baltic Germans during the 1920s remained satisfactory. But an undercurrent of anti-German feeling lingered among the Latvians, and in the early 1930s, with the onset of economic difficulties, it surfaced in an upsurge of strident Latvian nationalism, much of it directed against Baltic Germans.

The nationalist tide crested in May 1934 when President Kārlis Ulmanis introduced authoritarian rule. As his regime curtailed parliamentary democracy, the Germans lost their representation. Cultural autonomy also ended, as did German control over their own schools. In the economy, state regulations as well as unofficial, public measures such as boycotts threatened their economic survival. In general, the Baltic German position in Latvia deteriorated.

VoMi became involved with this minority as Baltic German fortunes were reaching their nadir, a factor instrumental in making the nazification of this group one of VoMi's easiest and most successful assignments. The long-time president of the Volksgemeinschaft, Wilhelm von Rüdiger, was sympathetic to the Nazi cause but was not sufficiently in step with Hitler's Reich to suit some Baltic Germans, Erhard Kröger, for one. Kröger, with the support of influential Reich patrons, challenged Rüdiger's leadership.[9]

Kröger's challenge made little headway until Lorenz's arrival. In July 1937 the new VoMi chief ordered Erich Mundel, who in 1935 had replaced Rüdiger as the leader of the Volksgemeinschaft, to bring Kröger into the leadership. As he had done with the minority in Estonia, Lorenz threatened to use control over subsidies to enforce his will.[10] In the fall of 1938 Mundel, under pressure from VoMi, resigned, making way for a compromise candidate, Alfred Intelmann, who was not a Nazi but was a confirmed believer in Hitler.[11] Intelmann served VoMi's purposes well, since he not only sympathized with National Socialism but also appealed to non-Nazi Baltic Germans. Intelmann was the formal head of the minority, but VoMi relied on Kröger as its man in Latvia.[12]

VoMi imposed its will in Latvia as it did in Estonia, not only through its control over financial subsidies and its recognition of the minority leadership but also through revisionist propaganda. Here too it raised the prospects of an eventual unification of all Germans, implying that the Reich would help restore the Baltic Germans to their former prominence. But all Hitler wanted of Latvia was its neutrality. And this rather modest goal was jeopardized by the activists, whose open espousal of Nazism and talk of revisionism angered the Latvian public and pushed it toward a more pronounced anti-German stance.

During the Czechoslovakian crisis, Latvians feared and Baltic Germans anticipated an imminent Reich invasion. German hopes subsided after Hitler declared that the Sudetenland was his final territorial demand. All Baltic Germans did not, however, accept his words at face value. Kröger, for one, without authorization from Berlin, assured his followers that the Führer had not abandoned them, implying that revision still remained a possibility. Behrends sympathized with the disappointed Kröger but admonished him to subordinate Baltic German wishes to Reich interests and to refrain from interpreting the Führer's words as he pleased.[13]

Despite such complications, VoMi successfully guided the Baltic Germans of Latvia along the desired course toward National Socialism. The result was a loyal minority, which in the fall of 1939 obeyed the summons of the Führer to leave its ancestral homeland and resettle in newly conquered Reich territories.

• • RUMANIA

The German minority of Rumania consisted of several distinct *Volks-gruppen*, differing in social composition, historic backgrounds, religious and cultural characteristics, and political experience. Prewar Rumania, consisting of Moldavia, Wallachia, and the Dobrudja, contained relatively few *Volksdeutsche*, but the territories that Rumania annexed in the wake of the war brought large numbers of Germans under its rule. From Russia it took Bessarabia; from Austria it seized Bukovina (Buchenland); and from Hungary it obtained not only the eastern Banat but also Transylvania (Siebenburgen) and the Crišana-Maramures (Sathmar) area west of Transylvania. Consequently, postwar Rumania contained more than 13 million Rumanians and nearly 5 million non-Rumanians, including over 750,000 Germans.[14]

Most of Rumania's *Volksdeutsche*, including the 230,000–300,000 Danube Swabians (Donauschwaben) of the Banat, were former Hungarian subjects. Their ancestors, originally from western Germany, had settled the middle Danube region in the eighteenth century as the Habsburgs reconquered it from the Turks. Residing farther to the east were some 230,000–240,000 Transylvanian Saxons. Their forefathers had colonized Transylvania in the twelfth century as the wards of the kings of Hungary. They came from the Rhineland, not Saxony, but at that time all Germans were called Saxons. The Crišana-Maramures, or the Sathmar region, contained over 60,000 Germans, whose predecessors, like those of the Danube Swabians, had settled there in the eighteenth century. Some of Rumania's *Volksdeutsche*, specifically the 90,000 Germans of Bukovina, were former Austrians. Others, notably those of Bessarabia, the land located northeast of Moldavia, had belonged to the Russian Empire. Nearly all of these estimated 80,000 Germans were peasant farmers whose ancestors had colonized the area between Kishinev and the Black Sea in the eighteenth and early nineteenth centuries.[15]

Immediately after the war, the Rumanian authorities promised to respect and protect the rights of non-Rumanians living in their state, including the *Volksdeutsche*. But in the early 1920s, with the ink scarcely dry on the written guarantees, they launched a Romanization campaign to restrict the cultural autonomy of their minorities. Although these measures hampered German cultural institutions and programs,

Romanization was more tolerable than the Magyarization many of Rumania's *Volksdeutsche* had endured under Hungarian rule.[16]

In Rumania, as elsewhere in eastern Europe, agrarian reform marked the low point in the relations between the *Volksdeutsche* and the authorities. Although the land reform of 1921–23 primarily targeted large Magyar landholdings, the Germans, being mostly farmers, were also affected adversely. With their acreage reduced, some emigrated, but the majority remained. The Rumanians soon realized the economic value of these industrious people and permitted many of them to reacquire their land. German contributions in areas other than agriculture were less noteworthy. Although they were well represented in the trades, as shopkeepers and artisans, very few were engaged in industry. During periods of prosperity, German tradesmen did well, but with the depression of the 1930s they suffered from ethnically motivated economic discrimination.

On the whole, the Germans of Rumania were among the most self-reliant of all *Volksdeutsche*. Distant from the Reich and never having belonged to it, they expected little help from there. In response to the land reform, they organized one of the most efficient and prosperous cooperative systems in Europe. And to counter the campaign limiting cultural autonomy, their churches assumed much of the responsibility for educational and other cultural programs. The VDA nevertheless provided some help, as did Reich churches. As Germany came to appreciate Rumania as an economic and political associate, it steadily increased aid to the minority, especially in the economic sector. Even before 1933, subsidies from the Ossa-Finanzkontore credit system ensured the survival of a prosperous and distinct German element within the Rumanian economy.

With the help of this industrious, economically successful, and politically loyal minority, the Reich hoped to draw Rumania onto a pro-German course. A factor facilitating the effort was a common antipathy on the part of the *Volksdeutsche* and the Rumanians toward their former Hungarian rulers. Whereas in many eastern European lands anti-Germanism was the principal national prejudice, in Rumania anti-Magyarism prevailed. As a result, Rumanian regimes looked with increasing favor toward the Reich, which proved to have influence—and later authority—over Hungary's irredentist ambitions. Rumania's *Volksdeutsche* often benefited from this inclination.

The self-reliance of these Germans also manifested itself politically.

But because of their diverse historical, cultural, social, and political backgrounds, achieving organizational unity proved difficult. The earliest step toward unity was the formation of the Deutsche Partei in 1920, a political coalition of all German representatives to the Rumanian parliament. In 1921 they created the Verband der Deutschen in Rumänien, which brought together all German organizations.[17] These two organizations represented the minority to the Rumanians, whose attitude toward the *Volksdeutsche* fluctuated with the vagaries of Bucharest politics. Some regimes treated them well, others not as well.

Most Germans were content living under Rumanian rule. But there were those, mainly among the youth, whose loyalties transcended the frontiers and sought out the German *Volk*. They were the founders of the *Erneuerungsbewegung*, which originated in Rumania. Its preeminent figure was the Transylvanian Friedrich "Fritz" Fabritius, who in 1923 had met Hitler in Munich, became convinced that National Socialism was the path to German destiny, and went on to found a Nazilike movement in Sibiu (Hermannstadt). His success in organizing the agricultural cooperative movement to counter the land reform had won him the gratitude and admiration of many Germans, a popularity he easily refocused on his new political movement. Encouraged by the growth of National Socialism in Germany and his own rising stature, in early 1932 Fabritius formally founded a Nazi party, which immediately made impressive electoral gains among the Germans of Transylvania and the Banat. Suspicious of its motives and wary of its ties to the Reich, the authorities soon disbanded it.[18]

The proscription of his movement only enhanced Fabritius's standing. In June 1935 he was elected chairman of the Verband der Deutschen in Rumänien. He reorganized it along Nazi lines, renamed it the Volksgemeinschaft der Deutschen in Rumänien, and set it on a more activist course. Its program demanded greater national autonomy for the minority and more freedom to cultivate ties with Hitler's Reich. Although Fabritius was decidedly pro-Nazi, for some he was not Nazi enough. One critic, Alfred Bonfert, organized a rival group, the Deutsche Volkspartei Rumäniens.[19] The ensuing rivalry jeopardized the effectiveness of the minority as an intermediary between the Reich and Rumania, since the rhetoric of the quarrel was often anti-Rumanian. The minority was becoming more of a liability than an asset in Reich relations with Rumania.

Since both sides in the dispute had already adopted National Socialism, and since non-Nazi groups had already been pushed aside, the task facing VoMi in Rumania was to resolve the dispute and unify the minority. At first VoMi tried to negotiate a settlement. In April 1937 Behrends summoned both Fabritius and Bonfert to Berlin, hoping to find grounds for compromise. Finding Bonfert less amenable to reconciliation and more determined to follow an independent course than Fabritius, the VoMi leadership sided with the latter and ordered all Reich ties with Bonfert severed.[20] Rebuffed but undaunted, Bonfert continued in his renegade ways, much to the consternation of the Foreign Ministry, which was worried about the negative impact this dispute was having on Reich-Rumanian relations. Frustrated with Bonfert's obstinacy and disruptive behavior, Behrends traveled to Rumania in January 1938 to bring him in line. Actually Behrends had a twofold mission. Not only was he to straighten out Bonfert, but he was also to transmit confidential instructions for Rumania's Germans to support the government of Octavian Goga in upcoming elections. It was in the Reich's interests to support Goga, a fervent anti-Semite, who had reversed the course of Rumanian foreign policy from a pro-Western direction to one more favorable to Germany.[21]

During Behrends's meeting with Bonfert, the latter demanded recognition for his Volkspartei as the equal of Fabritius's Volksgemeinschaft. He also balked at supporting Goga in the upcoming elections. Behrends, unaccustomed to having his instructions questioned—much less defied—blustered that this was not a request but an order from the Führer! When Bonfert demanded to see the order in writing, Behrends, livid with rage, proclaimed "open rebellion" and broke off talks. He repeated the total excommunication of Bonfert, but this measure so far had produced negligible results.[22] In the Rumania of 1938, which was still independent of Reich control, there was little else Behrends and VoMi could do. Out of the reach of the SS, Bonfert could defy VoMi with impunity and without fear of unpleasant consequences.

Before returning to Berlin, Behrends met with Goga and assured him that the minority would support his regime. His diplomacy enjoyed brief success, for on 6 February, Goga recognized the Volksgemeinschaft as the exclusive, official organ of the minority and correspondingly proscribed Bonfert's group.[23] But in the volatility of Rumanian politics, such goodwill was fleeting. Four days later, before the elections took place, King Carol dismissed Goga and established a monarchical dictatorship. Rumanian foreign policy then shifted in favor of the West, and the status of the minority was again insecure. But subsequent events prompted the Rumanians to reconsider their position. By August the government realized that Germany was becoming the dominant force in eastern Europe, and as a gesture of goodwill it granted the minority certain cultural privileges. And in January 1939 Bucharest reconfirmed the Volksgemeinschaft as the official German organ and included it as a member of the new national political coalition, the Rumanian Front of National Regeneration.[24]

The flexing of Reich muscles on behalf of the Sudeten Germans, along with Rumania's shift toward the Reich, eventually brought Bonfert into VoMi's fold. In November he agreed to recognize Fabritius as minority leader and accepted the post of deputy leader for himself. By the following summer, however, conflict again disrupted the minority, and Fabritius expelled Bonfert and his followers from the Volksgemeinschaft.[25] At a time when the Reich required complete cooperation from the minority in order to maintain sensitive Reich-Rumanian relations, the situation was coming apart. In conversations involving the VoMi leadership, the Foreign Ministry, and Heinrich Himmler himself, it was decided to remove both Fabritius and Bonfert and bring them to Germany for safekeeping. VoMi ordered Fabritius to Berlin, to remain for a year or longer. But fearful of leaving the safe haven of Rumania for the Reich, Fabritius procrastinated his departure. The Rumanian authorities had developed a liking for him because of his opposition to any territorial revisions detrimental to Rumania and demanded assurances for his safety.[26] Even with Reich assurances, Fabritius declined the invitation. As long as he enjoyed Rumanian protection, neither VoMi nor the SS could reach him.

But as Rumania's dependence on Germany increased, Rumanian support for Fabritius waned. Aware of Rumania's inclination to please the Reich, VoMi became more assertive with the minority, warning that Reich financial assistance would cease if its leader refused to follow orders. Fabritius finally relented and accepted his dismissal. He was replaced by Himmler's personal choice, Wolfram Brückner, who would serve until someone even better attuned to Himmler's means and purposes could be found.[27]

With the start of war, the relations between the minority and both

Germany and Rumania were completely subordinated to the economic, the diplomatic, and especially the military needs of the Reich. And as Rumania grew more dependent on the Reich, particularly as the result of certain events in 1940, Berlin's control over the minority increased proportionately. In the summer of 1940, Stalin decided to claim Bessarabia—which Hitler had promised him in the August 1939 treaty. When, on 26 June, the Soviets presented the Rumanians with an ultimatum demanding Bessarabia and northern Bukovina, the Reich urged the Rumanians to yield. Consequently King Carol agreed, and the Red Army occupied the territories in question. Having witnessed Soviet success in pressing for revisionist demands, the Hungarians and Bulgarians presented theirs. Rumania turned to the Reich for support, but to its dismay, the advice from Berlin was to make further concessions. The Rumanians had no alternative but to comply, and in the Second Vienna Award of 30 August 1940, Rumania lost two-fifths of Transylvania and other western regions to Hungary. A few days later, after concluding an agreement with Bulgaria, it surrendered the southern Dobrudja. Germany agreed to guarantee the remainder of Rumania.

The enormous territorial and population losses were too much for King Carol's regime to bear, and in response to violent protest demonstrations, on 6 September he abdicated in favor of his son, Michael. Subsequently General Ion Antonescu established an authoritarian, right-wing dictatorship. In October, on the pretext of securing Rumania's oil fields, German troops occupied certain strategic points throughout the country and thereby assured the retention of Rumania in the Axis camp.[28]

As Rumania was partitioned, so was the German minority. Without any say in the events whirling around them, many *Volksdeutsche* were pared from the minority and transferred, along with territory, to other states. A large segment came under the rule of the Hungarians, whose chauvinism and treatment of minorities made Rumanian nationalism seem moderate in comparison. Others were transferred to Bulgaria. The worst fate, however, befell the *Volksdeutsche* of Bessarabia and northern Bukovina, who were subjected to brutal Sovietization under Stalin. The two major *Volksgruppen*, residing in the remnants of Transylvania and the Banat, would remain under Rumanian authority for the rest of the war.

The relationship between the nearly 500,000 *Volksdeutsche* living in post–World War I Hungary and their Magyar rulers reflected a centuries-old love-hate paradox.[29] Although some Germans could trace their Hungarian residence back to the Middle Ages, most of their ancestors had settled in Hungary in the eighteenth century. They shared with the Magyars a common heritage as the ruling peoples of the Habsburg Empire as well as a mutual interest in suppressing the aspirations of the empire's Slavs and other nationalities. But after the 1867 splitting of the empire into Austrian and Hungarian halves, the Magyars asserted themselves by suppressing all manifestations of non-Magyar nationality—even that of the Germans.[30]

Magyar nationalism intensified in the wake of military defeat in World War I. Once the rulers of one of the largest political units in Europe, the Hungarians were left with a truncated state. Although obligated by treaties to respect minority rights, the Hungarians, extremely bitter about their defeat and the surrender of vast territories, exploited every opportunity to demonstrate national sovereignty, commonly by suppressing national minorities living under their rule. A campaign of Magyarization, pursued relentlessly by lower-level officials, aimed at forcing all non-Magyars into the Hungarian national mainstream. Those resisting assimilation could expect discrimination in employment, education, and other everyday activities.[31] One must keep in mind, however, that the Hungarians gladly accepted anyone willing to assimilate, and all ethnically based disabilities disappeared as soon as an individual identified with the Magyar national majority.

The Germans of Hungary resisted Magyarization through their highly developed political organization and their moderate, politically astute leadership, whose outstanding personality was Jakob Bleyer. An advocate of cooperation, Bleyer believed that maintaining the minority as a loyal but distinct element in the Hungarian state was the best way to preserve the German culture and position. In 1923 he organized the Ungarländischer Deutscher Volksbildungsverein (UDV), which the authorities recognized in 1924 as the minority's official representation.[32]

As Magyar pressures for cultural conformity intensified in the early 1930s—partly as a result of the worldwide economic crisis—younger

Germans responded with greater militancy and less patience for Bleyer's policy of cooperation. The leader of the activists was Franz Basch, who, on Bleyer's death in December 1933, challenged the authority of Bleyer's replacement, Gustav Gratz. The activists, admirers of National Socialism, considered Gratz a traitor to the German cause and in 1934 founded the rival Volksdeutsche Kameradschaft, which soon attracted an impressive following. The authorities, hoping to bolster the more pliant UDV, provided it with generous subsidies. When knowledge of these subsidies became public, Gratz lost credibility with most *Volksdeutsche*. In contrast Basch, arrested several times for his political activities, became more popular.[33]

The activists were elated with Hitler's ascendancy, but they were more eager to become Nazis and serve the Reich than the Reich was to accept them into the fold. Since the Hungarians looked unfavorably on any outside meddling in their internal affairs, Berlin discouraged any efforts to strengthen ties between the minority and Germany.[34] When Lorenz took charge at VoMi, the approach changed. He intended to increase Reich influence within the minority without angering the Magyars. Lorenz, who displayed a far greater personal interest in this minority than any other, used minority business as a pretext to make frequent trips to Budapest, one of his favorite haunts for the pursuit of the good life. He had expected the unity issue to be his primary task in Hungary, as it was elsewhere. But since Gratz had discredited himself in the eyes of many *Volksdeutsche* as a creature of the Hungarian authorities, most supported Basch's Kameradschaft. All that was left for VoMi to do was to recognize Basch formally as the leader and the pro-Nazi Kameradschaft as the official link between Berlin and the minority.[35]

Basch's rise coincided with Hungary's tilt toward the Reich. The Hungarians, like many other East Europeans, realized the growing influence of the new Germany in their corner of Europe. In the spring of 1938, Hungary took a decided turn toward Nazi Germany when the anti-Semitic Béla Imrédy government assumed office. Imrédy's regime adopted a more tolerant attitude with the minority and tended to look away as VoMi extended its influence over it. Hungary's new approach paid almost immediate dividends. The first Vienna Award of 2 November 1938, a settlement partitioning Czechoslovakian territory, honored Hungarian claims to a part of Slovakia and the whole of Ruthenia.[36]

Although relations between Hungary and Germany improved, as did everyday life for Hungary's Germans, the success of Hungarian revisionism and apparent Reich support for it disappointed many *Volksdeutsche*. Also disappointed were Germans living outside Hungary in the Hungarian irredenta, in particular the Banat and Transylvania. As they watched the succession of Reich annexations farther west, many of them expected this process sooner or later to reach them. But the concessions to Hungary dashed these hopes. VoMi feared that the resulting discontent could lead to unrest, which in turn could strain Reich-Hungarian relations.

Anxious about calming the situation and maintaining good relations with Budapest, Behrends convened a meeting at VoMi on 22 November 1938 to discuss the situation in Hungary. Attending, among others, were representatives of the Ministry of the Interior, the Ministry of Propaganda, and the Foreign Ministry. Behrends called for reserve and moderation on the part of the minority. But in view of *Volksdeutsche* displeasure toward the Reich's apparent sympathy for Hungarian claims, it was decided that despite the improving relations, the Reich must not support Hungarian revisionism too strongly.[37] Behrends, for one, believed that if the Reich, through VoMi, was to maintain influence with the minority, it should not appear to be in total agreement with the Hungarians. For their part the Budapest authorities, impressed and encouraged with the results of cooperating with Berlin, continued making concessions. On 26 November 1938 they recognized a reconstituted Kameradschaft, the Volksbund der Deutschen in Ungarn (VDU), as the official organ of the minority, with Basch as its leader. Gratz, having lost official Hungarian support, withdrew from the political scene.[38]

But official generosity toward the minority aside, some segments of the Magyar public, in particular the lower officialdom, continued to harass Germans. As a result VoMi had to maintain official cordiality while responding to the unfriendly treatment of *Volksdeutsche* by the lower bureaucracy and a large portion of the public.[39] One reason for the lingering animosity was the boldness of the recently legalized VDU, which interpreted official sanction as license for increased activity. In turn the Hungarian public became more resentful toward the Germans and more sensitive about any ties between the minority and the Reich, especially the financial connection, which was known to subsidize VDU's activities. VoMi's efforts to keep the financial strings out of public view were undermined when prominent figures such as Rudolf Hess boasted from nearby Graz that the Reich was pouring millions of marks into the minorities.[40]

Hitler's announcement of the resettlement program in October 1939, which was not clear on which minorities would be affected, created anxieties among Hungary's Germans. When faced with the prospects of abandoning homes, farms, and businesses, many suddenly realized that perhaps Hungarian rule was not so bad after all. *Völkisch* loyalties dissipated and devotion to the Führer waned as the prospects of having to make great personal sacrifices became very real. Some Germans suddenly reversed themselves and accepted Magyarization in order to be counted as Hungarians and thereby evade resettlement. VoMi and the VDU assured the *Volksdeutsche* that they would not be resettled, but to little avail.[41] The evacuations from eastern Poland beginning in late 1939 and the exodus from Bessarabia later that year seemed to contradict all assurances. Indeed these concerns were not entirely unfounded. As late as September 1940, Hitler divulged to the Hungarian minister, Döme Sztójay, that he would be prepared to accept an additional million Germans into the Reich— intimating that among them would be those of Hungary.[42]

Further developments appeared to confirm that relocation was not in store for the *Volksdeutsche* of Hungary, but they also seemed to preclude any hopes for closer ties to the Reich through some sort of territorial arrangement with Hungary. After the Soviet Union claimed Bessarabia in June 1940, the Hungarians also raised their primary revisionist claim, the reannexation of Transylvania. To settle the matter once and for all, Ribbentrop summoned Hungarian and Rumanian representatives to Vienna and on 30 August imposed a solution. As noted earlier, this Second Vienna Award transferred western Transylvania and some other Rumanian territories to Hungary.[43] On 20 November, Hungary strengthened its ties to the Reich by signing— along with Slovakia and Rumania—the Axis Tripartite Pact.

The Hungarians had to guarantee the minority rights of their newly acquired German citizens. Indeed both the Rumanian and the Hungarian governments were required to sign agreements redefining the relationship between them and their German minorities. In signing the agreements, Hungary reconfirmed the VDU as the official organ of Hungarian Germans and acknowledged its National Socialist nature. The VDU would henceforth determine who was and who was not a German. Adherence to National Socialism became a prerequisite.[44] Shortly thereafter Hitler met with Count Sztójay and impressed on him the importance of favorable treatment for the *Volksdeutsche*. He assured Sztójay of their loyalty to Hungary and even suggested that Hungary could become a center for the Germans of southeastern Europe. Face to face with Hitler, Sztójay welcomed the idea, but the sincerity of his response was questionable.[45]

The Second Vienna Award and the accompanying minority protection treaty elevated the German minority in Hungary to the status of a recognized, legitimate entity within the Hungarian state. It also ensured that the group would remain a minority for the foreseeable future and doused *Volksdeutsche* hopes for rejoining the main body of the *Volk* through some sort of territorial rearrangement. The ties between this enlarged minority and VoMi grew closer during the war years, as did those between VoMi and all other groups that remained as minorities. But VoMi could hardly claim responsibility for the nazification of Hungary's *Volksdeutsche*. The process had been an internal, voluntary affair, initiated locally. Perhaps for this reason the conversion was not complete. As would be demonstrated time and again, the *Volksdeutsche* of Hungary were among the most reluctant to sacrifice for the Reich's cause and seemed to assume the attitude that if they could accept National Socialism on their own volition, they could also renounce it.

• • YUGOSLAVIA

The overwhelming majority of Yugoslavia's 600,000–700,000 *Volksdeutsche* resided in areas that before World War I had belonged to Austria-Hungary. Only a small number lived in Serbia and the other non-Habsburg lands of the new state. Most of the estimated 40,000 former Austrian subjects lived in Slovenia, created from the southern part of Styria (Untersteiermark), all of Carniola (Krain), and parts of Carinthia (Kärnten). By far the largest group of Germans was the Danube Swabians, former Hungarian subjects. Some 450,000 lived in the Vojvodina, the land north of Belgrade and the Danube. Another 90,000 resided in Syrmia, a part of Croatia-Slavonia. The rest of Croatia-Slavonia contained 70,000 more Germans.[46] Most of Yugoslavia's *Volksdeutsche*, in particular those living in the Vojvodina, Yugoslavia's prime farming region, were engaged in agriculture. The far fewer urban Germans were employed primarily in the professions and business and were mostly former Austrians living in Ljubljana (Laibach) and Maribor (Marburg).

Although the leaders of this new multinational state signed minority protection treaties and pledged to respect the rights of national minorities, the treatment of the *Volksdeutsche* depended mostly on the whims of the dominant local Slavic nationality. The Slovenes, the majority Slavs living in former Austrian lands, had experienced German rule for many centuries, and even though that rule had been relatively benign, once the roles were reversed, they suppressed everything German. The Swabians fared somewhat better with the Serbs and even with the Croats, with whom they had shared a common, mostly unpleasant past as Hungarian subjects.

Another factor affecting the relations between the *Volksdeutsche* and their Yugoslavian neighbors was the ongoing conflict among the three major Slavic nationalities. The Slovenes and to a lesser degree the Croats, sensitive about what they perceived as their less-than-equal status with the more numerous Serbs, vented their frustrations through the exercise of local rule in their homelands. As a result, all national minorities—Italians, Hungarians, Germans, and even fellow Slavs, particularly Serbs—suffered from their intolerance.[47] Against this discrimination Yugoslavia's Germans relied mostly on their own resources. In 1920 they created the Schwäbisch-Deutsche Kulturbund (SDKB), headquartered in Novi Sad (Neusatz), which coordinated and supported cultural programs, schools, and churches. Even though these Germans were not entitled to official Reich aid—since no part of Yugoslavia had belonged to Germany—the VDA provided some assistance.

In the economic field the most successful *Volksdeutsche* endeavor and the key to their relative prosperity was the agricultural cooperative system, organized in response to the land reform of 1919–20. Actually the reform did not seriously threaten German agriculture, since few German farms were large enough to be affected. Furthermore, the local authorities, in particular the Serbs ruling the Vojvodina, recognized the importance of these industrious farmers to the country's economic health and refrained from applying the reform fully against them. The Reich also acknowledged their value as economic intermediaries with Yugoslavia and made their cooperative system eligible for financial assistance.[48]

The minority was less successful at political organization. The Slovenes were suspicious of German political activities and curtailed those of the former Austrians. Nonetheless, the Germans founded a nationwide political party in 1922, only to see it dissolved in 1929, as were all political parties in Yugoslavia. Consequently the cultural organization, the SDKB, assumed political significance. Although its rank-and-file membership was predominantly Swabian, the leadership was Austrian, from the Slovenian cities of Maribor and Ljubljana. Much of the prewar Swabian leadership, living in Timisoara (Temesvar), found itself after the war on the Rumanian side of the border, and the former Austrians, restricted in their political activities in Slovenia, assumed the nationwide leadership. By the early 1930s, however, a split developed between the mostly Austrian leadership and the Swabians.[49] Complicating matters was a third force, young Swabians, disenchanted with both factions and inspired by the *Erneuerungsbewegung* of Fritz Fabritius in neighboring Rumania. Hitler's success in Germany also stirred the youth. But even though National Socialism appealed to the younger generation, many Germans remained indifferent to it. This indifference, along with the escalating factionalism, made nazifying this minority and bringing it under Berlin's control a challenging task.

When Lorenz first became involved in Yugoslavia, he realized that the SDKB leadership was losing popular support. Younger leaders struck a more responsive chord.[50] VoMi therefore pressured the SDKB to accept some of the younger men into the leadership. Not until early 1939, after numerous entreaties and under the threat of having official Reich recognition revoked, did the SDKB accept VoMi's choice as minority leader, Sepp Janko, one of the more dynamic members of the younger generation. Through Janko, VoMi controlled the minority so thoroughly that by May, Behrends could boast to a group of reporters that the Germans of Yugoslavia would sooner or later all be Nazis.[51]

Having secured the leadership, VoMi began exploiting the group on behalf of Reich interests in Yugoslavia. As with most other southeastern states, during the late 1930s Reich interests required good relations between the minority and the authorities. The most advisable course for the minority to follow was to maintain a low profile and not to support any regime too enthusiastically. Yugoslav politics were too unpredictable to associate the minority too closely with a particular faction. Heeding this advice, the minority watched passively as regimes came and went, hoping that the latest changes would not bring harder times.

The outbreak of war in September 1939 threatened the safety of Yugoslavia's *Volksdeutsche*. Although Yugoslavia was not yet involved in the struggle, anxieties among the Slavs regarding Hitler's intentions intensified anti-German feelings, especially in Slovenia, a former possession of Hitler's homeland of Austria. By May 1940, reports reached Berlin of anti-German demonstrations and increased military activity.[52] The central government in Belgrade warned the local authorities in Slovenia to curb anti-German actions, but with little success.[53] Indeed, Slovene fears were not unfounded. Although the majority of *Volksdeutsche* did nothing to antagonize the Slavs, others, mostly from safe haven in the Reich, publicized their revisionist aims. Some emigré groups had even compiled lists of German officials to be installed after the reannexation of the borderlands.[54]

Both VoMi and the Foreign Ministry did their best to preserve decent relations between Berlin and Belgrade, a difficult task in view of the popular anti-German feelings and the growing militancy of *Volksdeutsche* activists. One measure the Reich considered in early 1941 was a minority protection treaty similar to those recently signed with Slovakia, Hungary, and Rumania.[55] The Foreign Ministry, trying to lure Yugoslavia into the Axis camp, looked favorably on the idea, but VoMi argued that Belgrade's record of abiding by such treaties was poor. Besides, the central government could not enforce the treaty in the provinces, especially in Slovenia, where local officials would flaunt their anti-Germanism to test the Reich's resolve. This would be worse than if no agreement existed at all. The Foreign Ministry accepted this reasoning and gave up the idea.[56]

The Reich's efforts to maintain decent relations with Belgrade seemed briefly to pay off on 25 March 1941. The Dragiša Cvetković government, realizing the futility of remaining neutral, reluctantly, and contrary to strong popular sentiment, signed the Tripartite Pact and brought Yugoslavia into the Axis camp. Two days later a military coup overthrew the regime. Although the new government insisted that it would honor all prior commitments, including the pact with Germany, the coup and the expected turn in Belgrade's foreign policy away from the Reich threatened Hitler's plans for dominating south-eastern Europe.

Hitler decried the changes in Belgrade and ordered German troops already assembled for an invasion of Greece to prepare for an attack on Yugoslavia as well. Some preparations inside Yugoslavia would also be necessary, since there was good reason to believe that the local *Volksdeutsche* would suffer for Germany's aggression. Widespread anti-German demonstrations were already occurring. Sepp Janko tried to calm the situation by pledging *Volksdeutsche* loyalty to the new regime and by ordering all potentially provocative German actions to cease.[57] But despite efforts by Belgrade and the minority leadership, tensions mounted, and unrest continued.

Rumors of an imminent German invasion seemed to be substantiated by a Yugoslav call-up of reserves and increased induction of new recruits. In the midst of this tumult the minority leaders turned to Berlin for advice, inquiring whether or not Germans should report for mobilization and induction. When the question reached Hitler, he advised the *Volksdeutsche* to evade mobilization by fleeing the country or going into hiding. While VoMi transmitted this highly confidential message to the minority, the Foreign Ministry arranged with the Rumanian and Hungarian authorities to allow fleeing Germans from Yugoslavia to cross their borders.[58]

The idea was also broached to orchestrate cries for help from the *Volksdeutsche* as justification for the invasion—as had been done in Poland and Czechoslovakia. VoMi, whose leaders were aware of at least some of the preparations for the invasion, offered its services, but events were moving so rapidly that incidental appeals for help made little difference in the overall scheme.[59] Besides, Hitler had already ordered the attack on Yugoslavia, and by April 1941 he was indifferent to world opinion and needed no justification.

The collapse of Yugoslavia was precipitous. Total dissolution followed the German invasion of 6 April 1941. On 10 April the Croats declared their independence. Then came further dismemberment, as most of Yugoslavia's neighbors—following precedents established in earlier German conquests—claimed the spoils. After Germany annexed most of the formerly Austrian borderlands, Italy took Montenegro, much of Carniola including Ljubljana, and part of the Dalmatian coastline. Hungary, hoping to redeem its entire irredenta, seized parts of the Vojvodina, while Bulgaria grabbed Macedonia. Even Albania took its small share. The Banat, the region containing most of the country's Germans, remained indefinitely under German military occupation. The rest of Yugoslavia, consisting of Serbia and parts of Bosnia-Herzegovina, was reconstituted as an autonomous Serbian state, under Serb administration but subject to German military occupation.

The dismemberment of Yugoslavia resulted in a corresponding disintegration of the German minority. *Volksdeutsche* residing in areas directly annexed by the Reich received Reich citizenship. So did those living in areas claimed by Italy, but only after their eventual resettlement to the Reich. As for the rest, at least for the time being they would remain members of a national minority. Those living in lands seized by Hungary rejoined their fellow Swabians in that state's growing German minority. The Germans of Serbia and parts of the Banat under direct German occupation, although members of a national minority, enjoyed a privileged status, as did the *Volksdeutsche* of the new state of Croatia, which was independent in name alone.

• • • THE WEST

Several western European states contained large numbers of *Volksdeutsche*, many of whom were former Reich citizens and were thereby entitled to official Reich concern. But since *Lebensraum* lay in the east, not in the west, only a few groups here assumed an importance in Hitler's plans comparable to that of the eastern minorities.

Germany's largest and most important western neighbor was France, which, through the reannexation of Alsace and Lorraine after World War I, possessed—by one 1935 German count—an estimated 1,580,000 *Volksdeutsche*.[60] But neither German nor French counts meant much here. It was personal preference that determined who was French or German. For those considering themselves Germans, the authorities granted no special status as members of a national minority. As one of the major victorious powers, France forced lesser states to adopt minority protection guarantees but accepted no similar obligations for itself. The French tolerated absolutely no links between their Germans and the Reich. A few German organizations existed, but they were strictly cultural or social in purpose, with no *völkisch* or political significance. VoMi eventually created a network of agents, but their activities were limited to gathering intelligence. They made little or no effort to organize or nazify the German population.[61]

As VoMi officials conceded, of all German minorities in the west, only that of Eupen-Malmédy in Belgium even approached the minorities in the east in importance. Interest in these 50,000 Germans, living in former Reich territory annexed by Belgium after the war, was based mostly on the Reich's obligation to its former citizens, not on their *völkisch* importance or even their place in Belgian-German relations. Evidently the Belgians were not as sensitive as their fellow victors the French and the Italians about permitting their Germans to maintain ties with the Reich. The minority in Eupen-Malmédy received aid from Reich and Prussian ministries through the Deutsche Stiftung and the Ossa-Vereinigte Finanzkontore, and the VDA serviced its cultural needs. Through these channels numerous Reich organizations, including Nazi groups after 1933, established contacts with this minority. As with other minorities, VoMi recognized only one organ and one leadership as its official representation, the Heimattreue Front.[62] After the invasion of Belgium in May 1940, Germany reannexed Eupen-Malmédy and granted Reich citizenship to the local Germans.

VoMi's involvement in Belgium extended beyond Eupen-Malmédy and beyond *Volksdeutsche*. Through its Gau representative in Düsseldorf, VoMi became involved with the Germanic, Flemish part of the population. In July 1937, the VoMi official Gunther Stier, in a conversation with Ribbentrop's office, alluded to certain undisclosed activities he was pursuing among the Flemings, "as Behrends had requested." Both Lorenz and Behrends were aware of his involvement and provided some funds.[63] This evidence suggests that in performing its duties, even in the prewar years, VoMi did not limit itself to *Volksdeutsche*. And although no documentation substantiates it, VoMi may also have been operating in other Germanic lands such as the Netherlands.

Another country in the west with a sizable German population was Switzerland, but here, as in Austria, the Germans were the majority nationality. As a result of Switzerland's peculiar course of historical development, *völkisch* attachment to Germany and the *Volk* was alien to the Swiss. Nevertheless, after 1933 the flood of Nazi propaganda calling on the Swiss to rally to the swastika seduced a few individuals.[64]

Several pro-Nazi groups were formed, but when their agitation became a nuisance, the authorities disbanded them. In December 1938 Lorenz, in the interest of preserving proper relations with the Swiss, instructed all VoMi regional offices, the VDA, and the Gestapo to sever all ties with their contacts in Switzerland. At least for the time being, the "*Volksdeutsche*" of Switzerland would be off limits for Nazi proselytizing. Furthermore, these organizations were to screen carefully all Swiss requesting membership in the Nazi party in the Reich. It was suspected that Swiss agents were trying to infiltrate the party.[65]

As the Germans of Switzerland were removed from the list of potential converts to the Nazi cause, so were the Germans of the tiny principality of Liechtenstein, a Swiss diplomatic dependency. Here too VoMi urged its people to use caution, since Liechtenstein's close ties with Switzerland could jeopardize Reich relations with the Swiss. But minuscule Liechtenstein, squeezed in a valley between Switzerland and Austria, was not immune to the contagion of National Socialism. Although VoMi warned several local groups not to engage in overtly pro-Nazi activities, a few renegades, with help from the Austrian SA, attempted a coup in the capital city of Vaduz on 22 March 1939. The local constabulary proved to be something more than a comic opera cast and subdued the conspirators. The Swiss, outraged by this crude attempt to subvert their tiny dependency, protested to Berlin. Shortly thereafter VoMi, having received instructions to nip in the bud any future disturbances, consulted a trusted contact in the Vaduz government. In return for a promise that Liechtenstein would take no action against the culprits, VoMi agreed to recall all Reich Germans involved in the coup and to prevent any recurrence.[66] It appears that the agreement was honored by both sides throughout the subsequent war years, and the Germans of Liechtenstein were spared the tragic experience of the main body of the German *Volk*.

• • • NORTH SCHLESWIG

The Germans of North Schleswig, the southernmost part of Denmark, were comparable to the *Volksdeutsche* of eastern Europe in terms of their political and ideological importance to the Reich. These 40,000 people became a national minority as a result of a plebiscite held in 1920 in which the majority of the population of North Schleswig, then a part of Germany, voted to join Denmark. Since most inhabitants were either bilingual or spoke a local, hybrid dialect of Danish and German, it was difficult to distinguish the local Germans from their Danish neighbors. Religion was not a distinction either, since the overwhelming majority of both Danes and Germans were Lutheran. And since most were engaged in agriculture, there were no pronounced social or occupational differences. Indeed, in North Schleswig, it was mostly one's personal preference that marked a Dane or a German.

The Germans of North Schleswig could raise very few legitimate grievances against Danish rule, since the Danes allowed them extremely generous cultural and political rights.[67] One valid objection was economic dislocation. The new frontier separated them from the regional economy of Schleswig-Holstein, of which they had been a part for centuries. But this dislocation had also disrupted the economic patterns of the area's Danes. Another issue facing these Germans was landownership. Although Denmark had no agrarian reform, which in other states undermined the economic and social status of the local Germans, German farmers came under financial pressure, especially with the onset of the depression. In Denmark the economic crisis hit agriculture very hard, and the government appeared to favor Danish farmers in providing assistance. Germans, for instance, found it increasingly difficult to arrange credit and as a result began losing land to foreclosure. Consequently they turned more frequently to the Reich for help. As former Reich citizens, they were able to tap into the resources of Ossa-Finanzkontore.[68] Reich credit, as well as direct subsidies, enabled them to retain their property and thereby reinforced German claims to the land.

In the prosperous days of the 1920s as well as the difficult times of the 1930s, the minority defended itself through its own political organizations, which the Danes sanctioned. In North Schleswig, where little else distinguished between nationalities, political affiliation became an important mark of national identity. In 1920 the Germans organized the Schleswiger Wahlverein, under the leadership of Pastor Johannes Schmidt aus Wodder. It was closely associated with the Schleswig-Holstein Bund (SHB), a Reich organization advocating the return of North Schleswig to Schleswig-Holstein.[69]

Hitler's ascendancy sparked hopes among these *Volksdeutsche* of fulfilling their revisionist goal of returning to the Reich. This expectation brought many of them to Nazism. But other factors besides the prospects of border revision also contributed to their conversion. Their predominantly rural society was extremely traditional, even antidemocratic, and many features of National Socialism found acceptance here. Another factor was the proximity of Schleswig-Holstein, one of the strongest enclaves of Nazi support in Germany. Although these factors prepared fertile ground for National Socialism in North Schleswig, it was the growing reliance on the Reich for subsidies that contributed most to the nazification of this minority.

Before 1933, the established leadership under Schmidt aus Wodder did not tolerate Nazi activities, but with the Nazi takeover to the south, the minority learned that if it wanted to keep receiving the subsidies, it had to cooperate with Berlin. After the SHB in Schleswig-Holstein adopted National Socialism in 1933, it pressured the Wahlverein to do the same. When Schmidt aus Wodder refused, the nazified SHB withdrew its backing from the Wahlverein and helped establish a Nazi party in North Schleswig as a rival.[70]

By the time Lorenz became involved, a factional quarrel had broken out between the Wahlverein and the new Nazi group. Various organizations inside the Reich patronized one or the other. It was not until the summer of 1938 that VoMi resolved the dispute in favor of the Nazi, Jens Möller. VoMi had presented the minority with a simple choice: either it followed orders, or the subsidies stopped.[71] Although effective initially, the tactic of using the subsidies as leverage became less so. By 1938, as the foreign-exchange situation for the Reich worsened, expenditures abroad, including funds for the minorities, were parceled out more sparingly. It became difficult for VoMi to fill all requests, and as this became apparent, the Germans of North Schleswig became less inclined to comply with VoMi's orders.

Compounding VoMi's problems in North Schleswig was the fact that Reich interests in Denmark clashed with the revisionist goals of the Volksdeutsche. Their hopes for reannexation conflicted with Hitler's desire to win over Denmark as a willing partner in his new European order. He and many other Nazi racists, particularly Heinrich Himmler and his SS ideologues, envisioned the Danes as the principal link to the racially valuable Nordic peoples of Scandinavia.[72] They wanted Danish cooperation and did not wish to alienate them by taking away territory. Thus, in the interest of persuading the Danes to join in the common effort, the Reich compromised the interests and goals of the local *Volksdeutsche*. They were to maintain their German identity as well as friendly relations with the Danes. They were also to set an example of neighborly cooperation with the Nordic peoples of Scandinavia. Whereas in Poland and Czechoslovakia the Reich encouraged and exploited *Volksdeutsche* revisionist demands, in Denmark it suppressed them.

The task of persuading these Germans to resign themselves to Danish rule fell to VoMi. The assignment became even more demanding as Hitler's diplomatic successes in 1938 and early 1939 stimulated their revisionist expectations. In the spring of 1939, Jens Möller, VoMi's choice as minority leader, resumed his demands for reunification while complaining ever louder about the Reich's inability to supply the minority with adequate funds. VoMi summoned Möller to Berlin to impress on him that the Führer demanded tranquil relations with Denmark. Möller replied that his demands only reflected the sentiments of his constituents, who, by the way, were desperate for financial assistance. He was promised the necessary foreign exchange, but on the condition that he ceased all talk of revisionism. Apparently the promised funds did not come through, and Möller continued his agitation. Lorenz again scolded him, threatening him with political ostracism if he did not relent.[73] Evidently Möller heeded the warning enough to suit Lorenz, since he managed to hold on to his post into the war years. But neither he nor most of the *Volksdeutsche* of North Schleswig abandoned their hopes for a border revision.

At least for the time being, reannexation was out of the question. But another solution to the nationality problem in the area became a possibility in October 1939—resettlement. After the announcement of the Baltic resettlement, rumors of an imminent departure spread throughout the German community. Many who had clamored for reannexation had second thoughts about rejoining the *Volk* when the most likely means became relocation. Assurances from the Foreign Ministry that resettlement was not anticipated for them allayed many fears. Sobered by the prospects of resettlement, and aware of their tenuous position, these Germans reluctantly resigned themselves to the fate the Führer selected for them. The situation in North Schleswig remained stable until April 1940, when Germany invaded Denmark.

The Soviet Union contained one of the largest German minorities in Europe, an estimated 1,240,000 *Volksdeutsche*.[74] But due to the isolation of the Soviet Union from the rest of Europe, neither the Reich nor VoMi had anything at all to do with these people during the interwar years. Hansa traders had established German enclaves in Russia in the Middle Ages, and Peter the Great had brought in all sorts of German engineers, advisers, technicians, and administrators to help modernize his empire. However, Germans did not arrive in great numbers until the reign of Catherine II and her efforts to colonize lands conquered from the Turks. The first German colonists settled around Saratov on the middle Volga and became the nucleus of the group known as the Volga Germans. In Lenin's Soviet Union, the Volga Germans had the right to organize themselves as a national entity, and in 1918 they created an autonomous region, which in 1924 became the Autonomous Soviet Socialist Republic of the Volga Germans. Most of these Germans were industrious, prosperous farmers of the "Kulak" class, which suffered terribly under Stalin's collectivization. Many were deported to Siberia, and others perished from the hardships of the program. Eventually Stalin abolished the republic.[75]

Another large group of Germans living in the Soviet Union comprised the Germans of the Ukraine, divided into the Volhynian and the Black Sea Germans. The estimated 50,000 Volhynian Germans had been separated from their neighbors in Poland by the border arrangement of 1921. The Black Sea Germans, a much larger group of nearly 400,000, had colonized the steppes along the Black Sea from Odessa to Rostov in the early 1800s. Most of them emigrated from southern Germany, but others came from Russian Poland and Habsburg lands. After the Communists took over the Ukraine, they created six German self-administration areas, bestowing on them names honoring German Communists, names like Spartakus-Grossliebenthal, Liebknecht-Landau, and Luxemburg bei Mariopol. Commonly the 44,000 Crimean Germans have been included among the Black Sea Germans, even though they had their own administrative raion in the Crimean Republic.[76]

The Germans of the Ukraine, like those of the Volga region, suffered greatly during collectivization. The extent of their hardships became known only after the German invasion in June 1941, when

German troops discovered survivors living under the most wretched conditions. It was only then that VoMi became involved with this distant branch of the German *Volk*.

• • *VOLKSDEUTSCHE* OVERSEAS

According to Hess's distribution of responsibilities in *Volkstum* matters, VoMi had authority over the *Volksdeutsche* of Europe and the United States, whereas the AO could deal with the rest. Contrary to postwar testimony in which Lorenz insisted that VoMi had nothing to do with Germans outside Europe, the office was deeply involved with Americans of German descent, enough to warrant the creation of an "overseas" (*Übersee*) section in the Berlin office.[77]

As early as October 1937 the Foreign Ministry realized that Reich involvement with Germans and people of German ancestry living in the United States, particularly with the members of the German American Bund (GAB), was creating bad feelings among Americans. Since VoMi was the Reich office most active in maintaining these ties, the ministry suggested that it cease its activities in the United States.[78]

VoMi agreed to curtail these activities, specifically with the GAB, but was unwilling to surrender its prerogatives as the Reich agency exclusively responsible for these "*Volksdeutsche*." At a meeting in early February 1938, Behrends promised to limit activities in the United States but insisted that when in the Reich, American Germans must deal only with VoMi.[79] In violation of these promises, some VoMi agents continued their activities. The Reich ambassador to the United States, Hans Heinrich Dieckhoff, complained to the Wilhelmstrasse that some VoMi official had recently promised aid to the Chicago branch of the GAB and that another was recruiting German Americans for repatriation to the Reich. He repeatedly warned Berlin that Americans were losing patience and pleaded that VoMi must immediately halt its activities.[80]

VoMi meanwhile was searching for alternative channels to America. Its officials had conferred with the Deutsche Auslands-Institut about the possibility of the latter expanding its cultural activities in the United States, since the DAI, on the surface an exclusively cultural institution, would arouse little suspicion. But by the summer of 1938, any hint of ties between German organizations in the United States and the Reich aroused the American public. The following year VoMi advised the DAI to suspend all contacts with the GAB.[81] VoMi had totally misunderstood and miscalculated the attachment that Germans in the United States had for the Reich. Although a few were unabashedly Nazi sympathizers and saw themselves as true *Volksdeutsche*, the vast majority regarded themselves as Americans and valued their Germanness merely as a cultural heritage, void of any political predisposition.

CHAPTER SEVEN

Wartime and Resettlement VoMi

On 6 October 1939, shortly after Germany's annihilation of Poland, Hitler stood before the Reichstag and proclaimed that with the recent victory, Germany's territorial demands had been satisfied and that he was henceforth interested only in peace. As evidence of his peaceful intentions, he solemnly announced that he would shortly resettle the remaining Germans of eastern Europe to the Reich and its newly acquired territories, thereby eliminating a potential source of friction and conflict.[1] The Nazi party newspaper, the *Völkischer Beobachter*, hailed his proposal as the "Magna Carta" of the European east.[2]

Although it is doubtful that Hitler's resettlement program will ever match the Magna Carta in lasting historical importance, it held great significance for Heinrich Himmler as well as for his "auxiliaries," the Volksdeutsche Mittelstelle and the *Volksdeutsche* of Europe. Indeed, with the inception of the program, the paths of the Reichsführer SS and the Volhynian *Volksdeutsche* began converging toward Przemysl.

The resettlement presented Himmler not only with another opportunity to extend his authority over the *Volksdeutsche* of Europe but also with prospects for launching the new racial order—his most cherished goal. As for the *Volksdeutsche* designated for resettlement, it would now be their turn to serve the Reich. First, they would serve Hitler by accepting relocation in the interest of his foreign policy. And second, they would serve Himmler by becoming the human building blocks of the new order. The resettlement would also be of great importance for VoMi, since the fulfilling of its resettlement duties, along with the circumstances of war, resulted in its further absorption into the SS system.

Events leading to Hitler's announcement on 6 October had been set in motion two weeks earlier. On the night of 25 September, the Reich ambassador in Moscow, Werner von Schulenburg, notified the Wilhelmstrasse that the Soviet leader, Josef Stalin, intended to redeem the Führer's promise to allow him a free hand in Latvia and Estonia, as agreed in the secret clause of the German-Soviet Friendship and Non-Aggression Treaty of 23 August 1939.[3] The treaty, which divided much of eastern Europe into German and Soviet spheres of interest, served Hitler's immediate foreign policy goals. It secured Soviet neutrality while he attacked Poland, and after Poland's defeat, it ensured Stalin's continued friendship while Hitler prepared for further aggression. But the *Volksdeutsche* living in the Baltic States and other territories destined to fall to the Soviets threatened the arrangement. Hitler anticipated that once Stalin seized these territories, these Germans would expect the Reich to rescue them. Hitler, who for years had championed Germans everywhere, would have to choose between maintaining good relations with Stalin and coming to the aid of his fellow Germans. Anxious to avoid this dilemma, Hitler decided to resettle first the Baltic Germans and eventually all Germans living in territories designated to fall to the Soviets. In the interest of his immediate foreign policy needs, the *Volksdeutsche* would have to sacrifice their homes and homelands.

Resettlement was far easier to proclaim than execute. Hundreds of thousands of people would be involved. They would first have to be identified as Germans, then registered, transported, and finally settled in new homes. They would have to be fed, housed, and cared for every step of the way. To complete this enormous task, Hitler at first turned to VoMi. A few days after receiving Schulenburg's notice, he summoned Werner Lorenz to the chancellery and placed him in command of the Baltic operation. The following day Hitler telephoned Lorenz to inquire about his progress. Lorenz reported that he had met with representatives of the Foreign Ministry, who had informed him of diplomatic preparations already under way, and with those of the Transportation Ministry, who had placed some forty ships at his disposal. No doubt Hitler was pleased with Lorenz's progress. But neither he nor Lorenz anticipated the reaction of Lorenz's SS superior, Heinrich Himmler, to learning of his subordinate's new responsibilities.[4]

Shortly after his conversation with Hitler, Lorenz unassumingly informed Himmler of his new assignment. Himmler was dumbfounded. He berated Lorenz for accepting these new tasks, which, so he fumed, exceeded both Lorenz's authority and abilities. Himmler evidently fancied himself the man best suited to direct the operation and stormed off to see the Führer, blustering that the decision of who would direct the resettlement was not yet final. The next evening he telephoned Lorenz at home and informed him that Hitler had reconsidered his earlier decision. He had placed Himmler in charge of the resettlement as the Reichskommissar für die Festigung deutschen Volkstums (RKFDV). Henceforth Lorenz would receive instructions from Himmler, not from Hitler directly.[5] Lorenz, true to the SS principle of unquestioning obedience, accepted his demotion without a fuss.

One may only speculate why a ruffled Himmler hastened to the Führer to protest the selection of Lorenz. One possibility is that since Hitler had appointed Himmler director of the South Tyrol resettlement the previous spring, he now considered himself the foremost expert and authority in such operations. Internal SS politics may also have prompted Himmler to question the choice. He may have feared that Lorenz's appointment would make him a much too independent force within the SS.

One likewise can only speculate why Hitler initially selected Lorenz and then changed his mind. Possibly the Führer first selected Lorenz because he appeared to be the most knowledgeable and experienced man in the *Volksdeutsche* business and because the other choice, Himmler, was still preoccupied with the South Tyrolean resettlement. But a more tenable explanation is Hitler's reluctance to enhance Himmler's already considerable power. Therefore, whatever ultimately swayed Hitler to change his mind outweighed these—or other—considerations.

Since nothing is known of Himmler and Hitler's conversation that resulted in Lorenz's demotion, one can only conjecture as to what dissuaded the Führer from his first choice. One strong possibility is the ideological implications of the resettlement. One may envision a scenario in which Himmler—after all other arguments to change Hitler's mind had failed, such as Lorenz's alleged incompetence—suggested that the time had come to begin the building of the new racial order. Victory on the battlefield and the Führer's diplomatic successes had liberated former German territory as well as acquired additional *Lebensraum* for the *Volk*, and only the SS, which over the years had proven itself the most diligent proponent of the Nazi racial idea, was capable of performing the task. The resettlement, under Himmler's guidance, would be the initial step toward that goal. Perhaps Hitler thought, why not let Himmler make a go of it?

It may never be known for certain what prompted Hitler's reversal, but the fact is that what resulted from this exchange between the most powerful and the second most powerful man in the Reich exceeded the scope of an evacuation—with which Hitler had at first charged Lorenz. Hitler's commission to Himmler consisted of three provisions, and only the first dealt with the evacuation. In his decree of 7 October 1939—the formal order for the "Strengthening of Germandom"—Hitler authorized Himmler to (1) retrieve the *Volksdeutsche* and the *Reichsdeutsche* (Reich citizens) from foreign lands and return them to the Reich for permanent settlement; (2) eliminate the harmful, alien segments of the population from the German *Volk* and its living area; (3) plan and implement the settlement of the land designated for the repatriated Germans.[6] These three provisions were the basis for a comprehensive racial program designed for building the new Germanic racial order. Himmler would be in control, and VoMi and the *Volksdeutsche* would both be vital participants.

• • • THE RKFDV

The Führer's decree of 7 October only commissioned the Reichsführer SS with certain responsibilities. It did not authorize the creation of a Kommissariat, nor did it even designate Himmler a Kommissar. Himmler, in recognition of the official nature of his commission to "Strengthen Germandom," simply designated himself as the Reichskommissar für die Festigung deutschen Volkstums.[7] Apparently Hitler did not object to this lofty title, and Himmler retained it for the duration of the program.

Hitler left the building of the RKFDV apparatus to Himmler, who, in executing his commission, could employ any state, party, and SS offices and agencies, including the preeminent office in *Volkstum* affairs, VoMi, which by then was already closely associated with the SS. As Himmler prepared for his monumental task, he constructed the RKFDV office as a coordinating center for participating organizations. Soon the RKFDV office, like most other Third Reich organs, assumed the character of its leader, which—since Himmler was the Reichsführer SS—was that of the SS. He let no opportunity pass to impose SS authority over the RKFDV operation and assigned RKFDV responsibilities to SS or SS-associated organs, including VoMi. As a result, the RKFDV system became yet another pillar of strength for Himmler and his SS.[8] It must be kept in mind, however, that even though the RKFDV program assumed the character and appearance of the SS, the commission for the "Strengthening of Germandom" was based on Reich authority, and state funds financed the project.

A measure anchoring the RKFDV more firmly within the SS system was Himmler's June 1941 elevation of the RKFDV office to a status equivalent (*gleichgestellt*) to that of an SS main office (*Hauptamt*) in all matters pertaining to the SS.[9] Henceforth it was the RKFDV Stabshauptamt, equal to, but not, an SS office. Few contemporaries bothered with the nuance and simply accepted it as a part of the SS. Himmler forged yet another link between the RKFDV and the SS when in June 1942 he placed everyone working for the RKFDV office under the jurisdiction of the SS police and court system.[10] Personal ties, however, in particular Himmler's dual role as RFSS and RKFDV, remained the most important links between the SS and the RKFDV operation. These he fortified by appointing SS officers throughout the RKFDV hierarchy, beginning with the selection of SS Brigadeführer Ulrich Greifelt, an administrative expert, as its chief.[11]

• • VOMI AND THE RKFDV

From the outset, the exact status of the RKFDV office, a state authority operating as an SS organ, was confused. So too was the status of other offices and organizations participating in the program. This was certainly true of VoMi. Before the launching of the resettlement program, it was clearly an NSDAP organ. But with Himmler's first order as RKFDV, in which he assigned to VoMi the responsibility for evacuating and transporting the resettlers to the Reich, its status was no longer so clear.[12] Whereas earlier Himmler's influence over VoMi had been personal, informal, and based solely on the fact that the VoMi leadership belonged to the SS, through the RKFDV program Himmler formalized his authority—but only in respect to its resettlement activities.

The 7 October 1939 RKFDV decree claimed no authority over VoMi's dealings with those *Volksdeutsche* living in states and regions unaffected by the resettlement. But since Himmler coveted complete sovereignty in *Volkstum* affairs, he sought authority over them as well. In this quest his primary target was Hess's position as VoMi's superior in its activities with the minorities. Determined to appropriate this position for himself, Himmler challenged Hess. His persistence paid off when, on 7 December 1940, Hitler transferred VoMi's former, pre-RKFDV authority to Himmler. Nothing is known about the politics and events resulting in the transfer. Nor is anything known of the specific contents of the Führer's order. Neither the Foreign Ministry nor even VoMi had copies.[13] The assumption here is that Himmler convinced Hitler that centralized, unified direction of all *Volkstum* activities—the RKFDV program as well as minority business—required another reallocation of authority. Once reallocated, party authority complemented Himmler's RKFDV state authority as he pursued primacy in the *Volkstum* field.

Himmler became VoMi's superior in party matters, but whether or not Hess retained any authority in *Volkstum* matters was unclear. In February 1941 Hess, presumably on Hitler's orders, acknowledged Himmler as the Führer's man in charge (*Sachbearbeiter*) in this area. He evidently reserved some authority for himself, since he designated Himmler as his own deputy, responsible for all *Grenz- und Volkstums-fragen*.[14] Hess's inexplicable flight to England in May simplified the issue. Hitler abolished the office of deputy Führer and replaced it with a party chancellery under Martin Bormann. Since he did not endow the new office with the authority of the old, Bormann did not inherit all of Hess's powers—definitely not any in *Volkstum* matters. Thus Himmler, as Hitler's *Sachbearbeiter* and Hess's former deputy in *Grenz- und Volkstumsfragen*, by default became the exclusive party authority in this field, answerable only to the Führer.[15]

Himmler was now VoMi's superior in every respect. As the chief party authority in *Volkstum* affairs, he was its boss in minority business, and as RKFDV, he was its superior in resettlement activities. It is significant that in neither instance was he acting in his capacity as Reichsführer SS. Nevertheless his leadership of the SS was crucial. As the commanding SS officer of all VoMi personnel belonging to the SS, Himmler reinforced both his RKFDV and party authority. In the same 11 June 1941 order in which he elevated the RKFDV office to a status equivalent to that of an SS main office, he bestowed a similar "honor" on VoMi. He claimed he had created (*errichtet*) a new office, the RKFDV Hauptamt Volksdeutsche Mittelstelle, and then awarded it status equivalent to that of an SS main office.[16] But in reality the "new" Hauptamt consisted of those VoMi sections that for nearly two years had already been performing resettlement tasks. The measure was no more than a sleight of hand reinforcing Himmler's monopoly in *Volkstum* matters by confusing even further VoMi's ties to the RKFDV and the SS.

The next step in Himmler's campaign to consolidate his authority in *Volkstum* matters was the creation of the Büro für Volkstumsfragen der NSDAP. This office was to coordinate all relevant party activities and serve as an intermediary between the NSDAP and the SS. The Büro had direct ties to two SS offices, RSHA and RuSHA; to a state office associated with the SS, the RKFDV Stabshauptamt; and to a party organ, VoMi. Bringing together VoMi and the RKFDV office with the two SS offices drew both deeper into the SS system through association.[17] Then on 12 March 1942, Hitler approved Himmler's creation of yet one more party office, the Hauptamt für Volkstumsfragen, whose offices in the Gaus handled local *Volkstum* business. In doing so, Hitler reconfirmed Himmler's position as the exclusive Reich authority in this field.[18] With Hitler's blessings, Himmler's control over the *Volksdeutsche* was complete, as was his authority over every aspect of VoMi's activities. Although VoMi formally remained a party office, in practice it functioned as a branch of the SS.

• • PERSONNEL

VoMi's additional resettlement responsibilities required the creation of new sections, units, and branches and, correspondingly, the enlargement of its staff. Expansion brought in new people whose presence significantly transformed its nature and character. It obtained personnel from various sources and by diverse means. For clerical and lower-level workers, the Berlin office simply advertised in the press and notified the local employment office of its needs. For higher-level officials, VoMi mostly relied on personal contacts and recommendations from throughout the Nazi and the SS systems.[19]

Many of the new, middle-level positions were filled—unlike in the preresettlement years—by SS men transferred from throughout the SS system. VoMi notified the SS personnel office of openings, and the latter arranged the transfers. Both the Allgemeine SS and those SS units soon to become the Waffen SS could order men to report to VoMi. It also became common practice for Waffen SS men on leaves of absence from the front, or while convalescing, to serve the SS in various capacities in the rear, including service with VoMi. SS men already employed at VoMi, when called to active duty with the Waffen SS, frequently were permitted to serve at least a part of their active tour with VoMi.

VoMi also acquired a portion of its manpower from outside the SS through conscription. The emergency personnel procurement order, the Notdienstverordnung of 15 October 1938 (Dritte Verordnung zur Sicherstellung des Kraftebedarfs für Aufgaben von besonderer staatspolitischer Bedeutung), authorized state agencies and party offices performing official state functions to draft civilians. The RKFDV had recourse to this order, and on 12 November 1939, Himmler empowered VoMi to use it to fill manpower needs.[20] VoMi conscripted people for the headquarters staff as well as for its many branch offices and special units. One should note that induction was for employment at VoMi, not induction into the SS. Most SS men transferred to VoMi from within the SS system were, however, considered inducted, since induction meant that the Reich, not the SS, would pay them.

With the growth of VoMi's staff, its personnel became more diverse. Increased reliance on the SS for manpower brought in a greater number of career SS men. Unlike the pre-October 1939 staff, which was mostly men who had a particular expertise—either in the *Volkstum* field or in some area of administration—and who enlisted with the SS only after they joined VoMi, the new arrivals were generally SS men first and administrators or *Volkstum* experts second, if at all. The drafting of civilian workers also brought in a few people with little or no previous involvement with the Nazi movement.

VoMi was fortunate in enlisting several capable men, whose backgrounds and qualifications compared well with those of the prewar staff. One such new addition was Waldemar Rimann, a *Volksdeutscher* from Danzig, who arrived in the fall of 1939. Before his employment, Rimann, like many of those who preceded him at VoMi, had belonged to the SA but not the SS and had sported an active if not distinguished political record. As a *Volksdeutscher*, he was familiar with *Volkstum* issues, and his legal training qualified him for the white-collar tasks of a VoMi bureaucrat.[21] Another was Heinz Brückner. A war veteran and a Nazi, Brückner had not belonged to the SS before his induction into VoMi. What probably brought him to the attention of VoMi was his work with the BDO, which was ultimately supervised by VoMi Chief of Staff Behrends.[22]

Unlike Rimann and Brückner, some others already belonged to the SS before coming to VoMi. Johann Sandler, an Austrian Nazi from Carinthia, had joined the SS in 1936. Sandler brought to VoMi a record of political activism as well as experience in the *Volkstumskampf*, the perfect combination for VoMi service. The leadership was no doubt pleased to find someone with Sandler's credentials. But as his case illustrates, SS men with such accomplished backgrounds were a rare commodity, and VoMi found it increasingly difficult to keep them in its service. Military and security needs enjoyed higher priority in the SS than *Volkstum* affairs. The Waffen SS activated Sandler in May 1942, and in 1943 it thought highly enough of him to send him to the elite SS Junkerschule Bad Tölz.[23]

Occasionally Lorenz and Behrends managed to delay or even rescind an official's transfer to active Waffen SS duty. But as the war continued, their efforts were usually futile. For instance, Lorenz managed to keep his adjutant, Ellermeier, for most of the war years, but eventually he lost Behrends to an assignment as HSSPF in Serbia. Horst Hoffmeyer, the leader of the resettlement commandos, left VoMi for an assignment as chief of security for the Ploesti oil fields. Although VoMi regularly lost personnel disputes to the Waffen SS, it more than held its own with other SS branches. The same frequency of personnel transfers between VoMi and the Waffen SS is not evident between VoMi and the other, nonmilitary SS branches. It appears that once an individual established expertise in an area of SS activity, he remained employed in that field.

SD men were something of an exception. Many were assigned to other SS units and branches, but at least in the case of those assigned to VoMi, they were not formally transferred from the SD. Most of them remained on SD rolls. This practice of assigning SD men to nonpolice SS branches was apparently a means that Heydrich employed for surveillance and for extending SD influence throughout the SS system. Heinz Brückner's pre-VoMi association with Behrends leaves open the possibility of an SD connection, even though he had some later problems with the Gestapo.[24] And then there was the career SD man Konrad Radunski, who became chief of VoMi's personnel section, the office responsible for maintaining liaison with the SS.[25] Another SD man was Dr. Klaus Siebert, who served VoMi and the SD mostly in the field, performing some of VoMi's most difficult and demanding resettlement tasks. Siebert's record, along with those of Behrends and Hoffmeyer, supports the generalization that VoMi's most dynamic and capable people had SD connections. Siebert's SS records provide a fascinating glimpse into the background of an energetic, fanatical, career SS man, hardly typical of the majority of the workers at VoMi.[26]

Another type to appear in increasing numbers at VoMi after the fall of 1939 was the resettled *Volksdeutscher*. Leonid von Cube, a resettler from Latvia and inlaw of Wilhelm von Rüdiger, a leader in the Baltic German minority in Latvia, offered to help with on-site preparations for the evacuation from Latvia. Afterward VoMi employed him in its Posen office to assist Baltic Germans in dealing with the problems of relocation. The local SD also enlisted his services.[27] Other *Volksdeutsche* served VoMi in a variety of capacities, from working with resettlement teams to accompanying VoMi Chief Lorenz as a temporary adjutant, as did Werner Krassowsky.[28]

It should be mentioned that the personnel buildup brought in a few undesirable characters. One such figure was Rudolf Kiepert, who came to VoMi in 1941 and served as chief of the Beratungsstelle für Einwanderer. Although he had an impressive record of service with the Hitlerjugend, he also had a reputation for financial improprieties. On top of that, Kiepert evidently was also something of a skirt-chaser with VoMi's women employees and was known to take pleasure trips on the pretext of business. As a result of his shortcomings, in October 1943 Kiepert's superiors relieved him of his duties at the BfE and reassigned him to VoMi's branch in Cracow, a measure tantamount at that time to bureaucratic exile.[29]

The critical shortage of manpower during the war years required a greater reliance on the use of women at VoMi—as was increasingly true throughout the German work force. VoMi hired and requisitioned women not only for clerical positions but also for staff positions. English-born Oberin Friede-Grace Koehler worked as a section chief in VoMi's health office. VoMi first employed her in September 1940 as a nurse in the Baltic resettlement.[30] One of the most active women on the staff was a Fräulein Reinhardt, who worked in the propaganda section. One of her many duties was accompanying dignitaries on tours of VoMi camps. One such luminary—whose reporting was critical of VoMi—complained that while he was touring resettlement operations in Poland, Fräulein Reinhardt constantly obstructed his efforts to investigate and report VoMi's activities.[31]

• • THE REORGANIZED BERLIN OFFICES

VoMi's new resettlement duties required the reorganization of its headquarters. The regional sections, the Länder Referate, which handled VoMi's preresettlement activities with the minorities, underwent a few changes. By October 1939, Austria, Czechoslovakia, the Memelland, and Poland no longer existed, and the corresponding sections were disbanded. The section responsible for the South Tyrol would soon follow, as would those for the Baltic States. But new ones appeared as the Reich created new client states, specifically Slovakia and later Croatia.

As for the sections defined by functions, Lorenz and Behrends created new ones as the need arose. As had been the case with the preresettlement organization, they could not anticipate which functions would be temporary and which would become permanent. For example, they did not expect that camp administration would become VoMi's most important activity, eventually requiring the greatest share of its attention and resources. At the same time, the evacuation, registration, and transportation of *Volksdeutsche* receded in importance.

Lorenz formally designated those sections of VoMi engaged in the resettlement as Volksdeutsche Mittelstelle, Abteilung Umsiedlung, and relocated them to new offices at am Karlsbad 20. Sometime in the summer of 1940, the headquarters section of the main office also moved, from Unter den Linden to Keithstrasse 29.[32] Lorenz and Behrends housed their offices here, as did most of the preresettlement sections. As in preresettlement days, Lorenz and Behrends set policy and tackled major problems in person and then left the details and routine matters to subordinates. Even though Lorenz appointed Ellermeier nominal head of the resettlement program, Behrends, as chief of staff, often superseded him in resettlement affairs. Behrends reinforced his control over resettlement matters by inserting SD man Klaus Siebert as Ellermeier's deputy.[33]

Although organizational changes began when VoMi assumed resettlement responsibilities, major restructuring did not occur until 1942, when it was reorganized into eleven departments (*Ämter*). Contrary to some contemporary accounts and later observations, which claimed that the reorganization split VoMi into two or more "VoMis," it remained one organization, officially known as the RKFDV Hauptamt Volksdeutsche Mittelstelle. Physical dispersal of sections was due to the need for more office space, not to an organizational split.

A brief look at the eleven sections provides some insights into VoMi's evolution as a Third Reich institution as well as into its activities and relations with other offices and agencies. Amt I, Amt des Dienststellenleiters, relocated to Keithstrasse 29, served as headquarters. It included both Lorenz's and Behrends's offices. Changes in this department reflected the increased presence of the SS. It eventually contained an SS legal officer and a Waffen SS company, to which were assigned all active Waffen SS men serving with VoMi. The personnel of Amt I, unlike the employees of most of the other departments, consisted entirely of SS men—with the exception of a few female clerical workers. As of November 1943, sections of this department were scattered across Berlin, as Allied bombings began taking a toll on VoMi's office space.[34]

Amt II, Organisation-Personal, functioned as VoMi's personnel office under the supervision of the career SD man Konrad Radunski. It is noteworthy that separate sections dealt with SS personnel and so-called civilian, or non-SS, personnel. For VoMi's purposes, the few people assigned to it from the Wehrmacht were grouped with the civilian employees. Although the minorities were the business of another department, Radunski dealt with their organizational affairs. It is likely that Behrends, in the interest of SD surveillance, gave this responsibility to a department headed by an SD man. Radunski could observe and supervise organizational and personnel matters, for VoMi as well as for the *Volksdeutsche*. The importance of Amt II increased during the final years of the war because of its role in allocating

Volksdeutsche manpower for the Reich labor force. The section Fachab-teilung maintained liaison with numerous Reich and NSDAP agencies requesting workers and supervised the placement of available *Volks-deutsche*.

Amt III, Finanzen- Wirtschafts- und Vermögensverwaltung, was the revamped finance office of preresettlement VoMi. Under the lead-ership of Heinrich Lohl, it continued financing VoMi's earlier, non-resettlement activities, the most important being the collection and distribution of funds for the remaining minorities. In these matters VoMi remained subordinate to Franz Xavier Schwarz, the NSDAP treasurer, and thus continued to function as a party organization.[35]

Amt IV, Presse, Berichterstattung und Verbandsarbeit, later re-named Information, was VoMi's press and propaganda department. Under the direction of Waldemar Rimann, it became VoMi's official mouthpiece. It documented and reported VoMi's activities and main-tained contact with Goebell's Propaganda Ministry as well as *Volkstum* organizations such as the DAI. It also supervised the publication of all *Volksdeutsche* journals, and all information regarding the *Volksdeutsche* passed through it for approval. Amt V, Deutschtumserziehung, super-vised by Dr. Adolf Puls, performed cultural and educational tasks among the minorities, for which the VDA had once been responsible.

Amt VI, Sicherung deutschen Volkstums im Reich, dealt with reset-tlers once they arrived in the Reich. It absorbed the Beratungsstelle für Einwanderer (BfE), which for years had been performing this function under VoMi's authority.[36] Although Amt VI provided certain services for all resettlers, its primary duty was toward those selected for permanent settlement in the Altreich, pre-*Anschluss* Germany. These "A-Cases," as will be discussed later, were politically the least reliable and racially the least desirable of the resettlers. Among these reluctant, racially questionable Germans were numerous Poles, Slo-venes, and Frenchmen, mostly deportees. One further function of Amt VI was *Patenschaftsarbeit* (sponsorship work), which meant look-ing after the material, spiritual, and cultural welfare and above all the political reliability of *Volksdeutsche*. Contrary to the postwar testimony of its department chief, Heinz Brückner, this office cooperated closely with the Gestapo and the SD, regularly reporting recalcitrant and politically objectionable *Volksdeutsche*.[37] Although on paper it func-tioned as a welfare agency, the presence of so many unwilling people under its care, as well as its connection with the most notorious SS security agencies, cast doubt on its purposes.[38] It received considerable postwar scrutiny because Brückner was one of only three VoMi men, along with Werner Lorenz and the finance officer Otto Schwarzenberger, tried at Nuremberg.

Amt VII, Sicherung deutschen Volkstums in den neuen Ostgebieten, performed tasks similar to those of Amt VI, but for the *Volksdeutsche* residing in eastern territories under German occupation, specifically in the Baltic States, unannexed Poland, and Russia. It established branch offices in Cracow, Riga, and Kiev, the latter two attached to the offices of the local HSSPF, the primary representative of the SS in the east.

Amt VIII, Kultur and Wissenschaft, was engaged in archival work, maintaining custody of records, archives, and cultural artifacts belonging to the minorities. Although it dealt mostly with the remaining minorities abroad, it served also as the curator for the treasures and documents brought along by the resettled groups.

Lorenz regarded Amt IX, Politische Führung deutscher Volksgruppen, which incorporated the old regional sections of the preresettlement VoMi, as the most important department. Subdivided into eight regional sections, it continued to provide political "leadership" and guidance to the minorities. Its responsibilities included (1) domestic *Volkstum* affairs, (2) relations between the minorities and the Reich, (3) relations between the minorities and their governments, (4) relations between the foreign states and the Reich regarding the *Volksdeutsche*, (5) relations between the minorities and non-German groups and organizations, and (6) liaison with the Foreign Ministry.

Amt X, Führung der Wirtschaft in den Deutschen Volksgruppen, was another remnant of preresettlement days. Under Lothar Heller, it directed the economies of the remaining minorities. Before the war, VoMi's economic duty toward the minorities was to ensure their solvency for their benefit as well as for Reich foreign policy interests. During the war, its primary goal became their exploitation in the interest of the Reich. This department set up sections for agriculture, industry, and credit and banking, as well as an office with the nebulous title of Volkswirtschaft, which was responsible for the Aryanization of the *Volksdeutsche* economies.

Amt XI, Umsiedlung, which originated as VoMi, Abteilung Umsiedlung A, was the most important resettlement office. Led by Walter Ellermeier, it directed VoMi's vast resettlement operation, supervising the financing of all resettlement activities and managing the camp network. It consisted of several sections, the most important being Umsiedlung-Lagerführung, commanded by Friedrich Altena. This section fed and housed the resettlers. It operated the growing camp system and coordinated the material, spiritual, and political care of the inmates as provided by various party, Reich, and SS offices. The Gaueinsatzführer, VoMi's resettlement officials in the Gaus, and the subordinate camp commanders all reported to this section. Since supervising all camp business was too much work for any one person, VoMi created section Umsiedlung Verwaltung (resettlement administration) to handle the financial side of the operation.[39]

BRANCH OFFICES AND FIELD UNITS

Although the Berlin offices remained the center of operations and decision making, the added resettlement responsibilities and wartime demands required the creation of numerous branch offices and field units, inside the Reich and in the annexed and occupied territories. At home the most important new office outside Berlin was that of the Gaueinsatzführer, or Gau placement officer, who was responsible for all resettlement matters within a Gau, in particular the administration of resettler camps.[40] As camp administration displaced other activities as VoMi's primary domestic concern, the Gaueinsatzführer replaced the Gaubeauftragter as VoMi's official in the Gaus. In most cases the Gaubeauftragter, a party functionary, simply assumed the new title and duties and became a state employee paid from RKFDV funds. Since the new post was far more demanding than the old, more attention was paid to administrative and command abilities. Nevertheless, as in the selection of Gaubeauftragter, mostly Gau party officials filled the new posts. Few Einsatzführer were career SS men.[41] In their selection, the local Gauleiter, whose cooperation was crucial for facilitating the resettlement on the local level, played a prominent role.

Most Gaueinsatzführer were NSDAP functionaries, but some had belonged to the SS before their appointments—and others joined afterward. It was their party activities, however, rather than SS membership that landed them their jobs. One "old" Nazi assigned as Gaueinsatzführer for Bayreuth was Arnulf Panzer, who entered the NSDAP in May 1925 with the relatively low party number of 5,521.

Einsatzführer duties involved mostly paperwork and routine business, but at times the unexpected disrupted the routine. For instance, in early 1944, Panzer had to find housing in Regensburg for 800 resettlers whose camp had been destroyed in an air raid.[42] Local VoMi officials constantly encountered such headaches and received little, if any, help from Berlin. When dealing with crises, they relied almost entirely on local resources, their own wits, and local party contacts. As the war continued, the disruption of central Reich authority resulted in considerable autonomy on the local level. Local authorities, such as the VoMi Einsatzführer, provided the leadership and services that enabled the Reich to function at the everyday, grass-roots level.

The first duty of the Gaueinsatzführer was to organize and supervise resettler camps, all of which needed commanders, administrators, cooks, nurses, teachers, even propaganda experts. Since the Einsatzführer was a RKFDV official, the majority of camp personnel were employed through the Notdienstverordnung, which entitled them to state benefits and pay. VoMi ordered all of its camp personnel, whether drafted or not, to apply for *notdienstverpflichtet* status.[43]

The most important camp employee was the camp commander, the Lagerführer. For the earliest resettlements, mayors and other local officials helped obtain camp commanders, but in January 1940, VoMi charged the Einsatzführer with this task. If qualified people were not available locally, the Berlin office would procure needed personnel through the SS or some NSDAP office.[44] All sorts of people with varied backgrounds served as camp commanders. Many, like August Deussen, were older Nazis and SS men. Deussen, for one, was quite reliable and competent. His experience in the 1930s as an SS camp commander came to the attention of VoMi, and in August 1942, it requisitioned him as camp commander at Regenwalde in Pomerania. Deussen, in his late fifties, made a perfect camp commander, projecting a mature, fatherly image.[45] Another older SS man serving as a camp commander was Hermann Baumgart, who joined both the NSDAP and the SS in 1932. Baumgart is an interesting case because he worked at two different kinds of SS-administered camps, the VoMi resettler camps and the notorious concentration camps. After attending the SS school at Dachau in 1938, he served at the Sachsenhausen concentration camp. In September 1939, VoMi conscripted him to supervise one of its refugee camps in Upper Silesia and, with the advent of the resettlement program, appointed him commander of a resettler camp.[46]

Baumgart and Deussen apparently were capable camp command-ers, but some others were not. The decentralized selection process and the Reich's manpower shortage resulted in a number of incompetents and rascals and created opportunities for graft, corruption, and black marketeering. One documented case of improper conduct was that of the SS man Anton Weidhaus, whom VoMi inducted into its service in October 1940 and assigned as commander for a camp at Heiligen-kreuz. Still only in his twenties, Weidhaus assumed the role of father to the resettlers. In time, word reached Berlin and VoMi that Weidhaus not only had exploited his post for personal financial gain but also had abused his authority to win sexual favors from women resettlers. Weidhaus was tried in an SS court, found guilty, expelled from the SS, and jailed for eight months. To prevent such misconduct, VoMi had implemented an inspection system, but as Weidhaus's case demon-strates, it was far from foolproof.[47]

VoMi also assumed new responsibilities outside the Reich and there-fore created branch offices abroad. One of the most important of these posts was VoMi Einsatzstab Litzmannstadt, the central transit point of the resettlement operation. Properly speaking it lay in Reich territory. Lodz, a major industrial city in central Poland, renamed Litzmann-stadt in the spring of 1940 after a World War I German general, was located in the newly created and incorporated Warthegau. Resettlers from the east passed through Lodz on the way to temporary camps inside the Altreich (pre-1938 Germany) and passed through again in the opposite direction if selected for eastern colonization. Like most VoMi officials serving outside the Altreich, the commanders at Lodz were all SS men. One was the Sudeten German Karl-Heinrich Per-then. Although active in clandestine SS activities even earlier, in 1938 Perthen officially began his SS career, which included training at the Dachau and Bad Tölz SS schools.[48]

Another important VoMi office located outside the Altreich was the one in Vienna, created shortly after the *Anschluss*. With time it re-focused attention from Austrian affairs to activities throughout south-eastern Europe. In 1944, with *Volksdeutsche* refugees from the east streaming into Austria, VoMi bestowed on the Vienna office the title of Verbindungsstelle Südost and listed it after the eleven Berlin depart-ments as the twelfth recipient of VoMi orders and communications.[49]

Three other foreign branches were the Cracow office for the Gen-eral Government; the Riga office, attached to the HSSPF for the

Ostland; and Sonderkommando R, the special unit for Russia, attached to the HSSPF Rusland-Süd, with its headquarters in Kiev.[50] All three came under Amt VII, Sicherung deutschen Volkstums in den neuen Ostgebieten. VoMi also maintained at least two offices in the west, in Paris and Brussels, both subordinate to the local HSSPF.[51] In addition, VoMi set up temporary headquarters for its resettlement teams, the Umsiedlungskommandos, whenever they operated in foreign lands. And in 1944, as the Red Army advanced into southeastern Europe, VoMi planted an office in Budapest to supervise the evacuation of *Volksdeutsche* from the region. VoMi's functions were so diverse and its operations so dispersed that there very well may have been other offices and units abroad not mentioned here.

The personnel staffing the offices and units outside the Altreich came to VoMi from many sources and by various means, but as far as can be determined, common to all was membership in the SS. There are several reasons for the preponderance of SS men in foreign positions. Most of these posts were attached to the local HSSPF and therefore required SS men. Furthermore, since central authority tended to diminish with distance from Berlin, Himmler protected his interests by appointing trusted SS men. Besides, it was only fitting that in the east, in the conquered *Lebensraum*, SS men represented his interests.

• • • SS INFLUENCE

The staff expansion at the main offices, as well as personnel additions in the Gaus and the new assignments abroad, resulted in an increased SS presence and thereby greater SS influence throughout VoMi. Some controversy, however, revolves around the nature of the SS membership of VoMi's personnel and brings into question SS membership as a factor promoting SS influence. Many former VoMi officials insisted after the war that although they had worn the SS uniform, they had not been genuine, active SS men. Heinz Brückner, for one, explained that he had joined the SS in 1940 as an officer because of his role in the Lithuanian resettlement. The Soviets had insisted that high-level participants wear uniforms and have officer rank.[52]

Assertions, such as Brückner's, that SS memberships were less than genuine, and indeed were forced on the officials, are untenable. Although the *NSDAP Organisationsbuch* recognized several categories of

SS officers, including both active and honorary, very few personnel records of SS men associated with VoMi indicate other than active SS service.[53] Many, particularly the leaders, were undeniably career SS men. Those drafted into VoMi's service through the Notdienstverordnung later pleaded they were not active SS men and had been forced to accept SS membership. But induction into VoMi did not confer automatic membership in the SS, which, at least in the Allgemeine SS, was entirely voluntary. Those with Waffen SS status were also active SS men, although their membership was not always voluntary.

Some claimed that SS membership was an absolute prerequisite for holding a high position at VoMi such as department head and that they therefore found it imperative to enlist. To the contrary, although one may have been ordered or at least pressured to enroll in the SS, one did not have to comply. As pointed out earlier, although most officials enlisted with the SS after their arrival at VoMi, some postponed doing so for some time. Two department heads, Adolf Puls and Lothar Heller, evaded SS membership at least until 1944.

One must conclude that the SS membership of the vast majority of VoMi's personnel was genuine and that most had joined voluntarily. Therefore the SS membership of so much of VoMi's staff was indeed a significant factor in establishing SS influence. Not only was Heinrich Himmler their ultimate boss as they went about either their RKFDV tasks or their activities with the remaining minorities under NSDAP auspices, but he was also their SS superior.

The SS further strengthened its hold over VoMi personnel by imposing certain obligations and practices. All SS men were aware—and if not, were reminded—of their racial obligations, specifically the one of propagating the *Volk*. Himmler prodded Walter Ellermeier to find a wife and begin siring children, and he reminded Horst Hoffmeyer, perhaps VoMi's most energetic officer, that one child was not enough for an SS man. VoMi's SS men knew their obligations and could expect such scoldings, but eventually these responsibilities were extended to its non-SS employees. For example, membership in Lebensborn, which promoted the procreation of racially valuable children, was a duty of every SS man. But during the 1942 membership drive, Lorenz ordered all employees—remiss SS men as well as non-SS employees—to enroll.[54] Another obligation, imposed in January 1943, required all VoMi personnel, non-SS as well as SS, to provide documented evidence of unblemished Aryan ancestry traceable to 1800.[55]

The SS imposed itself further by extending SS legal jurisdiction over everyone employed at VoMi. Himmler had already granted Lorenz the legal and disciplinary authority of an SS commander over his SS workers, but in a decree of 29 July 1942, everyone assigned to or working for any SS unit or the police came under the SS legal system. All non-SS employees had to waive their civil legal rights and declare their willingness to accept SS jurisdiction. Consequently VoMi's employees, including women, who wished to keep their jobs had to accept these conditions.[56]

SS presence, appearance, and influence, especially regarding its personnel, were overwhelming throughout VoMi during the war and resettlement years. This still did not make it formally part of the SS. The ambiguity of Himmler's order creating the RKFDV Hauptamt clouded the issue of whether VoMi was an SS, Reich, or NSDAP office. From all available evidence, Himmler never took the final step of incorporating it legally and organizationally into the SS. But such a measure was unnecessary. Himmler had extended his personal authority over all of VoMi's activities. As RKFDV, he was its superior in resettlement matters, and as Hess's successor as chief of party *Volkstum* affairs, he directed its remaining minority business. His control over its staff as their SS superior filled in whatever authority gaps remained. In practice, VoMi was drawn fully within Himmler's sphere of authority and performed its wartime duties under the assumption that it was a part of the SS. Its evolution as Himmler's auxiliary was complete.

. . . .

CHAPTER EIGHT

The Resettlement, I

Italy, the Baltic States, and Poland

. . . .

POLICY AND IDEOLOGY

Hitler's decision to resettle the *Volksdeutsche* appeared at first glance to be a reversal of Reich policy toward the minorities. Before 6 October 1939, it was assumed that his policy was revisionist, aiming to unite the *Volksdeutsche* with the main body of the *Volk* through annexations. This had been the case with the *Anschluss* of Austria, the dismemberment of Czechoslovakia, the reincorporation of the Memelland, and the invasion of Poland. The resettlement program therefore came as a surprise. Those most astonished and perplexed by the Führer's apparent reversal were the remaining *Volksdeutsche*, most of whom had viewed his expansion to date as previewing their own annexation to the Reich. Few, if any, had expected Hitler to bring the *Volk* together by removing them from their homelands and relocating them.

In one respect, Hitler's reversal was real. For years the Reich had discouraged *Volksdeutsche* emigration from disputed lands, since a reduced German population weakened German claims to these territories. By 1939, however, Hitler's diplomatic preparations for war had higher priority than revisionist claims based on the presence of German farmers. But emigration aside, the change in policy was more apparent than real. As discussed earlier, Hitler's foreign policy had both long-range and short-term objectives, and measures taken in pursuit of short-term goals at times seemed inconsistent with the ultimate goal of unifying the *Volk* in a new racial order. The resettlement was an example of an apparently contradictory short-range measure. Although removing the *Volksdeutsche* from lands presumed to become part of the *Lebensraum*, Hitler did not abandon these territories for good. At the price of surrendering these lands, he was preempting potential problems that could impede reaching the ultimate goal of creating the new order. The abandoned territories could be reclaimed as *Lebensraum* sometime in the future.

Appearances were further misleading in that the resettlement was consistent not only with Hitler's long-range effort to build the new order but also with his short-term, pragmatic approach to the minorities. His policy toward them was revisionist only when it suited his purposes. His general aim regarding the minorities was to win their loyalty and then to exploit them, group by group, in the interest of his immediate diplomatic needs. Each minority served the Reich as circumstances required. Some, such as the Sudeten Germans, performed as classic fifth columns, whereas others, such as the Germans of Poland, were for the most part passive pawns, pretexts for aggression. These groups had already served the Reich well, and in the fall of 1939 other minorities were expected to contribute to the cause by resettling.

From Hitler's speech, it was not clear which minorities were to be resettled, and it was widely assumed he meant all *Volksdeutsche*. But this was not to be. Some had other missions to fulfill for the Reich and would remain in place. No one knew which groups Hitler had designated for resettlement. It seems that even he was uncertain. A few days before his proclamation, he had confided in Italian Foreign Minister Galeazzo Ciano that besides the Germans of the South Tyrol, he also intended to relocate the Germans of Hungary and other East European states—a move that never materialized.[1]

The 6 October announcement created such a stir among *Volksdeutsche* that Reich missions abroad were swamped with frantic inquiries as to whether this or that minority was to be relocated.[2] Some regimes stoked the agitation. Hungarian authorities, for example, openly speculated about the removal of all Germans. As a result, many Hungarian *Volksdeutsche*, who for years had resisted Magyarization and had vowed to follow the Führer to the ends of the earth, now had second thoughts on how far they would follow and questioned the sacrificing of homes, businesses, and their relatively comfortable lifestyles for the uncertainties of resettlement. Suddenly their Germanness was not all that important as they rediscovered their Magyar heritage.[3]

As matters unfolded, the fears of the Hungarian *Volksdeutsche* and others were unwarranted. For the time being, Hitler, despite his musings with Ciano and others, used resettlement only to eliminate points of conflict with his two most important allies, Mussolini and Stalin. Although eventually the operation assumed ideological importance for Hitler and became an integral part of a comprehensive racial program involving all *Volksdeutsche*, at the outset it was an expedient measure serving his diplomacy of aggression. But for others, from the very beginning, the operation stirred their deepest *völkisch* sentiments. Himmler, as already noted, was perhaps the first to perceive the ideological implications. Even Werner Lorenz, by no means an SS ideologue, applauded the "Homecoming" in the press and spoke of the "blood ties" between the resettlers and the rest of the *Volk*.[4]

The media also emphasized the ideological side and romanticized the resettlement as the modern *Völkerwanderung* and the resettlers, once relocated in the conquered *Lebensraum*, as defenders of civilized Europe from the Asiatic hordes.[5] One eulogist disclosed a chilling prescience of the ideological implications of this operation. He predicted that in the new order, the resettlers would become the ruling class, the *Herrenvolk*, whereas the vanquished Poles would be relegated to subhuman, *Untermensch* status.[6] Nazi propaganda heaped special adulation on the most primitive resettlers, whom they contrasted favorably with contemporary urban Germans, allegedly spoiled by modernization. The Reich public was inundated with homespun bits of peasant wisdom revealing a simple trust in the *Volk* and the Führer. "The Führer calls!" became the slogan for the resettlement.[7] And in response, according to the propaganda, "a joyous echo answered the call."[8]

But contrary to such panegyrics, something besides the call of the Führer motivated the resettlers. Fear of, or firsthand experience with, Soviet rule accounted for most of the positive responses to the summons. Comparing the responses of *Volksdeutsche* living in lands either threatened by or already occupied by the Soviets with those of Germans free from the menace confirms this observation. The farmers of the South Tyrol, not in imminent danger of the Soviets, procrastinated their departure, and many never resettled. In contrast, the Germans of Bessarabia and Volhynia, who had already briefly tasted Soviet rule, answered the Führer's call enthusiastically and almost unanimously. It seems that Stalin, not Hitler, was the primary motivator.[9] The men working on the operation, on location, realized this fact, and most perceived their tasks primarily as humanitarian measures, rescuing fellow Germans from a horrible fate.

The SS men directing the resettlement at the top, such as Lorenz and Behrends, although aware of the Soviets as a factor, also understood very well the racial and ideological ramifications. From the outset, Himmler shared with them his vision of using the resettlement as the initial step in building the new order. He revealed his intentions in the highly confidential RKFDV decree of 7 October 1939, the basic document for the resettlement. All of the ranking participants knew that the evacuation of the *Volksdeutsche* was tied to the weeding out of "harmful influences" from the German *Volk* as well as to the Germanization of the conquered *Lebensraum*.[10] And on 30 October, Himmler issued another order, distributed to all leading participants in the RKFDV program, explicitly connecting the resettlement with the broader racial program. According to this order, the RKFDV, before placing resettlers in certain parts of conquered Poland, would remove all Jews, evict all Congress Poles (those who moved in from central Poland in the 1920s and 1930s) from Danzig–West Prussia, and deport known anti-German Poles from Posen, East Prussia, and eastern Upper Silesia.[11]

Fully cognizant of the resettlement ramifications, diplomatic as well as ideological, Lorenz, Behrends, and other SS men in the leadership directed VoMi's involvement through every phase of the resettlement, from beginning to end. To fully appreciate the complexity and extent of their involvement, and to understand the contribution of each resettlement to Hitler's diplomacy as well as to Himmler's construction of the new order, one must examine each operation individually.

• • • **ITALY**

When Hitler announced the resettlement program on 6 October 1939, one operation was already in progress. To eliminate the main point of contention between the Reich and Italy, Hitler had instructed Himmler, in March 1939, to relocate the former Austrians of the South Tyrol to the Reich. It was not until 23 June that Reich and Italian representatives met in Berlin to negotiate the resettlement. Participating were high-ranking SS men, including Heydrich and Karl Wolff, and from VoMi, Lorenz and Behrends. The South Tyroleans were not represented. Among other things, it was agreed that the Reich would remove the *Volksdeutsche* as soon as possible, beginning no later than 1940. A joint Reich-Italian commission would work out property compensation. A final treaty would specify the details.[12]

As director of the operation, Himmler appointed his liaison man with the Four Year Plan office, Ulrich Greifelt, soon to become head of the RKFDV office. In doing so, he passed over the most obvious man for the job, Werner Lorenz. Although he snubbed Lorenz, Himmler nevertheless relied heavily on VoMi's experience and resources. He selected Behrends's deputy, Wilhelm Luig, as chief of local operations in the Tyrol.[13] From time to time, other VoMi officials contributed, and VoMi received regular progress reports and compiled statistics on the resettlement.

The operation began when Luig arrived in Bolzano on 18 July to open an emigration office, the Amtliche Deutsche Ein- und Rückwandererstelle (ADEuRST). Meanwhile negotiations over the details continued, resulting in the treaty of 21 October 1939. The most difficult issue, property compensation, was resolved when the Italians agreed to compensate the Reich for property left behind, and in return the Reich, through a newly created agency, the Deutsche Umsiedlungs-Treuhandgesellschaft (DUT), would either reimburse individual re-settlers or provide them with property of equal value. All Reich Germans had to leave the South Tyrol within three months, but *Volksdeutsche* had until 31 December to declare whether they would resettle or remain. Those leaving had until 31 December 1942 to do so.[14] The treaty also set two important precedents for subsequent resettlements. First, the resettlements would be based on agreements concluded between the Reich and the resettlers' home state. Second, resettlement was optional. Officials from both sides, the Reich and the other state, would observe the option process to guard against coercion.

The resettlement was not officially announced until 26 October. Before then, the South Tyroleans knew of their fate only by way of rumors.[15] The first task of the resettlement officials was to persuade the *Volksdeutsche* to leave. This effort ran up against propaganda, coming from the local Catholic church as well as local Italian officials, urging them to stay. The reluctance of the Italians to see the Germans leave came as a surprise, considering their mutual dislike. Apparently many local officials, although eager to Italianize the region, also realized the importance of the German farmers to the local economy.[16] Furthermore, the initial number of Germans opting to leave was far greater than the Italians had anticipated, and they became concerned about the huge amount of compensation they would have to pay the Reich. The Reich protested the obstructionism, but the propaganda and interference continued.[17]

After initially choosing to leave, many *Volksdeutsche* had second thoughts as they faced the realities of abandoning farms and homes. Some rescinded their initial decision to relocate; others procrastinated their departure. By the end of 1942, the expiration date for completing the resettlement, only 82,681 *Volksdeutsche* had been evacuated, less than half of those who had opted to leave.[18] Several explanations account for these results. Antiresettlement propaganda took its toll, but perhaps the crucial factor was the absence of urgency. There was no fear of impending danger, as there was in the east, where the threat of Soviet rule loomed over all. Italian designs for the region were limited to assimilating the local Germans into the Italian state and society and thus did not threaten lives or property. For the South Tyroleans remaining behind, losing the right to transact official business in German was inconvenient but was certainly less of a sacrifice than abandoning homes and forsaking forever the familiar native countryside.

Other reasons for the poor results were technical and organizational. The ADEuRST office and staff did not actively seek out resettlers. Rather than traveling from village to village registering *Volksdeutsche* for resettlement, as their counterparts in the east did later, the staff in Bolzano opened a few branch offices and then sat back and waited for resettlers to come to them. Another obstacle was the lack of adequate settlement space. The first wave of resettlers, some 50,000, consisted mostly of propertyless Germans who were readily absorbed into the labor-short Reich economy. Landed farmers, however, could not be relocated until farms comparable to the ones left behind became available in the Reich. There was a shortage of such farms, particularly in the Austrian Gaus, the areas designated for Tyrolean settlement.[19] Himmler, aware of the problem, contemplated sending the Tyroleans east to Poland, but this plan never materialized. Nor did another one, which recommended the Crimea as an area of settlement. Hitler, who seldom intervened in resettlement matters, heard of the latter proposal and thought it an excellent idea.[20] It was fortunate for the South Tyroleans that he did not pursue this "excellent" idea further. Eventually most of these people were placed in the mountainous, formerly Austrian Gaus and in Bavaria.

The South Tyrol resettlement continued until the collapse of the Mussolini regime in 1943 and the subsequent Reich occupation of northern Italy. For the thousands of *Volksdeutsche* who had not left, the occupation confirmed their decision to remain. Not only had they retained their old homes and farms, but it appeared that annexation to the Reich would come after all. They were, of course, wrong. As for VoMi, the German occupation did not restore its authority over these people. Rather than receiving official status as a minority and thereby returning to VoMi's care, those remaining became the wards of the local HSSPF and the Reich military commander until the end of the war.

The South Tyrol operation was not the only one in Italy. Also designated for removal were *Volksdeutsche* living in an area of northeastern Italy known as the Kanaltal, with its principal city of Tarviso (Tarvis), and those living in nearby Grödnertal. Since they were to be moved no farther than to adjacent Carinthia, this evacuation went more smoothly than the Tyrolean. By the fall of 1940, an estimated 4,600 resettlers had been withdrawn from the Kanaltal and another 4,400 from Grödnertal.[21]

During the Kanaltal operation, a problem arose that plagued several later resettlements. Many non-Germans, mostly Slovenes, who composed some 20 percent of the population, wanted to resettle. Officials in Carinthia complained to VoMi that the influx of Slovenes would add to an already substantial, unwanted local Slavic population.[22] Although not directly responsible for this resettlement, and confronted with an issue not within its jurisdiction—the treatment of non-Germans—VoMi officials nevertheless recommended that Slovenes not be placed in Carinthia. Having to help decide the fate of these people forced VoMi beyond the limits of dealing exclusively with *Volksdeutsche* and into that part of the RKFDV program pertaining to the allegedly detrimental racial influences on the German *Volk*.

VoMi first became directly involved in the resettlement business in the evacuation of the Baltic Germans from Latvia and Estonia in the fall of 1939. As discussed in the preceding chapter, the planning and preparation for this resettlement produced the RKFDV system and first kindled *völkisch* imaginations. It was the first to be at least in part planned and executed with the ideological goal of reconstructing the east.[23] The Baltic Germans were descendants of crusading knights, associated with the romantic *Drang nach Osten* of the medieval past, and thus touched *völkisch* emotions in a way the South Tyroleans did not.

The operation was set in motion almost immediately after Hitler received Stalin's 25 September 1939 message that he was about to assert his influence in these two states. Stalin included Lithuania in his notice, but since it still lay within the German sphere of interest, he proposed its exchange for the Lublin and Warsaw districts of Poland, which belonged to the Soviets.[24] On 28 September, Ribbentrop, whom Hitler dispatched to Moscow to discuss Stalin's proposal, renegotiated the spheres of interest and agreed to the territorial exchange—under one condition. Germany would retain a strip of southwestern Lithuania bordering East Prussia in which the majority of Lithuania's Germans lived.[25] It was understood that whenever the Soviets cashed in their claim to Lithuania, Germany would keep this strip. Consequently there appeared to be no urgent need to resettle Lithuania's *Volksdeutsche* along with those of Latvia and Estonia.

While still in Moscow, Ribbentrop received a request from Himmler to arrange an agreement with the Soviets regarding the Baltic resettlement.[26] Even though Latvia and Estonia were still independent, Himmler was aware that shortly the Soviets would be the controlling power. No sooner requested than done. On the same day that Ribbentrop signed the agreement to alter the spheres of interest, he also concluded an agreement providing for the exchange of populations between the German and Soviet zones.[27]

Meanwhile the situation in the Baltic states was deteriorating. Even though the clause of the Nazi-Soviet treaty assigning them to the Soviet sphere was confidential, the Latvians and Estonians suspected Soviet designs. Reich diplomats in the two states began to fear for the safety of the local Germans, vulnerable to the wrath of the Baltic peoples.[28] Resettlement was becoming urgent.

Agreement with the Soviets was not enough. Since Latvia and Estonia were still sovereign states, treaties with both were necessary. It was not until 5 October, the day before Hitler's Reichstag speech, that the Foreign Ministry instructed its representatives in Riga and Tallin to inform the two Baltic governments of the Reich's intentions to resettle the *Volksdeutsche*. The Reich diplomats were to warn the two Baltic regimes that the Reich expected complete cooperation and that German warships would accompany the transport ships.[29] On the next day the ministry also notified the Baltic governments that negotiating teams would be sent to arrange a property settlement, determine evacuation procedures, and decide on dates for the departures. Included would be the chiefs of the two legations as well as VoMi officials. Lorenz sent Horst Hoffmeyer to Riga and Hans-Jochen Kubitz, the head of VoMi's Baltic section, to Tallin. Both were empowered to negotiate as well as to command the evacuations.[30] The Estonian discussions went smoothly, and by 15 October a treaty had been concluded and signed.[31] In contrast, the negotiations with the Latvians, who held out for a more favorable property settlement, dragged on until the end of the month.[32]

Both treaties regulated property transfer and compensation. On registering for resettlement, *Volksdeutsche* would transfer all immovable property to the Reich, which would hold it in trust until it could be turned over to the Latvian state. In return, the Reich would compensate individual resettlers when they arrived in the Reich, either in equivalent property or in a money payment. In December the Reich created two companies, the Umsiedlungs-Treuhand Aktien Gesellschaft (UTAG) in Latvia and the Deutsche Treuhandverwaltung in Estonia, which assumed responsibility for the resettlers' finances and dealt with the Baltic authorities in all economic and financial matters.[33]

Once the treaties were concluded, the evacuations could begin. For Kubitz and Hoffmeyer, who remained in the Baltic after the negotiations, registration became the next task. In this effort, as well as in the compilation of property lists, the two were assisted by the local minority organizations, not by well-prepared resettlement teams, as would be the case in subsequent operations.[34] They learned quickly that they could not depend on the cooperation of the Latvians and Estonians. The public and the authorities were reluctant to see the Germans depart, not out of love for them but out of dread of what the future held for a Baltic without Germans.

To counter antiresettlement propaganda predicting an uncertain future in the Reich and the loss of property, Kubitz and Hoffmeyer reassured the Baltic Germans that everything possible was being done to ensure a smooth transition.[35] The *Volksdeutsche* were inundated with placards and fliers extolling their reunification with the rest of the *Volk*. But for indecisive Germans, there also appeared warnings that in no uncertain terms spelled out what they could expect if they chose to stay in the Baltic.[36] Numerous Baltic resettlers later concurred that two considerations prompted them to leave. One, the Latvian and Estonian governments would no longer recognize the remaining Baltic Germans as a national minority. And two—the truly decisive factor—some "fatal changes" would await those left behind.[37] These "fatal changes" later materialized with the Sovietization of the two states.

The initial response to the resettlement was overwhelmingly positive. But as the negotiations dragged on, especially in Latvia, the original appeal lost its luster. The Soviet threat also abated as the supposedly imminent invasion did not occur. And as the urgency receded, so did the stream of applicants to leave. At this point the VoMi propaganda machine shifted into high gear, and emphasis decidedly turned from the idyllic to the terrible—from the theme of *völkisch* reunion to that of the Soviet menace. The latter became more convincing when the Soviets began installing military bases. Germans who had earlier hesitated, as well as many Latvians and Estonians who could produce proof of German ancestry, now hastened to register. A stir arose when the mother and the sister of Latvian Foreign Minister Vilhelms Munters applied to resettle.[38] Even some Jews sought to emigrate to the Reich, evidently preferring to accept the fate of racial enemies in the Reich to that of class enemies in a Soviet Baltic.[39]

Those registering the applicants paid little attention to racial criteria, but the inclusion of large numbers of non-Germans raised objections in the Reich. The SD instructed processing teams at the ports of arrival to accept only racially qualified non-Germans and to return the racially inferior.[40] In November the Foreign Ministry issued guidelines for determining and rejecting Jews. It did, however, attach a request for a list of doctors among the applicants, implying that exceptions might be considered.[41] A later order stipulated that the granting of citizenship to resettlers arriving in the Reich would proceed according to the Nuremberg Laws of 1935—in effect, excluding Jews.[42]

Before the conclusion of the formal treaties, only Reich Germans could leave. Thus, on 14 October, the first ship left Riga with 348 Reich Germans aboard. The first *Volksdeutsche* embarked from Estonia on 18 October. *Volksdeutsche* did not begin departing Latvia until 7 November. By the time the last ship left Riga on 21 December, a total of eighty-seven ships had transported 61,858 resettlers from Estonia and Latvia to Gdynia, Danzig, Stettin, Swinemunde, and recently annexed Memel.[43]

As originally planned, VoMi's responsibilities were to end when the resettlers boarded their ships. Local party offices assumed responsibility for their care once they arrived in the Reich. But the "Homecoming" reception was less than hospitable. Gauleiter Forster of Danzig–West Prussia was openly hostile to settling these Germans in his Gau. Although not hostile, Arthur Greiser, the Gauleiter of Warthegau, a new Gau created out of conquered Polish lands, was less than enthusiastic. Greiser resented the haughtiness of the class-conscious Baltic Germans and was leery of the high proportion of elderly people among them, who in all probability would be a burden rather than a benefit to the Gau.[44] Himmler had not anticipated such reactions and ordered VoMi to step in and help with the reception of the new arrivals. VoMi responded by establishing in Posen the Einwanderer Beratungsstelle, a resettler assistance office, and shortly assumed full responsibility for care of the resettlers after their arrival in the Reich.[45]

• • EASTERN POLAND

The resettlement that truly fired Himmler's *völkisch* sensitivities and set the RKFDV machine into full gear toward its goal of reconstructing the east was that of the 100,000–125,000 *Volksdeutsche* from the Volhynia, Galicia, and Narew regions of eastern Poland, all of which lay within the Soviet sphere of influence. The Soviets had occupied these regions during their attack on Poland, and for the same reasons that prompted the removal of the Baltic Germans—eliminating a potential source of friction with his ally Stalin—Hitler wanted to evacuate these *Volksdeutsche* as well. Executed during the bitter winter of 1939–40, this operation was the most ambitious and ideologically the most significant to date.

The SS propaganda machine exploited this resettlement for every ounce of ideological significance. It was the conclusion of this operation that would bring Himmler to the Przemysl bridge. One reason for Himmler's extraordinary interest in these people was their peasant nature. Except for the large community in Lvov, the overwhelming majority of these Germans were small farmers, suited perfectly by SS standards for settling in the east. These unaffected, rustic peasants entertained no lofty notions—as did the haughty Baltic Germans—of belonging to an elite class entitled to rule the east. Himmler, with a strong dislike for Alfred Rosenberg, had little patience for the arrogance of Baltic Germans, who might balk at accepting the SS vision. The farmers of eastern Poland, free of any ambitions, provided far more supple building material for the new order. They were the ideal colonists for an SS-planned and SS-dominated east.

On the same day they signed the treaty redrawing the spheres of interest, 28 September, Molotov and Ribbentrop also agreed in principle to exchange the Germans residing in the Russian zone of Poland for the Russians, Ukrainians, and White Russians living in the Reich's sphere.[46] Reich negotiators, including VoMi officials, departed for Moscow on 15 October to work out the details. According to the agreements, concluded on 16 November, this resettlement would be an exchange of populations, not a unilateral evacuation, as had been the case in the South Tyrol, Latvia, and Estonia. Attention was paid to every detail of the operation, from selecting the evacuation routes to requiring uniforms for all those involved in executing the action. German-Russian registration teams would examine all applicants and would then determine who was eligible for relocation. The treaty also spelled out the process of property transfer and economic compensation and specified the amount of property the resettlers could carry with them. The whole operation was to be completed by 1 March 1940.[47]

In the order of 30 October, Himmler assigned to VoMi the responsibility for registering these resettlers as well as collecting them and transporting them to prearranged border crossings. From there the Reich police would convey them to reception centers.[48] The greatest change from the process used in the Baltic action was in receiving the *Volksdeutsche*. Himmler had learned that delegating too much responsibility to the NSDAP and the local Gauleiters was a mistake. Not only were the Gauleiters causing unpleasantries and confusion, but assigning them responsibility also diminished SS control. Therefore, in the interest of efficiency, image, and his own authority, Himmler charged VoMi with tasks he had delegated to the party in the Baltic operation. The party would still help, but no group outside the SS would have any independent authority. Another innovative feature, the resettlement teams, or Umsiedlungskommandos, would be commanded and trained by the SS—under Behrends's supervision.[49] With the Volhynian-Galician resettlement, the SS, through the RKFDV system, became the exclusive authority in the planning and execution of all resettlements.

Another feature of the revised process was the designation of Lodz, later renamed Litzmannstadt, as the principal reception center. It was selected because it was the easternmost city of any size in the new Reich territories. It also had a large indigenous German community, from which VoMi planned to draw additional manpower. In contrast to the Baltic action, in which reception points were scattered along the Reich's Baltic coast, the Polish resettlement funneled all resettlers through Lodz for centralized processing. Trains and wagons carried them from the Soviet zone to the border and from there on to Lodz.[50]

On 9 December 1939, after a month's training, the resettlement teams, under the command of Horst Hoffmeyer, who had just completed the Baltic evacuation, crossed into the Soviet zone at Przemysl. Squads of four Germans each, accompanied by Soviet counterparts, traveled in bitter cold from village to village locating and registering resettlers. The Volksdeutsche enthusiastically welcomed the teams, sharing their meager provisions and lodgings.[51] Of the many difficulties the VoMi teams encountered, the two most serious were the weather and, as they learned for the first time, the Soviets. The winter of 1939–40 was one of the harshest in years, and the Soviets seemed bent on obstruction. They often vetoed applications in what appeared to be a random and arbitrary way.[52]

After completing the registration, the commandos began the evacuation. The urban Volksdeutsche, the old, the infirm, and most women and children rode Soviet trains to the border. The men and some of the sturdier women and children traveled on wagons. Operating from east to west, VoMi teams accompanied the trains and wagons, picking up more resettlers on their journey westward. The railways presented few problems, but the wagon caravans, consisting of 100 to 250 wagons each, were another story. The journey, lasting three to five days in the harshest winter weather, exacted a lethal toll. One source noted that as many as 10,000 died.[53] Although this figure seems to be exaggerated, perhaps even a misprint, it is quite likely that casualties were higher than expected. No documents or other sources examined so far mention the casualties, but most of the reports on this evacuation seem to emphasize the extensive medical and health precautions taken, as though those responsible for the operation were defending their performance. Even Himmler later spoke of the difficulties encountered in this operation and praised the resettlers for their endurance and sacrifices.[54] Nor were the VoMi officials immune: Werner Lorenz caught a cold during a brief inspection tour and had to spend several days in bed.[55]

On 26 January 1940, Himmler greeted in person the last wagons to cross the San River at Przemysl. VoMi commandos had scoured 200,000 square kilometers of eastern Poland, registering, collecting, and evacuating resettlers from more than 200 cities and towns and nearly 1,000 villages. According to one final count, they evacuated 134,950 people in 92 trainloads and 15,000 wagons.[56] The SS newspaper *Das Schwarze Korps* proudly reported the reception of the last arrivals and commended the work of the resettlement teams. Himmler's adjutant, Karl Wolff, in the presence of Behrends, decorated Hoffmeyer and the entire command for their services.[57] For Hoffmeyer and the commandos, more resettlements were in store, and for the resettlers, the evacuation was only the first step in their odyssey.

An important feature of the Volhynian-Galician resettlement was its reciprocal nature. The treaty of 16 November 1939 also provided for the resettlement of Russians, Ukrainians, and White Russians from the German sphere of interest—if they so desired. Following a meeting with Reich officials in Warsaw on 15 December, the Soviets evacuated those wishing to move to the Soviet zone, but without the urgency, enthusiasm, and fanfare of the German effort. Original estimates had projected as many as a million resettlers, but when on 18 February the first train departed for the east, only 295 people were aboard. By the end of the operation, only 11,000 had opted to relocate to the Soviet zone.[58]

The resettlement of *Volksdeutsche* in former Poland was not limited to those residing in the Soviet zone. In the spring of 1940 leading Nazis were debating the future status of German-occupied central Poland, labeled the General Government, and argued whether it should be annexed as Reich territory or set aside as a dumping ground for Jews and Poles. Meanwhile, in early May, Himmler decided to transfer westward at least those *Volksdeutsche* living east of the Vistula, first from the Lublin area. In principle, Polish farmers from the annexed Warthegau were to be exchanged for Germans living in the Lublin region—a village of Poles for a village of Germans. In practice, the majority of Poles, whose relocation was handled by the police and SD, were simply dumped into the easternmost reaches of the General Government.[59]

Himmler charged responsibility for this operation—the first to clearly manifest in practice the Nazi racial ideology and the inherent relationship between *Untermensch* and *Herrenvolk*—to the HSSPF for the General Government, Friedrich Wilhelm Krüger. Krüger enlisted VoMi to carry out the German side of the project, the evacuation of the *Volksdeutsche*. Lorenz again assigned Hoffmeyer to command the operation. By mid-July, VoMi had completed the registration, and in league with the police, it began transporting 30,758 German resettlers.[60] The Lublin operation, performed without signing a treaty with another state, was the first of several unilateral wartime actions, executed entirely within German zones of occupation.

THE *NACHUMSIEDLUNG* AND LITHUANIA

By the end of 1939, more than 60,000 Baltic Germans from Latvia and Estonia had resettled, but many had decided to remain behind. A few had received permission to stay longer to conclude business, but the majority of those remaining behind had simply ignored the Führer's summons and had decided to take their chances. As early as October, the Soviets had begun establishing military bases in the Baltic states, but seemed to respect their sovereignty and did not interfere in domestic affairs—until June 1940, when Stalin decided to assert total control. Events then followed in rapid succession. The Soviets invaded Latvia, Estonia, and Lithuania and by means of rigged elections forced them into the Soviet Union as member republics. For the Germans who in 1939 had chosen to remain in the Baltic, the situation drastically changed. Their worst fears proved true. Tens of thousands of arrests followed, mostly of Baltic national leaders, officials, military officers, and intelligentsia, but some *Volksdeutsche* also disappeared.[61] Anyone with even the remotest claim to being a German now flocked to the Reich legations, pleading for the Führer's protection and another chance to resettle.

Hitler left the fate of the remaining Germans in Himmler's hands. The latter felt little sympathy for their plight, since they had ignored the Führer's earlier order to leave. As he noted in a letter to Ribbentrop, giving them a second chance would set a bad precedent for *Volksdeutsche* elsewhere. They might likewise disregard the Führer's orders, knowing that if the situation later became difficult, they could still count on the Reich to save them. But one consideration tended to sway Himmler in favor of another evacuation. These people were of German blood—which for Himmler was of great importance.[62]

Another consideration that rekindled interest in the Baltic and raised the possibility of another resettlement was economic. By the time of the Soviet occupation, a large portion of the UTAG and Treuhandverwaltung property holdings still had not been transferred to the Baltic governments. Nor had the latter paid what they owed the Reich. Furthermore, the Russian takeover threatened other Reich investments in the region. Since the Reich stood to lose even more with Sovietization, it seemed the right time to discuss not only Reich economic interests but also the issue of removing the remaining *Volksdeutsche*.

The Soviet occupation of Lithuania, along with the two other Baltic States, for the first time placed the removal of the Lithuanian Germans on the agenda for serious consideration. Since most of them lived in the strip still assigned to Germany, the Reich had expected to acquire them through annexation. As for those living in the interior, the Reich had adopted a wait-and-see attitude. But in seizing Lithuania, the Soviets also occupied the border strip, which, along with Lithuania's *Volksdeutsche*, now became a vital issue.

After the Soviet takeover, the Reich legation in Kaunas reported that at least for the time being, the Russians were behaving properly toward the Germans. It noted, however, that the Lithuanian public, which associated the Reich and the local *Volksdeutsche* with the Russian invasion, was more menacing.[63] Aware of the deteriorating situation, VoMi drew up contingency plans for an evacuation, which Behrends submitted to Himmler on 25 June.[64] Himmler met with Ribbentrop, and the two decided that resettlement was necessary.[65] Available documents reveal no direct role for Hitler in deciding whether or when the

Lithuanian operation should take place, but one may presume he was consulted.

The next day VoMi, RKFDV, and Foreign Ministry officials discussed the resettlement. They decided to relocate entire villages in Lithuania to neighboring East Prussia and Danzig–West Prussia. VoMi would register the resettlers, transport them to the Reich, and construct camps in East Prussia as temporary housing.[66] Himmler suggested that Lorenz or Greifelt, chief of the RKFDV, personally meet with the local Gauleiters to discuss the placement of the incoming *Volksdeutsche*. Although he had denied the party any further responsibilities, he still respected the power of the Gauleiters and realized they were crucial for the final, settlement phase of the operation.[67]

Not until 11 July did the Foreign Ministry inform its legation in Kaunas about the resettlement, stressing that the Lithuanians were not to know of it until the Reich had received a response from Moscow. Reich diplomats were to present the resettlement to the Soviets as an extension of the Estonian and Latvian operations. They were to make clear that the Germans living in the disputed border strip, presently occupied by the Soviets, would not be affected by the resettlement.[68] This caveat underscored the Reich's claim to this land as part of the Reich sphere of interest.

Two days later Molotov informed the Reich ambassador Schulenburg that it would be inconvenient for the Soviets to surrender the strip and that Stalin was interested, in view of the "extraordinarily friendly relations between Germany and the Soviet Union," in finding some way for the Soviets to keep it. He suggested that the Germans living there could be relocated along with the rest of Lithuania's Germans. In relaying this message to Berlin, Schulenburg recommended using the border strip to settle outstanding economic questions in the region.[69] The Foreign Ministry evidently heeded Schulenburg's advice, for on 7 August the Soviets—after considerable thought on the matter—offered to discuss the economic issues and to negotiate a treaty for the resettlement of the Lithuanian Germans.[70] Although not mentioned in the Soviet offer, the strip of territory and the evacuation of the remaining Germans from Latvia and Estonia would also be discussed.

The Reich, for some inexplicable reason—perhaps not wanting to appear overly anxious—did not reply until 23 August.[71] In a counterproposal, Schulenburg offered creating two separate negotiating teams, one to handle the economic issues and the other to discuss the resettlement of the Germans from all three Baltic States. As far as can be determined, this was the first formal reference to a second resettlement in Latvia and Estonia. Molotov expressed great surprise—tongue in cheek, no doubt—that there were still Germans living in Latvia and Estonia.[72] Nonetheless, he agreed to the proposal, and on the following day, German negotiators departed for Moscow and for Kaunas.

The Moscow negotiations over the Lithuanian resettlement went smoothly, but the discussions regarding the remaining *Volksdeutsche* in Latvia and Estonia were embarrassing and arduous. The Soviet negotiators repeatedly pointed out the impossibility of resettling Germans from areas that, as of the fall of 1939, contained none.[73] They eventually agreed, in principle, to a second resettlement from Latvia and Estonia, the *Nachumsiedlung*. It was not until mid-September that a Reich delegation could travel to Riga to begin discussing the details.[74]

The Soviets also drove a hard bargain on the economic issues. After numerous claims and counterclaims, the Reich negotiators, anxious to settle the matter, agreed to a lump-sum payment from the Soviets far below Reich estimates of the value of German property in the Baltic. A treaty on the final disposal of Reich economic claims was signed on 10 January 1941, the same day that agreements were concluded on the Lithuanian and the second Estonian and Latvian resettlements.[75] Another agreement signed on that day transferred the strip of disputed Lithuanian land to the Soviets, who had made the resettlements contingent on the territorial issue. A few days before the signing of the treaty, Schulenburg had warned Ribbentrop that the Reich's refusal to give up the territory would jeopardize agreements on resettlement. Good relations with the Soviets, as well as the fate of an estimated 55,000 *Volksdeutsche*, depended on the territorial agreement.[76]

Once the agreements were signed, the evacuations could begin. VoMi had been preparing for the Lithuanian resettlement since August. Departing from the procedures of the earlier Baltic operations, in which it had relied primarily on local, *Volksdeutsche* manpower, it dispatched trained teams under the command of Heinz Brückner. As in preparing for the Polish evacuation, Behrends assembled and trained these teams at the SS barracks at Stahnsdorf.[77]

The teams in Lithuania registered the resettlers and their property and assembled them for evacuation. As in eastern Poland, prospective resettlers had to appear before a mixed panel of German and Soviet officials and declare their option to leave. Either side, Soviet or German, could deny any application. Even though it was commonly understood that anyone turned down by the commissions would suffer severe consequences once the Reich officials had departed, even non-Germans desperately clamored for resettlement. Brückner noted later that he personally had approved many non-Germans for evacuation. One Lithuanian army officer threatened with imminent arrest, a Lieutenant Colonel Sukuss, pleaded with Brückner for passage to Germany. Since there were no legitimate grounds for his resettlement, Brückner smuggled Sukuss across the border in the trunk of his car.[78] By February the relations between the Soviet and Reich officials on the registration teams had become so strained that Lorenz and Ellermeier hastened to Kaunas to protest Soviet behavior to higher authorities.[79] In spite of Soviet hindrances, by March the VoMi teams had registered and evacuated 50,904 people from Lithuania.[80]

The *Nachumsiedlung* from Estonia and Latvia was a more complex affair than the Lithuanian operation. It involved people who, according to the resettlement agreements of October 1939, were no longer recognized as Germans. Himmler's *völkisch* inclinations evidently outweighed other reservations and won him over to giving these desperate people another chance. On 14 August 1940 he notified the RKFDV office of his approval for another resettlement for Latvia and Estonia. The evacuees, however, would not receive resettler status, which would have entitled them to property compensation and other privileges. Instead they would be classified as refugees.[81]

In the official 19 August order for the *Nachumsiedlung*, Himmler insisted that only Germans were to be registered, and the registrars were to apply the strictest criteria in determining who was a German. Furthermore, since these people had rejected the Reich earlier, they were not fit to settle in the east, which was reserved for only the worthiest Germans, and would instead be sent to VoMi camps inside the Altreich to await final settlement there.[82] He ordered VoMi to examine applications, register those accepted, provide transportation and all material care for the resettlers during the operation, and construct temporary camps to house them in the Reich.[83]

On 22 August the Foreign Ministry informed its Baltic diplomats of the impending evacuation, which did not begin until after the signing of the treaties on 10 January 1941.[84] The commander of the VoMi resettlement team, the SD man Konrad Radunski, arrived in Riga a few days later with 125 men, many of whom were Baltic Germans who had resettled in the fall of 1939. From Riga, smaller teams dispersed to their assigned stations in Latvia and Estonia.[85]

As in earlier dealings with the Soviets, VoMi officials encountered all sorts of difficulties, both trivial and serious. In Narva, for example, the Germans and Russians quarreled over wall space for portraits of Hitler and Stalin. A far more serious obstacle was Soviet police harassment of prospective resettlers, many of whom were detained and arrested. One particularly spiteful Soviet practice was to deny passes to Germans serving in the military, thereby preventing them from appearing before the registration teams. One young soldier, denied a pass and thereby denied an opportunity to leave the country, committed suicide on the final day of registration.[86]

Most *Volksdeutsche* eventually registered and were resettled, often thanks to the intervention of higher Soviet officials who had been pressured by Reich counterparts to facilitate the process. As was the case in 1939 and in the Lithuanian operation, countless Baltic nationals, even some Russians, tried to leave. Since these unfortunate people had to petition mixed panels of Germans and Russians, few succeeded, and without exception those that did not were later deported. One Reich official working in Estonia observed that if the Soviets had allowed it, the vast majority of the Estonian population would have asked to resettle.[87]

According to the final report, 17,101 people were evacuated in the *Nachumsiedlung*, raising the total number of resettlers from Latvia and Estonia to 78,959.[88] For most of them, with the exception of those who would shortly return to the region as soldiers and administrators in a futile effort to rebuild a German Baltic, the *Drang nach Osten* initiated by their forefathers some seven centuries earlier was over.

• •

The Resettlement, II

The Southeast, the West, and the Soviet Union

• •

The primary reason for resettling the *Volksdeutsche* of Italy, the Baltic States, and eastern Poland was Hitler's concern that they could create difficulties with his allies, Stalin and Mussolini, and would thereby disrupt his foreign policy plans. But quite different considerations determined the wartime fates of the rest of Europe's *Volksdeutsche*, especially those of southeastern Europe. Instead of being seen as potential sources of conflict, they were regarded as crucial, mostly positive links between the Reich and the states and peoples of the region. It was not in the Reich's interest to remove them. But there were several exceptions to this policy. There were also *Volksdeutsche* outside of southeastern Europe who, because of wartime circumstances, required resettlement.

BESSARABIA AND NORTHERN BUKOVINA

The most notable exceptions to the policy of leaving the *Volksdeutsche* of southeastern Europe in place were the Rumanian resettlements in the fall of 1940, which served the same purposes as those discussed in the preceding chapter. In the secret protocol of the 23 August 1939 Nazi-Soviet Treaty, Hitler had also conceded the northeastern Rumanian province of Bessarabia to the Soviets. In June 1940, concurrently with his demands on the Baltic states, Stalin pressured the Rumanians to hand over not only Bessarabia but also the northern part of Bukovina, territory not mentioned in the agreement. After some haggling, the Reich agreed to support the Soviet claim to northern Bukovina and reconfirmed its own disinterest in Bessarabia. Out of concern for the problems that the local *Volksdeutsche* might create, on 25 June Ribbentrop expressed to the Soviets the Reich's wish to resettle them. The following day Molotov approved the request.[1]

Included in the German delegation that flew to Moscow in July to discuss the Rumanian operation were two VoMi officials, Horst Hoffmeyer, rapidly becoming the leading expert on resettlements, and Hans Brückner, who would shortly command the Lithuanian evacuation. The negotiations lasted well into August, and the final treaty was not signed until 5 September. It specified in the minutest detail everything related to the resettlement, from the amount of property the resettlers could take with them to the points of departure and routes of travel.[2]

Preparations had begun even before the conclusion of the treaty. As early as 10 June, both VoMi and the RKFDV office were collecting information on Rumania's *Volksdeutsche*. By early July, Behrends and Hoffmeyer were planning the logistics, which included boat transport up the Danube to the Reich.[3] Galati, on the Rumanian side of the Danube near the Black Sea, would be the port of embarkation. VoMi would construct a camp there as well as two others along the Danube in Yugoslavia, one at Prahovo, near the "Iron Gates," and the other at Zemun (Semlin), near Belgrade. Once Reich diplomats secured permission from Belgrade, Behrends sent VoMi's camp experts, Hans Hagen and Friedrich Altena, to Yugoslavia to supervise the construction. In mid-August he flew to Bucharest to discuss the resettlement in person with the Rumanian authorities.[4]

Himmler issued the formal order for the operation on 20 August, two weeks before the signing of the final agreement with the Soviets. In it he designated Danzig–West Prussia and the Warthegau as the settlement areas for the Bessarabians and the area around Kattowitz in Upper Silesia for the Bukovina Germans. He assigned to VoMi virtually the same duties as in the Polish operation: registration and evacuation of the resettlers.[5] According to VoMi's plans, the Bessarabians would travel by trucks, trains, and wagons from the interior to Galati, where they would board riverboats and travel to either Prohovo or Zemun. They would then continue by train to Villach or Graz. Most of their processing, the crucial racial and political examinations, would be conducted in camps inside the Reich rather than in Lodz. As for the Bukovina Germans, they would travel overland through Przemysl to camps in Upper Silesia.[6]

Hoffmeyer and his VoMi commandos arrived in Galati in early September, shortly after the signing of the treaty. From there they proceeded to Tarutino, the command post for the operation. As in Poland, the local *Volksdeutsche* welcomed them as saviors. Countless resettlers testified later that their brief experience with Soviet rule provided the incentive to leave.[7] After the commandos registered the *Volksdeutsche*, they collected and transported them to Galati. The first trucks and wagons arrived for the rendezvous with the ships with little difficulty. But those traveling in October encountered the local rainy season, which turned the operation into a quagmire. Despite the two major obstacles, the weather and the uncooperative Russians, the evacuation was completed by 23 October. Hoffmeyer insisted on remaining until he had secured the release of every *Volksdeutscher* known to be held by the Soviets.[8] As a testimonial to VoMi's efforts, the local Rumanian socialite, Countess Waldeck, observed the commandos in action and noted, "No matter what SS men were elsewhere, I thought amusedly, here they were a gentle, baby-kissing lot."[9]

The combined Bessarbian–northern Bukovina resettlement was the most ambitious of the evacuations from Soviet-controlled territory. VoMi evacuated a total of 93,548 Germans from Bessarabia and another 43,568 from northern Bukovina. Of these, some 80,000 Bessarabians were eventually classified as racially and politically worthy of settlement in the east, but only some 23,000 Bukovina Germans were acceptable.[10] One result of this operation was the growth of the RKFDV apparatus and the VoMi camp network to maximum size. Both systems, first organized for the Volhynia-Galicia resettlement, remained in service throughout the war years to process and care for the steady stream of resettlers and refugees arriving in the Reich.

• • • THE REST OF RUMANIA

With the Bessarabian and northern Bukovina resettlements under way, Reich officials began negotiating with the Rumanians for the removal of *Volksdeutsche* from two other parts of the country, the Dobrudja and southern Bukovina. As early as July 1940, resettlement from the Dobrudja, the area east and south of the final bend of the Danube, had been discussed, but it was postponed until after the completion of the Bessarabian operation. This resettlement and that from southern Bukovina were further exceptions to the Reich's policy of not removing *Volksdeutsche* from southeastern Europe. Neither territory was claimed by the Soviets, although the southern Dobrudja was about to be transferred to Bulgaria. In both cases, resettlement was mostly a matter of image. Unlike the two major groups in the southeast, the Transylvania Saxons and the Danube Swabians, who were economically important and positive contributors to German influence in the region, the Germans of the Dobrudja and southern Bukovina had little to offer. Indeed, their relative poverty and low local status were something of an embarrassment and stood in marked contrast to the superior image the Reich was trying to create for itself and the other German communities of the southeast.

On 22 October 1940, the Reich concluded an agreement with Rumania to resettle these two groups, and on 31 October, the RKFDV office issued the basic order for the operation. In general the responsibilities and procedures were the same as for the Bessarabian action. VoMi commandos found the registration and evacuation of the 15,399 *Volksdeutsche* from the Rumanian Dobrudja a relatively easy task. The local authorities created few problems, and the people, living in exclusively German settlements, were easy to identify as Germans. Once registered and collected, they embarked on ships and steamed up the Danube to the camps in Yugoslavia and from there on to the Reich.[11]

Things did not go as smoothly in southern Bukovina. The local authorities proved uncooperative and were reluctant to let the Germans leave. They believed the evacuation was the first step toward a fate similar to that of their neighbors farther north. Overall the local Germans responded positively to the appeal, as did large numbers of non-Germans. The prospect of Soviet rule—although not in store for them in the immediate future—was a prime motivator. Evidently VoMi officials performed a relatively slipshod screening here. On arrival in the Reich, many of these 52,107 resettlers were deemed racially unfit and had to be sent back.[12]

Some of the resettlers from Rumania had relatives who also wanted to leave, but they lived in parts of the country not designated for resettlement. The treaty of 22 October provided for their relocation as well as for the removal of Germans originally from the resettlement areas and presently living in other parts of Rumania. To facilitate their evacuation, VoMi set up centers in Bucharest, Sibiu (Hermannstadt), and Timisoara. These offices registered and sent on their way 5,000 more *Volksdeutsche*. There was also the question of numerous *Volksdeutsche* refugees, mostly deserters from the Rumanian army, who over recent years had fled to the Reich illegally and now sought permanent residency. As a solution, the Reich retroactively designated some 2,000 of these refugees as resettlers, thereby entitling them to resettler benefits.[13]

• • • CROATIA AND SLOVENIA

Before the April 1941 invasion of Yugoslavia, the Reich had no plans to resettle any of its *Volksdeutsche*, who, in the manner prescribed by Reich policy for the *Volksdeutsche* of the southeast, would maintain German influence in the region and serve as intermediaries between the Reich and the local Slavic population. As elsewhere, Hitler's resettlement speech caused considerable alarm here. The Reich Foreign Ministry had to reassure Yugoslavia's Germans they would not have to leave. The situation changed, however, with the April 1941 invasion, when the resettlement of some *Volksdeutsche* became necessary. Those living in parts of Yugoslavia transferred to Italy were to be removed for the same political reasons as the South Tyroleans. Another consideration was the safety of *Volksdeutsche* threatened by the partisan warfare launched shortly after the invasion.

The first resettlements from Yugoslavia removed *Volksdeutsche* from the Italian zones, from the Kočevje (Gottschee) area and the environs of Ljubljana (Laibach). Since this operation was considered an extension of the Italian resettlement, which was still in progress, the RKFDV office, with the help of the Sicherheitspolizei and the SD (Sipo-SD), assumed command. Processing began in October, and the evacuation itself, which removed 11,747 resettlers from Kočevje and 2,865 more from Ljubljana, began in mid-December and continued for about a month. Many of the Kočevje resettlers relocated to Lower Styria, while most of the Ljubljana Germans settled in Carinthia.[14]

Whereas VoMi did not operate in the Italian zones, it was responsible for evacuating *Volksdeutsche* from partisan-threatened areas in Serbia. As early as June 1941, its officials were pondering how to deal with the steady stream of Germans fleeing from these mountainous regions. VoMi soon assumed an active role, and by mid-November it had evacuated, with the assistance of the local military authorities, some 800 *Volksdeutsche* to the safety of Austria. For the first time, its personnel operated in hostile areas, vulnerable to enemy fire. VoMi commandos drove in armed convoys to remote settlements, loaded the *Volksdeutsche* and their possessions on trucks, and returned to Belgrade. From there the resettlers were transported to the Reich. By the end of 1942, VoMi had evacuated 1,925 *Volksdeutsche* from Serbia.[15] Throughout the remainder of the war, *Volksdeutsche* refugees continued to straggle into Belgrade as more areas of Serbia came under partisan attack.

Initially the Reich had no intention of removing Germans from the newly created state of Croatia, but the threatening partisan situation, particularly in Bosnia, necessitated yet another exception to the rule of not resettling *Volksdeutsche* from the southeast. When Himmler raised the issue with Ribbentrop in early September 1942, the latter argued against a wholesale resettlement from Croatia. He feared the adverse effect it would have on the Croats, who regarded the German presence as a guarantee of continued Reich support. Consequently, only the *Volksdeutsche* of Bosnia, facing annihilation by the partisans, were to be removed. On 30 September 1942, the Reich concluded a treaty with Croatia sanctioning the evacuation.[16]

As soon as the order to evacuate the Bosnian *Volksdeutsche* reached VoMi, it sent additional commandos, under the leadership of Otto Lackmann, to Belgrade. By early October, VoMi squads were venturing into the Bosnian mountains to evacuate the *Volksdeutsche*. As in the Serbian operation, they went from village to village, accompanied by the military. They found many communities already victims of partisan raids and even came under attack themselves. By the end of November, VoMi's commandos had evacuated some 18,000 *Volksdeutsche* from Bosnia.[17] Lorenz himself went to Bosnia to lend a hand. Unfortunately for him, the adventure had an unhappy ending. During one of his forays into the mountains, his speeding automobile failed to negotiate a turn on one of Bosnia's treacherous roads and crashed. Seriously injured, Lorenz spent several months convalescing in hospitals in Serbia and Austria.[18]

One of the population transfers the Reich performed in Yugoslavia did not involve *Volksdeutsche*. On 18 April 1941, Himmler ordered the construction of a strip of purely German settlements across Slovenia and Croatia, some twenty kilometers wide, separating German lands to the north from Slavic lands to the south. Building this racial barrier required the expulsion of the resident Slovenes.[19] On 6 May, representatives of VoMi, the RKFDV, several Reich ministries, and the military commander in Serbia met at Maribor (Marburg) to discuss the project. Various suggestions were offered, including deporting the Slovenes to Serbia, Bulgaria, and even Italy.[20] Himmler, however, had concluded that Slovenes possessed enough German blood to be converted into Germans. Being racially kindred to the Germans, the Slovenes, with some reeducation in the Reich, could fit very nicely into the *Volk*. Indeed, some could even be permitted to settle in the east, the holy cradle of German posterity.

The expelled Slovenes would be replaced by German settlers from the Kočevje and Ljubljana operations. A racial examination would determine which Slovenes would be transported to the Reich to undergo Germanization and which, having failed the examination, would be deported to Serbia.[21] The racial examinations, however, slowed down the deportations and created a bottleneck in the Germanization of the border strip, prompting grumblings from some of those in charge of the expulsions, among them Adolf Eichmann.[22]

In mid-October Himmler charged VoMi, which up to that point had played no part in the deportations, with a vital role. Himmler, disposed favorably toward the Slovenes, wanted experienced VoMi resettlement commandos rather than the less sensitive Sipo-SD men to transport the racially acceptable Slovenes to the Reich. Once inside the Reich, they would live in VoMi camps and become its wards. Friendly, Germanizable Slovenes would receive the same treatment as German resettlers. Eventually they would even be eligible for Reich citizenship.[23] Forced to work with the Slovenes, VoMi departed from its usual practice of dealing exclusively with Germans and became deeply involved in the non-German side of building the new order.

Although Himmler fancied himself as being generous to the Slovenes, the fact remained that "resettlement" to the Reich for the purpose of transforming them into Germans was a forced deportation. Consequently, by 1942, Slovene resistance to the deportations stiffened. So did the resolve of the partisans to carry their struggle to all corners of Yugoslavia, including the northern borderlands. Angered by Slovene ingratitude and frustrated by partisan successes, on 24 January 1942 Himmler ordered the shooting of all "bandits" and their accomplices, hoping that such stern measures would demoralize the resistance.[24] Not only did the draconian approach fail to deter the partisans, but it also created an entirely new problem—disposing of the dependents of the executed guerrillas.

One proposed solution was to deport the families of known and suspected partisans to the Reich, thereby undermining the morale of the resistance. It was finally decided that the dependents of executed partisans, as well as the families of those in the field, would be sent to the Reich, where VoMi would house them in its camps. On 25 June 1942, Himmler issued an even more brutal order for dealing with the "bandits." The men were to be executed, the women placed in concentration camps, and the children sent to the Reich and placed in VoMi's care.[25]

Himmler, as the Reich's security chief and its prime authority in implementing the Nazi racial ideology, never did resolve his Slovene dilemma. On the one hand he was determined to eradicate the "bandits," but on the other he believed in their racial value. Thus the deportations, for both racial and deterrence purposes, continued. So did the antipartisan measures. By the end of June 1942, more than 34,000 Slovenes had been sent to the Reich, and by the end of the war, a total of some 55,000.[26] The vast majority passed through the VoMi camp system. VoMi's involvement with the Slovenes demonstrated in practice the inherent, inseparable ties between the *Untermensch* and the *Herrenvolk* in the Nazi racial scheme. In both planning and execution, it became impossible to draw neat, clear lines between activities related to one group or the other.

• • • BULGARIA AND GREECE

VoMi performed two other, minor resettlements in southeastern Europe, in Bulgaria and Greece. The resettlement of Bulgarian *Volksdeutsche* was accomplished in several separate operations in the winter of 1940–41, another in December 1941, and yet another in the late spring of 1943. Altogether, VoMi commandos resettled some 2,500 people from Bulgaria.[27] This resettlement was another exception to the policy of not removing *Volksdeutsche* from those areas of the southeast not threatened by a Soviet takeover. But as was the case of some of the groups in Rumania, the minority in Bulgaria was in no condition economically, politically, or culturally to serve as a viable link between the Reich and the host state. Most of these Germans, including those transferred with the southern Dobrudja from Rumania, were destitute and failed to convey the same industrious, positive image as did the Transylvania Saxons or the Danube Swabians. Their presence in Bulgaria was more of a liability than an advantage. Therefore, mostly in the interest of the Reich's image, Himmler and his associates decided to resettle these poorer examples of the *Herrenvolk*.

The resettlement of a small colony of Greek Germans from the village of New Heraklion near Athens in early 1942 accounted for 144 more resettlers. They were descendants of Bavarian farmers who had followed their Wittelsbach prince, Otto, to Greece when he had become King of the Hellenes. Having discovered these Germans after the Reich's occupation of Greece in 1941, Himmler hoped to exhibit them as evidence of generations of biological exclusivity. But to his disappointment, his SS racial experts classified only one of them as being racially suited for colonization in the east—a meager dividend for his troubles.[28]

FRANCE AND LUXEMBURG

The resettlement of western *Volksdeutsche*, from France and Luxemburg, in certain respects compared with the population transfers in Yugoslavia. People were resettled from certain areas under German military occupation either to the Reich or to adjacent border regions. These operations also entailed the movement of non-Germans with the purpose of enhancing the German character of designated areas.

After the campaign in the west in the summer of 1940, the German military occupied France and Luxemburg. France was divided. About two-fifths, the southern and central parts—so-called Vichy France—for the time being remained nominally independent and free from military occupation. Most of the rest—including the north, the entire Atlantic seacoast, and Paris—came under direct military control. As for Alsace and Lorraine, which for centuries had been contested by France and Germany, the Reich did not immediately incorporate them but awarded them, along with Luxemburg, special status tantamount to annexation.

Each of the three—Alsace, Lorraine, and Luxemburg—came under the rule of a chief of civil administration. The chief for Lorraine was Gauleiter Josef Bürckel of Gau Westmark; for Alsace, Gauleiter Robert Wagner of Gau Baden; and for Luxemburg, Gustav Simon, Gauleiter of Koblenz-Trier. In the summer of 1940, Hitler told Bürckel and Wagner that they had ten years in which to Germanize their domains. They and Simon tackled this chore at once.[29] Once Germanized, through the removal of racial and political undesirables and the settling of more Germans, including *Volksdeutsche*, the three lands would be incorporated into the Reich. These three chiefs, not Himmler, took the initiative in rearranging the ethnic composition of their realms.

Gauleiter Bürckel of Lorraine took the first steps. In November 1940 he expelled, to interior France, all the politically unreliable— known anti-Nazis and individuals who preferred French rule to German. Similar deportations followed in Alsace and Luxemburg. By the end of 1942, an estimated 295,000 people had been removed to France.[30] Just as vital to the ethnic transformation of these lands was the settlement of additional Germans. It was at this point that the RKFDV entered. Himmler appointed his HSSPFs in Strassburg, Metz, and Luxemburg as his RKFDV deputies and ordered them to work with the three chiefs.[31] Since resettled *Volksdeutsche* were to be a vital source of new German blood, VoMi also became involved.

The main source of *Volksdeutsche* for Alsace and Lorraine was the rest of France. People with German ancestry as well as all refugees who had fled from the border provinces when hostilities began could apply to return. Applicants were classified in three categories: (1) those designated to return to Alsace and Lorraine; (2) the racially most valuable, designated for resettlement in the east; and (3) those unsuitable either for the east or for Alsace and Lorraine. The latter were to be deported to the Altreich. VoMi did not participate in these resettlements, which began in 1941 and continued into 1942, but it did become involved with resettlers designated for placement either in the east or in the Altreich. Their odysseys included stays in VoMi camps while they awaited their permanent settlement.[32]

Himmler's relations with Bürckel and Wagner were bumpy. The three differed on several issues, including what criteria to use in determining the final placement of resettlers from France. Neither Gauleiter took race seriously and judged resettlers coming to their provinces on political reliability and cultural characteristics, particularly language. Their reluctance to settle politically and culturally deficient people simply because they possessed certain racial characteristics clashed with Himmler's precepts, which allowed for other shortcomings if an individual displayed Germanic physical features. The two applied the same criteria for deportations from the provinces. For example, Wagner wanted to expel the politically unrepentant along with the racially inferior, but Himmler emphatically opposed deporting to France any of the politically errant who displayed valuable physical traits. They should be removed, but not to France. They should be sent to the Reich for reeducation and an eventual reunion with the *Volk*.[33]

The disagreement between the Gauleiters and Himmler reached Hitler, who in August 1942 decided that the politically undesirable but racially acceptable would no longer be sent to France. Depending on their racial type, they would be settled either in the Altreich or in the east.[34] The Gauleiters got rid of the unreliable and unwilling, and Himmler was able to salvage all good German blood, both the willing and the unwilling. To help with the preservation of reluctant German blood, Himmler turned to VoMi. On their arrival in the Reich, the deportees would be placed in VoMi camps, where racial examiners would determine their fate.[35] Lorenz and Behrends balked at being forced into this activity. But it seems that their opposition was more a matter of not wanting to add inmates to already overcrowded camps than a matter of concern for moral principles. Moreover, these involuntary inmates would create more headaches than the resettlers from the east, who more or less came by choice.

The situation in Luxemburg was similar. Gauleiter Simon informed Himmler that he too was about to begin Germanizing his land. When Himmler referred the proposal to VoMi, it questioned the idea of a wholesale population rearrangement at this time, suggesting that such measures should be postponed until after the war. Behrends sent Heinz Brückner to Luxemburg to forestall Simon's efforts, but VoMi could not deter him for long. Simon, anxious to purge his realm of undesirables and to strengthen its Germanness, proceeded with deportations to the Reich. To keep from being left out altogether, VoMi reluctantly agreed to help, mostly by caring for the arriving deportees in its camps. As in the case of the Slovenes, VoMi was taking in reluctant resettlers, including dependents of deserters, "renegades," outspoken anti-Nazis, and in general those refusing to be good Germans.[36] The resettlements from the west further belie the claim that VoMi was involved only with *Volksdeutsche* who had volunteered to resettle. By far the majority from the west did not arrive on their own free will. Nor did they wish to become Germans.

• • • THE SOVIET UNION

In the summer of 1941 VoMi became involved in the Soviet Union. Resettlements here differed from most others, and correspondingly so did VoMi's responsibilities. From the outset these operations were urgent evacuations rather than planned measures contributing to the racial reconstruction of the east. And they certainly did not serve the purpose of removing potential for conflict.

During the first two years of German rule, resettlement here was limited to relocating scattered, vulnerable communities of Germans either to the Reich or to more secure areas of Russia. In the summer and fall of 1941, as the Reich's forces drove deeper into Russia, they discovered isolated pockets of Germans that the Soviets had failed to remove to the interior. SD Einsatzgruppe A, following in the wake of the military toward Leningrad and executing political and racial enemies along the way, came across some Germans still living in the outskirts of the city. As was common with most German groups found by Reich forces, the Soviets had deported the younger men, leaving behind only women, children, and the elderly, barely surviving in the most wretched conditions. The SD men, who regularly performed their diabolical duties with calculated ruthlessness and cold detachment, were moved by the plight of these survivors and immediately notified VoMi.[37] In response Behrends sent Paul Eilers to Russia to establish a liaison with the SD and, with its cooperation, to begin registering these people. Meanwhile Behrends made arrangements for their evacuation. In January 1942, VoMi commandos, with the help of the SD, transported them by truck to Tallin and then by train to VoMi camps in West Prussia. By April, 3,441 *Volksdeutsche* from the Leningrad region had been evacuated to the Reich.[38]

The Leningrad group was the largest contingent of resettlers from the Soviet Union during the first two years of the Russian campaign. A few others trickled in, and by the summer of 1942, 4,635 *Volksdeutsche* from the Soviet Union had arrived in VoMi camps.[39] But resettlement for most of the Germans still living in the Reich-occupied Soviet Union was not yet contemplated. Because of overburdened facilities, lack of transportation, and the fact that they already inhabited the proposed *Lebensraum*, they were to remain in place. With VoMi's guidance, they would serve, to the best of their abilities, in the most remote, eastward outpost of the German *Volk*.

• •

CHAPTER TEN

The Resettlement, III

Home in the Reich

• •

When the resettlers answered the call of the Führer, packed their belongings on wagons, trains, and boats, and bid a final farewell to their ancestral homelands, they had some misgivings about their future, but overall they felt confident that their lives would somehow go on. Few, however, could have imagined what awaited them. As they experienced the harsh realities of life in the Third Reich, the euphoria of the initial welcomes, especially for those privileged to have someone of Himmler's stature present at their arrival, quickly dissipated.

They first encountered a bewildering series of physical, racial, occupational, and political examinations to determine their degree of Germanness. They soon learned that in the eyes of Himmler's SS racial examiners, all Germans were not equal. Physiognomic features such as nose size, prominence of cheekbones, the color and texture of hair, and the potential for propagating positive racial traits determined their value and, accordingly, their final placement. Those passing the tests with the highest marks had the dubious privilege of colonizing the new *Lebensraum*, the conquered east. For many of those not selected as colonists, a final settlement never materialized. Provisional camp internment became their permanent way of life in the Third Reich. VoMi, responsible for the resettlers' care and housing, participated both directly and indirectly in every step of the process that carried them from their homelands to their final settlement.

Himmler's RKFDV program for strengthening Germandom, of which the final placement of the resettled *Volksdeutsche* was an integral part, determined the fate of these people. The resettlers were to Germanize the recently acquired *Lebensraum*. Their addition to the indigenous German population would enhance the German character of these lands. The resettlers were to be the infusion needed to tip the racial balance in favor of the German *Volk*. Concurrently the non-German population would be reduced by various means.

The first plan that Himmler seriously considered for reconstructing the east did not originate on the drawing boards of the SS but came from within the party's Racial Political Office. In early December 1939 its chief, Walter Gross, forwarded to Himmler a thirty-six-page paper on Germanizing the east. In it he proposed using the indigenous German population of Poland as the nucleus. *Volksdeutsche* from other lands would account for the rest. Another source of German blood was the Poles themselves. According to Gross, an estimated 1 million Poles contained enough German blood to make them suitable for assimilation into the German *Volk*. The rest, along with Jews, would be expelled to the remotest eastern reaches of Poland to live in Polish and Jewish reservations.[1] Parts of the plan, especially those pertaining to the *Volksdeutsche*, pleased Himmler, and he passed it on to Greifelt for closer scrutiny. Subsequently the RKFDV produced a modified version, which Himmler presented to Hitler in late May 1940. Hitler quickly skimmed over the first few pages and conferred on it his complete, enthusiastic approval. With Hitler's sanction, Himmler had a virtually free hand to reconstruct the east.[2]

Although Hitler had approved Himmler's plan, others interested in the Germanizing of the east were not as supportive. Gauleiter Forster of Danzig–West Prussia, for whom racial considerations were secondary to the political and economic order of his Gau, was skeptical of the scheme. As far as he was concerned, anyone willing to accept German rule could remain in his Gau. He wanted to ensure stability for his realm, which the wholesale population transfers envisioned in Himmler's plan could disrupt. He believed the future of his Gau depended on the indigenous population, both German and Polish, and not on *Volksdeutsche* resettlers.[3]

The preferences of Arthur Greiser, chief of the neighboring Warthegau, another prime *Lebensraum* area, were more compatible with Himmler's schemes. His realm contained far fewer local Germans than did Forster's, and therefore he was more willing to accept resettlers to help Germanize his mostly Polish province. Greiser concurred also with the SS view that only racially suitable individuals could join the *Volk*. He envisioned constructing a human wall of peasant soldiers to defend Germany from the eastern masses by resettling *Volksdeutsche* and Reich Germans alongside the local German population.[4]

• • • THE VOMI CAMP SYSTEM

When the first Baltic resettlers began arriving in the Reich in late October 1939, it became apparent that the relocation process would not be a simple matter of transferring them from old homes to new ones. The process would be far more complicated than anyone had anticipated. First, the dispersal of the resettlers to several ports of arrival made control difficult, and their receptions varied from one location to another. Gauleiter Forster was particularly uncooperative. Consequently, as the operation continued, VoMi rerouted the resettlers from Forster's Danzig to Greiser's Warthegau. Although Greiser personally cared little for the Baltic Germans, his views on Germanization impressed Himmler, who decided to consolidate the receiving and processing of the resettlers in Greiser's Gau, first in Poznan (Posen), then in Lodz.

In the interest of centralizing the reception and of maintaining SS control over the entire operation, Himmler assigned total responsibility for the housing and care of the resettlers to VoMi. This charge set it on the path toward becoming one of the Reich's foremost "social services" agencies as well as a major camp administrator. VoMi resettler camps became the *Herrenvolk* counterparts to the concentration and forced-labor camps housing "subhumans" and "asocials" of all sorts. The two camp systems, both run by the SS, were further manifestations of the *Herrenvolk-Untermensch* dichotomy. The VoMi camps, however, had no organizational or command connection with the concentration camps or with their parent organization, the SS Wirtschafts- und Verwaltungshauptamt.

Having received its new responsibilities, VoMi sent Ludwig Doppler to Lodz in late October to secure housing for some 40,000 people.

Rather than construct new facilities, Doppler sought out existing buildings, such as schools, factories, cloisters, and hotels. In fact, the majority of camps in the VoMi network did not conform to the common image of camps in the Third Reich, that of the tent cities or army-style frame barracks. Finding living space in Lodz was simple. First, all unoccupied space was requisitioned. Then Doppler's commandos, with the help of the local police and *Volksdeutsche*, evicted Poles and Jews to create more vacancies. The dispossessed were either thrown out onto the streets or sent to special camps. The housing search presented many opportunities for looting. Doppler kept for himself a cache of some fifty bottles of vodka he discovered in one of his raids.[5]

By late November, Doppler had secured enough housing in Lodz for VoMi to begin processing some of the later Baltic arrivals as well as the first of the Volhynians. By Christmas, twenty-one camps were in operation, and another nineteen were ready for use.[6] But as the Volhynian operation reached its peak in early 1940, even these facilities could not accommodate the influx of resettlers. Thus Himmler modified the process once more by sending resettlers who had completed their processing to the Reich to await their final placement. By shifting the process to the Altreich, Himmler and VoMi had to bring the party back into the resettlement business. It was at this point that VoMi created the post of Gaueinsatzführer and enlisted the Gau organizations to help with the care and housing of the processed *Volksdeutsche*. The Einsatzführer used his local party influence to help obtain facilities for camps and to assemble camp staffs.

Acquiring space had been far easier in Poland than in the Altreich, where one could not clear out entire city blocks to make room for resettlers. VoMi's Einsatzführer first made use of all available public buildings, such as schools, castles, museums, and vacant camps. Then they sought out private facilities, negotiating rents and arranging leases. Often owners of hotels and pensions rented entire buildings, and in many such cases VoMi appointed the owners as camp commanders. VoMi settled for every imaginable kind of shelter. Palace Hübertusburg in Saxony, the site of the signing of the peace treaty ending the Seven Years War, served as a VoMi camp. At Fürth, the town hall provided some space, and in Roth, some resettlers lived in Bruns's cigar factory.[7]

Conventional means did not always produce enough housing, and VoMi frequently relied on requisitioning, based on a law of 1 September 1939 permitting local officials such as mayors to seize property for official use. VoMi initially relied on these officials and the local Gestapo, but eventually Himmler granted VoMi the authority to expropriate housing space on its own.[8] Churches became VoMi's favorite victims, since their buildings, especially cloisters, were well suited for communal housing. The anti-Christian attitude of National Socialism and of the SS in particular made confiscation of church property even more palatable. Some church property used by VoMi, such as the Klosterberg monastery overlooking Passau, was rented. In this instance VoMi allowed the resident brothers to remain there and even mingle freely with the inmates. When existing space could not be found, VoMi had to construct new housing, such as the wood-frame barracks at Linz, built in the style that comes to mind as the standard "Nazi camp."[9]

Overall, VoMi was successful in procuring housing space. In the peak years of 1940 and 1941, the system reached its maximum size of between 1,500 and 1,800 camps.[10] But after the large numbers of resettlers from the Baltic States, eastern Poland, and northern Rumania passed through the system, VoMi found it increasingly difficult to justify holding on to empty, unutilized space. As vacant housing became a scarcity in the Reich, VoMi had to surrender many camps, mostly to the Waffen SS and the Wehrmacht. The loss of camps did not pose serious problems until 1944, when refugees from the east began arriving in greater numbers.

VoMi designated three kinds of camps, each serving a specific purpose. The first camps the resettlers encountered were transit camps, *Durchgangslager*, hastily constructed facilities in which the resettlers seldom spent more than a night or two on the way to the Reich. From the transit camps the resettlers were transported to assembly camps, *Sammellager*. Here they were housed for several days, or up to a week, while processing was completed and a decision was reached on their final placement. For the early phase of the Baltic action, these camps were set up in Poznan, but they were soon relocated to Lodz, which also served as the assembly center for the Volhynian resettlement.

Once the processing was completed, the resettlers were assigned to observation camps, *Beobachtungslager*, for at least four weeks. Here they were observed for any signs of political deviations or physical and spiritual deficiencies that might have slipped past the examiners. Time spent here also served as a quarantine period, since many of the resettlers came from regions that fostered diseases uncommon to Germany.[11] Beginning with the Bessarabia-Bukovina resettlement, Himmler relocated all of the observation camps to the Altreich. Since much of the preliminary processing previously performed at the Lodz assembly camps had already been completed either at the transit camps along the Danube or aboard ship, the assembly camps were eliminated from the process. The final examinations and processing took place in the observation camps inside the Reich. As the pace of the resettlement program slackened after 1941, the observation camps assumed new functions. Resettlers selected for colonization in the east were sent to Lodz and then on to final settlement. But those found unfit for eastern settlement and designated to remain in the Altreich stayed in the observation camps, which for many became permanent homes.[12]

• • • THE PROCESSING

Himmler created the Einwandererzentralstelle (EWZ), the Central Immigration Office, as the main processing office under the auspices of the Sipo-SD. Founded in early October 1939 for the Baltic operation, the EWZ included representatives of various Reich, party, and SS offices involved in the classification and placement of the resettlers.[13] The procedures of the EWZ evolved along with the resettlement program. For the Baltic resettlement, the EWZ sent teams to the Baltic ports of entry as well as to Poznan and later Lodz to process the new arrivals. But the examiners, because of the decentralization, processed the resettlers either improperly or not at all.[14] Therefore, in the Volhynia-Galicia resettlement, the processing was consolidated at Lodz. It was again decentralized for the Rumanian operation. Preliminary registration was completed en route, and the final work was done inside the Reich by special, mobile EWZ teams, the Fliegende Kommissionen, which traveled from one VoMi camp to another.[15]

Each of the five or six EWZ teams consisted of some sixty to one hundred people, including representatives of the Ministry of the Interior, Ministry of Finance, Reich Health Office, and Reich Labor Office. The two most important agencies were SS organs: the Sipo-SD, which handled the political and criminal investigations, and RuSHA, the SS racial office, whose experts examined each individual's racial qualities.

A team descended on an area or Gau, broke up into smaller units of ten or twelve, and visited the camps in that area to process all new arrivals.[16]

VoMi's role in the processing was minimal. Its camp commanders and Einsatzführer were, however, responsible for scheduling and arranging for the EWZ teams to visit the camps. The camp commanders also supervised the resettlers' progress through the process, after which they transferred the resettlers to new camps, if necessary. VoMi also kept track of the mounds of paperwork that accompanied each resettler family. Occasionally VoMi officials tried to interfere in the processing, but the EWZ quickly rebuffed such attempts.[17]

Entire families were processed and examined together, a procedure taking three to four hours to complete. At the first station, a policeman scrutinized the family's papers and added any missing forms. The second station prepared identification papers and compiled all personal information. After a photographing session at station three, the family proceeded to station four, at which all property matters were settled. The amount of property left behind was ascertained, and the resettlers were issued receipts stating how much and what type of compensation they were to receive.[18]

The fifth stop was the most important. Designated as the physical examination station, it in fact performed racial examinations. The examiners had instructions to be discreet, since Himmler wanted the resettlers to think that these inspections were medical, not racial. Here the family endured all sorts of probing and measuring by physicians and SS racial examiners, resulting in individual as well as composite health and racial profiles for the entire family.[19] Most resettlers were unaware they were undergoing a racial selection. One resettler described how the examiners studied skull formations and facial angles and recalled how some people found the probing and measuring so comical that they broke out laughing. One examiner, annoyed by this frivolity, sternly admonished them: "Don't laugh. If you knew how important this examination was for you, you would trouble yourself to be serious."[20] How right he was.

At station six the Sipo-SD determined the political status of the family, which they based primarily on documented political activities. Reliable witnesses from the homeland frequently were on hand to add their knowledge of the family's politics. Whereas this inquiry turned up few objectionable people from the eastern resettlements, the ma-

jority of those from the west did not pass the tests of political reliability.[21]

Officials at station seven determined a resettler's occupation, which,
along with the results of the racial and political evaluations, decided a
family's placement. Himmler had envisioned most of the resettlers as
peasant-soldier colonists, but since not all were farmers, classification
by occupation became necessary. The majority of rural people, if
acceptable politically and racially, were designated for the east to
become Himmler's cherished colonists, whereas the inferior ones were
to remain in the Altreich as agricultural laborers. Nonfarmers with
skills vital to the war economy were placed in appropriate occupations,
both in the east and in the Altreich. As a rule, unless someone possessed a particularly crucial skill, racial and political considerations
took precedence in determining a family's final placement.[22]

The results of the evaluations were passed on to the final station,
where a special EWZ panel determined the classification of a family
and issued identification cards and papers. The two basic, most common classifications were the O-cases (Ost), those selected as colonists
in the east, and the A-cases (Altreich), those designated to remain in
the Reich. The primary consideration for both was racial quality. The
racial examiners had classified the resettlers into one of four categories: group I, racially above average; group II, average; group III,
below average; group IV, unacceptable for the east.[23] Families classified in racial groups I and II—and some in group III, if found
politically reliable, German in culture, and through their occupations
capable of contributing to the colonization of the east—were designated O-cases. Resettlers acknowledged to be German in culture but
either classified in racial groups III and IV or labeled politically unreliable, or for some other reason thought unsuitable for the east, received A-case labels. Those judged to be non-Germans but having
group I and II racial features also were to remain in the Altreich,
to undergo Germanization. Non-Germans belonging to either racial
group III or IV were classified "S" and were either sent back to their
country of origin or deported to the General Government. The classifications were kept secret from the resettlers, and only the colors of
their identification cards indicated that not all were equal within the
Volk.[24]

After their processing and classifying, the resettlers were redistributed to new observation camps accordingly, where they waited for

their final placement. It was at this point that VoMi, through its camp commanders, could intervene to change a classification or a final destination. If, for instance, any shortcoming appeared in a resettler during the observation period, the camp commander reported it, and the EWZ, on VoMi's recommendation, could revise the original classification.[25]

The camp commanders could also influence the final placement of resettlers through temporary work assignments. As early as March 1940, Himmler decided that rather than languishing in the camps waiting for a final settlement, resettlers could perform valuable services in the Reich's manpower-short economy, and he ordered all able-bodied resettlers to work.[26] Although making resettlers work contributed to the Reich's economy and relieved the monotony of camp life, it created new problems. Once a resettler was employed, both he and the employer were reluctant to part, and if the job happened to be vital to the war industry, every effort was made to keep the resettler permanently. As a result, the RKFDV office had to remind camp commanders and employers that employment was only temporary and that the resettlers had to leave when summoned. RKFDV officials were most distraught over the loss of the valuable O-cases, the future peasant soldiers, to jobs in the Altreich.[27]

• • • **CAMP LIFE**

It was during their stay in the VoMi camps that the resettlers first experienced life in the Third Reich. They arrived at camps decorated with banners welcoming them to the Fatherland. The SS newspaper, *Das Schwarze Korps*, boasted that henceforth everything would be provided for the resettlers—housing, food, clothing, health care, even spiritual and political care.[28] The camps varied both in size, housing anywhere from a few dozen to thousands of resettlers, and in facilities, utilizing every kind of shelter. But everyday life and the rules regulating it were basically uniform throughout the system. The most decisive factor distinguishing life in one camp from that in another was the camp leadership. The camp commander was the most important Reich official to have immediate contact with the resettlers. He supervised all their dealings with the outside world. Their welfare, as well as the quality of their camp stay, depended on his competence and integrity.

Each camp was officially designated a community, and each commander enjoyed authority at least equivalent to, if not greater than, that of a German mayor. Each commander had police powers and was expected to keep order without involving local authorities from outside the camp, who had no jurisdiction over him or his resettlers. He was accountable only to the Gaueinsatzführer, who in turn answered to VoMi in Berlin. Much was expected of the commander. He was to be a capable leader but at the same time a friend and confidant to the resettlers. Above all, he was to set an example as a good Nazi.[29]

All evidence seems to indicate that VoMi did everything possible under extremely difficult conditions to make camp life comfortable. Himmler himself took a personal interest in the welfare of the resettlers, especially in their provisions.[30] Although when they arrived in the camps the resettlers had to surrender all foodstuffs, they were relatively well fed. According to a regulation of 21 February 1940, VoMi camps received the status of convalescent camps, entitling their residents to rations 20 percent higher than those of the average German.[31] Many inmates nevertheless complained about the food, grumbling that camp officials were eating delicacies like schnitzel while they had to eat more common fare.[32] VoMi took great pains to investigate these complaints and correct any deficiencies, but more often than not these resulted from circumstances beyond anyone's control—from boredom, crowded living quarters, anxieties over an uncertain future, and wartime shortages.

VoMi also cared for the resettlers' cultural, recreational, and educational needs, providing all sorts of sporting, musical, dramatic, and literary activities. On special holidays it arranged festivities. The resettlers could organize activity groups but were prohibited from forming any political or *völkisch* associations. Surprisingly, many Nazi political activities were not permitted. Martin Bormann explicitly forbid party recruitment in the camps, since conferring NSDAP membership on someone who might later be rejected as an inadequate German could prove embarrassing. A resettler who had not belonged to the NSDAP before the resettlement had to wait a year after leaving the camp before he could apply and be admitted into the party.[33]

Although camp inmates could not join the NSDAP, they nonetheless became a captive audience for a barrage of Nazi propaganda and education. Along with instruction in the German language—in which many resettlers were less than proficient—and other courses necessary for their entry into the *Volksgemeinschaft*, the newcomers were deluged by an interminable stream of political and racial lectures. VoMi also made certain they had suitable reading material by ordering all camps to subscribe to the *Völkischer Beobachter*, *Der Angriff*, *Das Schwarze Korps*, and *Der Stürmer*. Every family was to receive the VoMi newsletter, *Wir sind daheim*, and for Christmas each resettler received a copy of the national bestseller *Mein Kampf*.[34]

In evaluating the quality of everyday life in the camps, one needs to examine the issue of labor. With the use of resettlers as temporary workers arose the question of forced labor. Many former inmates testified that they had worked voluntarily, and Lorenz noted that many of them had complained of boredom and had asked for work.[35] But the evidence is overwhelming that in the case of able-bodied, healthy resettlers, there was no choice in the matter—they had to work. VoMi even designated several camps for incarcerating shirkers.[36]

Even though the resettlers had little choice, at least for the majority the work was hardly slave labor. Those who had voluntarily resettled understood that they would receive Reich citizenship and that along with it came obligations. They were required to do no more or no less than Reich Germans, who were expected to work for the war effort and could be inducted into virtually any area of that effort—in industry, agriculture, public services, or the military. Besides, they were compensated for their work at the same rate as Reich Germans. As for non-German resettlers, such as the Slovenes, and others sent to the Reich against their will, the conditions of their employment—as will be discussed shortly—might justifiably be characterized as forced labor.

Another important consideration in determining the quality of camp life is the degree of liberty the camp residents enjoyed. VoMi reminded the commanders that the camps were not jails. The resettlers could come and go and associate with the local population, although for security reasons locals were not permitted to enter the camps. There were times, however, when the resettlers were restricted, such as quarantine periods, during processing, and while a transfer from one camp to another was impending. The camps had guards, most of whom were resettlers themselves, but at least at the regular camps they were not uniformed, and their only distinguishing mark was an armband with the emblem or name of the camp on it. VoMi prohibited the wearing of swastika armbands by the camp guards to avoid giving the impression that the guards represented the party.[37] It cannot be determined whether or to what extent they were armed.

FINAL SETTLEMENT

The final stage of the resettlement was the permanent placement of a resettler family in business, in industry, or on the land. Himmler designated the conquered Polish lands as the primary settlement area, particularly the annexed Gaus of the Warthegau, Danzig–West Prussia, and Upper Silesia. In late 1942 he decided that the Warthegau, the prime settlement area, had absorbed as many settlers as it could hold, and he designated the Lublin region of the General Government—an area from which he had earlier removed *Volksdeutsche*—for settlement.[38] To a much lesser degree he used the Sudetengau, the Protectorate, Alsace, Lorraine, and even Luxemburg as settlement areas. The annexed regions of northern Yugoslavia were also designated for settlement but were reserved mostly for *Volksdeutsche* from other parts of that country.

Himmler ordered the priorities for receiving land, property, and even positions in the settlement areas. Local *Volksdeutsche* had first claim, the resettlers were next, and last came any Reich Germans, whose turn would come after the war.[39] Himmler would have preferred to rank the resettlers first, but to avoid alienating the local Gauleiters even further and in deference to the indigenous Germans, he decided on this ranking.

Few measures demonstrated so graphically the racial dichotomy between the *Herrenvolk* and the *Untermensch* as did the removal of Jews and Poles to make room for the *Volksdeutsche*. As early as 11 October 1939, Himmler declared that deportations would precede the final placement of German settlers.[40] And at a conference on 30 January 1940, Heydrich tied the deportations of Jews and Poles to the settlement of the Volhynian *Volksdeutsche*. He estimated that some 120,000 Poles would have to be expelled before the Germans could be settled.[41] Since the VoMi official Hans-Jochen Kubitz was present, the VoMi leadership was apprised of the inherent connection between the final placement of the *Volksdeutsche* and the deportations of non-Germans.

VoMi's role in the final, settlement stage, above all in the placement of O-cases, was nil. Responsibility for locating land and farms, evicting the residents, and replacing them with *Volksdeutsche* settlers belonged to the RKFDV and other SS offices. The most important was the Ansiedlungsstab Litzmannstadt, headed by Wilhelm Koppe, the HSSPF for the Warthegau.[42] VoMi's only duty in regard to the O-cases was to coordinate with the Ansiedlungsstab the transfer of the "O-cases" from camps in the Reich to Lodz (Litzmannstadt).[43] Occasionally VoMi intervened in individual, select cases. For instance, it sought a suitable estate in the east for Fritz Fabritius, the erstwhile leader of the German minority in Rumania.[44]

Once the Ansiedlungsstab located space, it notified VoMi, which in turn alerted its local camp officials to prepare the resettlers. It summoned an entire village of *Volksdeutsche*, and camp commanders throughout the Reich had to locate everyone from that village classified as O-cases and send them to Lodz. From Lodz they were delivered to their new homes. The final placement was as simple as it was ruthless. Officials of the Ansiedlungsstab, accompanied by the police or other SS security services, drove the *Volksdeutsche* to Polish or Jewish dwellings or farms, most of which were already vacated. But occasionally farms and homes were still inhabited. In these instances the residents were ordered to vacate the premises immediately. Often they were hauled away in the same trucks that had delivered the *Volksdeutsche*. They were then usually deported, either to the General Government or to the Altreich as laborers. Some dispossessed Polish farmers were permitted to remain in the area as agricultural laborers, but they could not live among the German settlers.[45]

In contrast to its minimal role in the settling of O-cases, VoMi's responsibilities for finding work and housing for the A-cases were great. As early as 1940, VoMi was prodding its Einsatzführer and camp commanders to expedite the placement of A-cases in order to clear out camp space for incoming resettlers.[46] VoMi placed most A-cases, but it simply could not place all, especially the infirm and the aged, who for the most part were transferred to welfare homes or VoMi's own special camps for the elderly.[47] The disposal of the aged and infirm raises a troubling question. Since the euthanasia program was in progress at the time of the early resettlements, one wonders whether any resettlers met their end as a result of it. Available evidence discloses no connections between the two programs. But since the euthanasia program was veiled in euphemistic subterfuge such as "transfer to homes for the elderly," which was exactly the same terminology that VoMi often used, some suspicion lingers.

Another problem in placing resettlers was the desire of many to return to their homes. After the German invasion of Russia rolled back the Soviet threat to their former homelands, many *Volksdeutsche* wanted to return. For most of them, especially the precious O-cases and those already placed in vital, permanent jobs in the Reich, a return was absolutely out of the question.[48] The elderly, however, as well as those difficult to place, the racially unfit, and any non-Germans who had made their way to the Reich, were permitted to return.

Contrary to Reich propaganda glorifying the resettlement, life as resettlers, in particular as colonists in the east, was anything but romantic and seldom rewarding. As a rule, the high expectations were not met, and disappointment inevitably followed. Many resettlers found occupying businesses, homes, or farms from which the former occupants had been forcibly evicted, sometimes before their very eyes, difficult to reconcile. Also, readjustment to a new land and environment—a trying transition even in the best of times—was simply too demoralizing under wartime conditions. Some farmers complained about inadequate facilities and equipment, and others, who had been industrious, diligent workers back home, increasingly relied on cheap Polish labor and assumed the roles of indolent gentlemen farmers.[49]

By far the greatest source of anxiety and despair was the vengeance of the dispossessed people. Both Hitler and Himmler had envisioned a system of military outposts to protect the settlements. Himmler even boasted to a group of resettlers that they had no reason to fear the Poles, since the police and the SS would protect them: "The Pole knows that this is Germany, that here is German territory, in which no German may be touched. If you bother just one hair of a German family, you and all Polish men in your village will lose your lives."[50] But despite such assurances, Himmler could not back them up with adequate security. The colonists soon became targets for terrorist attacks, and after the reversal of German fortunes in Russia, partisan bands raided German settlements with impunity.

By 1944, as the German military position eroded, the resettlers found themselves on the road again, fleeing westward from the vengeful *Untermensch* and the advancing Red Army. The "human wall" crumbled under its first test, the onslaught of the "Asiatic hordes." By the war's end, the O-cases fleeing from the east were thrown together inside the Reich with A-cases, newly arrived *Volksdeutsche* refugees, non-German laborers and refugees from all across Europe, and Reich Germans. Segregated earlier according to racial, political, and occupational criteria, the resettlers discovered the true *Volksgemeinschaft* in the common experience of flight, refuge, and devastating defeat. Visions of the new order vanished. But even though Himmler and his SS minions fell short of their goal of Germanizing the *Lebensraum*, they had briefly previewed what could have been. Hitler had predicted that someday 20 million Germans would be settled in the *Lebensraum*.[51] His prophecy fell considerably short of the mark. Statistics vary, but one can estimate that the RKFDV program resettled some 600,000 *Volksdeutsche*.[52]

• • • VOMI AND THE NON-GERMANS

As discussed earlier, VoMi was not involved exclusively with *Volks-deutsche*. It was an active accomplice in certain SS activities dealing with non-Germans, among them Polish *Volksdeutsche* whose Germanness was questionable. In early 1940, Himmler's planners formulated a procedure for determining an individual's degree of Germanness. By identifying and evaluating certain racial traits, political preferences, and other criteria, SS examiners determined whether and to what degree an individual was a German. Those evaluated as Germans, to one degree or another, were enrolled on the Deutsche Volksliste (DVL), the German Ethnic List.[53] In March 1941, Himmler officially introduced the DVL as the standard procedure for determining citizenship in the conquered territories.

The DVL acknowledged four categories of Germanness. Categories I and II comprised racially and politically acceptable Germans. Categories III and IV contained a mixed bunch who, although still regarded as Germans, did not measure up to acceptable political, cultural, and especially racial standards. Members of groups I and II became Reich citizens and usually were allowed to remain in their homes in the east, whereas those registered in groups III and IV, whose value as Germans was lower, were sent to the Altreich to receive training in becoming better Germans. VoMi had little or nothing to do with the people in categories I and II or those rejected altogether by the DVL, but it was directly involved with categories III and IV, who were to be housed and cared for in VoMi camps while undergoing their Germanization in the Reich.[54]

Since the people belonging to categories III and IV were formally recognized as Germans, one could argue that in its involvement with them, VoMi was still dealing with Germans. But there could be no doubt about the non-German nature of the Slovenes, whom Himmler ordered VoMi to lodge in its camps. As discussed in the previous chapter, the purpose of shipping them to the Reich was Germanization, for which the local HSSPF, not VoMi, was responsible. But since the process was to take place in VoMi camps, VoMi had to provide a proper environment. VoMi camp officials also helped determine when an individual was properly Germanized and was ready to enter the mainstream of everyday life in the Third Reich.[55]

The treatment of Slovenes varied from camp to camp, from individual to individual. Those selected for Germanization, as long as they cooperated, were apparently treated well. Himmler even considered colonizing some of the more cooperative ones in the east. But since the Slovenes strongly objected to being sent even farther from home, Himmler gave up the idea.[56] If, however, they expressed any reluctance to becoming Germans or proved ungrateful, they suffered severe consequences, including sentencing to labor and concentration camps. With time, cases of insubordination, refusal, and even escape increased, requiring progressively sterner disciplinary measures. As early as November 1941, all Slovene camps were closely watched, and by 1942 all railway traffic to southern Austria came under police surveillance. In September 1942, Himmler decreed that all escapes were to be reported immediately to the Gestapo and that the fugitives as well as any accomplices were to be hanged. Their families were to be sent to concentration camps.[57]

One particularly incriminating aspect of VoMi's involvement with the Slovenes was its complicity in disposing of the orphaned children of executed partisans. When in June 1942 Himmler ordered the shooting of all Slovene guerrillas, VoMi received the unpleasant task of receiving the orphans. It planned to hand over racially superior children under twelve to Lebensborn, the SS organization promoting the procreation of racially pure children, which would place them for adoption in German homes. VoMi ordered its local officials to take especially good care of the orphans, and Lorenz personally inspected the camps to ensure compliance.[58]

The camp business and the Germanization process brought VoMi into contact with yet another group of non-Germans, American prisoners of war. In 1942 Himmler became intrigued with the prospects of retrieving American prisoners of war of German descent for the *Volk*. He instructed Lorenz to study this possibility and in January 1943 ordered him to set up a camp for potential recruits.[59] VoMi obliged by reserving a camp at Kobenz bei Knittfeld in Styria. Meanwhile Behrends broached the idea to the Foreign Ministry and the military for their opinions. Receiving a cool response, he proceeded most reluctantly. Waldemar Rimann, the VoMi official in charge of the scheme, interviewed a few potential candidates for retrieval and concluded that these efforts would be futile. Unlike European *Volksdeutsche*, the Americans refused to have anything to do with the Reich. Lorenz hesitated to tell Himmler the negative results and postponed informing him until January 1944.[60] It appears that by this time Himmler, perhaps already aware of the response of the GIs, had lost interest in the effort.

Himmler did not pursue the Germanization of Americans, but he hoped to convert other POWs. In late January 1944 he ordered VoMi to compile a list of all POWs with German names. If cooperative, they were to be released to undergo Germanization.[61] It is not known whether this scheme brought results, but the listing of POWs was shortly extended to inmates of concentration camps in the east. On Himmler's insistence and in cooperation with VoMi, Oswald Pohl, chief of the concentration camp network, compiled a list of inmates with German names—1,222 men and 431 women. Pohl offered to collect the men at Sachsenhausen and the women at Ravensbruck and turn them over to VoMi, which would make the final selection as to who was or was not Germanizable. Lorenz later claimed that nothing came of this idea—as was the case with many measures planned toward the end of the war. Its final outcome, like that of the POW recruitment, remains unknown.[62]

• • • THE VOMI CAMPS AND THE KZS

From the time VoMi became involved in the camp business, some of its camps served purposes other than housing transient *Volksdeutsche*. These special camps bring to mind the infamous concentration camps, the Konzentrationslagers (KZs). Indeed, the Nuremberg prosecution attempted to associate these VoMi camps—as well as all other VoMi camps—with the other SS facilities. Although organizationally the VoMi camps were not at all related to the concentration camps, allegations that the purposes of and treatment of inmates in these camps were not much different from those of the concentration camps have some validity. These special VoMi camps isolated "asocial" and other harmful influences from the other resettlers and reeducated those who were reluctant to accept the ways of the Third Reich—precisely the functions of the concentration camps.

Many resettlers brought to the Reich against their will, most notably Slovenes and the politically unreliable but racially acceptable deportees from Alsace, Lorraine, and Luxemburg, created disciplinary problems. For them as well as for resettlers refusing work assignments, VoMi constructed "education camp" Rotes Luch, near Waldsieversdorf, Brandenburg. Friedrich Altena, the administrative chief of the VoMi camp network, regarded sentencing to Rotes Luch as so serious—just one step short of a concentration camp—that he insisted on being informed of every case. He observed that a stint at Rotes Luch improved the attitudes of troublesome resettlers and that concentration camps should be resorted to only if Rotes Luch proved ineffective.[63]

This in-house arrangement did not last long. In late 1941 Vomi was ordered to close down Rotes Luch, and in the future it was to refer all serious disciplinary cases to the Gestapo. One suspects that the Gestapo, which coveted complete control over all security and police matters, was behind this move, since VoMi, operating its own "education" camp, infringed on the Gestapo's turf. Altena instructed his subordinates to abide by this new regulation but also told the Einsatzführer to inform him of all cases referred to the Gestapo.[64] Lorenz, however, was not prepared to surrender all disciplinary authority over the resettlers to the Gestapo. After the closing of Rotes Luch, he instructed each Einsatzführer to construct or designate a work camp for troublemakers and those refusing to work.[65]

The camps for Slovenes and the deportees from the west had many of the features of concentration camps. One such camp was Jeschwetz, near Trebnitz, Silesia, which kept in close touch with the Gestapo and sequestered reluctant resettlers from Luxemburg. A VoMi official later conceded that the fifty or sixty people confined to Jeschwetz either had not fit in well with fellow resettlers or were deemed "aso-cial."[66] At Lodz, VoMi operated another facility, Konstantinow, for non-Germans who had arrived with the resettlers and for persons generally regarded as "unreliable." In February 1940 a DAI investiga-tor visited Konstantinow, which he specifically referred to as a *Konzen-trationslager*. He noted, however, that the rumors of inhumane condi-tions at this camp were exaggerated and that the treatment of the residents was no worse than that of *Volksdeutsche* elsewhere.[67] These bits and pieces of evidence alluding to camps such as Rotes Luch, Jeschwetz, and Konstantinow contradict postwar claims that VoMi camps were not at all like the SS concentration camps.

› • • VOMI AND THE FINAL SOLUTION

One further issue requiring examination is VoMi's participation in the final solution, the destruction of the Jews. After the war, Lorenz and other VoMi officials testified that they had had nothing to do with the final solution, concentration camps, deportations, and the like. They also emphasized their lack of anti-Semitism and even cited instances of individual efforts to save Jews. Granted, VoMi was not a hotbed of anti-Semitism, but claims of total innocence in these matters and assertions of ignorance about atrocities are incredible. All VoMi per-sonnel were familiar with the SS position toward Jews and with their own personal obligations as SS men to eliminate the Jews from the *Volk*. Furthermore, the divisions of labor within the RKFDV system were not always meticulously honored, and since VoMi, supposedly involved exclusively with *Volksdeutsche*, did participate in RKFDV pro-grams dealing with some non-Germans, one can reasonably suspect that its involvement could have also extended to Jews.

Individual acts of kindness toward Jews aside, evidence reveals that in certain situations VoMi and the people working under its authority either assisted in anti-Jewish measures or exploited the plight of Jews to benefit the *Volksdeutsche*. One of the earliest of VoMi's activities in this respect was the preparation of Lodz as a reception center for resettlers by expelling Jews from their homes. Witnesses described outrageous scenes of Jews being evicted from apartments. One ob-server told how VoMi's crews rounded up a thousand Jews to clean apartments selected for the resettlers.[68] But when the living conditions of Lodz's Jews deteriorated to the point that epidemics threatened to break out, Ludwig Doppler, the VoMi man in charge, prohibited any further entry of Jews into the VoMi camps and decreed that *Volksdeutsche* could no longer communicate or transact any business with Jews. Other VoMi officials were less hesitant to utilize cheap, readily available Jewish labor. For instance, a VoMi camp near Kattowitz requested Jewish stable hands to care for resettlers' horses.[69]

VoMi not only availed itself of Jewish labor and expropriated their homes and apartments, but it also made use of their personal belongings, from furniture to socks and shoes. Enormous quantities of clothing became available as the deportations and the final solution commenced. In late September 1942, Hans Frank, the chief of the General Government, wrote to Auschwitz suggesting that the clothing and other personal belongings of the inmates be given to VoMi for distribution to the resettlers. Himmler approved the plan and recommended to Lorenz and Oswald Pohl, the chief of the concentration camps, that goods from the Auschwitz and Lublin camps be collected and used as Christmas presents for the *Volksdeutsche* in the Ukraine. Pohl, unable to deliver the goods to the Ukraine because of transportation difficulties, sent them instead to Lodz, from where VoMi could distribute the loot as it saw fit.[70]

The Christmas present idea was a prelude to a broader program known as *Action Reinhard*. Clothing, shoes, and other personal articles from Auschwitz and other eastern camps were collected and shipped to the Reich. One of the primary recipients was VoMi. Lorenz later pleaded ignorance, although Himmler had written him about the *Action*. One of Lorenz's top subordinates, Hans Hagen, recalled receiving five or six trainloads of goods from Auschwitz for VoMi camp inmates through *Action Reinhard*.[71] In December 1942, Himmler also ordered all formerly Jewish property in the General Government, including home furnishings, to be placed at the disposal of the resettlers.[72]

The RKFDV program for strengthening Germandom was a comprehensive scheme combining a variety of operations—such as the Germanization of the east, the annihilation of allegedly racially inferior people, and the resettlement of the *Volksdeutsche*—into a bizarre but purposeful whole. VoMi's contribution, which included the resettlement, care, and housing of *Volksdeutsche* resettlers as well as some categories of non-Germans, illustrated the inherent relationship between the ruling German *Herrenvolk* and the non-German *Unter-mensch* in the Nazi racial ideology. The strengthening of the first depended on the corresponding destruction of the second. As VoMi's *Volksdeutsche* took their places in the new order, the resettlers displaced the *Untermensch* by occupying the non-Germans' homes, farms, and businesses and literally stepping into their socks and shoes.

CHAPTER ELEVEN

The Minorities in the War Years

An Overview

• •

Resettlement did not eliminate all German minorities from foreign lands. The *Volksdeutsche* of Slovakia, Hungary, most of Rumania, the two successor states of partitioned Yugoslavia (Croatia and Serbia-Banat), Denmark, and the Soviet Union remained in their homelands. Reich policy toward these groups continued as in the prewar period, preserving them as distinct ethnic-racial entities and using them as Reich interests required. Far more, however, was expected of them. These *Volksdeutsche*, no less than Reich Germans and the resettlers, would have to contribute to the war effort, as defined and directed by Himmler and the SS. Consequently VoMi assumed dual and sometimes conflicting responsibilities. It supervised the contributions of the minorities to the war effort while at the same time it tried to preserve them as distinct entities. In the process VoMi, already serving as Himmler's auxiliary, made SS auxiliaries of them as well.

VOMI'S AUTHORITY

Two developments made fulfilling VoMi's wartime responsibilities to the remaining minorities more difficult. One was its concurrent involvement in the RKFDV program, which demanded much of its attention and resources. The second was the continued erosion of its authority. As discussed earlier, with Himmler assuming direction over the resettlement and with the launching of the RKFDV program, step by step VoMi lost its exclusive authority in *Volkstum* affairs. Although the RKFDV commission did not give Himmler power over *Volksdeutsche* not affected by the resettlement, he nevertheless regarded them as vital to his schemes. He was determined to extend his authority over them as well.

It appears that the VoMi leadership did little to forestall Himmler's efforts. Just as Lorenz had quietly accepted Hitler's transfer of responsibility for the Baltic resettlement to Himmler, he and his colleagues dutifully accepted a greater role for Himmler and the SS in the affairs of the remaining minorities. Accounting for this meekness was not only deference of SS subordinates to the Reichsführer SS but probably also the realization that the new arrangement made little difference in VoMi's everyday tasks.

Himmler's growing influence in *Volkstum* matters and the creation of the RKFDV encouraged various groups and individuals—which in the past two years had come under VoMi's authority—to turn against VoMi, hoping to regain some lost independence. The VDA, for one, stirred up some dissent and propagated rumors that Lorenz's days as chief were numbered. Talk of serious differences between Lorenz and Behrends and of Himmler's dissatisfaction with both abounded.[1] The dissent, however, failed to strengthen the critics. Himmler exploited the various charges to increase his control over VoMi, but he had no intention of restoring the independence of the groups under VoMi's control. He only became annoyed with the attacks, which began to reflect negatively on the internal harmony of the SS. Indeed, VoMi actually tightened its grip over its critics while Himmler in turn asserted greater control over VoMi and extended his monopoly over all *Volkstum* activities.

VoMi's hold over the *Volkstum* organizations remained as firm as before, but with Himmler as its ultimate boss, VoMi found itself challenged with increasing success from within the SS system, especially by Gottlob Berger, the head of the SS Hauptamt and the SS Erganzungshauptamt and, by virtue of the latter post, the chief Waffen SS recruiter. Berger's relationship with Lorenz and VoMi was paradoxical. On the one hand, as fellow SS officers, they often stood united against outsiders meddling in the affairs of the minorities. But on the other, within the SS they were rivals by virtue of their mutual but contradictory interests in the *Volksdeutsche*. Berger valued the minorities as a supplementary source of manpower for the Waffen SS, a purpose conflicting with VoMi's efforts to maintain the minorities as viable, distinct entities for the postwar period.

The only authority outside the SS system to retain any say in *Volkstum* matters was the Foreign Ministry. Under Ribbentrop, the ministry, with Himmler's support, had repelled several party forays into foreign affairs, but in the process the SS had implanted its influence in the field. And once the SS had staked a claim, it was there to stay. As a result, relations between Himmler and Ribbentrop became strained, and their disagreements over the role of the SS in foreign affairs became a permanent consideration in VoMi's wartime dealings with the minorities.

Differences between Himmler and Ribbentrop came to a head in January 1941, when Ribbentrop admonished Lorenz to clear with his ministry all activities related to the minorities. These were inherently foreign affairs and therefore within his sphere of authority. Ribbentrop emphasized that he, not Himmler, was the ultimate authority in this field.[2] When Himmler heard of Ribbentrop's pretensions, he dismissed the claims. By then Hitler had transferred all of VoMi's authority in minority matters to Himmler. After some heated exchanges, on 31 March the two signed an accord redefining jurisdiction in *Volkstum* matters. Ribbentrop conceded that Hitler had transferred VoMi's authority to Himmler, and the latter in return agreed that the Foreign Ministry was to be consulted in all matters of diplomatic importance. He ordered all SS offices, including VoMi, to respect this arrangement.[3]

Despite the understanding, tensions simmered. Himmler, through the RKFDV program, SD intelligence activities, and Waffen SS recruiting, was pursuing what amounted to an independent SS foreign policy. His SS subordinates regularly ignored the Wilhelmstrasse on important issues. On one occasion, in July 1942, Himmler even rebuked Lorenz for complying too scrupulously with the Ribbentrop agreement. Himmler had instructed Lorenz to deal with some sensitive matters regarding the resettlement of *Volksdeutsche* from France. Faithful to the agreement, Lorenz informed Ribbentrop before taking action. When Ribbentrop raised the matter with Himmler—the last thing Himmler had wanted or expected—the latter informed Lorenz that he had had a "very nice conversation with the foreign minister."

He warned Lorenz that in the future he was to carry out his orders, not discuss them with others. If the Reichsführer SS wanted to communicate with the foreign minister—so fumed Himmler—he did not need VoMi, he could use the post office.[4]

It would be wrong to conclude that in this dispute Himmler held an overwhelming advantage and that Ribbentrop was fortunate to eke out any concessions. Ribbentrop still enjoyed credit with Hitler, enough to deal Himmler one of his few reverses. On 4 November 1942, Hitler designated Ribbentrop as the authority responsible for regulating all party activities abroad, in particular those of the AO.[5] The charge, however, was worded so ambiguously that Ribbentrop, as had the AO years earlier, interpreted it to extend to activities among the minorities as well. With this Führer decree in his pocket, Ribbentrop continued to meddle in *Volksdeutsche* affairs and to challenge Himmler's monopoly. Ironically Ribbentrop's boldness—directed against VoMi as well as Himmler—served VoMi well. As long as Himmler's authority over the minorities was not complete, VoMi was left a little room to maneuver independently of its SS boss.

• • • **VOLKSTUMSARBEIT**

Wartime brought far greater demands on the minorities, especially in three areas: first, in contributing economically to the Reich war effort; second, in supplementing the Reich labor force; and third, in providing manpower to the Reich's armed forces, specifically the Waffen SS. In return for their contributions, the minorities could expect continued political and material assistance from the Reich. The Reich also assisted the minorities less directly. Heightened Reich military and political presence in their states improved their domestic status. The host governments, coming increasingly under the Reich's influence and anxious to demonstrate their goodwill, granted them concessions, usually in the form of greater political and cultural autonomy.

Although wartime circumstances brought the minorities certain political advantages, material support from the Reich diminished. As the Reich mobilized and allocated its resources more sparingly, it cut back on financial support, especially for cultural and educational activities. The most pressing reason for the cutback was the critical shortage of foreign exchange. To cope with the shortage, the Reich's economic leaders arranged a clearing system whereby the Reich and its trade partners scrutinized all goods and currencies exchanged, ensuring an equitable balance of trade and payments. Strategically important goods, as well as activities and services abroad that contributed most to the war effort, enjoyed the highest priority on the clearing lists and in the allocation of precious foreign exchange. Since cultural activities among the *Volksdeutsche* ranked low, VoMi had difficulty procuring funds for them. It also faced obstacles in distributing these funds. Because many cultural activities also served political purposes, at times the host states obstructed the transfer of funds for such activities. Furthermore, other Reich authorities, in particular the Foreign Ministry, concerned about alienating allies such as Hungary and Rumania, often disapproved funds for purely political activities.

One might have expected the scarcity of funds to undermine the Reich's leverage over the minorities. But this was not the case. With the increased Reich presence in the host states, the subsidies were no longer needed to win the minorities over to National Socialism and to enforce compliance with the Reich's wishes. VoMi had already more or less secured their loyalties, and with the increased Reich military presence, as well as that of security organs such as the SD and the Gestapo, financing receded in importance as a means for enforcing obedience. Less subtle, more direct ways were now at the Reich's disposal. Also, the governments of these states recognized a special relationship between the Reich and the local *Volksdeutsche* and granted the Reich a freer hand in dealing with them, especially in matters such as determining their political leaderships. Consequently, during the war years, financing, or lack of it, made little difference in controlling the minority leaderships or steering them in a pro-Reich direction.

The Reich, although at times remiss in financing cultural activities, did everything in its power to provide adequate funds for *Volksdeutsche* economic needs. Support for their enterprises brought tangible earnings in the form of production for the Reich's war effort. The greatest *Volksdeutsche* economic contribution came in the agricultural sector. While the Reich itself concentrated on industrial production, most of its associate and subject nations were expected to produce food. In many client states, the *Volksdeutsche* were among the most efficient farmers, and their economic well-being was a fundamental prerequisite for continued agricultural production.

In the procurement and distribution of funds, VoMi remained under the supervision and control of the foreign minister and Reich treasurer Schwarz. But here too Himmler staked a claim. He formalized his entry into the financing side of *Volkstumsarbeit* first in the 31 March 1941 agreement with Ribbentrop that delineated their areas of competence and then in an agreement in August 1942 with Schwarz.[6] As a result, VoMi was no more than a cashier, distributing funds to the minorities, with Himmler, Ribbentrop, and Schwarz making the major decisions.

But even as a cashier, VoMi still handled a substantial sum of money covering the cost of numerous activities and programs, such as maintaining a tuberculosis sanatorium in Slovakia, supporting kindergartens, and paying supplements for teacher salaries.[7] A representative VoMi wartime budget was that of April 1941 through March 1942, a sum of 31,832,741 RM. Approximately one-third covered regular operating expenses, including those of VoMi itself and the minority organizations, and the rest consisted of one-time payments, such as purchases of buildings and opening clinics.[8] Although the subsidies for cultural, health, and educational programs no longer served the purpose of ensuring political compliance, they continued to reap political dividends. As was the case before the war, the subsidies demonstrated to foreign states as well as to the *Volksdeutsche* the Reich's interest in them and underscored its commitment to those who supported its cause.

The VoMi department responsible for financial and economic matters, Lothar Heller's Amt X, worked closely with the Foreign Ministry's economic sections, particularly Kultur B and the Verinigte Finanzkontore. VoMi usually did not distribute funds directly to the minorities but used the Finanzkontore, which deposited money in banks in neutral lands, mainly in Switzerland and, until the spring of 1940, in the Netherlands. From there the funds were "laundered" to banks and credit institutions in the *Volksdeutsche* homelands. Heller's office also coordinated the returns on the Reich's investment. Its local liaison men, attached to each minority, not only supervised the allocation of the Reich subsidies but also coordinated the economic contributions of each minority.[9]

The economic dividends the *Volksdeutsche* repaid the Reich went beyond producing for the war economy. As before the war, but to a greater degree, they served as a supplementary work force. As early as

January 1939, Himmler was counting on them as an auxiliary labor force and designated VoMi as the office in charge of their recruitment.[10] Unlike non-German laborers, most *Volksdeutsche* were racially acceptable, a vital consideration for Himmler. Furthermore, since most of them were recruited to work voluntarily in the Reich, they were more productive than non-German laborers, most of whom were deported to the Reich against their will. Employment of *Volksdeutsche* also overcame the language barrier, which in certain skilled positions was a crucial consideration.

In cooperation with the Reich Labor Office and the Labor Front, VoMi helped recruit *Volksdeutsche*, and by the end of 1943 some 46,000, not including the resettlers, were working in the Reich. It appears, however, that VoMi officials were not overly enthusiastic about recruiting *Volksdeutsche* from abroad. VoMi worried that extensive recruitment would deplete the minorities of their most productive elements and would lead to their demise.[11] Others, however, did not share these concerns. In early 1942, Hitler's plenipotentiary for the procurement of labor, Fritz Sauckel, renewed efforts to import foreign labor, including *Volksdeutsche*. He ordered his subordinates to contact the minority leaderships and enlist the aid of Reich diplomats. Sauckel, however, neglected to consult either VoMi or Himmler, and an aroused Reichsführer SS, learning of these efforts, ordered Sauckel to work through VoMi. With the excuse that recruitment from some minorities would do irreparable harm to their stability and well-being, Himmler placed certain groups off-limits to Sauckel.[12]

• • • THE *VOLKSDEUTSCHE* AND THE WAFFEN SS

Before concluding that Himmler's efforts to protect the minorities from wholesale labor looting was out of concern for their welfare, one must examine another SS interest in the *Volksdeutsche*. Whereas Himmler bristled at exploiting them for the Reich labor force, he had no qualms about depleting the minorities through Waffen SS recruitment. VoMi stood side by side with Himmler to repel non-SS efforts to exploit the *Volksdeutsche*, but when confronted with Waffen SS demands on their services, VoMi more often than not found itself as their sole protector, in opposition to Himmler. Although in some exceptional instances Himmler realized that Waffen SS recruitment threatened the stability of a certain minority and intervened in its favor, as a rule he supported the efforts of Gottlob Berger and his recruiters.

The Waffen SS, or the armed SS, had originated in 1933 as a special, armed body guard for Hitler and had evolved over the years as the combat branch of the SS. In March 1940 these armed units officially became the Waffen SS, although they had been referred to as such for some time. Administratively the Waffen SS was under the command of Himmler as Reichsführer SS, but at the front, in combat, its units were subordinate to field commanders, usually Wehrmacht generals. Since it performed official state functions, first as a body guard to the Führer and later as a component of the Reich's military, the Reich, through the Ministry of the Interior, financed it and, through the Wehrmacht, supplied and equipped it.

Membership in this branch of the SS, unlike general SS (Allgemeine SS) membership, counted as fulfilling one's Reich military obligation. For Hitler, the Waffen SS was a private army, duty-bound to him personally, not to the state. For Himmler, it provided not only another source of power within the Third Reich but also an opportunity to advance his goal of making the SS the vanguard of National Socialism. Members of the Waffen SS, the elite of the racially elite SS, were to be the peasant soldiers of the new racial order.

The unique feature distinguishing the Waffen SS from the regular armed forces, the Wehrmacht, was its racial rather than official state nature. It was racial and physical being, not Reich citizenship, that qualified a young man for the Waffen SS. Therefore, all racially and physically qualified young men, including *Volksdeutsche* and other Germanics, were welcome to join. Years before the outbreak of the war, the Waffen SS was already courting them as supplementary manpower.

After Lorenz assumed command of VoMi in January 1937, Himmler began to exploit his subordinate's position to help recruit *Volksdeutsche* for the armed SS units. VoMi reluctantly cooperated. It consented to the recruitment of *Volksdeutsche* refugees arriving in the Reich on their own, but it frowned on the recruitment of young men abroad, directly from the minorities.[13] It often assisted the Waffen SS by arranging physical training programs and athletic visits for young *Volksdeutsche* in the Reich. These visits were a cover for SS recruitment, a fact that many youths discovered only after their arrival. While in the

Reich, some succumbed to SS entreaties to enlist, but others did not. As long as the numbers of recruits remained few and did not upset the stability of the minorities back home, VoMi cooperated. From the outset, the Foreign Ministry viewed the practice as hazardous to the Reich's foreign relations and sought VoMi's help in curbing these recruitments. Although Lorenz tended to agree with the ministry and interceded with the SS, it was to no avail. Other, more powerful SS interests were determined to continue these efforts.[14]

With the outbreak of war, the recruitment escalated, and in response VoMi took a stronger stand against the practice. Its apprehensions about the diplomatic ramifications remained. But its primary concern was that the siphoning off of the very best *Volksdeutsche* youth to the Waffen SS would undermine VoMi's own efforts to maintain the minorities as viable social, political, and economic entities. Another consideration, an important one for SS racists, was that the removal of these young men would deplete the biological pool and threaten the racial growth of the minorities.

Dismissing VoMi's misgivings—which its leaders time and again voiced in protest—the Waffen SS chief recruiter, Berger, launched the first major recruitment campaign abroad in early 1940. Limited in the voluntary enlistment of Reich citizens by Wehrmacht-imposed quotas, and not having authority to induct, Himmler and Berger turned to the minorities as a rich and still relatively untapped source of manpower. Since *Volksdeutsche* were citizens of other states, the only limits to their recruitment were the effectiveness of the Waffen SS appeal and the degree of cooperation or obstructionism on the part of foreign governments.

For the 1940 campaign, Berger drew on both kinds of *Volksdeutsche*: the resettlers, already wards of the RKFDV; and those still residing abroad as members of minorities. The resettlement had placed tens of thousands of *Volksdeutsche* at the direct disposal of the Waffen SS. Although as resettlers they received Reich citizenship, assumed Reich military obligations, and entered the pool of manpower controlled by the Wehrmacht, the SS—by virtue of its ties with the RKFDV and VoMi—got a crack at recruiting them first. Between the time the resettlers departed their homes and the time they became Reich citizens, the SS found ample opportunities to recruit them. For instance, in January 1940, Ulrich Greifelt of the RKFDV ordered officials of the Tyrolean resettlement to compile a list of resettlers eligible for the military—before their arrival in the Reich. And during the construction of the transit camps along the Danube for the Bessarabian operation, the Waffen SS sent recruiters to the sites, not only to await the arrival of the resettlers but also to recruit any local *Volksdeutsche* employed on the construction crews.[15]

The VoMi camps became prime recruiting grounds. VoMi instructed its camp officials to cooperate fully with SS recruiters, but granted no comparable favors to the Wehrmacht. It even denied entry into the camps to the Wehrmacht without the prior consent of the local Einsatzführer. If resettlers managed to enlist with the army, the camp commanders were instructed to secure an immediate release on the grounds that enlistment interfered with their final placement. With the same sweep of the pen, VoMi explicitly excepted voluntary enlistment with the Waffen SS from this regulation.[16]

Although VoMi was generous in providing the Waffen SS with resettler recruits, it was less cooperative in recruiting from the minorities. Whereas the resettlers, once they left the camps and became Reich citizens, were no longer VoMi's wards, maintaining the welfare, health, and stability of the minorities abroad remained a primary obligation, one that VoMi's leaders apparently took seriously. They also viewed recruitment within the minorities as an encroachment on VoMi's authority. Before Himmler's appropriation of all authority in *Volkstum* matters in late 1940 and early 1941, VoMi limited Berger's ambitions and balanced the interests of the minorities with those of the Waffen SS. But after Himmler's ascendancy, VoMi had to heed his commands, which more often than not favored the Waffen SS.

Even with the enlistment of *Volksdeutsche* from the minorities, the Waffen SS could not meet its manpower needs. Consequently there arose the issue of a *Volksdeutsche* military obligation. By early 1942 it was apparent to Himmler and Berger that voluntary enlistment was inadequate and that perhaps conscription was the answer.[17] There was no question that when resettlers received Reich citizenship, they assumed a military obligation. But it was an entirely different matter for the *Volksdeutsche* still living abroad, who, as foreign citizens, had military obligations in their own states.

VoMi opposed the Waffen SS on the issue of a general *Volksdeutsche* military obligation. It argued that conscription, which such an obligation legitimized, would create tremendous hardships on the minorities and would undermine their stability and general welfare. More important, in consideration of overall Reich interests, a military obligation could jeopardize the Reich's dealings with the host states. They would rightly perceive such claims on their German citizens as further infringements on their national sovereignty. Apparently, after years of involvement and contact with the *Volksdeutsche*, VoMi's officials had grown sympathetic toward their wards and were becoming genuinely concerned for their welfare. They believed that a general *völkisch* military obligation was not in the best interest of the *Volksdeutsche*. Lorenz, for one, drew the attention of the SS to the precarious position of the minorities and cautioned against an extensive induction of *Volksdeutsche*. He acknowledged the need for *Volksdeutsche* to contribute to the war effort through limited military service, but not through mass inductions.[18]

Himmler thought otherwise, and by 1942 his views, not those of Lorenz, counted. As far as Himmler was concerned, all members of the *Volk*, irrespective of formal citizenship, shared in its fate and therefore shared obligations—including a *völkisch* military obligation.[19] According to Himmler, this obligation did not have to be formalized. It was simply understood to exist. Although an ambiguous *völkisch* obligation was good enough for the Reichsführer SS, it was not good enough for Lorenz or for some of the minority leaders, such as Sepp Janko of Yugoslavia. Himmler, annoyed with their contrariness, referred the question to his SS legal advisers for a ruling. They concluded, as one could have expected, in favor of Himmler. They argued that an obligation of military service existed, but because of its potential for diplomatic complications, it could not be formally codified. Besides, the Reichsführer SS's declaration that such an obligation existed was sufficient validation.[20]

Having received a positive ruling, in early August 1942 Himmler instructed Lorenz to notify all minority leaders confidentially, and only orally, that a *völkisch* military obligation to the Reich existed for all *Volksdeutsche*.[21] But to allay the qualms of people such as Lorenz and some of the minority leaders, Himmler had Ribbentrop conclude agreements with the respective foreign governments authorizing further recruitments and granting to the Reich broad, unprecedented powers in this effort. As will be discussed in some detail in the next chapter, the specific provisions of each treaty varied, but in general they cleared the way for Himmler to launch his most ambitious campaign to date in February 1943. Despite a lack of enthusiasm, VoMi helped with the campaign, which focused on the large minorities in Hungary and Rumania.[22] By the end of 1943, VoMi had been at least partly responsible for the enlistment and induction of 139,567 *Volksdeutsche* from southeastern Europe alone. Of these, nearly 10 percent (12,210) were already dead or missing.[23] According to some sources, long before the end of the war, *Volksdeutsche* outnumbered Reich Germans in the ranks of the Waffen SS.[24]

Although in numbers their contribution was great, the military value of the *Volksdeutsche* was questionable. One authority had concluded that the best Waffen SS divisions were the predominantly Reich German units and that a negative correlation existed between the percentage of *Volksdeutsche* in a division and its combat proficiency: "the higher the percentage of ethnic Germans, the lower the level of performance."[25] Theodor Eicke, the commander of the SS Division Totenkopf, observed in late 1941 that not only the physical quality of the *Volksdeutsche* was poor but that they were also spiritually deficient, which resulted in disciplinary problems and cowardice.[26] Hitler was also aware of their poor reputation. When he inquired about two new SS divisions, Florian Geyer and Maria Theresa, in a 1944 conversation with General Alfred Jodl, he was relieved to hear that even though one was 40 percent *Volksdeutsche* and the other 70 percent, the rest of the troops were Reich Germans, who would compensate for the *Volksdeutsche*.[27]

As members of the Waffen SS, the *Volksdeutsche* performed various tasks. Besides combat duty, many filled positions in the rear, from service with VoMi to duty as concentration camp guards.[28] One activity for which many *Volksdeutsche* were particularly well suited was counterinsurgency in their own homelands. The most notorious antipartisan fighters were the men of the Prinz Eugen Division, operating in their native Yugoslavia. They compiled a grisly record of massacres, torture, murder, and village burning. Regardless of the variety of the *Volksdeutsche* duties and the quality of their contributions, the casualties they suffered while fighting in the ranks of the Waffen SS were the greatest sacrifices the minorities made for the *Volk*, the Reich, and the Führer.

• •

CHAPTER TWELVE

VoMi and the Minorities, III

The War Years

• •

After prewar territorial changes, resettlements, and the earliest hostilities, only seven major groups of *Volksdeutsche* remained as national minorities into the war years: in Slovakia, Hungary, Rumania, the two successor states of Yugoslavia (Croatia and Serbia-Banat), Denmark, and the Soviet Union. The term *minority*, with its negative connotation of second-class citizens, referred only to their numerical size. The Reich's military presence and dominant influence in these states helped elevate them to a privileged status equal to or even superior to that of the majority nationalities. They paid a price for their improved status, however, in contributions to the Reich's war effort. And it was Himmler and the SS, specifically VoMi, that directed these contributions, in ways usually beneficial to the SS.

SLOVAKIA

The declaration of Slovakia's independence on 14 March 1939 was a bitter disappointment for its estimated 130,000 Carpathian Germans. Many had hoped that Slovakia, like the Protectorate of Bohemia-Moravia, would come under direct Reich rule. But Hitler's support for Slovak independence determined that at least for the time being, they would remain a national minority. It was small consolation that in Nazi schemes for the future, Slovakia was to be Germanized and that they would be the nucleus for the effort.

Thanks to the compliant regime in Bratislava and the Reich's prevailing presence, everyday life for these Germans was not much different from what it would have been under direct Reich rule. The Slovaks recognized them as a legal entity and guaranteed them extensive cultural, political, and social privileges not granted other national minorities. They even created a special post of Secretary for German Affairs for minority leader Karmasin and recognized the minority's nazified political organization, the Deutsche Partei (DP), as its exclusive, official organ.[1]

The Reich's presence in Slovakia, most notably that of the SD, ended VoMi's role as the exclusive Reich office dealing with the Carpathian Germans. Nevertheless, its participation was still essential, especially in their economic affairs. VoMi continued to look after their economic enterprises and provided assistance through the Finanzkontore. But in return, these Germans were expected not only to produce for the Reich but also to supply manpower for its labor force. They responded positively, for by the end of 1943, 20,356 were employed in Germany, a manpower contribution greater than that of any other minority.[2]

VoMi also provided funds for cultural and political purposes. But as the war progressed, it became more difficult to do so, not only because of the shortage of resources in the Reich but also—as discussed in the preceding chapter—because of currency transfer problems. The Reich treasurer, Schwarz, regarded Slovakia as one of the least cooperative states in this respect.[3] Although it was pliant on most issues, Slovakia, like other client states, was surprisingly assertive in regulating and accounting for foreign exchange. Evidently this was one of the few ways in which the clients could exercise their limited sovereignty.

Not satisfied with the minority's privileged position, Karmasin refused to accept Slovak independence as final. Annoyed with Karmasin's obstinacy, VoMi sent its southeastern expert, Karl Henniger, to Bratislava in mid-January 1940 to admonish the minority leader to follow orders. The visit must have made an impact, for in May Karmasin, anxious about keeping his position and eager to demonstrate his devotion to the Nazi cause, invited Gunther Pancke, the head of the SS racial office, RuSHA, to Slovakia for a racial inspection of the minority. Pancke was impressed and praised Karmasin's efforts to enhance the minority's racial well-being.[4]

Occasionally Karmasin still grumbled about the Reich's lack of support for his minority's interests. But even though the Reich's own interests as well as those of the Slovaks seemed to have precedence, by no means had the Reich abandoned this minority. For instance, in February 1942, Lorenz intervened when the Slovakian Catholic church tried to force German Catholics to send their children to Slovak parochial schools. And in June he interceded again, to object to proposed legislation limiting the minority's autonomy.[5]

One area in which Karmasin, an avowed racist, enthusiastically complied with the Reich's wishes was the racial purging of the minority. When, in early 1942, the Slovaks introduced anti-Jewish measures modeled on the Nuremberg Laws and began deporting Jews to the Reich, the minority followed suit. In July, to help the minority remove "asocials"—political nonconformists and racial undesirables, mostly Jews—VoMi sent Otto Lackmann to Bratislava. With the aid of the police and the minority's paramilitary organization, the Freiwillige Schutzstaffel (FS), Lackmann rounded up and deported more than 600 German "asocials." Karmasin assured Himmler that most of the deportees were delighted to have the opportunity to emigrate to the Reich and that the remaining *Volksdeutsche* were just as happy to see them go. In the Reich, they were supposedly registered as resettlers and placed in VoMi camps.[6] Their ultimate fate, however, is unknown. Based on the fate of other reluctant "resettlers," one suspects that the majority ended up in concentration camps and that some were eventually exterminated.

Another area of collaboration between the Reich and these Germans was the procurement of manpower for the Waffen SS. Although a few had joined the Waffen SS earlier, they did not enlist in significant numbers until Slovak independence. In its efforts to recruit, the Waffen SS at first competed with the FS. But shortly the SS extended control over the FS by training its cadre and assigning SS officers as advisers. It also created an Allgemeine SS unit within the FS, the ET-Sturmbann, from which the Waffen SS recruited the best men for itself.[7]

By the end of 1941, this practice had yielded only 600 recruits, not enough to suit Gottlob Berger. Therefore, in late 1942, when Himmler and Berger decided to launch a major recruiting effort the following year, the minority in Slovakia became a prime target. The Foreign Ministry paved the way with a treaty according to which the Slovaks consented to the voluntary enlistment of *Volksdeutsche* in the Waffen SS. Those who joined would retain their Slovak citizenship. The Slovaks also agreed to facilitate the transfer of funds from the Reich for paying allowances to the recruits' dependents.[8]

The SS was now free to recruit openly, and the minority leadership was expected to cooperate. The agreement did not sanction induction, but the forceful measures the DP employed to get young men to enlist stopped just short of that. VoMi's participation was minimal, limited mostly to publicizing the recruitment and relaying orders to the DP leadership. Although the 1943 campaign brought in 5,390 Carpathian Germans, Berger and Himmler were still not satisfied.[9] Therefore, in January 1944, as the Reich's military situation worsened, Berger, with the approval of both the Foreign Ministry and VoMi, imposed not only a mandatory Reich military obligation on Slovakia's Germans but also mandatory labor service. It was not until June, however, that the Slovaks, demoralized by their declining fortunes in the war, agreed to place their *Volksdeutsche* at the exclusive disposal of the Reich's armed forces, which in practice meant the Waffen SS. They even transferred the 1,700 Germans still serving with what was left of the Slovak army to Reich military units.[10] In effect they had surrendered to the Reich all authority over their German population, whose minority status, for all practical purposes, had ended.

Before 1944, the war had not been overly difficult for the Carpathian Germans. Other than contributing manpower for both the Waffen SS and the Reich labor force, they had suffered few hardships. Food supplies were adequate, as were most other necessities. And above all, the battle front remained far away. But by 1944 the situation had worsened. The eastern front was rapidly approaching, and by summer, Allied bombing had reached Bratislava. Another cause for alarm was increased resistance. Karmasin reported that the Slovak army was disintegrating and deserters were joining the "communists." Most vexing were rumors of Germans fighting in the resistance. As attacks on *Volksdeutsche* settlements increased, Karmasin pleaded for Reich assistance.[11]

The 23 August 1944 coup in Rumania, which resulted in its reversal from an ally to an enemy of the Reich, encouraged resistance throughout southeastern Europe. On 29 August an uprising erupted in Slovakia, directed against both the German presence and the pro-German regime. The Reich poured troops into the country, and all *Volksdeutsche* men were mobilized into a militia, the Heimatschutz. The local Germans suffered terribly, especially in central Slovakia, the center of the revolt. Mass executions, abductions, plunder, rape, and countless other outrages were perpetrated against the *Volksdeutsche*.[12] These atrocities previewed what *Volksdeutsche* living throughout German-occupied eastern Europe could expect as the protection of the Reich military collapsed.

With the uprising, the issue of evacuation became critical. On 5 September, Karmasin suggested the complete removal of the minority, but VoMi, hesitant to countermand the Reich's policy of maintaining a German presence in the region, consented only to a partial withdrawal. In the midst of these hostilities, VoMi commandos, working with the local militia and Reich military units, began removing women and children to safer ground. Not until November did Himmler order all Germans removed from Slovakia—by force, if necessary. By then the uprising had been suppressed, but the Soviet menace was at hand. The Red Army had entered Slovakia during the last days of October.[13]

The evacuation served more than humanitarian purposes. Not only were the *Volksdeutsche* rescued, but much industrial and agricultural equipment was salvaged—or, from the Slovak perspective, plundered. In this endeavor VoMi collaborated with the Four Year Plan Office, removing not only equipment but also recently harvested grain. By mid-October much machinery had been relocated to Cracow, still considered a relatively secure area. The Slovak regime, realizing that the end was approaching and they were being abandoned, became uncooperative, even obstructive.[14]

The evacuation and the German military retreat ended the centuries-old German presence in the Carpathian region. On 4 April 1945 the Soviet army entered Bratislava. By then most of the *Volksdeutsche* had been evacuated, but a large number had refused to leave and chose to take their chances with the Russians and the returning Czechoslovakian authorities. According to some sources, as many as 20,000 remained behind.[15]

Events in the late summer of 1940 drew Hungary firmly into the Axis camp and consequently altered the status of its German minority. The most notable event, the Second Vienna Award of 30 August, transferred to Hungary the northwestern regions of Rumania, including northern Transylvania and the Sathmar area, along with their estimated 45,000 *Volksdeutsche*. In appreciation for the Reich's support in the process and as a gesture of goodwill, the Magyars officially recognized the German minority as a legal, corporate entity and sanctioned the Volksbund der Deutsche in Ungarn (VDU) as the group's official organ.[16]

Just two weeks earlier, a lesser event, the dedication of the new VDU headquarters in Budapest, underscored the importance of Hungary's Germans in the wartime relations between Hungary and the Reich. The presence of Reich and Hungarian dignitaries, among them several SS men—including a frequent visitor to Budapest, Werner Lorenz—accentuated the significance of these *Volksdeutsche*.[17] Lorenz's organization, VoMi, remained primarily responsible for directing the minority in the interest of maintaining the German-Hungarian partnership. Whereas in neighboring Slovakia, Reich security agencies such as the SD enforced the obedience of the local German minority, in Hungary, which enjoyed far greater independence, the Reich could not act as brazenly. VoMi's more discreet methods were less likely to arouse the Magyars and served the Reich better. VoMi's goal was to nurture good relations between Germans and Magyars and thereby reinforce the formal ties between Hungary and the Reich. At the very least, it hoped to prevent the minority from creating difficulties that could complicate the partnership.

The goodwill generated by the Vienna Award was fleeting. By the end of March 1941 clashes were occurring between Magyars and Germans.[18] Straining Reich-Hungarian relations further was the status of Hungary's unredeemed southern irredenta, still held by Rumania and Yugoslavia. At Vienna the Magyars had unsuccessfully sought these territories as well, but Rumania kept the eastern Banat, and the Yugoslavian share, the Vojvodina, was never at issue. The latter region, however, became a contested prize of war in the spring of 1941. The Reich had led the Hungarians to believe that in return for their participation in the invasion of Yugoslavia, they would receive this territory. Having different views were many of the *Volksdeutsche* living in the region, who anticipated an outright annexation to the Reich, or at least some sort of autonomous status under German rule.[19] Reconciling these conflicting expectations, as VoMi discovered, was no easy matter.

After the invasion of Yugoslavia, the actions of the Hungarian military, which occupied some of these disputed lands, did little to bolster the Reich-Hungarian alliance. For instance, the Hungarian commander in Novi Sad ordered the removal of all Nazi emblems and banners and declared that henceforth the Führer of the region was the Hungarian regent Miklos Horthy, not Adolf Hitler.[20] Hearing of this and other incidents, Lorenz rushed to Novi Sad. The local Germans complained to him that when hostilities had begun, before the arrival of the Hungarians, they had disarmed the Serbs with little bloodshed. But when the Hungarians appeared, they began to shoot indiscriminately, even at Germans, and treated the Germans much worse than had the Serbs.[21]

In part the Magyar quest for the irredenta succeeded. The Reich allowed Hungary to annex Bačka and the Baranya (parts of the Vojvodina) and a small section of Slovenia known as Prekomurje (Murgebiet). These additions brought an estimated 175,000 more *Volksdeutsche* under Hungarian rule, thereby increasing the size of the minority to 700,000 and making it the largest organized German minority group in Europe. Many of the transferred *Volksdeutsche* had expected to come under some sort of German rule and were bitterly disappointed. Minority leader Franz Basch tried to calm them, but when the more vocal activists ignored his appeal to cooperate with the Magyars, he turned to VoMi. VoMi, aware of the importance of the Reich's territorial deal with Hungary, warned the dissidents to accept Hungarian rule and obey their VDU leaders.[22]

One reason for maintaining tranquil relations was Hitler's plan to expand the role of the Hungarian army in Russia in the fall of 1941. Several Magyar generals had openly expressed their annoyance with *Volksdeutsche* agitation, and ruffled feathers at the highest levels of the military could impede securing Hungarian cooperation. In mid-November, VoMi summoned Basch to Berlin and stressed the importance of improving relations. This scolding had little effect, and in

February, Behrends personally ordered Basch to cease all criticism of the Hungarians, even when they were violating minority rights. The *Volksdeutsche* must give the authorities no cause for complaint.[23]

Since no Reich authority in Hungary was in a position to impose its will directly on the *Volksdeutsche*, VoMi found enforcing its orders difficult. Its most effective leverage remained its control over Reich subsidies. But even this method was becoming less effective. Although Hungary's recognition in 1940 of the special relationship between the minority and the Reich facilitated the distribution of funds to the minority—since the Reich embassy in Budapest no longer had to distribute these funds secretly—a new complication arose. The clearing process, to which Hungary adhered scrupulously, obstructed the transfer of currency. By March 1942 the Reich had already accumulated a deficit of 240 million RM with Hungary.[24]

Another reason for regulating *Volksdeutsche* behavior was the Reich's interest in tapping this reservoir of German manpower for the Waffen SS. This enterprise, no less than that of securing Hungarian military participation in the war against the Soviet Union, depended on the good graces of Budapest. Before the Vienna Award, very few Hungarian *Volksdeutsche* enlisted in the Waffen SS. But as of August 1940, the SS exploited the officially recognized relationship between the minority and the Reich to escalate its efforts. SS recruiters lured young *Volksdeutsche* to the Reich on the pretext of participating in work or play. Once there, they were subjected to propaganda and military training, with an option to join the Waffen SS. Himmler's boldest attempt came in January 1941 when he instructed VoMi to arrange to bring 500 young men to the Reich on the pretext of working at the Hermann Göring Works.[25]

But such ploys brought limited results, as well as the displeasure of the Reich Foreign Ministry, which had to placate irate Magyar authorities who got wind of these activities. Finally, in January 1942, Himmler asked Ribbentrop to get Budapest's permission for open SS recruitment. After arduous negotiations, in February the Hungarians agreed to a voluntary recruitment of 20,000 *Volksdeutsche*. They insisted, however, that on enlistment, the recruits immediately lost their Hungarian citizenship. Furthermore, Germans serving in the Honved, the Hungarian armed forces, were off-limits.[26]

The recruitment of 1942, conducted openly, enlisted more than 18,000 *Volksdeutsche*. Enlistment was voluntary, but pressure on young

Germans from the SS, the VDU, and even from home left them with little real choice but to sign up. Those who did not enlist were publicly reviled.[27] The Hungarians, who had expected a meager turnout, were both surprised and dismayed at the response. They obstructed the recruitment, at the local level by enforcing the agreement to the letter and at the higher reaches by strictly controlling currency exchange. Because of exchange shortages on the Reich side, payments to SS dependents living in Hungary were often in arrears, and the authorities did nothing to help. As a result, the morale of SS soldiers declined, which in turn had a negative effect on recruitment.[28] VoMi did its best to alleviate the day-to-day hardships of SS dependents and countered negative publicity about SS service with its own more upbeat propaganda.

In early March 1943, following the German disaster at Stalingrad, Himmler ordered yet another levy of 30,000–50,000 recruits from Hungary. VoMi officials doubted whether that many young men would still be available in the civilian population. But what Himmler had in mind were the *Volksdeutsche* in the Honved. The Foreign Ministry approached the Hungarians on the issue, and by late April they had consented to another recruitment. On 22 May the Reich and Hungary signed an agreement whereby Germans serving in the Honved would become eligible.[29] After their own military debacle at Voronezh, the Hungarians had lost their enthusiasm for the war and were willing to let their *Volksdeutsche* fight all they wanted and with whom they pleased. By August, Lorenz reported that the campaign had netted 22,000 men, 18,216 of whom were accepted into the Waffen SS. By the end of 1943, a total of 22,125 *Volksdeutsche* from Hungary were fighting in the Waffen SS, and another 1,729 had managed to find their way into the Wehrmacht—much to Himmler's displeasure. Still, an estimated 35,000 remained in the Honved, apparently declining the opportunity to enlist with the Waffen SS.[30]

In early 1944, as the Waffen SS continued to suffer horrendous casualties and as the Reich's military fortunes worsened, Himmler planned for another muster. His opportunity came with the Reich's military occupation of Hungary on 19 March. Increased Hungarian reluctance to pursue the war prompted the Reich to preempt a possible reversal of Hungary's alliance. Hungary was reduced to only a semblance of independence, and the Reich lost most of what remained of pro-German sympathies among Hungarians. The public mood toward the *Volksdeutsche* turned hostile.

The occupation resulted in a new, far more compliant government under Döme Sztójay, which on 14 April concluded yet another treaty on military service. According to this treaty, *Volksdeutsche* no longer enjoyed the option of choosing between the SS or the Honved. They had to serve in the SS. Furthermore, they were allowed to keep their Hungarian citizenship, an important provision, since it underscored the consent of Budapest. With this treaty, Hungary transferred to the Reich its sovereignty over the military service of its German subjects. As a result, whether they chose to or not, 40,000 additional men entered the Waffen SS. By the end of the war, some 120,000 *Volksdeutsche* from Hungary and its annexed territories had served in Himmler's units.[31]

Most *Volksdeutsche* welcomed the March occupation. Reich military presence helped allay their anxieties over the advancing Red Army and their increasingly hostile Magyar neighbors. But the new situation troubled many of them, since the Reich was demanding even greater sacrifices. The Waffen SS conscripted virtually all males, and to keep in step with the anti-Jewish campaign of the Sztójay regime, the VDU launched its own belated, but thorough, racial purging. The minority also had to satisfy greater economic demands as the VoMi economic staff insisted on a total mobilization for the war effort.

Whatever hopes these *Volksdeutsche* had for a favorable end to the war were dashed with the Rumanian coup of 23 August. With Rumania's reversal, the front was suddenly at the Hungarian border, and the safety of the *Volksdeutsche* was in jeopardy. Although the Sztójay regime was decidedly pro-German, the Reich felt insecure about the Hungarian commitment, and in view of the Rumanian turnabout, it helped orchestrate a coup on 15 October that removed the head of state, Admiral Miklós Horthy, and installed a true puppet, Ferenc Szálasi. By this time many *Volksdeutsche* were already fleeing westward, not far ahead of the invading Soviet army, which crossed into Hungary at the end of October. By Christmas the Soviets had occupied most of Hungary east of Lake Balaton and Budapest. German forces in Budapest fiercely held out until February 1945, a desperate resistance resulting in the destruction of the beautiful city. Employed in its defense were several Waffen SS divisions with large contingents of Hungarian *Volksdeutsche*. Most of Budapest's defenders, including the *Volksdeutsche*, and indeed the majority of Hungary's *Volksdeutsche*, did not escape. Despite VoMi's efforts to evacuate them, many, for reasons that will be discussed in the next chapter, did not leave.

• • • RUMANIA

Three events occurring in the late summer and early fall of 1940 marked the beginning of the wartime period for the German minority in Rumania: the Vienna Award of 30 August; the appointment in September of Andreas Schmidt, Gottlob Berger's son-in-law, as the leader of the minority; and the Bessarabian-Bukovina resettlement of September and October. VoMi's subsequent policy toward this minority, determined in part by these events, followed the Reich's overall policy toward Rumania. Hitler regarded it as the key state in south-eastern Europe and a crucial element in his wartime strategy. He anticipated utilizing Rumanian manpower on the eastern front and included Rumania's agricultural production and oil resources in his strategical calculations. To gain Rumanian cooperation in providing manpower and sharing its resources, the Reich tended to favor the interests of the Rumanians over those of the German minority.

Keeping the minority satisfied and willing to contribute to the war effort while at the same time persuading the minority to accept its subordinate position was VoMi's task in Rumania. The events of 1940 simplified this mission somewhat. The Vienna Award, which deprived Rumania of northern Transylvania and the Sathmar region, along with the resettlement from Bessarabia and Bukovina, reduced the minority by about 200,000 people. The more than half a million remaining in the rest of the country constituted a more prosperous and more homogeneous minority, far easier to keep unified and disciplined. Furthermore, even though the Rumanians harbored some resentment toward the Reich for its role in the territorial concessions, they now found themselves far more dependent on the Reich and thus became more obliging on most matters, including the *Volksdeutsche*.

The Vienna Award also served VoMi's purposes by obligating the Rumanians to abide by the minority protection laws already on their books but not respected in the past. On 20 November the Rumanian leader, Marshal Ion Antonescu, recognized the Deutsche Volksgruppe in Rumänien (DVR) as the official organ of the minority, a step that in effect created an autonomous German state within Rumania.[32] Although the Rumanians cooperated on most issues, they, like most other clients, stood firm on the clearing arrangements, thereby obstructing Reich efforts to subsidize the local *Volksdeutsche*.

The other fateful event for the minority in the fall of 1940 was the installment of the SS man Andreas Schmidt as its leader, replacing long-time leader Fritz Fabritius. Schmidt, a Rumanian *Volksdeutscher* and son-in-law of Gottlob Berger, first attracted VoMi's attention in early 1940 during a clandestine Waffen SS recruitment. His energetic efforts impressed Himmler as well as the VoMi leadership, which came to rely on Schmidt as one of its most trusted men in Rumania.[33] Shortly after assuming his new post, Schmidt reorganized the minority more along Nazi lines, formally renaming the DVR as the NSDAP der Deutschen Volksgruppe in Rumänien and bringing its paramilitary formation, the Einsatzstaffel, under SS control.[34]

Indebted to VoMi and the SS for his position, Schmidt was far more dependent on them than were his counterparts Basch in Hungary and Karmasin in Slovakia, both recognized by their constituents as legitimate leaders. Schmidt, although a local *Volksdeutscher*, was seen as an imposition from the outside. Loyal to VoMi in most ways, on the issue of Waffen SS recruitment, Schmidt stood firmly with his father-in-law, Berger. He tended to view and promote Waffen SS interests as SS and Reich interests. He was prepared to go to any lengths and take any measures to fill recruitment quotas, even if doing so impeded other SS activities or interfered with other aspects of the Reich's war effort. This tendency often frustrated VoMi, which was balancing several interests, as well as the Foreign Ministry, which was responsible for maintaining good relations with Rumania.

VoMi became entangled in the SS recruitment business in Rumania before the war. The first recruits were refugees who either had fled Rumania to evade induction into the military or, already in the ranks, had deserted. The Rumanian military was notorious for its harsh treatment of non-Rumanians, and as a result many Magyars and Germans deserted. By the fall of 1939, as Rumania prepared for war and stepped up its inductions, the flow of defectors increased. To VoMi fell the task of housing them in its refugee camps, where they became easy prey to the Waffen SS.[35]

Fearing diplomatic repercussions, VoMi ordered the minority leadership to halt the desertions. But Berger had instructed Schmidt to muster another 1,000 men. Evidently neither VoMi nor the Foreign Ministry knew about this scheme. In fact, many of the deserters arriving in the Reich were among Schmidt's clandestine 1,000, those who had been unable to obtain valid exit visas. Having discovered the secret operation and faced with an accomplished fact, VoMi and the Foreign Ministry sought to legitimize the campaign. On the personal intercession of Ribbentrop, the Rumanians granted permission for 1,000 young *Volksdeutsche* to leave the country under the pretext of going to the Reich as agricultural laborers. But rather than applying the permission retroactively to those already enlisted, the SS regarded it as sanction for another levy. VoMi dutifully assisted in the operation, and by mid-June 1940, 1,060 "agricultural laborers" traveled by ship up the Danube to enlist in the Waffen SS.[36]

In January 1941, Himmler, encouraged by his earlier success, ordered yet another 1,000 recruits from Rumania. This operation, like the preceding one, was overtly a labor recruitment.[37] But in the meantime the Rumanian political situation changed. Marshal Antonescu had crushed a revolt of the Iron Guard, a Rumanian fascist organization, and had thereby strengthened his position. He was eager to enhance Rumania's ties to the Reich in hopes of gaining its support for territorial revisions. As evidence of his commitment, he ordered a military buildup, which meant the induction of more *Volksdeutsche*. As a gesture of goodwill toward the Reich and in an effort to make service in the Rumanian armed forces more palatable to *Volksdeutsche*, Antonescu ordered better treatment of German recruits and declared an amnesty for all deserters who wished to return to Rumania.[38]

Desiring good relations with Rumania and in consideration of the upcoming military effort in Russia—which required Rumanian participation—the Reich could not ignore the marshal's generosity or bother him with further requests for *Volksdeutsche* recruits. The overzealous Schmidt, however, was already seeking out more. Ribbentrop was furious when he learned of this, but rather than halt the recruitment, he approached Antonescu one more time to obtain retroactive consent. The marshal agreed, and 500 more young men departed for the Reich. Berger still was not satisfied, and the Waffen SS continued to encourage desertions. Incensed with Berger, Ribbentrop ordered an immediate stop to all recruitment of Rumanian *Volksdeutsche*. Evidently he had Hitler's support, for a few days later Himmler informed both Lorenz and Berger that after discussing the matter with the foreign minister, he too was ordering a moratorium on enlistments from Rumania. In view of upcoming events, the Rumanian military buildup deserved the Reich's support.[39]

German desertions continued. The stream turned into a flood in early 1943 after the Rumanians shared in the devastating defeat at Stalingrad. Rumanians retreated in disarray and in a mutinous mood. In the confusion, *Volksdeutsche* serving with the Rumanian forces simply walked over to German units. Berger suggested to Himmler that conditions were opportune for a recruitment, since the demoralized Rumanians would now be willing to let their Germans continue fighting—in Reich units, if they wished. Himmler agreed and asked the Foreign Ministry to obtain Antonescu's permission to recruit some 20,000–30,000 more men. The marshal agreed but did not approve recruiting from within the Rumanian armed forces—the primary target of the SS.[40]

The Waffen SS recruiters went to work. Disregarding Antonescu's prohibition, they enlisted many Germans still in the armed forces. The Rumanian authorities, disheartened by the war and disillusioned with the German alliance, looked the other way. The recruitment went smoothly, but problems arose regarding the financing of the new troops. As elsewhere, the exchange problem impeded providing for dependents, and Antonescu adamantly refused to make any concessions. By the fall of 1943, desperate dependents were taking to the streets to demonstrate their plight. Rumors began to circulate that the minority leadership had misappropriated money for SS families, prompting demands for Schmidt's removal. Schmidt, who had been at best tolerated as minority leader, pleaded with Lorenz—and probably with his father-in-law as well—to have Himmler take the issue to Hitler, who in turn could address Antonescu.[41] Schmidt's entreaties were in vain. The currency problem continued, and his popularity plummeted. But he had been a highly successful recruiter. By the end of 1943, 54,000 Rumanian *Volksdeutsche* were serving with the Waffen SS.[42]

The notion began to spread among Rumania's *Volksdeutsche* that they were making far greater sacrifices than Germans elsewhere. Their resentment focused on Schmidt, who had overtly served the interests of the Waffen SS rather than theirs. Demands for his ouster became more vocal. The German Lutheran church in Transylvania openly criticized the leadership. Many *Volksdeutsche*, fed up with the war and unfulfilled promises, spoke derisively of "*Adolf von Berchtesgaden und Schmidt von Bergers Gnaden.*"[43]

The defection of Germany's primary ally, Italy, and the collapsing eastern front in 1943 further eroded *Volksdeutsche* morale. Adding to their anxieties was the growing disenchantment among Rumanians over the German alliance. Only the most radical of the fascist Hora Sima supporters could be relied on as friends of Nazi Germany. The Rumanian authorities—usually renowned for their anti-Semitism—were reluctant to follow the Reich's example in Jewish matters, which VoMi interpreted as evidence of their weakening resolve. By March 1944, VoMi was reporting increased "bandit" activity in some areas of Rumania.[44]

After the German occupation of Hungary on 19 March 1944, many Rumanian *Volksdeutsche*, concerned for their safety, hoped for a similar takeover in their country. But the Rumanians remained in control. Indeed, Rumania was the only Reich ally in the southeast that never officially surrendered all of its authority over its German subjects. Whereas by the end of the war the other client states had transferred to the Reich the right to deal with their *Volksdeutsche* as it saw fit, Rumania, although making concessions, managed to evade the final, ultimate surrender.

On 23 August 1944 the Reich's and the minority's worst fears materialized. The Soviet offensive into Rumania prompted King Michael and the opposition to depose Antonescu. On the following day, the new regime reversed Rumania's alliances and declared war on Germany. Reich officials as well as the local *Volksdeutsche*, although aware of growing anti-German feelings, were caught completely by surprise. The Reich military managed to withdraw in order, but the *Volksdeutsche* were not as fortunate. Events were so precipitous that only those of northern Transylvania and the western Banat managed to escape. The rest, including virtually the entire *Volksgruppe* in the rest of Transylvania, were left to an uncertain fate. In Sibiu, the headquarters of the DVR, the Rumanians arrested the entire minority leadership, except for Schmidt—who was nowhere to be found.[45]

After the 23 August coup, VoMi lost all contact with the *Volksdeutsche* in the interior. With the leadership in custody and Schmidt gone, the anti-Nazi Hans Otto Roth became the minority's spokesman. Roth sought the best possible terms from Juliu Maniu, one of Rumania's new leaders, but Maniu promised him nothing. There was absolutely nothing VoMi, or for that matter anyone in the Reich, could do for the captive minority. VoMi officials decided that the most prudent policy was to refrain from any action and hoped that Roth's merits as a known anti-Nazi could ensure the safety of the *Volksdeutsche*.[46]

Schmidt, having surfaced in the Reich, refused to accept the inevitable. He wanted to return to Rumania and organize resistance against the Soviets. Himmler approved and ordered Otto Skorzeny, the hero of Mussolini's rescue, to help Schmidt prepare commandos for a guerrilla war in Transylvania. On the night of 6 November, Schmidt and seven others, equipped for waging guerrilla war for six months, were flown over Sibiu for an airborne assault, but a heavy cloud cover prevented their jump. On the return flight the plane developed mechanical problems, and the crew and the commandos parachuted behind enemy lines in Hungary. The pilot and one commando found their way back to Budapest, but Schmidt was not heard from again.[47]

Schmidt's foolhardy, desperate mission ended the Reich's and VoMi's contacts with a large part of the minority in Rumania, in particular the Transylvania Saxons. Their fate—arrests, deportations, expulsion, life in Communist Rumania—is a topic beyond the scope of this study. As for the rest, those living farther west, including many of the Danube Swabians of the Banat, their ties with the Reich and VoMi continued, at least for the time being. They were among the first of the refugees from the southeast to flee to the Reich seeking safe haven.

• • • SERBIA-BANAT

The dismemberment of Yugoslavia after its defeat in April 1941 was complete. As its territory was partitioned, so was its German minority. The *Volksdeutsche* living in lands annexed directly to the Reich assumed Reich citizenship, as did most of those in Italian areas, from which they were resettled to the Reich. As for the rest, they would retain minority status, either by having their lands transferred to Hungary or by remaining in Croatia or Serbia-Banat, the two successor states of Yugoslavia. These latter *Volksdeutsche*, by virtue of the special relationships between their two states and the Reich, enjoyed privileges and status placing them above the majority peoples.

After the conquest, the Reich set up a puppet Serbian administration, under General Milovan Nedić and subordinate to the German military commander in Belgrade. Attached to Serbia was an autonomous Banat, that part of the former Vojvodina east of the Tisza (Theiss) River and north and east of Belgrade. The resident Danube Swabians opposed its transfer to Hungary—as Hitler had promised Horthy—and advocated instead that all territories inhabited by Swabians be unified into a separate German land. The Reich rejected that idea, for it would have meant not only divesting Rumania of even more territory but also defaulting on its promise to restore these lands to Hungary. The Reich's partnerships with Rumania and Hungary were more important than the wishes of the Swabians. The Reich delivered two sections of the Vojvodina, Bačka and Baranya, to Hungary but kept the Banat under Reich occupation. The reason appears to have been strategical. Hitler regarded Belgrade as the key to controlling southeastern Europe and believed that the city would be more secure if the Banat remained in German hands.[48]

The military occupation of Serbia brought the local *Volksdeutsche* special privileges, including complete cultural and political autonomy. Although nominally under the Serbian administration, in reality they answered only to the German military commander, the real power in Belgrade. Here VoMi also came under the same authority, through the local HSSPF attached to the commander.[49] VoMi had little input in making important decisions and mostly performed routine, technical functions such as providing cultural, social, and economic care for the minority. Its most vital, regular duty was supervising the agriculture of the fertile Banat and ensuring that its produce reached the Reich. Another task was providing security to partisan-endangered German communities and, as discussed earlier, evacuating the Germans when the threat became critical. One problem VoMi did not face in Serbia-Banat was that of currency exchange. Since Reich control was total, the puppet Serbs did not dare exercise even this limited measure of self-assertion, as did other Reich clients.

Himmler's appointment of VoMi Chief of Staff Behrends as HSSPF for Serbia-Banat in the fall of 1943 strengthened VoMi's position, for it appears that in his new job, Behrends continued to look after VoMi's interests. But by then his primary chore was directing antipartisan operations and evacuating endangered *Volksdeutsche*. The general wartime rule that VoMi's influence and authority over a minority decreased in proportion to the Reich's increased control over a client state held true for Serbia-Banat.

Despite losing much of its authority over the minority, VoMi managed to retain Sepp Janko as minority leader. It installed him as chief of a new organization, the Deutsche Volksgruppe in Serbien und Banat (DVSB), which replaced the Schwäbisch-Deutsche Kulturbund as the official organ of the minority. Like other wartime minority organizations, the DVSB was restructured along the lines of the NSDAP. Its most important branch was the paramilitary formation, the Deutsche Mannschaft, which here, as elsewhere, came under the control of the SS.[50] Janko and the DVSB cooperated fully with VoMi, and as a step in the minority's total nazification, it even introduced a system of classifying the local *Volksdeutsche* similar to that used by the DVL in Poland. One advantage in belonging to the highest category—group A, racially and politically acceptable members of the German community—was entitlement to better food rations than were allotted to the rest of the population.[51] But after the war, belonging to this classification spelled certain doom—deportations, incarceration, or even death.

The overriding issue in Serbia-Banat affecting the minority was recruitment for the Waffen SS. Whereas in other, more independent states the local authorities played a decisive role, in Serbia-Banat the Serbs had no voice at all in this matter. Neither did VoMi. Because of the overwhelming Reich presence, including that of a powerful HSSPF, VoMi's discreet, if not always clandestine, approach to recruitment was unnecessary.

Few *Volksdeutsche* from Yugoslavia enlisted in the Waffen SS before its collapse, although in late December 1940, Himmler had instructed Berger to recruit 200 men from there. This operation, like those in Hungary and Rumania, was to be camouflaged as a labor recruitment.[52] When VoMi learned of the operation, Lorenz and Behrends met with Ribbentrop. They agreed that the situation in Yugoslavia was volatile and feared that its discovery could ignite the situation. They instructed their contacts in Belgrade to halt the campaign. When Himmler heard that VoMi had countermanded his orders, he summoned its two leaders for a tongue lashing, after which they dropped their opposition to the recruitment.[53] This was one of the more serious confrontations between the VoMi leaders and their SS superior over SS priorities and interests.

Yugoslavia's defeat opened the door to unhindered SS recruitment. The Waffen SS immediately enlisted 600 *Volksdeutsche*, and in July it announced plans for the formation of an exclusively German regiment. But in the Banat the SS encountered competition from the Wehrmacht, which had in mind sponsoring its own unit, a militia force of some 8,000 men. Himmler, alarmed by this development, took the case to Hitler and secured permission not only to create a new, exclusively *Volksdeutsche* SS division but also to take over the Wehrmacht's militia. Lorenz traveled to Serbia to announce in person the creation of the new SS formation.[54]

Himmler appointed the Transylvanian Arthur Phleps as commander of the new division, which officially became the 7th SS-Gebirgsdivision Prinz Eugen, named after the early-eighteenth-century Habsburg general Eugene of Savoy, who had campaigned in the Balkans against the Turks. But after the initial rush of *Volksdeutsche* to join, voluntary enlistments tapered off, and the new unit did not reach division size. Therefore, in August 1941, the SS discarded the voluntary approach, and after a favorable judgment from the SS court in Belgrade, imposed a mandatory military obligation on all *Volksdeutsche* in Serbia-Banat, the first of its kind for non-Reich Germans. Sepp Janko protested, but after Himmler ordered Lorenz—who also held reservations about the legality of the measure—to take Janko "by the tie" and inform him that the Reichsführer SS was displeased, Janko changed his tune.[55]

The mandatory military obligation became a fact of life, and by the end of December 1943, more than 22,000 Germans from Serbia-Banat were serving in the armed forces of the Reich, most of them in the Prinz Eugen Division. Although this unit consisted mostly of locals from Serbia-Banat, Germans from Rumania, Hungary, and especially Croatia found their way into its ranks. It operated almost entirely in Yugoslav territories in counterinsurgency warfare, earning a reputation for ferocious fighting and cruel atrocities. After its surrender in Slovenia in 1945, most of its members fell victim to bloody retaliation.[56] Another *Volksdeutsche* military unit, Michel Reiser, was formed in September 1944 to defend the Banat against the approaching Red Army, but little is known about its origins and exact status.[57]

The *Volksdeutsche* of Serbia were among the first German civilians to suffer directly at the hands of the enemy, beginning with the partisan offensive of July 1941, which required their evacuation. As for the Banat Germans, as late as January 1944, VoMi reported them in high spirits. Subsequent reports, however, reflected pessimism and eroding morale.[58] When the Rumanian reversal of August 1944 brought the war to the Banat frontier, VoMi decided to remove the Swabians as well. It persuaded many of them to leave, but surprisingly large numbers chose to remain. In October the Soviets occupied the Banat, and on 20 October, Tito's partisans captured Belgrade, snuffing out Hitler's hopes of constructing a German "Prinz Eugen" land.

• • • CROATIA

On 10 April 1941, four days after the invasion of Yugoslavia, Croat separatists proclaimed the independent state of Croatia, which included much of the historic crownland and most of Bosnia. Although the new state was nominally independent, there could be no doubt that it owed its new status to the Reich. The Croats conducted their foreign and domestic policies accordingly, particularly toward their 180,000 *Volksdeutsche*. The overwhelming majority lived in Slavonia-Syrmia, the region west of Belgrade between the Drava-Danube and the Sava rivers, with its principal city of Osijek (Esseg). The Croats granted the minority generous rights, including complete cultural autonomy and some political autonomy. Acknowledging the special ties between the *Volksdeutsche* and Germany, the Croats allowed them unhindered contact with the Reich, the wearing of Nazi uniforms, the display of swastikas, and the open espousal of National Socialism. One concession the Reich had sought for them but did not get was dual citizenship.[59]

In Croatia, as elsewhere in German-dominated southeastern Europe, preponderant Reich influence meant a lessening of VoMi's influence. Nevertheless, VoMi preserved for itself some authority—certainly more than in neighboring Serbia-Banat. In the face of strong opposition from other Reich interests, VoMi appointed Branimir Altgayer, its former liaison man in the area, as the leader of this new minority. VoMi's eternal nemesis, the AO, alleged that Altgayer not only was out of step with National Socialism but also was a reputed alcoholic and even a drug addict. Berger also tried to block the appointment, probably because Altgayer would be more concerned for the welfare of his constituents than for the manpower needs of the Waffen SS.[60]

Formerly members of the nationwide Schwäbisch-Deutsche Kulturbund, the Germans of Croatia founded the Nationalsozialistische

Deutsche Gefolgschaft (NSDG), which the Croats recognized as their official organ. As its name suggests, the NSDG modeled itself on the NSDAP. The Croats also created a state secretary post for Altgayer, who, perceiving some independence in this office, became a chronic source of trouble for VoMi. Because of his popularity with the Croatian authorities as well as his German constituents, Altgayer increasingly disregarded VoMi's instructions, especially when he believed that Reich demands conflicted with the best interests of his *Volksdeutsche*.[61]

VoMi's tasks in Croatia would have been relatively easy had it not been for Himmler's population schemes and Berger's recruitment drives. Himmler's designs for an exclusively German settlement area stretching across northern Yugoslavia interjected the *Volksdeutsche* into the historic, ongoing nationality struggle among Serbs, Croats, Slovenes, and Moslem Bosnians. The plan, which required the immediate removal of Slovenes by the Germans and of Serbs by the Croats, aggravated the nationality situation and resulted in violence and countless atrocities. The local *Volksdeutsche*, who over the years had stood apart from these quarrels, were now drawn in. And since they were also associated with the German invaders, they became targets of partisans as well as victims of the fighting between the Croatian paramilitary organization, the Ustaša, and the Serbian Chetniks.[62]

Some *Volksdeutsche* were evacuated, but as for the rest, the situation required their military preparation. The SS organized some into militias, but it also tried to recruit them for its own ranks. Immediately after the collapse of Yugoslavia, the SS began recruiting in Croatia, but the initial results were disappointing. One reason was the generosity of the Croats, who created exclusively German units within the Croatian army and even accepted the minority's paramilitary formation, the Einsatzstaffel der Deutsche Mannschaft, into the Ustaša. These arrangements enabled the local Germans to serve together and nearer to home. Therefore the Waffen SS, which sent them to fight in foreign lands, was not as attractive to them as it was to the Germans in Hungary and Rumania.[63]

The SS was displeased with these military arrangements and wanted greater access to Croatia's *Volksdeutsche*. In September 1941 the Croats agreed to make 10 percent of all eligible *Volksdeutsche* available to the Waffen SS and the Wehrmacht, which still competed for recruits in Yugoslavia. Until the summer of 1942, recruits from Croatia were assigned to various Waffen SS units, but in June, Himmler decided to place them exclusively in the Prinz Eugen Division, operating in nearby Serbia. Doing so would make the Waffen SS more attractive. The recruits would remain closer to home and would be fighting against forces menacing their Croatian homeland. Recruitment improved, but Himmler and Berger also wanted access to the Germans serving in the Croatian army. In July, Ribbentrop initiated talks with the Croats on the transfer of these units to the Prinz Eugen Division.[64] Although the Croats would not agree to such transfers, they were willing to place all *Volksdeutsche* not yet serving in their military at the full disposal of the Reich. But Berger refused to honor this agreement and continued to recruit whomever he pleased. Lorenz became especially incensed when Berger—in violation of the recently concluded agreement—attempted to enlist the entire *Volksdeutsche* contingent of the Croatian labor service.[65]

As long as Himmler ordered more levies, Berger filled the orders. By mid-November 1942, the SS had enlisted some 4,000 *Volksdeutsche* from Croatia, but far more were needed.[66] The defeat at Stalingrad in early 1943, along with bolder partisan activity closer to home, increased the demand for more soldiers. A few months earlier, in December, Hitler had ordered the Prinz Eugen Division to extend its area of operations to Croatia, placing additional pressure on the minority to support the Waffen SS. Finally, in the spring of 1943, the Reich coerced the Croats to introduce obligatory military service for their Volksdeutsche in the armed forces of the Reich, which in practice meant the Waffen SS. The Croats also conceded the transfer of German units from their army to the SS. By year's end, 17,538 Croatian *Volksdeutsche* were serving in the ranks of the Waffen SS, almost all in the Prinz Eugen Division.[67]

The Foreign Ministry and VoMi occasionally protested the recruitment methods and the heavy sacrifices demanded of this minority. But by mid-1943 one reason for their complaints, fear of alienating the Croats, was no longer valid. The situation in Croatia had deteriorated to the point that Himmler declared most of the country a combat zone, and the Reich military and security forces paid little attention to the Zagreb regime. All able-bodied Germans were mobilized. Those working in the Reich were recalled home. It should be noted that all of Croatia's *Volksdeutsche* did not fight on the side of the Reich. By August, an anti-Reich German guerrilla band—the Ernst Thälmann company, named after a German Communist—was operating in Slavonia. Other *Volksdeutsche*, as individuals, were joining the partisans.[68]

As early as June 1942, at the time of the Bosnian resettlement, Lorenz and Himmler had discussed the possibility of evacuating the *Volksdeutsche* from Croatia but had decided against it, since it would have appeared to be a prelude to abandoning Croatia.[69] By the end of 1943, though, the plight of Croatia's Germans was critical. By then, disappointing the Croats no longer mattered, and evacuation became a strong possibility. In January 1944, Lorenz visited Croatia to appraise the situation firsthand. He met with various officials, including the Croatian leader, Ante Pavelič. The situation was hopeless. The only tangible results of Lorenz's trip were an agreement to establish a German-Croatian friendship society and Pavelič's conferring on him the Great Order of the Crown of King Zvonimir.[70] Decorations and trappings were all that was left of shortlived Croatia.

Throughout the spring of 1944, reports told of countless atrocities against *Volksdeutsche*. The only option was evacuation. During the summer, VoMi commandos, along with the military, mostly from the SS, evacuated some 24,000 *Volksdeutsche* to east Syrmia, the last bastion of Germandom in Croatia.[71] Other Germans fled north to the Reich on their own. Until August the evacuations were piecemeal, but with the defection of Rumania and the advance of the Russians, a total evacuation could be delayed no longer. Rumors that both the partisans and the Chetniks had ordered the liquidation of all Germans added a sense of utmost urgency.[72]

It was not until September that VoMi received permission to begin the general evacuation of Croatia, which was not concluded a day too soon. As the partisans and Russians were entering Belgrade on 20 October, the last caravans of *Volksdeutsche* were departing Syrmia and Slavonia for Austria and Hungary. Most of the evacuees were women, children, and the elderly. The majority of the men remained in Croatia fighting the partisans and the Soviets until the final German capitulation.

• • NORTH SCHLESWIG

The only organized German minority outside southeastern Europe that continued to exist as such during the war years was that of North

Schleswig. After invading Denmark on 9 April 1940, Hitler hoped to control it with a minimum of resources and effort. He expected all Germanic peoples, including the supposedly racially superior Scandinavians, to rule alongside Germans as *Herrenvolk* over the new European racial order.[73] The Danes were important in Hitler's plans as a bridge to the Scandinavians, and in order to gain their cooperation, he planned to make the occupation of Denmark as benign as possible. During the first two years, the Reich Plenipotentiary for Denmark, Cecil von Renthe-Fink, pursued a lenient, conciliatory policy, as did all Reich interests and authorities in the country, including VoMi.

The Reich's policy toward the Germans of North Schleswig followed the general policy toward Denmark. On the day of the invasion, the Foreign Ministry instructed VoMi Chief of Staff Behrends to inform the minority what was expected of it. By setting an example of neighborly relations with the Danes, the 40,000 *Volksdeutsche* of North Schleswig would preview how Germanic peoples were to live together in the new racial order. Above all, they were to silence their demands for a border revision. Annexation to the Reich, at least for the time being, was out of the question.[74]

VoMi relayed the message to the minority, but minority leader Jens Möller was reluctant to comply, since border revision was the top priority of his constituents.[75] Another group unhappy with the Reich's policy was the indigenous Danish Nazi Party, the Dansk National Socialistik Arbejder Partiet (DNSAP), led by Fritz Clausen. The Danish Nazis had hoped for a coup of some sort that would have given them at least some say in Copenhagen. Instead, the Reich refrained from any immediate changes. Any significant concessions to the minority or to the Danish Nazis—who enjoyed very little popular support—would have upset the Danes and undermined Hitler's policy for Denmark.[76]

Responsibility for maintaining order and balancing the interests of the Reich, the majority of Danes, the Danish Nazis, and the German minority fell to Renthe-Fink. But it was VoMi's duty to keep the minority in check and prevent it from disrupting the delicate balance. Its officials soon realized this would be no simple matter, and in November they summoned Möller to Berlin. They stressed again the importance of suppressing the border issue and voiced concern about the close ties between the minority and the Danish Nazis, whom the overwhelming majority of Danes disliked. The Reich's attitude toward the Danish Nazis was ambivalent. Although the Reich wanted to distance itself and the minority from the Nazis, the latter were the only Danes who wholeheartedly supported the Reich and its plans to include Denmark as a partner in the new racial order.[77]

In accordance with Hitler's wishes to respect Danish national sovereignty as much as possible, at least for the first two years of occupation, Reich security forces in Denmark kept a low profile and minimized their activities. As a result, VoMi's dealings with the minority hardly differed from its prewar approach. It relied on political recognition and financial support as the most effective means for enforcing compliance. But a major obstacle was the exchange problem. Denmark, cooperative in most other respects, persisted in a business-like adherence to the clearing system. Consequently, VoMi's payments to the minority were constantly in arrears, and its political leverage at times lacked sufficient clout. These subsidies were also vital to the German farmers of North Schleswig, an important source of agricultural products for the Reich. VoMi's economic section helped organize the farmers for war production, but as long as the subsidies were inadequate or irregular, getting the produce to market was no easy task.[78]

Another major issue in North Schleswig was military service. It was more complicated here than in the southeast. Whereas in the southeast, SS recruitment at least initially was limited to Germans, in Denmark, from the outset, the SS also aimed at enlisting the supposedly racially valuable Danes. Indeed, enlistment of Danes became the primary goal of the SS, since the manpower that the relatively small German minority could muster was negligible in comparison with the large number of potential Nordic soldiers among the Danes.

Here, as elsewhere, the SS recruited *Volksdeutsche* before the war, but it was not until after April 1940 that it escalated its efforts. Hitler had a personal interest in SS activities in Denmark and ordered the stationing of a Waffen SS company in North Schleswig. He hoped it would attract both Danes and Germans to the new Germanic SS division, Wiking. The initial response of Danes was disappointing. Not until after the invasion of the Soviet Union in 1941, when Himmler created separate SS national legions for Flemings, the Dutch, Norwegians, and Danes—rather than mix them with Germans in regular SS units—did Danish enlistments grow. By the end of 1941, more than 1,000 Danes were serving in the exclusively Danish Freikorps Dänemark. During the same period, the SS enlisted only 600 *Volksdeutsche* from Denmark.[79]

Recruitment of Danish *Volksdeutsche* did not improve much with time. It seems that most of those inclined to enlist did so in 1941, and further efforts to recruit yielded meager returns. By the end of 1943, only 1,292 *Volksdeutsche* from North Schleswig had joined the Waffen SS. In comparison, some 6,000 Danes had volunteered. One reason for the poor results was that the Danish authorities refused to surrender sovereignty over their Germans, and the enlistments remained on a voluntary basis. Yet even though these Germans were slow in responding to the Führer's call to arms, their record in providing labor manpower was much better. By the end of 1943, some 6,000 of them were working south of the border.[80]

Although the Danes generally had cooperated and had created no serious difficulties, Renthe-Fink's relatively mild rule did not suit Berlin. He failed to eliminate all resistance, and the satisfactory response of the Danes to the SS recruitment aside, the "carrot" approach had not succeeded in forging a true friendship between the future racial partners. It was time for applying the "stick." Prompted by widespread sabotage in the summer of 1942, Hitler reversed his policy and replaced Renthe-Fink with Werner Best, a staunch SS-SD man who ruled Denmark with a firmer hand. But even he could not suppress the growing resistance, which culminated in a general strike in August 1943. Best then declared a state of emergency and introduced martial law. From that point on, the Reich abandoned even the pretense of an independent Denmark.

After the Reich gave up hope for Danish cooperation, the behavior of the German minority made little difference. The Reich was more interested in its contributions in manpower and agricultural production than in its relations with the Danes. VoMi continued its routine business with the minority, but with the heightened Reich presence, it relinquished much of its authority to Best. Actually VoMi's diminished role in North Schleswig worked out well, since the threatening situation in the southeast demanded more of its attention and energy.

Because of their location, the *Volksdeutsche* of North Schleswig did not share the fate of the Germans in the southeast. Not threatened by the Red Army, they did not have to evacuate to the Reich. In fact, the refugee stream flowed in the opposite direction as North Schleswig's countryside, lacking industrial bombing targets, provided the urban populations of northern Germany a haven from Allied air raids. The North Schleswig Germans nevertheless paid a price for their close association with the Reich as the Danish resistance increasingly targeted them for attack. For instance, on Christmas Day 1943 their community center in Hadersleben was blown up.[81]

By early 1944, the *Volksdeutsche* feared what the Danes hoped for—the Reich's defeat. Although anti-German terror was not as prevalent in Denmark as in lands such as Slovakia, Serbia, or Croatia, enough occurred to trouble the *Volksdeutsche*. After the Normandy invasion in June 1944, talk of an Allied invasion of Denmark became common, and evacuation was contemplated. Although minority leader Möller objected to the idea and believed that Anglo-American invaders would not harm the minority, VoMi nevertheless favored withdrawing the group to the Reich. Himmler was in complete agreement.[82]

The invasion of Denmark did not materialize, nor did an evacuation of the *Volksdeutsche*. And as the war came to an end, their worst fears did not come to pass. Their wartime behavior, in part the result of Reich policies forced on them by VoMi, had not provoked among the Danes the intense desire for vengeance that consumed the peoples of eastern Europe. The *Volksdeutsche* had not established themselves as a ruling race, nor had the Reich authorities attempted to elevate them to a status superior to that of the majority Danes. Reich policy had denied them a lofty, privileged position, which elsewhere had aroused passions for revenge. The Germans of North Schleswig had survived the war without completely alienating their neighbors.

• • • THE SOVIET UNION

The isolation of the more than 1 million *Volksdeutsche* of the Soviet Union from the rest of the German *Volk* ended with the German invasion of June 1941. The separation had been total. Developments affecting the other German minorities of Europe, including prewar nazification, heightened expectations over Hitler's annexations, and the resettlement program, had passed them by.

As the German armies advanced into Russia in the summer of 1941, they discovered small groups of *Volksdeutsche* that the Soviets had overlooked in their efforts to evacuate all Germans to the east. Very few were found in the westernmost areas, since Stalin, anticipating an eventual showdown with the Reich, had deported most Germans from the frontiers long before the invasion. Farther to the east, the Soviets had not been able to remove everyone. As a rule, they had abducted the men but left women, children, the old, and the infirm behind. Some communities were passed by entirely and were left intact. Deeper in the interior, however, where the Soviets had more time, not many *Volksdeutsche* had evaded deportation. From the Crimea and the Caucasus, the Russians had deported tens of thousands of Germans to Siberia and Kazakhstan before the Reich's armies could reach them. The largest concentration of *Volksdeutsche*, the Volga Germans, shared a similar fate, even though the invading armies never reached their territory.[83]

Since the majority of the remaining *Volksdeutsche* were women, children, and the elderly, all barely surviving, emergency care became vital. The military and the accompanying SS Einsatzkommandos did whatever they could, but they were unprepared to care for tens of thousands of these pitiful people. After all, the SS and the military were in Russia for purposes other than saving lives. When news of the discovery of the *Volksdeutsche* reached Himmler, he assigned responsibility for them to his most reliable man in these matters, Werner Lorenz, who immediately dispatched VoMi commandos to Russia. On site, they came under the authority of the local HSSPF. Himmler instructed the Einsatzkommandos to assist VoMi in every way possible. Ironically, these SS death squads, assigned to maintain security behind the lines and to liquidate political and racial undesirables, assisted in a life-saving mission.[84]

Although the plight of the *Volksdeutsche* moved Himmler, it appears that it was the opportunity to claim a greater share in ruling the occupied Soviet territories that prompted him to respond so quickly to their needs. In the scramble for power, Himmler competed with several other authorities, including the Wehrmacht, Hermann Göring's economic enterprises, and Alfred Rosenberg, whom Hitler had appointed the supreme civilian authority. Himmler was already in charge of security and police functions in these lands, but the discovery of *Volksdeutsche* provided him with an additional claim.

Lorenz sent his most capable, most experienced officer, Horst Hoffmeyer, and Hoffmeyer's deputy, Klaus Siebert, an SD man, to direct VoMi operations in Russia. In early September the two arrived in the Ukraine, the region with the largest number of surviving *Volksdeutsche*. Hoffmeyer and Siebert were attached to the SD office in Kiev, under the command of the HSSPF Rusland Süd. Hoffmeyer organized his team as VoMi Sonderkommando R. Its area of operations extended beyond German-occupied territories to Rumanian-controlled lands. After the invasion, the Reich had allowed its Rumanian allies not only to reoccupy Bessarabia but also to control the area to the northeast, between the Dniester and Bug rivers, which included the city of Odessa. In this area, known briefly as Transnistria, the Einsatzkommandos had discovered large numbers of *Volksdeutsche*. After lengthy negotiations, Hoffmeyer and the Rumanian governor agreed that these 135,000–160,000 people would be organized as an autonomous political entity, under VoMi's authority. In Transnistria, Hoffmeyer was accountable only to Himmler, not to an HSSPF.[85]

One of Hoffmeyer's first tasks was to take a head count. By mid-March 1942, VoMi teams along with SD commandos had registered 185,408 Germans in the occupied southwestern Soviet Union. During the survey, Hoffmeyer's men learned of the extent of the deportations. They accounted for 41,462 *Volksdeutsche* deported before the outbreak of hostilities and another 24,700 between June 23 and the arrival of the German military. An additional 3,547 were known to be serving in the Red Army.[86]

As Sonderkommando R registered the *Volksdeutsche*, it also began organizing and consolidating them into larger, more viable and defensible communities. Hoffmeyer subdivided his jurisdiction into seven regions, assigning a commander for each. As these commanders completed the registrations, they issued identification cards for food rations. They also introduced a German registry, similar to the DVL. Enrollment on the registry was a matter of life or death, for in the occupied territories, the SS practiced its racial ideology even more relentlessly and ruthlessly than in Poland.[87]

Having completed the registration and the consolidation, VoMi next turned to reviving the local economies, building schools and clinics, and organizing self-defense militia units. Its commanders relied heavily on the SD Einsatzgruppen for logistical support, utilizing their transport, communications, and personnel. Before organizing the militia units, VoMi also depended on the SD for security. It is uncertain whether VoMi's militias, once operational, assumed all SD responsibilities, including executions. It is known that Hoffmeyer's deputy, Siebert, commanded some antipartisan operations and that the militia units collaborated with the Einsatzgruppen in many activities, which—one suspects—covered the entire spectrum of SD responsibilities in Russia.[88]

In August 1942, Himmler created a new office, the Volksdeutsche Leitstelle, replacing the Sonderkommando R as the agency responsible for the *Volksdeutsche* in Russia. VoMi, although still involved, no longer enjoyed exclusive authority. The creation of the Leitstelle may very well have been another instance of Himmler's making a change on paper that in practice made little difference. The "new" SS office, with Hoffmeyer as commander and with its headquarters in Zhitomir, assumed the duties of the Sonderkommando R and came directly under the HSSPF Rusland Süd. It was to coordinate the activities of several SS and SS-associated offices, including the RKFDV, RuSHA, the SS Wirtschafts- und Verwaltungshauptamt, and VoMi. The Leitstelle eventually extended its operations to the Crimea and the northern Caucasus, where a few more *Volksdeutsche* surfaced.[89]

From all corners of Hoffmeyer's realm came glowing reports of the regeneration of the *Volksdeutsche* communities. Especially rosy were reports from Transnistria. In the summer of 1942, making his easternmost venture into the field, Lorenz personally inspected the region and commented on its flourishing agriculture.[90] Hoffmeyer had provided the *Volksdeutsche* with the best collective farmlands and with machinery from abandoned machine-tractor stations. To help rebuild the industrial sector, VoMi sought Reich firms to build plants in the more secure areas. It even considered relocating some textile factories from Belgium.[91]

The *Volksdeutsche* of the Soviet Union were hardly in a position to produce for the Reich. Yet they could contribute in one area—labor manpower. It probably would have been in their best interest to evacuate them from the devastated, hostile land to the relative security and comfort of the Reich. But Himmler steadfastly opposed such a move, mostly for ideological reasons. He wanted to keep them in Russia as a nucleus for its future Germanization. The only workers Himmler approved sending to the Reich were *Volksdeutsche* girls to serve as household help for large German families. According to most accounts, these girls were only too glad to get out of Russia.[92]

Because of the critical shortage of men among these Germans, Himmler did not attempt a full-scale recruitment for the Waffen SS. Instead, VoMi organized militia units. The militias, placed under SS command, participated mostly in antipartisan actions in their own localities. In Transnistria, VoMi organized a formidable troop of 8,000–9,000 men and in the Ukraine a unit of 7,000. To hinder the Wehrmacht's efforts to enlist these men as interpreters and for other purposes, Himmler ordered them registered in the Waffen SS.[93] In February 1943, a few days after the surrender at Stalingrad, Himmler violated the understanding that the militias were to be used only locally. He ordered Berger and Lorenz to redeploy some 3,000 men from Transnistria to the Ukraine, where the situation had become more threatening.[94] In effect, these militia units had become SS auxiliaries.

After Stalingrad, partisan activity and the Soviet counteroffensive threatened the *Volksdeutsche* communities and prompted VoMi to consider their evacuation. But Himmler had something far more comprehensive in mind. On 13 February 1943 he ordered his HSSPFs for the Ukraine and the central front to remove the entire population, non-Germans as well as Germans, leaving behind a completely depopulated countryside.[95] VoMi was especially concerned for the safety of the estimated 10,000 Germans of eastern Byelorussia, where guerrilla resistance had become particularly threatening. Behrends sent a squad of ten men with a few trucks to begin their evacuation, which was not completed until July.[96] After all, it was no simple task for ten men to relocate 10,000 people.

The major evacuation effort, which was the initial step in the eventual evacuation of Germans from all of eastern Europe, began in the late summer of 1943, with the resumption of the Russian offensive. In August, VoMi evacuated an estimated 70,000 Black Sea Germans from the southeastern Ukraine. They set out on their slow journey west using every available means, including trains, trucks, wagons, and feet. Along with them fled a multitude of non-Germans—Cossacks, Caucasians, Ukrainians, and Russians—who had collaborated with German rule. Although Himmler had ordered the forced evacuation of the entire population, most refugees, especially the *Volksdeutsche*, needed no prodding. Those very few Germans who refused to leave lost their ration cards as well as their protection. On paper, and in the cases of some non-Germans, the evacuation was a mandatory deportation, ordered by the Reichsführer SS. In reality, and for the overwhelming majority of the evacuated *Volksdeutsche*, it was an escape.[97]

The evacuation of the central Ukraine began in October. The entire population was to be removed. In Kiev, security forces tried to round up as many people as they could, but not enough transportation was available to meet the demands of those clamoring to leave, much less to deport the unwilling. These estimated 70,000 refugees from the central Ukraine were joined in late October by some 50,000 more from the western Ukraine.[98]

In comparison with the earlier resettlement operations, these evacuations were prepared and executed haphazardly. There were few, if any, rest camps or sheltered accommodations along the way. And since Himmler had waited until the last moment to give the order to depart, the refugees found themselves on the road at the onset of a Russian winter. They had to endure every kind of tribulation, not only exposure to the harsh weather but also attacks by partisans and advance Red Army units. They ran a veritable gauntlet all along the route to Poland. Although escorted by the Wehrmacht, the Waffen SS, and their own militias, some columns were intercepted and completely annihilated—men, women, and children. The survivors reached Poland in the spring of 1944.[99]

As the Ukrainian *Volksdeutsche* were arriving in Poland, those of Transnistria were only beginning their trek. Himmler had also waited until the last moment to decide on their evacuation, and it was not until 12 March that Hoffmeyer received orders to proceed. Hoffmeyer, who had organized the Bessarabian operation in 1940, hoped to use it as a model for this evacuation. After crossing Bessarabia on wagons, the refugees were to board ships on the Danube for the remainder of the journey. By 28 March every village was evacuated, · but on reaching the Danube, Hoffmeyer and his host discovered that shipping was not available and they would have to proceed overland to the Reich. He placed some 20,000 aboard trains, but the rest, the sturdiest, were divided into two groups for the long journey. One column of 70,000 people marched through northern Rumania and Hungary toward the Warthegau. The second column, some 40,000, followed the river westward. Both columns set out in early April and reached the Warthegau in May and June. With their arrival, VoMi had led an estimated 300,000 *Volksdeutsche* out of the Soviet Union.[100]

The *Volksdeutsche* of Rumania, Hungary, and Serbia-Banat watched sullenly as the Transnistrian columns trudged past their settlements. Ominous illustrations of the reversal of German military fortunes, these evacuations previewed what lay ahead for them. The same was true for the Germans of Poland, many of whom had only recently been resettled there. The sight of Ukrainian *Volksdeutsche* passing through the General Government to the Warthegau warned them that their turn was not far off. Indeed, as early as March 1944, all Germans residing in the Lublin area and not engaged in vital activities were ordered to evacuate to Lodz. And so the first of the resettled *Volksdeutsche* were on the road again, to be followed shortly by the rest. The new racial order, displayed briefly but dramatically in all of its brutal inhumanity by Himmler and his SS, was crumbling. The Volksdeutsche Mittelstelle had shared in the construction of the racial order, and now it was helping to salvage what it could.

• •

CHAPTER THIRTEEN

Götterdämmerung

• •

THE EVACUATION

As early as March 1943, shortly after Himmler's initial order to evacuate the *Volksdeutsche* from Russia, Lorenz alerted minority leaders Schmidt, Altgayer, and Karmasin about the possibility of evacuating *Volksdeutsche* from southeastern Europe.[1] Planning for an evacuation was an extremely sensitive matter, since any preparations of this sort—especially at this early date—smacked of defeatism and ran counter to Hitler's intent to fight to the end. Consequently, all references to evacuation were couched in provisional terms, implying a later return, once the military situation improved.

According to VoMi's master plan, its RKFDV sections as well as those dealing with the minorities would participate in the evacuation. The department responsible for nonresettler *Volksdeutsche* living and working in the Reich would supervise refugee housing and physical care while the BfE would register the refugees—who were to be classified as provisional Reich Germans—and handle all paperwork. VoMi's resettler camps were to be readied for the anticipated influx. Its planners envisioned the evacuation as an orderly process, not much different from the resettlements. But as events unfolded, it was anything but orderly.[2] Carefully laid-out plans more often than not were ignored. Exigency, not blueprints, dictated the course of the operation.

Although some *Volksdeutsche* from southeastern Europe had begun fleeing westward on their own before the 23 August 1944 coup in Rumania—which caught everyone on the German side by surprise— VoMi had taken few steps beyond preliminary planning. Even after the coup, its leaders, aware of Hitler's determined stand against any withdrawals, hesitated to act. By the time they came to their senses and confronted the calamity in Rumania at a meeting on 2 September, it was too late for most Transylvania Saxons. The Russians had reached Brasov, the headquarters of the minority, on the previous day and would occupy Sibiu, with its large German community, a week later.[3]

At that meeting Lorenz, having conferred with Himmler, consulted his experts on the southeast. From the conversation, which focused on the evacuation of 40,000 *Volksdeutsche* from northern, Hungarian Transylvania, it appears that Lorenz had already written off as lost not only the *Volksdeutsche* of Rumanian Transylvania but also the Swabians of the Rumanian Banat. Lorenz appointed Hans Weibgen, an SS man with a background of varied service, in charge of evacuating the southeast. He ordered Weibgen to set up a command center in Budapest, the Südost Kommando der Volksdeutsche Mittelstelle.[4]

After sending Weibgen to Budapest, Lorenz soon followed, to be closer to the action. But finding one of his favorite cities in a state of high anxiety, and not at all the gay Budapest of better times, he declared it too remote for proper supervision of the evacuation and returned to Berlin. Weibgen, however, remained and proceeded with his duties. He inquired about the situation in Transylvania, but little was known. One of the last reports from there had noted a column of people moving south from Brasov, but it was not clear whether this was a fleeing refugee column or *Volksdeutsche* being led away by the Russians for deportation.[5]

Reports from the Banat were no more reliable. Weibgen, hoping to rescue at least some of Rumania's *Volksdeutsche*, quickly collected some eighty men and sent them to the Banat, into the unknown, with orders to evacuate as many as perhaps 300,000 people.[6] The order and expectations were unrealistic. If the Red Army had not already occupied the Banat, it was most certainly approaching it. Furthermore, the response of the Rumanians was unpredictable—would the former allies be hostile or cooperative? And the idea that eighty men could retrieve and lead to safety some 300,000 people was logistically preposterous.

Having reached the Banat with their small convoy of trucks, Weibgen's commandos were relieved to discover they had arrived ahead of the Russians. But to their astonishment, they encountered a new and totally unexpected phenomenon. Even with the Red Army approaching, many Germans refused to leave. Only with the greatest effort could they dislodge some 20,000 of the anticipated 300,000 Swabians. As would be the case throughout the region, many *Volksdeutsche* refused to leave their homes. Unlike the Germans of the Soviet Union, those of southeastern Europe were hard to convince that evacuation was a matter of life and death. Their hesitancy was reinforced from another quarter, their churches, which, having earlier acquiesced to nazification, chose this most inopportune time to call on the faithful to renounce the Führer and to demonstrate their defiance by remaining in place.[7]

The evacuation from Rumania was a dismal failure. In part it was Hitler's stubbornness on the issue of retreat and evacuation, in part it was the indecision and confusion of his subordinates, specifically Himmler and VoMi, and in part it was logistical difficulties that accounted for the fiasco. But the hundreds of thousands of Rumanian Germans left behind, especially in western Rumania, must also shoulder blame. More than any other factor, it was their reluctance to leave until it was too late that sealed their fate. The entire episode evoked bitterness and recrimination, such as that reflected in a letter from an SS soldier who lamented that the "worthless" Russian Germans had been saved but the 700,000 "first class" Rumanian Germans had been shamefully betrayed.[8]

After attempting to evacuate the Rumanian Banat, Weibgen and his crew tackled the removal of an estimated 40,000 people from northern, Hungarian Transylvania. Here they ran into new obstacles. The Foreign Ministry worried about the harm the evacuation could do to Reich-Hungarian relations. After all, evacuation acknowledged defeat. Another problem was the Hungarians, who were uncooperative and impeded the process at every turn. In addition, the VoMi commandos found transportation inadequate and discovered that moving large numbers of people westward along roads on which military units were advancing eastward was next to impossible.[9] But the greatest obstacle hindering VoMi's efforts in Hungary was the attitude of the *Volksdeutsche*. Many refused to leave, renounced their ties to the Reich, and reaffirmed loyalties to Hungary. Hoping to evade evacuation, they accepted what for years they had denied—that they were Hungarians. As they defied the Reich's summons to evacuate, or procrastinated flight, they found their escape routes cut off and the evacuation commandos gone.

By the end of September, as the Russians reached points along the Tisza River in eastern Hungary, most of the *Volksdeutsche* of northern Transylvania, some 34,000, had eventually heeded VoMi's orders and were heading west. Next, in early October, VoMi began clearing the more western Sathmar region. The *Volksdeutsche* there, in greater numbers than any others, renounced their ties with the Reich, and only some 4,000–6,000 out of an estimated 40,000 opted to leave.[10] They fell in line with *Volksdeutsche* already in flight from the Yugoslavian and Rumanian Banat. Lorenz, who had earlier declared Budapest "too remote," returned to supervise the evacuations in person. It is not known whether some higher authority ordered him back to the action or whether he decided to return on his own. Whichever the case, he began with the evacuation of Bačka, the part of southern Hungary between the Tisza and Danube rivers.[11]

Although VoMi had been planning and directing evacuations since March 1943, beginning with those from the Soviet Union, it was not until mid-October 1944 that Himmler formally charged it with receiving and caring for the refugees. He retroactively sanctioned the evacuations as a RKFDV action, financed by the state. As VoMi officials were feverishly preparing for the arrival of the refugees in the Reich, their greatest problem was finding enough housing. The VoMi camp system, which had peaked in size in 1942, had been eroding ever since as various Reich authorities appropriated the precious commodity of living space. Himmler, sympathetic to VoMi's plight, ordered an immediate halt to any further requisitioning.[12]

Another vital task was the distribution of refugees. As a result of Allied air raids, large numbers of Reich Germans had fled to less populated, more remote corners of Germany, which also happened to be the areas designated for the incoming refugees. Local authorities were not pleased with the prospects of more new arrivals demanding a share of already overextended resources. VoMi officials as well as Himmler himself assured the authorities that the refugees would return to their homelands as soon as conditions permitted.[13]

One might presume that at this point Himmler had secured Hitler's permission to evacuate the *Volksdeutsche*, but this was not the case. A serious snag appeared when on 12 October, Lorenz informed Himmler that he expected the first of some 215,000 refugees to reach the Reich any day. He was astonished to learn that Himmler would still have to get Hitler's permission before they could enter. Apparently, at this late date, either Hitler knew nothing about the evacuation or Himmler, fearing the Führer's wrath at learning of the retreat, had not informed him of its true extent and nature. Compounding Himmler's fears was the fact that he, as the RKFDV, was responsible for the strengthening of Germandom. Yet it was he who had ordered abandoning the German position in the southeast. It was, no doubt, a meek Himmler who approached the Führer to seek permission for the refugees to enter the Reich. And it was surely a relieved one that informed Lorenz the following day that Hitler had approved accepting the *Volksdeutsche*.[14]

While VoMi officials in Germany were preparing to receive the multitudes, the columns of *Volksdeutsche* slowly moved westward. More refugees fell in line as the front approached. On 13 October, Himmler ordered the evacuation of Syrmia, home for the largest concentration of Germans in Croatia. Once the Russians reached the Banat and the Danube, their advance north was rapid, adding greater urgency to the evacuations. By the end of October, some 150,000 refugees from the southeast had arrived in the Reich, and it was thought that as many as 200,000 were still on the way.[15] In November, Lorenz, who had decided to remain in Budapest and direct the evacuations to the end, selected the Baranya, the part of southern Hungary west of the Danube, as the next region for evacuation. With the battlefront perilously close, Lorenz assumed personal command of this operation. He came to appreciate the difficulties of the task, especially when criticized for the shortcomings. In response to complaints from the Foreign Ministry about the slow progress in clearing the Baranya, a vexed Lorenz challenged the diplomats to send him the "wise man" who could do better.[16] Adding to his difficulties was the wavering resolve of the minority leader, Franz Basch. At this critical hour Basch no longer wanted to lead and chose to retire to a remote village and teach school. Lorenz chided Basch for quitting under fire, but rather than press the issue, he allowed the leader to step down.[17]

By early December the Russians had advanced to Kapsovar, just south of Lake Balaton. Of the estimated 200,000 *Volksdeutsche* of the Baranya, only some 30,000 had fled. The rest, for whatever reasons, had remained behind. The last *Volksdeutsche* to leave the southeast, those living in northwestern Croatia, westernmost Hungary, and parts of Slovakia, did so by the end of December. By the beginning of 1945, VoMi had completed removing the *Volksdeutsche*—those willing to leave—from southeastern Europe.[18] As the battlefront relentlessly crept westward, more refugees joined the exodus. In February, Karl H. Frank, the chief of the Protectorate of Bohemia and Moravia, ordered the evacuation of Germans from his domain.[19]

There is no accurate count of the number of *Volksdeutsche* from southeastern Europe that fled to the Reich. Numbers vary, but one may estimate approximately 500,000.[20] This does not include those serving in the armed forces who managed to find their way back to Germany at the end of the war. Nor does it take into account those already working in the Reich. Once inside the Reich, these refugees merged with a far larger flood of refugees from the northeast, Reich Germans as well as *Volksdeutsche*.

As early as 1943 many of the *Volksdeutsche* resettled in the General Government had already begun their flight to the Reich—not long after being settled in their share of the *Lebensraum*. They were shortly joined by other uprooted resettlers from the Warthegau, and then by others from areas farther to the west, as the retreating front continued to constrict the Reich's domain. As they arrived in the Reich, many of them no doubt recalled the ceremonies welcoming them as resettlers only a few years earlier. The circumstances as well as the receptions now were quite different as they returned to a Reich whose total defeat was only a matter of time. On 15 January 1945 began the symbolically most notable evacuation. Lodz, the center of the RKFDV program for the reconstruction of the east and the building of the new order, was abandoned.[21]

DISINTEGRATION OF VOMI

Although by January 1945 the outcome of the war was a foregone conclusion, Werner Lorenz at least publicly still professed confidence in victory. In his New Year's address he summoned his subordinates to rededicate themselves to the struggle and challenged them to work even more diligently for the cause. He reaffirmed his steadfast faith in both the Führer and the *Volk*.[22] But events were moving inexorably in another direction, and as defeat approached, the Third Reich and its component parts crumbled. VoMi was no exception. It too disintegrated. By 1945, as a result of Allied bombing and several direct hits on VoMi's headquarters—destroying most of its records—the offices were relocated throughout Berlin and the surrounding Brandenburg countryside. This physical dispersal accelerated the unraveling of its centralized operation, which barely continued to exist. Besides, with the completion of the evacuations, the severing of contact with what was left of the minorities, and the removal of resettlers from the east, VoMi had lost much its purpose for being. Individuals responsible for the housing and care of the resettlers and refugees continued to do the best they could, relying mostly on local resources and their own ingenuity.

VoMi's demise paralleled the disintegration of its leadership. As early as the fall of 1943, Himmler assigned Behrends as HSSPF for Serbia. Serving in this capacity at war's end, Behrends was captured by Yugoslav partisans, tried, and hanged in 1946. In 1944, VoMi's prime troubleshooter, Horst Hoffmeyer, became chief of security for the Rumanian Ploesti oil fields. He was eventually reported missing in action. The climax of the disintegration at the top came in February 1945 with the transfer of Lorenz. Since VoMi had been so closely associated with him, his departure marked VoMi's end as an institution and force in the Third Reich.

According to Lorenz's postwar testimony, he had regularly requested a Waffen SS combat command.[23] Himmler, apparently regarding him more valuable as chief of VoMi, and perhaps not impressed with his potential as a combat commander, denied these requests. But with the conclusion of the evacuations, Lorenz's services at VoMi were no longer needed, and in February 1945, Himmler finally granted him his wish by bestowing on him the active rank of a Waffen SS general and appointing him commander of the Ordnungstruppen stationed in the rear of Army Group Vistula (Weichsel). As such, he was responsible for maintaining order among the retreating troops. In May, after serving in his new command for only a few months, Lorenz surrendered to the British in Holstein.[24]

As for VoMi's superior, Heinrich Himmler, the master architect of the new order and the chief Germanizer of the *Lebensraum*, his fate was also sealed. After betraying the Führer's trust by attempting to negotiate independently with the Allies, Himmler, dressed in civilian clothing, was captured by the British while attempting to flee. But before facing trial for his wartime criminality, Himmler committed suicide by swallowing a cyanide capsule. His capture and cowardly death brought down the final curtain on the new racial order.

• • EPILOGUE

The fate of the *Volksdeutsche* in the immediate postwar period is beyond the scope of this study, but it deserves at least a brief summary and some comment. All *Volksdeutsche* finding themselves inside the Reich at the final hour as resettlers, wartime laborers, recent refugees, and soldiers experienced the disastrous *Götterdämmerung*, the "twilight of the gods," the dramatic, but in this instance ironic, epitaph to the Wagnerian-like new order envisioned by Hitler, Himmler, and others. The final demise was unheroic and hardly Wagnerian, certainly as far as Hitler and Himmler were concerned. Both took the coward's way out.

The *Volksdeutsche* located in the Reich at this critical moment shared the misery and hardships of the disaster alongside Reich Germans. Their fate was tragic and difficult but overall not as lamentable as the fate of those left behind in their homelands. With few exceptions, those who either had opted not to evacuate or had found their escape cut off paid dearly for the wartime deeds of the Reich at the hands of the people the Reich had subjugated.

The majority of the *Volksdeutsche* left behind, for various reasons and in different degrees, had associated their destinies with those of the Reich, the *Volk*, and the Führer and now reaped the dividends of their folly. Granted, some had opposed the association, and others at least had not cooperated actively. But most—if only passively—had attached themselves to the Third Reich. Their non-German neighbors, aware of this affiliation, ascribed to them—to the guilty as well as to the innocent—general culpability for the wartime actions of the Reich. After years of brutal treatment, Poles, Czechs, Slovenes, Serbs, Russians, and others took grim vengeance against the most visible and accessible remnants of Reich domination—the *Volksdeutsche*.

In Czechoslovakia and Poland, where the Reich's occupation had been especially inhumane, the Germans, both indigenous and resettled, suffered terribly. These *Volksdeutsche* reaped not only the consequences of the Reich's occupation but also retribution for their own active participation in the destruction and occupation of their states. In both countries, individual *Volksdeutsche* as well as the official minority organizations had willingly collaborated. They either had offered their services to the Reich's cause or at least had served as pretexts for its aggression. During the years of Nazi rule they had benefited from occupation policies that not only elevated them above the non-Germans as the elite ruling race but also provided them with Polish and Czech land, homes, and businesses. Although as individuals many *Volksdeutsche* were innocent of collusion, or had not accepted the benefits coming to them as *Herrenvolk*, in the eyes of the former *Untermensch* they were still guilty, at least by association. As a result, repressed hatred erupted in countless atrocities of every imaginable kind against them. Germans have subsequently referred to these acts, in dark irony, as "hundreds of Lidices," alluding to the Nazi wartime eradication of a small Czechoslovakian town.

In view of the Reich's harsh rule and the complicity of the *Volksdeutsche*, the victorious Allies at the postwar Potsdam Conference approved Czech and Polish requests to expel all Germans. Although the Allies expressly stipulated that these operations proceed in an orderly, humane manner, they were anything but that. Plunder and maltreatment characterized these deportations, and countless people died along the way. The result was the virtual, if not complete, extirpation of the German minorities from Czechoslovakia and Poland. By 1955 less than 200,000 of the more than 3 million prewar German population remained in Czechoslovakia. An estimated 300,000 Germans still lived in Poland, but even that number was declining.[25]

The expulsion of Germans from Hungary also became official postwar policy, but it was not the result of popular hatred. Although the wartime allegiances of the majority of Hungarian *Volksdeutsche* had been with the Reich, and their relationship with the Reich had offended the Magyars, they had not turned against Hungary in the same way as the *Volksdeutsche* of Poland and Czechoslovakia had against their states. And at the final hour many of them renounced their allegiances to the Führer and, rather than flee to the Reich, chose to remain in their native land. Anti-German feelings simply were not as intense here. Besides, for most of the war the Hungarians had been willing accomplices of the Reich and had benefited territorially from the partnership. They could hardly blame their ultimate fate on the

Reich alone or on its most visible remnants, the remaining *Volks-deutsche*.

The expulsion from Hungary was the work of Soviet authorities, who forced this measure on the Hungarians as a means to help revolutionize the country. By removing the *Volksdeutsche*, the Soviets and their Hungarian Communist cohorts were eliminating mostly propertied farmers and urban professionals who were unsuited for Sovietization. On the pretext of getting rid of a potentially troublesome fifth column, the Soviets managed to include their expulsion on the agenda of the Potsdam Conference, which approved this deportation along with those from Poland and Czechoslovakia. Since the Hungarians were not enthusiastic about the expulsion, it was not thorough, and many Germans evaded deportation. In 1955 the Hungarian government still listed more than 200,000 German-speaking citizens.[26]

In Rumania, large numbers of *Volksdeutsche*, including most Transylvanian Saxons, were unable to escape after the reversal of alliances on 23 August 1944. From most reports, Rumanian treatment of these Germans was humane. Rumania, like Hungary, had spent most of the war years as the Reich's ally, and although its *Volksdeutsche* had enjoyed certain privileges and considerable autonomy—which many Rumanians resented and regarded as an affront to their national sovereignty—the Reich had not elevated them to a dominant status at the expense of the Rumanians.

In contrast to Rumanian treatment, Russian behavior toward these *Volksdeutsche* was bestial. They were the first Germans to fall into Russian clutches in large numbers, and the Russian soldiers vented years of anger on these unfortunate people. In addition, the Soviets pressured the Rumanians to hand the *Volksdeutsche* over as slave labor. Over Rumanian protests, the Russians deported an estimated 60,000–65,000 to the Soviet Union. It should be noted that Rumania was the only country in southeastern Europe that did not expel its German minority, although expropriation of property belonging to "collaborators" and subsequent socialization measures undermined the minority's economic base and reduced its overall influence. In 1948 the minority in Rumania still amounted to nearly 350,000 people.[27]

The fate of the *Volksdeutsche* trapped in Yugoslavia was perhaps the worst of all. As in the case of the German minorities in Poland and Czechoslovakia, the minority in Yugoslavia had played an active role as the Reich's accomplice both in the country's destruction and during its subsequent occupation. At the end of the war, most *Volksdeutsche* had managed to escape, but those that remained behind, in particular the members of the Prinz Eugen Waffen SS Division, experienced the wrath of a population that had endured the most heinous atrocities and deprivation under German occupation. The emotions generated by the grisly partisan warfare carried over into the war's aftermath. *Volksdeutsche* falling into Yugoslav hands were herded into concentration camps, in which thousands died. The Yugoslavs then turned over an estimated 100,000 of these people to the Russians for deportation to the Soviet Union as slave labor. They had requested approval from the Allied powers for the expulsion of the remaining Germans, but since the Allies did not respond, the Yugoslavs went about this business in their own way. By deporting thousands to the Soviet Union and pressuring the rest to leave, they effectively eliminated the Germans as a significant national minority. By 1953 only some 60,000 Germans remained in Yugoslavia.[28]

The German minorities in North Schleswig and the South Tyrol fared far better than those left in eastern Europe. Thanks to the roles they were forced to play in the relations between their states and the Reich, there were no expulsions of *Volksdeutsche* from either Denmark or Italy. The Reich's policy of subordinating the revisionist aspirations of these *Volksdeutsche* to the interest of maintaining special relationships between the Reich and these two states proved fortuitous for them in the postwar period. In the case of the South Tyroleans, the Reich had ignored their wishes for reannexation and spurned their offers to serve the Reich against Italy. Instead, Hitler eliminated them as an issue of contention with Mussolini by resettling them. Some left, but many, either feeling betrayed or simply not wanting to abandon their homes, remained. Wartime relations between Germans and Italians in the South Tyrol did not produce the legacy of national hatred generated in other parts of Nazi-dominated Europe. In fact, postwar agreements regarding the status of the South Tyroleans permitted many of those who had chosen to resettle in 1939 to return and reclaim their Italian citizenship.[29] Over the years they have reestablished their influence in the region along with a certain degree of autonomy.

The Germans of North Schleswig experienced no worse. Although Germany had occupied Denmark, the occupation had been mild, at least in comparison with the German rule in the east. Furthermore,

Reich policy for these *Volksdeutsche* had demanded restraint and coexistence with the Danes. Their revisionist goal of reannexation to the Reich was subordinated to the Reich's interest in including the Danes as willing partners in the new racial order. Although during the occupation they had enjoyed some privileges, the Reich had not elevated them far above the Danes. Consequently, after the war, popular feelings of revenge were not focused on the *Volksdeutsche*, who, on the whole, received decent treatment. Incidents against them did occur, but revenge was meted out on an individual basis, not as collective retribution. Danish collaborators, rather than Germans, bore the brunt of local vengeance. The German minority on the whole could continue living in the southern borderland more or less as it had before the war.

With the exception of the South Tyroleans and the Germans of North Schleswig, the *Volksdeutsche* who had remained in their homelands at the end of the war were shocked by the maltreatment they received at the hands of their non-German neighbors. Most perceived their complicity and participation in the events of the preceding years as circumstantial. As they saw it, their only fault was being German. In many cases this was true, but they still failed to realize that in the minds of the non-Germans, this very fact of their Germanness justified their fate. Poles, Czechs, Serbs, and others had endured the brutal rule of the Third Reich, a rule founded on the precept that by virtue of inherent racial superiority, the Germans were fit to rule and that non-Germans, because of their racial inferiority, were suited only for servitude. In the eyes of many non-Germans, the *Volksdeutsche*, through their self-imposed and self-perpetuated cultural exclusivity and their subsequent acceptance of National Socialism—even if only passively—had collectively associated themselves with the Third Reich and its deeds. It remains to be seen to what degree the memories of this experience will affect the future relationship between the new, reunified Germany and the new regimes of eastern Europe.

Similarly, when the leader of the Volksdeutsche Mittelstelle, Werner Lorenz, was charged after the war with a long list of crimes against humanity, he could not understand why he was being tried as a criminal for performing wartime tasks that he regarded as humanitarian and whose objective had been the welfare of the German *Volk*. In his trial before the United States War Crimes Tribunal at Nuremberg— for which the British released him from a POW camp in England— Lorenz and fellow VoMi officials questioned as witnesses repeatedly emphasized that their exclusive responsibility and interest had been the welfare of the foreign segment of the *Volk*, the *Volksdeutsche*. They insisted that they could not be held accountable for all of the crimes of the Third Reich and the SS, certainly not for the mistreatment of non-Germans.

But what Lorenz and many others would not concede, and what most *Volksdeutsche* victimized by postwar vengeance could not comprehend, was that VoMi's efforts to enhance the well-being of the foreign segment of the German *Volk*, and the latter's determination to maintain *völkisch* exclusivity, had served the ultimate objective of the Third Reich—the creation of a new racial order in which Germans would rule over others. Both the United States Tribunal at Nuremberg and the non-German persecutors of the *Volksdeutsche* perceived this connection and held both the *Volksdeutsche* and the leader of VoMi accountable. The VoMi chief received a twenty-year sentence, which he did not complete. With the help of his influential son-in-law, the Hamburg publisher Axel Springer, Werner Lorenz was released in 1955.[30] Most of the *Volksdeutsche*, as noted above, suffered far more. As for the fate of Himmler's once featured "auxiliary," the Volhynian peasant whom the Reichsführer SS greeted at Przemysl on that cold, winter's day in January 1940, it is unknown.

N O T E S

• •

The following citation system will be used for primary sources and documents.

Documents from major archives will cite the document, the abbreviation for the archive, and the collection or file identification. The following abbreviations will be used:

PA AA   Auswärtiges Amt, Politisches Archiv, Bonn.
BA   Bundesarchiv, Koblenz.
BDC   Berlin Document Center, Berlin. (BDC SSO refers to SS officer personnel files located at the BDC.)

Unless explicitly cited otherwise, documentation from postwar trials (such as testimonies, closing statements, etc.) will be from Case 8, United States of America v. Ulrich Greifelt et al., United States Tribunal at Nuremberg, deposited at the National Archives, Washington, D.C. (copies also available through the Center for Research Libraries, Chicago).

Microfilmed documents will be cited as follows. For National Archives microfilms: document, followed by "T" number/roll number/frame numbers. For Foreign Ministry microfilms: document, T-120/roll number/series number/frame numbers. Consult the Bibliography for a complete listing of "T" numbers and their corresponding collections.

Citations for documents from major published collections will list the document, abbreviation for the published collection, volume number, page number. The collections will be abbreviated as follows (consult the Bibliography for complete information):

DGFP   *Documents on German Foreign Policy, 1918–1945.* (*DGFP* will include series letter "D" before volume number.)
Expulsion   *Documents on the Expulsion of the Germans from Eastern-Central Europe.*
IMT   *Trial of the Major War Criminals before the International Military Tribunal.*
TWC   *Trial of War Criminals before the Nuremberg Military Tribunals.*

For published documents from single-volume collections with one editor, the citation will list the document, followed by editor's last name and short title.

CHAPTER ONE

1. Johst, *Ruf des Reiches*, p. 22. ("Our father has called us! We have come, now here we are!!")

2. Ibid., pp. 30–31. See also Zantke, "Die Heimkehr der Wolhyniendeutschen," pp. 169–71; Engelhardt-Kyffhäuser, *Der Grosse Treck,*; Bosse, *Der Führer ruft,* pp. 169–70, 189–91; *Das Schwarze Korps,* 25 January 1940, p. 11, 1 February 1940, pp. 11–12, 15 February 1940, p. 4

3. Himmler quoted in *Der Untermensch.*

4. Himmler, Posen Speech, 24 October 1943, T-175/17/2520786–808.

5. Hitler, *Hitler's Table Talk,* 1–2 November 1941, p. 106.

6. Gauss, *Das Buch vom deutschen Volkstum,* p. 7.

7. Winkler, *Statistisches Handbuch,* and *Deutschtum in aller Welt.*

8. "Nationale Minderheiten," October 1925, T-120/2298/4555/E147365–372.

9. Krähmer-Möllenberg, Deutsche Stiftung, to Economic Minister, 10 June 1936, T-120/1451/3023H/D598507–508.

10. "Bericht," 31 December 1934, T-120/1178/2168/470900–959. See also Jacobsen, *Aussenpolitik,* pp. 166–67.

11. Fittbogen, *Was jeder Deutsche,* title page. ("Volk service is God's service.")

12. Jacobsen, *Hans Steinacher,* is the authoritative work on the VDA. See also Jacobsen, *Aussenpolitik,* p. 165.

13. "Der Nationalsozialist als politischer Soldat des Ostens," NSDAP Gau Schwaben, 1941, BA, R59 80; "Das Volk—der Ausgangspunkt und das Endziel der nationalsozialistischen Innen- und Aussenpolitik," NSDAP Gau Oberschlesien, 17 October 1941, BA, R59 89.

14. Smelser, "The Betrayal of a Myth."

15. Strobel, "Kritik der Zeit."

16. Friedrich Lange, *Deutsches Volk in 15 Staaten,* pp. 7–8.

17. Hitler, *Hitlers zweites Buch,*

18. Hitler, *Secret Conversations,* pp. 527, 63–64.

19. Himmler, 27 November 1943, BA, R49 19.

CHAPTER TWO

1. Jacobsen, *Aussenpolitik,* pp. 170, 608–9. Section "Geheime Zentralization der Volkstumsführung" provides the foremost study of Reich *Volkstumspolitik* in the prewar years.

2. Ibid., pp. 167–76.

3. Ibid., p. 168; Jacobsen, *Steinacher,* pp. 59–60.

4. Jacobsen, *Steinacher,* pp. 15–16; *Aussenpolitik,* pp. 167–76.

5. Jacobsen, *Aussenpolitik,* p. 176; Jacobsen, *Steinacher,* pp. xliii, 399.

6. Steinacher, "Die Bildung des Volksdeutschen Rates im Oktober 1933," and Steinacher Memo, 24 February 1935, "Aufgaben und Stellung des Volksdeutschen Rates," both in Jacobsen, *Steinacher,* pp. 34–41, 271–81. See also "Die Funktionen des VR" in Jacobsen, *Aussenpolitik,* pp. 178–86.

7. Wilhelm Ernst Bohle, "Germans Abroad," in *Germany Speaks,* pp. 326–30. See also de Jong, *The German Fifth Column,* pp. 12, 138–39.

8. Ehrich, *Die Auslands-Organisation der NSDAP,* p. 7.

9. Jacobsen, *Aussenpolitik*, pp. 599–600.

10. "Die Dienststelle Ribbentrop," in ibid., pp. 252–318. See also Seabury, *The Wilhelmstrasse*, pp. 41, 50–67.

11. "Die Dienststelle Ribbentrop," in Jacobsen, *Aussenpolitik*, p. 252.

12. Ibid., pp. 284–91. See also Höhne, *The Order of the Death's Head*, pp. 314–16; Seabury, *The Wilhelmstrasse*, pp. 63–65, 102–3.

13. Jacobsen, *Steinacher*, pp. 23–24, 582; Jacobsen, *Aussenpolitik*, pp. 197–201.

14. Jacobsen, *Steinacher*, pp. 162–64; Jacobsen, *Aussenpolitik*, p. 215.

15. Jacobsen, *Aussenpolitik*, pp. 218–22. See also McKale, *The Swastika Outside Germany*, pp. 55–58, 97; Smelser, *The Sudeten Problem*, pp. 24–26, 77–79; Jacobsen, *Steinacher*, pp. 239, 247–48.

16. Jacobsen, *Aussenpolitik*, pp. 222–28. See also McKale, *The Swastika Outside Germany*, p. 97; Smelser, *The Sudeten Problem*, pp. 127–29. For Steinacher's account of these events, refer to "Das Büro Kursell" in Jacobsen, *Steinacher*, pp. 244–46. Also, Hess to von Neurath, 23 April 1936, T-120/1451/3023H/D598607.

17. Engel, Labor Ministry, to Volksdeutsche Parteidienststelle, 17 November 1936, PA AA, Inland IIg, 222, Bd. 3; Letter with letterhead "Büro von Kursell," 14 July 1936, T-120/1323/2425/D512459; also Hess letters, March and 1 April 1936, PA AA, Inland IIg, 220, Bd. 1.

18. Jacobsen, *Aussenpolitik*, pp. 228–30. See also Foreign Ministry Decree, 1936, T-120/1451/3023H/D598504–506.

19. Meeting, 18 March 1936, Kursell and Foreign Ministry, T-120/1451/3023H/D598496–501.

20. This is a theme in Aronson, *Reinhard Heydrich*.

21. Smelser, *The Sudeten Problem*, pp. 169–74.

22. Levine, "Local Authority and the SS State," p. 350.

23. Smelser, *The Sudeten Problem*, pp. 183–87; Jacobsen, *Aussenpolitik*, pp. 231–32.

24. Karl Haushofer to Hess, 10 December 1936, T-253/56/512012–013.

25. Ibid.

26. Jacobsen, *Aussenpolitik*, p. 232; Jacobsen, *Steinacher*, p. 385; Smelser, *The Sudeten Problem*, p. 187.

27. Hess to von Neurath, 27 January 1937, PA AA, Inland IIg, 222, Bd. 3. Lorenz Testimony, pp. 2605–6; Kubitz Testimony, p. 2852.

28. Jacobsen, *Aussenpolitik*, p. 234.

29. Memo, Kultur A to Foreign Minister, 1 February 1937, PA AA, Inland IIg, 222, Bd.3. See also Jacobsen, *Aussenpolitik*, pp. 234–35; Jacobsen, *Steinacher*, pp. 385–86.

30. Csaki, DAI, Report of 5 February 1937, BA, R57 DAI/339; Jacobsen, *Aussenpolitik*, p. 235.

31. Smelser, *The Sudeten Problem*, p. 157, speaks of VoMi as a "radical SS agency . . . under an imperialist-minded director." He also states, p. 190, that 1937 was a year of triumph for the radicals in *Volkstumspolitik* as the SS gradually consolidated its hold on the field. Jacobsen, *Aussenpolitik*, p. 240, observes that Lorenz intro-

duced a harder line, but it is incorrect to assert that Lorenz's leadership signified a radicalization of *Volkstumspolitik*.

32. Smelser, *The Sudeten Problem*, p. 182.

CHAPTER THREE

1. Krausnick et al., *Anatomy of the SS State*, p. 284; NSDAP, *Organisationsbuch, 1936*, p. 286; Berger to Himmler, 4 June 1942, T-175/125/2650298–302; Ellermeier Testimony, pp. 2781–86.

2. Führer Decree, 2 July 1938, PA AA, Inland IIg, 232, Bd. 13. This decree was highly confidential, circulating only among the highest party and state officials.

3. Kubitz Testimony, p. 2852.

4. Lorenz Affidavit, NO-4701, Prosec. Doc. Book I, Lorenz; Lorenz Testimony, pp. 2605–6.

5. Reitlinger, *The SS*, p. 129; Jacobsen, *Aussenpolitik*, p. 237. Also see "Quatre generaux: Werner Lorenz, Gottlob Berger, Oswald Pohl, Karl Wolff," in Bayle, *Psychologie et Ethique du Nationalsocialisme*.

6. Wolff to Lorenz, 11 April 1939, BDC SSO Lorenz.

7. BDC SSO Lorenz. See also Lorenz Testimony, pp. 2603–4; also *TWC* 4, Case 8, pp. 1176–78; Koehl, "Toward an SS Typology," pp. 115, 124.

8. Rauschning, *Men of Chaos*, p. 25.

9. Waldeck, *Athene Palace*, pp. 304–5.

10. Ibid.

11. Rauschning, *Men of Chaos*, p. 25.

12. Milch Testimony, doc. no. 40, Doc. Book I, Lorenz, p. 88.

13. Skowronski Testimony, pp. 1–2.

14. Jacobsen, *Steinacher*, pp. 389–90.

15. BDC SSO Lorenz; Prosecution Closing Brief, Lorenz, p. 15; Lorenz Testimony, p. 2612; Koehl, "Toward an SS Typology," p. 117. Lorenz's NSDAP membership number was 397,994; his SS number was 6,636.

16. BDC SSO Lorenz; Lorenz Testimony, pp. 2604–5, and *TWC* 4, Case 8, pp. 1177–78.

17. Lorenz to Himmler, 9 July 1933, BDC SSO Lorenz.

18. Lorenz Dienstlaufbahn, Promotion Notification, BDC SSO Lorenz. Rauschning, *Men of Chaos*, pp. 25–27.

19. Lorenz Testimony, p. 2614.

20. Ibid., pp. 2614–15; Skowronski, Doc. No. 2, Doc. Book I, Lorenz.

21. Seniority List of the SS, 9 November 1944, in *TWC* 13, Case 11, pp. 1176–88. Ahead of Lorenz were Himmler, four *Oberstgruppenführer*—Franz Xavier Schwarz, Josef "Sepp" Dietrich, Kurt Daluege, and Paul Hausser—and nine *Obergruppenführer*: Walther Darré, Walter Buch, Udo von Woyrsch, Friedrich-Wilhelm Kruger, Erbprinz zu Waldeck und Pyrmont, Max Amman, Karl von Eberstein, Philipp Bouhler, and Friedrich Jeckeln. Lorenz also outranked Hans

Prützmann, Erich von dem Bach-Zalewski, Oswald Pohl, Gottlob Berger, Hans Jüttner, Odilo Globocnik, Otto Ohlendorf, Gunther d'Alquen, and Karl Wolff.

22. Wolff Testimony, p. 2612.

23. Jacobsen, *Steinacher*, p. 389; Wolff Testimony, p. 1925.

24. Lorenz to Karl Haushofer, 31 December 1937, T-253/57/514482.

25. Lorenz Testimony, p. 2607; Closing Brief of the Prosecution, Lorenz, p. 7; Lorenz Affidavit, NO-4701, Prosec. Doc. Book I, Lorenz.

26. Bormann, Rundschreiben 39/42, 1 August 1942, BDC SSO Lorenz.

27. Lorenz Testimony, pp. 2607–8; Wolff Testimony, p. 1925.

28. BDC SSO Behrends.

29. Aronson, *Reinhard Heydrich*, pp. 161–62.

30. Behrends to Himmler, 29 December 1942, BDC SSO Behrends. See also Koehl, *The Black Corps*, pp. 127, 147; Smelser, *The Sudeten Problem*, p. 189 n. 95; Aronson, *Reinhard Heydrich*, pp. 202–3.

31. BDC SSO Behrends.

32. Letters in BDC SSO Behrends, including Behrends to Himmler, 29 December 1942.

33. Final Plea, Lorenz Defense, pp. 13–14.

34. BDC SSO Ellermeier.

35. Personal-Bericht, Beurteilung by Lorenz, 12 November 1943, BDC SSO Ellermeier; Ellermeier Testimony, p. 2767.

36. BDC SSO Ellermeier.

37. Jacobsen, *Aussenpolitik*, pp. 235–36, 609.

38. Collection of lists, addresses of units, etc., T-175/32/2540815–854.

39. Schmidt to Lorenz, 10 January 1938, BDC SSO Lorenz; Lorenz Affidavit, NO-4701, Prosec. Doc. Book I, Lorenz; Lorenz Testimony, p. 2606.

40. Lorenz Defense Opening Statement, p. 5; Jacobsen, *Aussenpolitik*, pp. 239, 245, 278; Lohl Affidavit, Doc. No. 10, Doc. Book I, Lorenz, p. 33; BDC SSO Stier; BDC SSO Wehofsich; Karl Haushofer to Hess, 17 December 1936, T-253/46/499839–840.

41. BDC SSO Wehofsich.

42. In a comparison of the April 1943 and June 1944 VoMi organization plans, both Heller and Puls were "Pg" (parteigenossen) in 1943 but held SS ranks in 1944. BDC, Research Division, Notebook RFSS 31.

43. Lohl Affidavit, Doc. No. 10, Doc. Book I, Lorenz, p. 32.

44. BDC SSO Wehofsich; BDC SSO Kubitz; Kubitz Testimony, pp. 2849–50, 2856; Jacobsen, *Aussenpolitik*, p. 238.

45. RSHA to SS Main Office, 3 February 1941, BDC SSO Henniger; Dienststelle Heissmeyer to SS Personnel Main Office, 3 April 1944, BDC SSO Henniger.

46. Wehofsich to "Lieber Onkel Karl," 1 August 1943, T-253/58/514618.

47. Refer to BDC SSO Kubitz, Luig, and Minke.

48. Neusüss-Hunkel, *Die SS*, p. 23.

49. Lerner, *The Nazi Elite*, pp. vi–vii.

50. BDC SSO Hoffmeyer. For the prototype, see Waite, *Vanguard of Nazism*.

51. Von Pfeffer to Koch, 21 June 1935, BDC SSO Hoffmeyer; Von Pfeffer Bescheinigung, 9 December 1935, BDC SSO Hoffmeyer.

52. Lorenz to Schmidt, SS Personnel Main Office, 8 March 1939, BDC SSO Hoffmeyer; Institut für Zeitgeschichte, *Gutachten*, p. 261; Jacobsen, *Steinacher*, p. 390.

53. Sydnor, *Soldiers of Destruction*.

54. No complete organizational plan for VoMi has turned up for the preresettlement period. Jacobsen, *Aussenpolitik*, p. 245, provides a basic, but incomplete, plan for 1937.

55. Jacobsen, *Aussenpolitik*, p. 245.

56. Brückner Testimony, pp. 2738–39.

57. Jacobsen, *Aussenpolitik*, p. 236.

58. BDC SSO Hube.

59. BDC SSO Kubelke.

60. Globocnik, 16 May 1938, BDC SSO Maier-Kaibitsch; 90. SS Standarte Dienstleistungszeugnis, 17 June 1939, BDC SSO Maier-Kaibitsch.

61. Wehofsich to Luig, 29 July 1938, BA, VoMi, R59/92.

62. BDC SSO Altena.

63. BDC SSO Hagen; Hagen to RFSS, 23 January 1939, BDC SSO Hagen; Hagen Affidavit, NO-5160, Prosec. Doc. Book XIIIB.

CHAPTER FOUR

1. Jacobsen, *Steinacher*, pp. 386–91.

2. Jacobsen, *Aussenpolitik*, p. 248; *Steinacher*, p. xxvi; Smelser, *The Sudeten Problem*, p. 192.

3. Jacobsen, *Steinacher*, p. 393.

4. Twardowski, Foreign Ministry, 14 January 1937, T-120/1451/3023H/D598566–575.

5. Jacobsen, *Steinacher*, p. xxvii; Jacobsen, *Aussenpolitik*, p. 249.

6. Hess to Steinacher, 19 October 1937, in Jacobsen, *Steinacher*, p. 413; Jacobsen, *Aussenpolitik*, pp. 249–51; Steinacher to Hess, 20 October 1937, PA AA, Inland IIg, 224, Bd. 5, Deutschtum.

7. Lorenz Testimony, p. 2608; also Lorenz, NO-4701, Prosec. Doc. Book I, Lorenz.

8. Jacobsen, *Aussenpolitik*, p. 169.

9. Pfundter, RMI, to Deputy Führer and Foreign Ministry, 3 September 1937, PA AA, Inland IIg, 224, Bd. 5. See also Jacobsen, *Aussenpolitik*, p. 249; Lorenz Testimony, pp. 2608–9; Lorenz, NO-4701, Prosec. Doc. Book I, Lorenz; Closing Brief, Prosec. Lorenz, pp. 6–7.

10. Hess, no. 5/39, 3 February 1939, T-175/119/2644543–545; also Jacobsen, *Steinacher*, pp. 504–5.

11. Richtlinien, unsigned, 2 February 1937, T-253/54/509443.

12. "Besprechung mit Lorenz," 23 April 1937, in Jacobsen, *Steinacher*, pp. 423–24.

13. Trampler to Karl Haushofer, 15 July 1940, T-253/55/510–983.

14. Bormann, to all NSDAP offices, 31 August 1937, BDC, Research Division, Folder 169–182; Robert Ley, "Anordnung," 15 May 1941, T-175/32/2540202.

15. Garben, Dienststelle Ribbentrop, to Luig, VoMi, 13 December 1937 and 15 December 1937, both in PA AA, Dienststelle Ribbentrop, 16/2 VoMi.

16. Albrecht Haushofer to Karl Haushofer, 10 February 1938, T-253/46/500006–011.

17. Supplement to Führer Order sent by Hess to Himmler, May 1938, T-175/21/2525778–779.

18. Unsigned memo, 19 March 1938, PA AA, Inland IIg, 226, Bd. 7.

19. "Entwurf," 29 March 1938, T-120/716/1078/315–994.

20. Supplement 5c, 19 March 1938, PA AA, Inland IIg, 222, Bd. 3; Bureau of Foreign Minister to Stieve, 29 March 1938, T-120/716/1078/315993.

21. Hitler, Decree of 2 July 1938, PA AA, Inland IIg, 219, 1941–1944.

22. Smelser, "The Betrayal of a Myth," p. 274. See also Rechnungshof to Reich Finance Ministry, 27 February 1943, PA AA, Inland II-D, 64-01-9/B1002.

23. Jacobsen, *Aussenpolitik*, p. 670.

24. Lohl Affidavit, Doc. Book I, Lorenz, pp. 32–33. Jacobsen, *Aussenpolitik*, pp. 676–77, 692–93. See also Deutsche Stiftung, 1937, T-120/1451/3023H/D598621–622.

25. Lorenz, VoMi to Lorenz in Kultur A, Foreign Ministry, 3 March 1939, T-120/1451/3023H/D599049; Memo, Kultur A, "Geldmittel," 19 March 1938, PA AA, Inland IIg, 226, Bd. 7.

26. Fabritius Testimony, Doc. Book III, Lorenz, p. 45; Jacobsen, *Aussenpolitik*, pp. 243–44.

27. Rabius, "Die Kirche im Volkstumskampf."

28. 1937 Kulturfond Budget, T-120/716/1080/316270–271; Heckel, to Reich Minister of Church Affairs, 18 June 1938, T-120/716/1080/316263–268.

29. Ribbentrop, 25 May 1938, T-120/1451/3023H/D599002.

30. Pieger Testimony, p. 2791.

31. Rödiger, Foreign Ministry, 2 March 1937, T-120/1323/2425/D512582–584.

32. Schröder, "Südosteuropa als 'Informal Empire' Deutschlands."

33. Himmler to Lorenz, 27 June 1938, BDC SSO Lorenz.

34. Luig to Dienststelle Ribbentrop, 26 January 1939, PA AA, Dienststelle Ribbentrop, 16/2 VoMi; Affidavit Hagen, NO-5160, Prosec. Doc. Book XIIIB; Wehofsich to Luig, VoMi, 29 July 1938, BA, VoMi R59 92.

35. RMI, "Deutsche-Volkszugehörigkeit," 29 March 1939, Doc. No. 63, Doc. Book I, Greifelt, p. 13.

CHAPTER FIVE

1. Hitler, *Mein Kampf*. See also Jacobsen, *Aussenpolitik*; Weinberg, *Foreign Policy of Hitler's Germany*.

2. This is one of the major themes in Weinberg, *Foreign Policy of Hitler's Germany*.

3. Wolfe, *The German Octopus*, pp. 18–19; *The Brown Network*, p. 11.

4. Albrecht Haushofer to Karl Haushofer, 3 February 1938, T-253/49/504318–321. See also Gehl, *Austria, Germany, and the Anschluss*; Jacobsen, *Aussenpolitik*, pp. 435–40.

5. Reports to Capra, undated, T-253/49/504287–288, and 8 January 1938, T-253/49/504272–273; Kraus to Karl Haushofer, 2 February 1941, T-253/55/510895–898;

6. Sievers to Behrends, 20 May 1938, BA, R59 92.

7. Winkler, *Deutschtum in aller Welt*, pp. 74–75. Fittbogen, *Was jeder Deutsche*, pp. 66–69, 94–99, estimates 212,500 Germans out of a total population of 260,491.

8. "Zur Lage in Österreich-Südtirol-Liechtenstein," in Jacobsen, *Steinacher*, pp. 403–9; also Latour, "Germany, Italy, and South Tyrol," p. 95.

9. Latour, *Südtirol und die Achse Berlin-Rom*, pp. 20–21, 96; Jacobsen, *Steinacher*, p. 573.

10. Koehl, *RKFDV*, p. 40; Bismarck, Foreign Ministry, to Hess, 6 April 1938, in *DGFP*, D, 1, no. 734, pp. 1068–69.

11. Memo, 19 May 1938, T-120/2529/520256–259; Stieve, Kultur A, to Ambassador in Rome, May 1938, T-120/1451/3023H/D598938–941.

12. VoMi, 20 January 1939, in *DGFP*, D, 6, no. 163, pp. 198–99 n. 2.

13. Latour, *Südtirol und die Achse Berlin-Rom*, p. 24; Minke, VDA, to Karl Haushofer, 21 April 1939, T-253/52/1507274–275.

14. Hassell, 16 January 1937, T-120/2127/4132/462800–803.

15. Latour, "Germany, Italy, and South Tyrol," pp. 98–99; Memo of Ciano and Ribbentrop talks on 6–7 May 1939, dated 18 May 1939, in *DGFP*, D, 6, no. 341, pp. 450–52.

16. Von Hassell, *The Von Hassell Diaries*, pp. 45–47.

17. Luig, VoMi, No. 44, 7 July 1939, PA AA, Dienststelle Ribbentrop, 16/2 VoMi.

18. Winkler, *Deutschtum in aller Welt*, pp. 46–47; Fittbogen, *Was jeder Deutsche*, pp. 86–92.

19. For a survey of the extent of financial aid the Reich granted the Sudeten-landers, see Smelser, "The Betrayal of a Myth"; also Svatosch, "Zum Untergang," pp. 83–98; Arndt, "Ständische Ideologie im Henleinfaschismus"; Jacobsen, *Steinacher*, p. 26.

20. Smelser, *The Sudeten Problem*, pp. 29, 43; idem, "Sudeten German Party Elites"; Brügel, "Deutsche Demokraten."

21. Smelser, *The Sudeten Problem*, pp. 49–52, 120; Luža, *Transfer of the Sudeten Germans*, pp. 49, 68, 74–79; Jacobsen, *Aussenpolitik*, pp. 441–42; Jacobsen, *Steinacher*, pp. 575, 585–90.

22. Woermann, Foreign Ministry, 19 August 1938, in Král, *Die Deutschen*, no. 186, pp. 277–78; Smelser, *The Sudeten Problem*, pp. 97, 172–73.

23. Smelser, *The Sudeten Problem*, pp. 196–200.

24. Twardowski to Stieve, 18 August 1937, T-120/1451/3023H/D598711–713.

25. Fries to Stieve, 23 August 1937, PA AA, Inland IIg, 223, Bd. 4.

26. Lorenz to Bundesleiter Sudetendeutscher Heimatbund, 23 October 1937, PA AA, Dienstelle Ribbentrop, 16/2 VoMi.

27. Altenburg to Foreign Minister, 9 December 1937, T-120/1451/3023H/D598720–721.

28. Memo of 14 February 1938, T-120/716/1078/315938–939; Luig, VoMi, to Dienststelle Ribbentrop, 26 August 1937, PA AA, Dienstelle Ribbentrop, 16/2 VoMi.

29. Foreign Ministry, 28 March 1938, in Král, *Die Deutschen*, pp. 162–63. Also "Bericht Konrad Henleins über seine Audienz beim Führer," in Král, *Die Deutschen*, p. 163.

30. Memo of 29 March 1938, in *DGFP*, D, 2, no. 109, pp. 203–4; Reference to Frank testimony, in *IMT* 7: 205–6.

31. Henlein Report, 31 March 1938, T-120/716/1078/315955.

32. Eisenlohr to Foreign Ministry, 4 April 1938, in Král, *Die Deutschen*, no. 107, pp. 172–73; Luig, VoMi, to SA, 9 April 1938, in Král, *Die Deutschen*, no. 116, p. 184; Weizsäcker memo, 9 April 1938, in *DGFP*, D, 2, no. 124, p. 228.

33. Operation Green, 30 May 1938, in *DGFP*, D, 2, pp. 357–62.

34. Memo, 13 August 1938, in *DGFP*, D, 2, no. 350, pp. 556–57.

35. Altenberg, 14 September 1938, in *DGFP*, D, 2, no. 472, pp. 757–58.

36. "Adolf Hitlers Richtlinien . . . vom 18 September 1938," in Král, *Die Deutschen*, no. 226, pp. 312–13; Henlein to Freikorps, 20 September 1938, no. 6, in Král, *Die Deutschen*, no. 229, pp. 316–17.

37. Viererbl, "Auslandsdeutsche Rundschau," pp. 80–84; also "Die Einigung des Sudetendeutschtums vollzogen."

38. Foreign Ministry, 2 November 1938, T-120/402/309269–272; Meeting at VoMi, 4 November 1938, PA AA, Inland IIg, 246, Bd. 1.

39. Stieve, Kultur A, 7 November 1938, PA AA, Inland IIg, 246, Bd. 1; Twardowski to RMI, Minister of Education, the OKW, RFSS, and VoMi, 11 November 1938, T-120/2559/5199H/E307678; Declaration of 20 November 1938, T-120/402/1022/309277–278.

40. Schliep, Pol. Abt. V, 9 November 1938, in *DGFP*, D, 4, no. 109, p. 138.

41. Ribbentrop to Czechoslovakian government, 14 March 1939, in Král, *Die Deutschen*, no. 279, p. 380.

42. Lumans, "The Ethnic German Minority of Slovakia."

43. Hoensch, *Die Slowakei*, pp. 72–73; Henlein to Karmasin, 15 October 1937, in Král, *Die Deutschen*, no. 76, pp. 130–31.

44. Karmasin to Henlein, 21 April 1938, in Král, *Die Deutschen*, no. 126, pp. 198–99.

45. Altenburg, Pol. Abt. IV, 19 May 1938, in *DGFP*, D, 2, no. 167, pp. 291–92; Hoensch, *Die Slowakei*, pp. 179 n. 36, 190.

46. Lorenz (not Werner), Foreign Ministry, to Foreign Minister, 15 October 1938, T-120/402/1022/309240–248; Kundt draft, 31 October 1938 T-120/402/1022/309262–263; Kundt draft, undated, T-120/402/1020/309227–229.

47. Rabl to Daluege, Prague, 20 September 1942, in Král, *Die Deutschen*, no.

395, pp. 496–97; Druffel, Bratislava, to Woermann, Foreign Ministry, 15 November 1938, in *DGFP*, D, 4, no. 119, pp. 149–51.

48. Meeting, 12 February 1939, in *IMT* 3:149; also Hoensch, *Die Slowakei*, pp. 226, 129–31.

49. Karmasin to Henlein, 16 March 1939, Král, in *Die Deutschen*, no. 282, pp. 384–85.

50. Wagner, *Die Deutsche in Litauen*; Fittbogen, *Was jeder Deutsche*, p. 195; "Litauen," T-120/1305/2334/486810–813.

51. Akademie für Deutsches Recht, "Die Deutsche Volksgruppe in Litauen," March 1939, T-120/1305/2334/486769–774; "Übersicht Litauen," 1939, T-120/1305/2334/486810–813. See also Broszat, "Die Memeldeutschen Organisationen"; Hubatsch, "Das Memelland."

52. Massmann, VDA, 29 June 1936, in Jacobsen, *Steinacher*, pp. 671–75.

53. Broszat, "Die Memeldeutschen Organisationen," pp. 273–75; Gentzen, "Die Rolle der 'Deutschen Stiftung,'" pp. 75–78.

54. Gentzen, "Die Rolle der 'Deutschen Stiftung,'" p. 93; Koch, Königsberg, to Foreign Ministry, 11 August 1937, T-120/3214/7573H/E542842.

55. Twardowski to Stieve, 19 August 1937, T-120/3214/7573H/E542845–846; State Secretary to Stieve, Kultur A, 20 August 1937, T-120/3214/7573H/E542847; Gestapo to RMI, 26 March 1938, PA AA, Inland IIg, 227, Bd. 8.

56. Woermann, 23 July 1938, in *DGFP*, D, 5, no. 349, p. 462; Weizsäcker to Memel, 28 September 1938, in *DGFP*, D, 5, no. 353, p. 469.

57. Saucken, Memel, to Foreign Ministry, 5 November 1938, in *DGFP*, D, 5, no. 361, pp. 482–84; Grundherr, Pol. VI, 25 November 1938, in *DGFP*, D, 5, no. 364, pp. 487–90.

58. Grundherr, Pol. VI, "Report to the Foreign Minister," 1 December 1938, in *DGFP*, D, 5, no. 369, pp. 494–95; Doertenbach, Pol. VI, 5 December 1938, in *DGFP*, D, 5, no. 371, pp. 494–95.

59. Grundherr to Zechlin, 2 January 1939, in *DGFP*, D, 5, no. 381, pp. 506–9.

60. Saucken, Memel, to Foreign Ministry, 15 January 1939, in *DGFP*, D, no. 384, pp. 512–13; Lorenz to Hess, 4 February 1939, in *DGFP*, D, 5, no. 388, pp. 515–16; Saucken, Memel, to Foreign Ministry, 8 February 1939, in *DGFP*, D, 5, no. 390, pp. 517–18; Woermann, Foreign Ministry, to Saucken, Memel, 14 March 1939, in *DGFP*, D, 5, no. 393, p. 520; Dortenbach, Pol. VI, 18 March 1939, in *DGFP*, D, 5, no. 398, p. 524.

61. Twardowski, Foreign Ministry, 27 July 1939, T-120/1451/3023H/D599073.

62. Winkler, *Deutschtum in aller Welt*, p. 114. Gauss, *Das Buch vom Deutschen Volkstum*, p. 7, claimed 300,000.

63. Fittbogen, *Was jeder Deutsche*, p. 182, claims 500,000 Germans lived in Congress Poland and Cholmerland before the war. In 1926 the Poles counted only 242,000, whereas German sources noted 320,000. Winkler, *Deutschtum in aller Welt*, p. 114, counted 223,067 in 1921 and 311,574 in 1931.

64. For Teschen, see Fittbogen, *Was jeder Deutsche*, pp. 188–90. For Galicia, Winkler, *Deutschtum in aller Welt*, p. 114, estimated 40,000, and Fittbogen, *Was jeder Deutsche*, pp. 190–95, counted 60,000.

65. Fittbogen, *Was jeder Deutsche*, pp. 36–42; Winkler, *Deutschtum in aller Welt*, p. 114; Gauss, *Das Buch vom Deutschen Volkstum*, p. 7. Also see Levine, *Hitler's Free City*.

66. "Entrechtungen . . . ," 1939, T-120/120/1305/2334/486813–825; "Die Rechtslage . . . Deutsche Volksgruppe in Polen," March 1939, T-120/1305/2334/486725–739.

67. Jacobsen, *Steinacher*, pp. 532–42.

68. Ibid.; Jacobsen, *Aussenpolitik*, pp. 583–86.

69. Jacobsen, *Steinacher*, pp. 526–31, 541–42; Jacobsen, *Aussenpolitik*, pp. 241–42, 596–99. For a survey of the situation in Poland at the time of Lorenz's arrival at VoMi, refer to "Polen-Volkstumsarbeit" 9 January 1937, T-120/3214/E542935–940.

70. Behrends to Twardowski, Meeting of 6–8 April 1937, dated 15 April 1937, T-120/1451/3023H/D598667–671; "Entwurf," 26 January 1937, T-120/3214/7507H/E543372–386; Consul General in Posen to Foreign Ministry, 2 September 1936, T-120/1323/2425/D512466–469.

71. Foreign Ministry memo, 12 May 1938, T-120/1451/3023H/D598964–965; Lorenz to leaders in Poland, 18 May 1938, T-120/1451/3023H/D598960–963.

72. Luig, VoMi, 7 July 1939, PA AA, Dienststelle Ribbentrop, 16/2 VoMi; Zembek to von Moltke, 20 October 1938, T-120/1305/2334/486686–687.

73. Lorenz to Ribbentrop, 5 November 1938, T-120/1305/2334/486677–681.

74. Ibid.

75. Twardowski to Stieve, 12 November 1938, PA AA, Inland IIg, 230, Bd. 11.

76. Seeber, "Der Anteil der Minderheitsorganisation 'Selbstschutz,'" pp. 10–11; Schwager, Kultur A, 27 October 1938, T-120/1178/2168/470991–992; Foreign Ministry memo to Kultur B, 15 November 1938, T-120/1178/2168/470995.

77. Twardowski, to Stieve and State Secretary, 8 February 1939, T-120/1305/2334/486702–703.

78. Memo, Kultur B, "Hilfsaktion . . . ," 15 July 1939, T-120/1495/3064H/D611815–817.

79. Schliep, Pol. Abt. V, to Veesenmeyer, Danzig, 22 August 1939, in *DGFP*, D, 7, no. 182, p. 190; Veesenmeyer, Danzig, to Foreign Ministry, 23 August 1939, in *DGFP*, D, 7, no. 196, p. 207; Schliep memo, 23 August 1939, in *DGFP*, D, 7, no. 195, pp. 206–7.

80. Heike, "Die ersten Opfer des Zweiten Weltkrieges."

CHAPTER SIX

1. Boelitz, *Das Grenz- und Auslandsdeutschtum*, pp. 97–99; Winkler, *Deutschtum in aller Welt*, pp. 128, 136; Gauss, *Das Buch vom deutschen Volkstum*, p. 7.

2. Akademie für Deutsches Recht, "Die deutsche Volksgruppe in Estland," March 1939, T-120/1305/2344/486775–784; "Übersicht Estland," T-120/1305/2334/486803–805; Weiss, "Das Volksgruppenrecht in Estland."

3. "Übersicht . . . Estland," T-120/1305/2334/486803–805; Bahr, *Volk jenseits*

der Grenzen, pp. 58–59; Luig, VoMi, memo, 7 July 1939, PA AA, Dienstelle Ribbentrop, 16/2 VoMi.

4. Lorenz to Wrangell and Lutz, 27 January 1938, T-120/716/1080/315788–789.

5. Frohwein, Tallin, to Foreign Ministry, 7 October 1938, T-120/1305/2334/486644–647.

6. Ibid.; Frohwein to Berlin, 13 October 1938, T-120/1305/2334/486656; Richter to Pol. VI, 21 October 1938, T-120/1305/2334/486648; Frohwein to Berlin, 7 October 1938, T-120/1305/2334/486644–647.

7. Legation in Tallin to Twardowski, 3 May 1939, T-120/1451/3023H/D599058–060.

8. Bahr, *Volk jenseits der Grenzen*, pp. 59–63; Akademie für Deutsches Recht, "Die deutsche Volksgruppe in Lettland," March 1939, T-120/1305/2334/486761–768; "Übersicht . . . Lettland," T-120/1305/2334/ 486808–810.

9. Jacobsen, *Steinacher*, p. 548; Rimscha, "Zur Gleichschaltung," pp. 36–37; Lundin, "The Nazification of the Baltic German Minorities"; Loeber, *Diktierte Option*.

10. German Legation, Riga, to Foreign Ministry, 24 July 1937, PA AA, Inland IIg, 223, Bd. 4.

11. Rimscha, "Zur Gleichschaltung," p. 47.

12. Luig, VoMi, 7 July 1939, PA AA, Dienststelle Ribbentrop, 16/2 VoMi.

13. Legation in Riga to Foreign Ministry, 1 October 1938, T-120/1054/1861/421294–297; Schack, to Foreign Ministry, 29 October 1938, T-120/1054/1861/421319–321.

14. Winkler, *Deutschtum in aller Welt*, p. 111.

15. Ibid.; Gauss, *Das Buch vom deutschen Volkstum*, p. 7; Fittbogen, *Was jeder Deutsche*, p. 137.

16. Akademie für Deutsches Recht, T-120/1305/2334/486740–748; Kultur A . . . Rumänien, 17 June 1940, T-120/1305/2334/488983–989; Wiese, *Auslanddeutsche Erneuerung*, p. 29; Jacobsen, *Steinacher*, pp. 80–81; Komjathy and Stockwell, *German Minorities*, pp. 103–24.

17. Boelitz, *Das Grenz- und Auslandsdeutschtum*, pp. 83–84; Jacobsen, *Aussenpolitik*, pp. 570–71; Paikert, *The Danube Swabians*, pp. 250–52; "Aufzeichnung . . . die deutsche Volksgruppe in Rumänien," 17 June 1940, T-120/1305/2334/488983–989.

18. Jacobsen, *Aussenpolitik*, pp. 570–74; *Expulsion* 3:33–34; VoMi, "Deutsche Volksgruppe in Rumänien," 26 October 1942, NO-3526, Prosec. Doc. Book IIB, Case 8; Albrich, Christ, and Hockl, *Deutsche Jugendbewegung im Südosten*, pp. 99–100.

19. Jacobsen, *Steinacher*, pp. 560–61; Jacobsen, *Aussenpolitik*, pp. 573–74

20. Twardowski to Bucharest, 11 May 1937, PA AA, Inland IIg, 233, Bd. 4; Wehofsich, VoMi, to Kultur A, 10 May 1937, PA AA, Inland IIg, 223, Bd. 4; Behrends, VoMi, to Twardowski, 21 May 1937, PA AA, Inland IIg, 223, Bd. 4; VoMi, "Abschluss Protokol," 24 April 1937, T-120/1323/2425/D512631.

21. Fabricius, Bucharest, to Foreign Ministry, 27 January 1938, T-120/716/1078/315795–797.

22. Ibid.

23. Jacobsen, *Aussenpolitik*, p. 581; *Expulsion* 3:35.

24. Hegemann, "Die Deutsche Volksgruppe in Rumänien," p. 374; Akademie für Deutsches Recht, T-120/1305/2334/486740–748.

25. Luig, VoMi, 7 July 1939, PA AA, Dienststelle Ribbentrop, 16/2 VoMi; Minke to Karl Haushofer, 22 July 1939, T-253/51/506297–298.

26. Twardowski, 25 July 1939, T-120/1305/2334/486837–838; Henniger, VoMi, to Foreign Ministry, 1 August 1939, T-120/1305/2334/486842; Twardowski to Bucharest, 2 August 1939, T-120/1305/2334/486840; Legation in Bucharest to Foreign Ministry, 12 October 1939, T-120/1305/2334/486848–850.

27. "Aufzeichung . . . die deutsche Volksgruppe in Rumänien," 17 June 1940, T-120/1305/2334/488983–989.

28. For background, see Hillgruber, *Hitler, König Carol, und Marschall Antonescu*; Komjathy and Stockwell, *German Minorities*.

29. Winkler, *Deutschtum in aller Welt*, pp. 66–67; Fittbogen, *Was jeder Deutsche*, p. 106. See also Gauss, *Das Buch vom deutschen Volkstum*, pp. 294–303; Boelitz, *Das Grenz- und Auslandsdeutschtum*, pp. 70–72.

30. Paikert, *The Danube Swabians*, p. 143. See also Jacobsen, *Steinacher*, pp. 552–53; Komjathy and Stockwell, *German Minorities*, pp. 43–64, 147–156.

31. Akademie für Deutsches Recht, "Die deutsche Volksgruppe in Ungarn," March 1939, T-120/1305/2334/486754–760.

32. Jacobsen, *Aussenpolitik*, pp. 521–22; Tilkovsky, "Die deutsche Minderheit in Ungarn," pp. 59–60; Paikert, *The Danube Swabians*, pp. 91–92; Steyer, "Das Deutschtum in Ungarn," p. 695; Jacobsen, *Steinacher*, pp. 550–51; *Expulsion* 2:22–24.

33. Paikert, *The Danube Swabians*, pp. 114–15, 200–201; Tilkovsky, "Die deutsche Minderheit in Ungarn," pp. 59, 70–72; Akademie für Deutsches Recht, T-120/1305/2334/486754–760; Jacobsen, *Aussenpolitik*, pp. 521–24; Jacobsen, *Steinacher*, p. 551; *Expulsion* 2:22–24; Steyer, "Das Deutschtum in Ungarn," p. 695; "Entrechtungen . . . Ungarn," 1939, T-120/1305/2334/486829–832.

34. Jacobsen, *Aussenpolitik*, pp. 523–26; Twardowski, 18 September 1936, T-120/1323/2425/D512503–513.

35. Paikert, *The Danube Swabians*, pp. 139–40; Jacobsen, *Steinacher*, p. 393.

36. *Expulsion* 2:24–25; Door, "Zur Vorgeschichte," p. 109; Paikert, *The Danube Swabians*, pp. 116–17; Schechtman, "The Elimination of German Minorities," p. 162.

37. Twardowski to Foreign Minister, 23 November 1938, T-120/1325/2446H/D514863–864.

38. Arató, "Der 'Volksbund der Deutschen in Ungarn,'" p. 290; Paikert, *The Danube Swabians*, pp. 116–17; "Entrechtungen," 1939, T-120/1305/2334/486829–832; "Die deutsche Volksgruppe in Ungarn," March 1939, T-120/1305/2334/486754–760.

39. Viererbl, "Auslandsdeutsche Rundschau," pp. 82–83; Akademie für Deutsches Recht, T-120/1305/2334/486754–760; "Entrechtungen," T-120/1305/2334/486829–832; Gestapo to Reich Foreign Ministry, 28 April 1939, T-120/1451/3023H/D599062–063.

40. Erdmannsdorff, Budapest, to Foreign Ministry, 3 August 1939, T-120/1451/3023H/D599077–079; VoMi, Henniger, to Foreign Ministry, 31 August 1939, PA AA, Inland IIg, 233, Bd. 14.

41. AO to Foreign Ministry and VoMi, 10 November 1939, T-120/1305/2334/486852.

42. Memo, 10 September 1940, in *DGFP*, D, 11, no. 41, pp. 49–54.

43. Paikert, *The Danube Swabians*, pp. 116–17; Broszat, "Deutschland-Ungarn-Rumänien," p. 94; Tilkovsky, "Die deutsche Minderheit in Ungarn," p. 74.

44. Paikert, *The Danube Swabians*, pp. 117–18; Tilkovsky, "Die deutsche Minderheit in Ungarn," p. 75.

45. Memo, 10 September 1940, in *DGFP*, D, 11, no. 41, pp. 49–54.

46. Gauss, *Das Buch vom deutschen Volkstum*, p. 7; Fittbogen, *Was jeder Deutsche*, pp. 109–20.

47. Akademie für Deutsches Recht, "Die deutsche Volksgruppe in Jugoslawien," March 1939, T-120/1305/2334/486749–753.

48. Ibid.; Lorenz, Foreign Ministry, 27 June 1940, T-120/1306/2363/488977–982. For background, see Wuescht, *Jugoslawien*; Komjathy and Stockwell, *German Minorities*, pp. 125–45.

49. Paikert, *The Danube Swabians*, p. 270; Wuescht, *Jugoslawien*, p. 258; Jacobsen, *Steinacher*, p. 562.

50. Twardowski, Foreign Ministry, to VoMi, 16 June 1937, PA AA, Abt. VI, Kultur A, Bd. 17; Lorenz to Legation in Belgrade, 22 October 1937, PA AA, Inland IIg, 225, Bd. 6; Jacobsen, *Steinacher*, pp. 568, 573; VoMi report, 23–29 January 1938, T-253/49/504269–270; Luig, VoMi, memo, 7 July 1939, PA AA, Dienststelle Ribbentrop, 16/2 VoMi.

51. Jacobsen, *Steinacher*, p. 568; Wuescht, *Jugoslawien*, pp. 254–55; Foreign Ministry, 27 June 1940, T-120/1306/2363/488977–982.

52. Carstanjen, Graz, to Dienststelle Ribbentrop, 25 May 1940, PA AA, Inland IIg, 236, Bd. 17.

53. Reich Legation, Belgrade, to Foreign Ministry, 5 June 1940, T-120/1451/3023H/D599216–218.

54. Twardowski to State Secretary, Foreign Ministry, 15 April 1939, T-120/1325/2446H/D514909; Auslandsdienst report, "Jugoslawien," 12 June 1940, PA AA, Inland IIg, 236, Bd. 17.

55. Sipo-SD to Foreign Ministry, Luther, 18 January 1941, PA AA, Inland IIg, 239, Bd. 20.

56. Rimann, VoMi, to Foreign Ministry, "Sudslawien," 1 February 1941, T-120/1451/3023H/D599330–331; Triska, Foreign Ministry, 6 February 1941, T-120/1451/3023H/D599332–334.

57. Carstanjen, Graz, to Foreign Ministry, 29 March 1941, T-120/2415/4670H/

E221510; Abwehrabteilung II to Chef Z Ausl., 28 March 1941, T-120/2415/4670H/E221505–506.

58. OKW, Abwehr, to Foreign Ministry, 28 March 1941, T-120/2415/4670H/E221506; Rintelen, Foreign Ministry, 28 March 1941, T-120/2415/4670H/E221507; Weizsäcker to Bucharest, 29 March 1941, T-120/2415/4670H/E221480; Kubitz, VoMi, to Foreign Ministry, 16 April 1941, PA AA, Inland IIg, 251, Jugoslawien; Wuescht, *Jugoslawien*, pp. 260–61; Paikert, *The Danube Swabians*, pp. 276–77.

59. De Jong, *The German Fifth Column*, p. 232.

60. Fittbogen, *Was jeder Deutsche*, pp. 16–17; Gauss, *Das Buch vom deutschen Volkstum*, p. 7.

61. VoMi, Report, 10–15 January 1938, T-253/49/504266; Report of 8 January 1938, T-253/49/504267–268.

62. Luig, VoMi, 7 July 1939, PA AA, Dienststelle Ribbentrop, 16/2 VoMi; Gauss, *Das Buch vom deutschen Volkstum*; Fittbogen, *Was jeder Deutsche*, pp. 28–33; Karl Haushofer papers, 24 September 1929, T-253/47/501350–362; Boelitz, *Das Grenz- und Auslandsdeutschtum*, p. 15; Vollert, RMI, to Foreign Ministry, 16 June 1939, T-120/1451/3023H/D599069–070.

63. VoMi, 21 July 1937. PA AA, Dienststelle Ribbentrop, 16/2 VoMi.

64. Jacobsen, *Aussenpolitik*, pp. 509–17.

65. Lorenz, 17 December 1938, T-120/1325/2446H/D514888.

66. Rintelen, Foreign Ministry, 16 March 1938, in *DGFP*, D, 5, no. 509, pp. 675–76; Lorenz to Ribbentrop, 31 March 1939, in *DGFP*, D, 6, no. 141, pp. 176–78; Hahner, Reichsnährstand, to Dienststelle Ribbentrop, 16 February 1939, PA AA, Dienststelle Ribbentrop, 16/2 VoMi; Garben, Foreign Ministry, to Stier, VoMi, 27 February 1939, PA AA, Dienststelle Ribbentrop, 16/2 VoMi; Lorenz to Ribbentrop, 31 March 1939, in *DGFP*, D, 6, no. 141, pp. 176–78.

67. Akademie für Deutsches Recht, "Die deutsche Volksgruppe in Dänemark," March 1939, T-120/1305/2334/486785–789; and "Übersicht . . . Dänemark," 1939, T-120/1305/2334/486801–802.

68. Tägil, *Minderheit in Nordschleswig*, pp. 11–12; Joesten, *Rats in the Larder*, pp. 176–78; Tönnesen, "Aus dem deutsch-dänischen Grenzland."

69. Jacobsen, *Aussenpolitik*, pp. 170–72; Tägil, *Minderheit in Nordschleswig*, pp. 9–12.

70. Tägil, *Minderheit in Nordschleswig*, chapter 4.

71. Meissner, VoMi, to Dienststelle Ribbentrop, 15 January 1938, T-120/1372/2627/D526235–236; Luig, VoMi, 7 July 1939, PA AA, Dienststelle Ribbentrop, 16/2 VoMi; Vereinigte Finanzkontore to Foreign Ministry, Reich Ministry of Finance, and VoMi, Behrends, 1 December 1938, T-120/1372/2627/D526154–157; Schwagerer, Foreign Ministry, 5 January 1939, T-120/1372/2627/D526151–153.

72. Jacobsen, "Nordische Schicksalgemeinschaft," in *Aussenpolitik*, pp. 483–95; Memo, Hitler-Quisling conference, 16 August 1940, in *DGFP*, D, 10, no. 352, pp. 491–95; Hitler and Danish Foreign Minister Scavenius, 27 November 1941, in

DGFP, D, 13, no. 510, pp. 861–64. See also "Die Schicksalstunde des Nordens," Schulungsbrief der NSDAP-Nord Schleswig, no. 12, T-120/1378/2714/D531595–598.

73. Grundherr, Foreign Ministry, to Renthe-Fink, Copenhagen, 23 May 1939, in *DGFP*, D, 6, no. 432, pp. 571–72; Renthe-Fink, Copenhagen, to Grundherr, Foreign Ministry, 1 July 1939, in *DGFP*, D, 6, no. 600, p. 825; Woermann, Foreign Ministry, to Reich Legation, Copenhagen, 2 September 1939, in *DGFP*, D, 7, no. 536, p. 510.

74. Gauss, *Das Buch vom deutschen Volkstum*, p. 7; Winkler, *Deutschtum in aller Welt*, p. 139.

75. Boelitz, *Das Grenz- und Auslandsdeutschtum*, pp. 101–7; Fittbogen, *Was jeder Deutsche*, p. 164.

76. Fittbogen, *Was jeder Deutsche*, pp. 171–74, 177; Boelitz, *Das Grenz- und Auslandsdeutschtum*, pp. 108–10; Winkler, *Deutschtum in aller Welt*, p. 140.

77. Lorenz Testimony, p. 2620.

78. Freytag, Foreign Ministry, 11 October 1937, in *DGFP*, D, 1, no. 414, pp. 634–38; Siegfried, Foreign Ministry, 17 December 1937, in *DGFP*, D, 1, no. 426, p. 657.

79. Goecken, Foreign Ministry, 3 February 1938, in *DGFP*, D, 1 no. 438, pp. 687–88.

80. Dieckhoff, Washington, to Foreign Ministry, 28 February 1938, in *DGFP*, D, 1, no. 443, p. 693; Dieckhoff to Foreign Ministry, 2 June 1938, in *DGFP*, D, 1, no. 455, p. 709.

81. Arthur L. Smith, *The Deutschtum of Nazi Germany*, p. 44.

CHAPTER SEVEN

1. Hitler's Speech, 6 October 1939, in Loeber, *Diktierte Option*, no. 72, pp. 79–81.

2. *Völkischer Beobachter*, 11 October 1939, p. 2.

3. Schulenburg to Foreign Ministry, Berlin, 25 September 1939, in *DGFP*, D, 8, no. 131, p. 130.

4. Lorenz Testimony, pp. 2620–21; Lammers to Himmler, 29 September 1939, in *TWC* 13, Case 11, p. 138.

5. Lorenz Testimony, pp. 2620–21; Lammers to Himmler, 29 September 1939, in *TWC* 13, Case 11, p. 138. See also Koehl, *RKFDV*, pp. 49–50.

6. "Erlass des Führers . . . ," 7 October 1939, BA, R49 25.

7. Koehl, *RKFDV*, pp. 55–57; Krausnick et al. *Anatomy of the SS State*, p. 277; "Erste Anordnung," undated, T-74/15/387211–213.

8. Koehl, *RKFDV*, p. 31.

9. Himmler, Decree of 11 June 1941, NO-4047, Prosec. Doc. Book IIB.

10. RKFDV Anordnung no. 72, 29 June 1942, NO-4026, Prosec. Doc. Book IIB.

11. BDC SSO Greifelt; Greifelt Testimony, pp. 1371–72, 1377–78; Final Plea Greifelt, 25–27; Wolff Testimony, pp. 1915–19.

12. "Erste Anordnung," T-74/15/387211–213. See also Koehl, *RKFDV*, pp. 249–50.

13. Goecken, Foreign Ministry, to Krümmer, 27 November 1941, a list of the most important documents on *Volkstumsarbeit*, T-120/2424/4699/E227047. See also "Vereinbarung über die Zuständigkeit in Volkstumsfragen," 31 March 1941, PA AA, Inland IIg, 240, Bd. 21.

14. NSDAP, Reichsverfügungsblatt, 8 March 1941, Ausgabe A, Anordnung A 7/41, 26 February 1941, BDC, Research Division.

15. Führer Decree, 29 May 1941, in NSDAP, *Organisationsbuch, 1943*, p. 151.

16. Himmler, 11 June 1941, BDC, Research Division, Notebook 30 RFSS.

17. "Anordnung des RFSS . . . ," 28 November 1941, BA, R49 13.

18. NSDAP Partei Kanzlei, "Errichtung eines Hauptamtes für Volkstumsfragen," Hitler, Verfügung V 2/42, Reichsverfügungsblatt, Ausgabe A, 11/42, 16 March 1942, BDC, Research Division, Notebook 29 RFSS.

19. Creutz Testimony, pp. 1381–82.

20. Himmler, Anordnung 7/III, 12 November 1939, T-74/15/387131; Kaltenbrunner Testimony, in *IMT* 11:311; Behrends, 25 November 1940, T-81/267/2386342.

21. BDC SSO Rimann; Rimann Affidavit, Doc. No. 3, Doc. Book I, Lorenz, pp. 19–20.

22. BDC SSO Brückner; Final Plea Brückner, p. 3; Schoepke Affidavit, Doc. No. 1, Doc. Book I, Brückner, p. 4; Brückner Affidavit, NO-5041, Prosec. Doc. Book I, Brückner.

23. BDC SSO Sandler.

24. Lorenz evaluation of Brückner, BDC SSO Brückner; Schoepke, Doc. Book I, Brückner, pp. 4, 8.

25. BDC SSO Radunski.

26. BDC SSO Siebert.

27. BDC SSO Cube.

28. BDC SSO Krassowsky.

29. BDC SSO Kiepert.

30. Koehler Affidavit, doc. no. 15, Doc. Book I, Lorenz, p. 41.

31. DAI Report, Rüdiger, 21 April 1940, T-81/273/2393598.

32. DAI Büro, Berlin, to "L," 4 July 1940, T-81/273/2392474–475.

33. Siebert, VoMi, 12 December 1940, BA, R59 8.

34. VoMi, "Organisation und Geschäftsverteilungsplan," 15 April 1943, BDC, Research Division, Notebook 31 RFSS; Lohl to Reichsschatzmeister, 25 November 1943, BDC SSO, Lohl; "Organisation und Geschäftsverteilungsplan," 15 June 1944, BDC, Research Division, Notebook 31 RFSS.

35. Schwarz to Kommerzbank, 8 December 1943, BDC SSO, Lohl; Schwarz to VoMi, Lorenz, 15 October 1943, BDC SSO, Lohl; Schwarz to Lohl, 28 April 1944, BDC SSO, Lohl; Schwarz, "Vollmacht," 9 March 1942, BDC SSO, Lohl.

36. Cube, February 1944, BDC, Research Division, Notebook 31 RFSS; Brückner Affidavit, NO-4717, Prosec. Doc. Book IIB; "Organisation und Geschäftsverteilungsplan," 15 April 1943 and 15 June 1944.

37. Brückner Defense Opening Statement, p. 1260; Schoepke Testimony, Doc. Book DB I, Brückner, p. 6; "Organisation und Geschäftsverteilungsplan," 15 April 1943 and 15 June 1944.

38. Radunski Testimony, p. 2897; Klingsporn Testimony, p. 2830; "Organisation und Geschäftsverteilungsplan," 15 April 1943 and 15 June 1944.

39. "Organisation und Geschäftsverteilungsplan," 15 April 1943 and 15 June 1944. Summary of the department functions is based on these two annotated plans.

40. Panzer Affidavit, NO-5362, Prosec. Doc. Book VIIID; VoMi to all Einsatzführer, 29/42, 21 April 1942, T-81/269/2388119–120; VoMi, undated, T-74/1/371312.

41. List of Einsatzführer, 1940, T-81/273/2393171–172; List of Einsatzführer, March 1942, T-74/3/373327–332.

42. BDC SSO Panzer; NO-5362, Prosec. Doc. Book VIIID.

43. Einsatzführung Schwaben, Rundschreiben 385, 6 January 1943, T-81/283/2405917–918; Einsatzstab Litzmannstadt, Perthen, 27 July 1942, T-81/267/2386550; VoMi, Behrends, 25 November 1940, T-81/267/2386342; VoMi to Landrat, Tauber-Bischofsheim, 9 November 1940, T-81/279/2400111–112.

44. Einsatzführung Pommern, Anordnung 30, 8 September 1942, T-81/282/2404321; Einsatzführung Pommern, Anordnung 6, 3 March 1941, T-81/282/2404351.

45. BDC SSO Deussen.

46. BDC SSO Baumgart.

47. Lorenz, April 1942, T-81/282/2404237–240; SS Police Court III, Berlin, Lorenz, 20 April 1942, T-81/278/2399211–215; Heitz Testimony, Doc. Book I, Lorenz, p. 58; Einsatzführung Bayerische Ostmark, 16 March 1942, T-81/278/2399229–233.

48. BDC SSO Perthen.

49. VoMi, BDC, Research Division, Notebook 30 RFSS; Note to Verbindungsstelle Südost der VoMi, 29 September 1944, T-120/1757/3579/E025304.

50. "Organisation und Geschäftsverteilungsplan," 15 April 1943 and 15 June 1944.

51. Ibid.

52. Brückner Testimony, p. 2694.

53. NSDAP, *Organisationsbuch, 1943*, pp. 428–29.

54. Perthen, Litzmannstadt, Sonderanweisung Nr. 44, 27 July 1942, T-81/267/2386549.

55. Einsatzführung Schwaben, Nr. 389, 26 January 1943, BA, R59 55, and T-81/283/2405907.

56. Einsatzstab Litzmannstadt, Nr. 182, 15 October 1942, T-81/268/2386707–708.

CHAPTER EIGHT

1. Memo, Hitler and Ciano on 1–2 October 1939, in *DGFP*, D, 8, no. 176, pp. 184–85; "Umsiedlungschronik," undated, T-81/294/2418768–769.

2. Weizsäcker, to all Missions, 3 November 1939, T-120/1451/3023H/D599113–115.

3. Twardowski to RMI, VoMi, AO, RKFDV, 13 December 1939, T-120/1451/3023H/D599125–127.

4. *Völkischer Beobachter*, 1 January 1940.

5. "Der Nationalsozialist als politischer Soldat des Ostens," undated, unsigned, BA, R59 80.

6. Auhagen, "Die Ansiedlung deutscher Bauern. . . ." BA, R49 20.

7. Bosse, *Der Führer ruft*, p. 107; Engelhardt-Kyffhäuser, *Das Buch vom Grossen Treck*, p. 33.

8. *Baltenbriefe zur Rückkehr*, p. 10; Achterberg, "Der deutsche Osten-Aufgabe," p. 17.

9. Winger, doc. no. 67, Doc. Book III, Lorenz, pp. 27–28; DAI, 30 April 1941, T-81/289/2412924–930.

10. "Erlass des Führers," 7 October 1939, T-74/15/386792–794.

11. Himmler, 30 October 1939, T-81/266/2384351; also Greifelt to RFSS, 23 July 1940, T-175/119/2645119.

12. "Memorandum," 12 December 1939, T-175/53/2566738–772; Woermann to Reich Embassy, Rome, 24 June 1939, in *DGFP*, D, 6, no. 562, pp. 778–79.

13. Latour, *Südtirol und die Achse*, pp. 44–46; Kaspar to Kutschera, 7 November 1939, T-81/279/2400443–445; "Südtirol," T-175/194/2732992–993; "Südtirol," in *Menscheneinsatz*, December 1940, p. 5, T-74/16/387–850; Latour, "Germany, Italy, and South Tyrol," pp. 100–103.

14. "Richtlinien," Bene and Mastromattei, 21 October 1939, BA, R49 204; "Italien," 18 December 1942, T-81/290/2414464–466.

15. "Memorandum," 12 December 1939, T-175/53/2566738–772.

16. Mackensen, Rome, to Foreign Ministry, 27 September 1941, in *DGFP*, D, 13, no. 362, pp. 575–81.

17. "Memorandum," 12 December 1939, T-175/53/2566738–772; Luig and Bene, "Erläuterungen," 17 November 1939, T-175/194/2733237–239; Bene to Foreign Minister, 9 December 1939, T-175/53/2566833–838.

18. "Gesamtzahl," 1 January 1943, T-175/194/2733184; RKFDV Report, 30 April 1943, BA, R49 14; Latour, *Südtirol und die Achse*, p. 69.

19. Latour, *Südtirol und die Achse*, p. 75; also "Südtirol," RKFDV to Gauleiters, T-175/194/2732992–993.

20. "Denkschrift," undated, T-175/53/2567513–532; Hitler, *Table Talk*, p. 548, 2 July 1942; Greifelt to RFSS, 28 September 1942, T-175/53/2567509–512.

21. Luig, VoMi, to Maier-Kaibitsch, 28 November 1939, T-81/279/2400431–435; Maier-Kaibitsch to Greifelt, 13 December 1939, T-81/279/2400424–425; Folkerts, "Die Aufgabe des RFSS als RKFDV," T-175/194/2733378–397.

22. Maier-Kaibitsch, 18 November 1939, T-81/279/2400439–441; Maier-Kaibitsch to Kaspar, T-81/279/2400439–441.

23. Himmler, 11 October 1939, NO-4613, Prosec. Exhibit No. 290, in *TWC* 4, Case 8, pp. 854–55.

24. Schulenburg to Foreign Ministry, 25 September 1939, in *DGFP*, D, 8, no. 131, p. 130.

25. Secret Protocol, German-Soviet Border and Friendship Treaty, 28 September 1939, in Loeber, *Diktierte Option*, no. 24, p. 28.

26. Weizsäcker to Foreign Minister, 28 September 1939, in *DGFP*, D, 8, no. 153, p. 162.

27. Secret German-Soviet Protocol, 28 September 1939, in Loeber, *Diktierte Option*, no. 41, p. 46.

28. Sthamer, Riga, to Chief of AO, 28 September 1939, in Loeber, *Diktierte Option*, no. 1, p. 3; Weizsäcker to Foreign Minister, 28 September 1939, in *DGFP*, D, 8, no. 154, p. 45.

29. Weizsäcker to Riga and Tallin, 5 October 1939, in Loeber, *Diktierte Option*, no. 58, pp. 61–62.

30. Weizsäcker to Riga and Tallin, 6 October 1939, in Loeber, *Diktierte Option*, no. 67, pp. 74–75; Weizsäcker to Foreign Minister, 6 October 1939, in Loeber, *Diktierte Option*, no. 69, pp. 76–77; Lorenz Testimony, p. 2622.

31. "Protokol . . . ," 15 October 1939, in Loeber, *Diktierte Option*, no. 250, pp. 471–76.

32. "Vertrag über die Umsiedlung," 30 October 1939, in Loeber, *Diktierte Option*, no. 270, pp. 515–26.

33. Loeber, *Diktierte Option*, refer to sections on DUT.

34. Lorenz Testimony, pp. 2620–23; RKFDV No. 4/II, 3 November 1939, T-74/1/371021; Rüdiger, DAI, 21 April 1940, T-81/273/2393592–594; Ribbentrop to Riga and Tallin, 9 October 1939, in Loeber, *Diktierte Option*, no. 94, p. 108; Kotze, Riga, to Foreign Ministry, 20 December 1939, in Loeber, *Diktierte Option*, no. 169, pp. 240–41.

35. "Aufbruch der Volksgruppe," Tallin, 15 October 1939, in Loeber, *Diktierte Option*, no. 102, pp. 115–17.

36. Pamphlets, October 1939, T-81/290/2413735–747.

37. Westermann, Doc. No. 59, Doc. Book IV, Greifelt, pp. 23–24.

38. Valters, *Mana Sarakste*, p. 120.

39. Dietrich, no. 54, Doc. Book III, Lorenz, pp. 21–22; Sintenis, no. 57, Doc. Book III, Lorenz, pp. 23–24.

40. Sipo-SD, to EWZ Gotenhafen (Gdynia), 17 October 1939, T-81/290/2414552.

41. Grosskopf to Riga, 22 November 1939, in Loeber, *Diktierte Option*, no. 124, pp. 157–58.

42. RSHA to EWZ Nordost, 8 December 1939, T-81/290/2414553.

43. Loeber, *Diktierte Option*, no. 170, pp. 242–43; Folkerts, "Die Aufgaben des RFSS als RKFDV," T-175/194/2733378–397; EWZ Nordost, Posen, Report, 1 January 1940, T-81/290/2414094–100.

44. Rüdiger, DAI, 21 April 1940, T-81/273/2393592–594.

45. Himmler, 3 November 1939, T-81/267/2385385; RFSS, "Der Einsatz der Balten," 9 July 1940, BA, R43II 1412; VoMi to DAI, 12 April 1943, BA, R59 1; Folkerts, T-175/194/2733378–397.

46. Secret Protocol, 28 September 1939, in Loeber, *Diktierte Option*, no. 41, p. 46.

47. Koehl, *RKFDV*, p. 92; Lorenz Testimony, pp. 2623–24; "Bericht über den Vortrag," 23 May 1940, T-81/289/2412668–670; Brückner Testimony, pp. 2694–98; List of Treaties, T-175/194/2732990–991; Koehl, *RKFDV*, p. 94.

48. Himmler, 30 October 1939, T-74/15/387136.

49. Lorenz Testimony, p. 2624; *Das Schwarze Korps*, 15 February 1940, p. 3; Himmler, 30 October 1939, T-74/15/387136.

50. *Das Schwarze Korps*, 8 February 1940, p. 9; Tschiersky, EWZ Lodz, to EWZ, 2 December 1939, T-81/266/2384700; Sommer, *135,000 gewannen das Vaterland*, p. 59; "Unser Beitrag," 1 June 1940, T-81/294/2418779.

51. Bosse, *Der Führer ruft*, pp. 169–90; *Das Schwarze Korps*, 15 February 1940, p. 4.

52. Bosse, *Der Führer ruft*, pp. 169–90; *Das Schwarze Korps*, 15 February 1940, p. 4. See also Hagen, Doc. 3, Doc. Book I, Lorenz, pp. 27–28; Csaki, DAI report, 9 December 1939, T-81/273/2393445.

53. *Der Treck der Volksdeutschen*, p. 9.

54. Himmler, *Geheimreden*, Speech of 29 February 1940, pp. 129–30, 136–38.

55. Rüdiger, DAI, 18 January 1940, T-81/273/2393549–550.

56. *Das Schwarze Korps*, 15 February 1940, p. 4; "Gesamtzahl," 1 January 1943, T-175/194/2733184; "Es wurden umgesiedelt," 1 January 1943, T-81/266/2384348–350; EWZ, 15 November 1944, T-81/264/2381873.

57. *Das Schwarze Korps*, 28 March 1940, p. 3.

58. "Bericht," Dengel to Hoffmeyer, T-81/294/2418812–815; Report, 27 February 1940, T-81/294/2418831–832; Memo, 2 March 1940, T-81/294/2418825–830.

59. Himmler, 9 May 1940, T-81/194/2733067–068; also Koehl, *RKFDV*, p. 131.

60. Quiring to DAI, Lodz, 30 October 1940, T-81/294/2393710–712; "Es wurden umgesiedelt," 1 January 1943, T-81/266/2384348–350; "Gesamtzahl," 1 January 1943, T-175/194/2733184.

61. Mommsen, no. 97, Doc. Book IV, Greifelt, pp. 28–30.

62. Himmler to Ribbentrop, 3 July 1940, in *DGFP*, D, 10, no. 102, pp. 113–14.

63. Zechlin to Foreign Ministry, 22 June 1940, in Loeber, *Diktierte Option*, no. 180, pp. 263–64; Behrends to RFSS, 25 June 1940, T-175/128/2654272–274.

64. Behrends to RFSS, 25 June 1940, T-175/128/2654272–274.

65. Ribbentrop to Weizsäcker, undated, in *DGFP*, D, 10, no. 22, p. 23.

66. Gradman, EWZ, 28 June 1940, T-81/266/2384648–649; Memo, 28 July 1940, T-81/293/2418107–108.

67. Himmler to Greifelt, to Lorenz, 2 July 1940, T-175/128/2654–261; Himmler, 22 July 1940, T-74/15/387116–118.

68. Weizsäcker to Kaunas, 11 July 1940, in *DGFP*, D, no. 154, p. 192.

69. Schulenburg to Foreign Ministry, 13 July 1940, in Loeber, *Diktierte Option*, no. 184, p. 268.

70. Soviet Foreign Commissariat to the Reich Government, 7 August 1940, in Loeber, *Diktierte Option*, no. 191, pp. 279–81.

71. Legation in Kaunas to Foreign Ministry, for VoMi, 21 August 1940, in Loeber, *Diktierte Option*, no. 185, p. 269.

72. Schulenburg to Foreign Ministry, 23 August 1940, in Loeber, *Diktierte Option*, p. 291 n 1.

73. Clodius, Foreign Ministry, to Moscow, 26 August 1940, in Loeber, *Diktierte Option*, no. 195, pp. 290–91.

74. Wiehl, Foreign Ministry, to Moscow, 13 September 1940, T-120/3560/9321/E661030; Benzler, mid-September, in Loeber, *Diktierte Option*, no. 198, pp. 295–97.

75. Schnurre and Schulenburg to Foreign Ministry, 28 November 1940, in Loeber, *Diktierte Option*, no. 200, pp. 301–2; "Abkommen," Mikoyan and Schnurre, 10 January 1941, in Loeber, *Diktierte Option*, no. 286, pp. 578–83.

76. Schulenburg to Foreign Minister, 7 January 1941, in Loeber, *Diktierte Option*, no. 201, pp. 302–3; Foreign Ministry note to Soviet government, 21 June 1941, in Loeber, *Diktierte Option*, no. 211, pp. 327–29.

77. Schoepke, Doc. Book I, Brückner, pp. 1–2; Memo, 19 September 1940, T81/293/2418131–134.

78. Brückner Testimony, p. 2700; Schoepke, Doc. Book I, Brückner, pp. 2–3.

79. Memo, 7 February 1941, T-81/293/2417615; Memo, 8 February 1941, T-81/293/2417613.

80. RKFDV, "Die Ostumsiedlung, Jahresbericht 1943," BA, R49 14.

81. Protocol of 15 August 1940, in Loeber, *Diktierte Option*, no. 193, pp. 283–87.

82. Himmler, 19 August 1940, T-74/15/387114–115; Loeber, *Diktierte Option*, no. 202, pp. 303–4; Keppler, Foreign Ministry, to RFSS, 12 August 1940, T-175/32/2540058.

83. Greifelt, 20 August 1940, T-74/15/387188–191.

84. "Vereinbarung," 10 January 1941, Benzler and Botschkarew, in Loeber, *Diktierte Option*, no. 285, pp. 545–65.

85. Resettlement Commission, 3 January 1941, T-81/290/2413882.

86. Report from Riga, 22 February 1941, in Loeber, *Diktierte Option*, no. 207, pp. 315–22.

87. Mommsen, Doc. 97, Doc. Book IV, Greifelt, pp. 28–30.

88. Memo, 26 March 1941, in Loeber, *Diktierte Option*, no. 209, p. 324; "Die Ostumsiedlung," 1942, BA, R49 14.

CHAPTER NINE

1. Ribbentrop to Schulenburg, 25 June 1940, in *DGFP*, D, 10, no. 13, pp. 12–13; Schulenburg to Ribbentrop, 26 June 1940, in *DGFP*, D, 10, no. 20, p. 21.

2. Quiring, DAI, to Csaki, DAI, 20 July 1940, T-81/274/2393730–732; Stumpp, DAI, to Csaki, DAI, 16 July 1940, T-81/274/2393683; Brückner Testimony, pp. 2697–98; Koehl, *RKFDV*, pp. 95–96;

3. Kruse, DAI, to Stumpp, DAI, 13 June 1940, T-81/273/2393429; Kruse, Memo, 5 July 1940, T-81/273/2393428; Stumpp, DAI, to Csaki, 16 July 1940, T-81/274/2393683.

4. Stumpp, DAI, to Csaki, DAI, 15 August 1940, T-81/274/2393682; "Bericht

der DAI," 29 August 1940, T-81/273/2393430; "Schlussbericht," undated, T-81/273/2393155–158; "Lagebericht Jugoslawien," T-81/273/2393527–532; Behrends to Personal Hauptamt, 23 September 1940, BDC SSO, Perthen.

5. Himmler, 20 August 1940, T-74/15/387112–113.

6. VoMi, "Sonderanweisung," August 1940, T-74/10/382576–591.

7. Jawarowski, Doc. Book I, Lorenz, pp. 79–80; Winger, no. 67, Doc. Book III, Lorenz, pp. 27–28; DAI, "Bericht," 9 January 1941, T-81/273/2393491–493.

8. Stumpp to DAI, Csaki, 2 November 1940, T-81/274/2393629–630; Thoss, "Die Umsiedlung und Optionen," p. 131; Thoss, "Die Umsiedlung der Volksdeutschen aus Bessarabien," p. 166.

9. Waldeck, *Athene Palace*, pp. 306–7.

10. "Die Ostumsiedlung," 1942, BA, R49 14.

11. Greifelt, 31 October 1940, T-81/267/2385408; Thoss, "Die Umsiedlung der Volksdeutschen aus Bessarabien," pp. 166–67; Thoss, "Die Umsiedlungen und Optionen," pp. 131–32.

12. Thoss, "Die Umsiedlung der Volksdeutschen aus Bessarabien," p. 166; Thoss, "Die Umsiedlungen und Optionen," p. 131; EWZ, November and December 1940, T-81/307/2435311–333; "Die Ostumsiedlung," 1942, BA, R49 14.

13. EWZ, 3 December 1940, T-81/307/2435317–318; EWZ, undated, "Rumänien-Siebenburgen und Banat," T-81/288/2412487; Memo for Behrends, 5 December 1940, T-81/300/2425982–986.

14. Grosskopf to Luther, 7 August 1941, T-120/2424/4699/E226946; Report on Kočevje, 6 November 1941, T-81/306/2433944–950; Greifelt, T-81/306/2433953–955; EWZ, Gottschee Report, 18 November 1941, T-81/306/2433938–943; "Abschlussbericht," T-81/306/2433592–647; "Vorläufiger Bericht," 24 February 1942, T-74/3/374075–078.

15. Gradmann, 14 November 1941, T-81/307/2435350–351; Memo, 8 May 1942, T-81/307/2435338–339; "Umsiedlung Restserbien," 22 January 1942, T-81/266/2384373–374; "Die Ostumsiedlung," 1942, BA, R49 14.

16. Lorenz Testimony, p. 2627; Stier to Brandt, 8 September 1942, T-175/21/2526878; Reichel, 25 February 1943, T-120/1003/1658/394158–159; Final Plea Greifelt, pp. 18–19; Preusse, no. 4, Doc. Book I, Brückner, p. 23.

17. "Abschluss Bericht," T-81/307/2434782–820; "Bericht . . . Bosnien," 3 November 1942, T-81/307/2435091; Lorenz to RFSS, 10 December 1942, NO-3012, Prosec. Doc. Book VC.

18. Lorenz, p. 2636; Radunski Testimony, p. 2888; Altena, no. 58, Doc. Book III, Lorenz, p. 6.

19. Himmler, "Aussiedlung . . . Südteiermark," 18 April 1941, BA, R43II 1409.

20. Goecken, 28 April 1941, T-120/2415/4670H/E221529; Benzler, Belgrade, to Foreign Ministry, 6 May 1941, T-120/2415/4670H/E221534–535; Koehl, *RKFDV*, pp. 129, 166–68.

21. Himmler to RKFDV, 18 May 1942, BA, R49 968; Himmler, "Wiedereindeutschung," 4 June 1941, T-175/194/2733312–313; Harriman, "Slovenia as an Outpost," p. 225.

22. Luther to Benzler, Belgrade, 30 August 1941, in *DGFP*, D, 13, no. 261,

pp. 416–17; Heydrich to Foreign Minister, 26 September 1941, in *DGFP*, D, 13, no. 360, pp. 570–71.

23. Stier, "Absiedlung der Untersteiermark," 18 October 1941, T-81/267/2385463–466; RKFDV, "Umsiedlung . . . Slowenen," 9 June 1942, BA, R49 968; Himmler, 15 December 1942, T-74/15/387115.

24. Himmler, "Richtlinien . . . Oberkrain und Untersteiermark," 25 June 1942, T-175/53/2567700–701.

25. Ibid.

26. Harriman, "Slovenia as an Outpost," p. 228; Wuescht, *Jugoslawien*, pp. 59–61; Altena to Ellermeier, 26 June 1942, NO-5306, Prosec Exhibit 707, in *TWC* 4, Case 8, pp. 1057–59.

27. Greifelt, 22 January 1942, T-175/194/2733218–220; Lorenz to RFSS, "Schlussbericht," 22 March 1942, T-175/19/2523468–473; "Abschlussbericht," March 1942, T-175/19/2523437–466.

28. "Bericht . . . Neu-Heraklion," 21 April 1942, T-81/307/2435407–414; EWZ, "Abschlussbericht," T-81/307/2435353–365.

29. Jäckel, *Frankreich*, p. 313.

30. Foreign Ministry to Ambassador Abetz, Paris, 2 November 1940, in *DGFP*, D, 11, no. 278, p. 456; "Bericht . . . Umsiedlung in Lothringen," 16 October 1942, T-81/277/2397500–505; RKFDV, "Tätigkeitsbericht, 1942," T-175/194/2732994–995; Jäckel, *Frankreich*, pp. 230–31.

31. Koehl, *RKFDV*, p. 128.

32. Brückner Testimony, p. 2709; "Westumsiedlung," 22 January 1942, T-81/289/2413325–327; EWZ Paris, 23 March 1942, T-81/289/2413311–312; EWZ Paris, 28 August 1941, T-81/289/2413232; Himmler, "Anordnung . . . Frankreich," 17 June 1942, NO-2552, Prosec. Doc. Book VD.

33. Jäckel, *Frankreich*, pp. 229, 317.

34. Ibid., pp. 231–32, 317–18.

35. Rassenamt, 28 September 1942, NO-1499, Prosec. Doc. Book VF.

36. Brückner Testimony, pp. 2701–3, 2712; Eilers, Doc. Book I, Brückner, p. 11; Lorenz to Personal Staff, 5 July 1941, NO-1792, Prosec. Doc. Book VF.

37. Preusse, Doc. Book I, Brückner, pp. 21–22; Wallrabe, Doc. Book I, Brückner, pp. 25–26.

38. "Bericht . . . Leningrad Gurtel," T-81/294/2419062–081; Wallrabe, Doc. Book I, Brückner, pp. 26–27; Lorenz Testimony, p. 2635; Wallrabe, "Erlebnisbericht," 14 April 1942, T-81/294/2419088–092; Preusse, Doc. Book I, Brückner, pp. 21–22.

39. "Abschlussbericht," T-81/294/2418955–9060.

CHAPTER TEN

1. Rassenpolitisches Amt, 25 November 1939, BA, R49 75; T-74/9/380572–611.

2. RFSS, 28 May 1940, T-175/119/2645120–122.

3. Bach-Zalewski Testimony, p. 447; Forster, "Der Reichsgau Danzig-Westpreussen," p. 35; "Anordnung" 14 December 1940, T-74/15/387139–158.

4. Greiser, "Die Grossdeutsche Aufgabe im Wartheland."

5. Doppler, undated, T-81/268/2387136; *Das Schwarze Korps*, 8 February 1940, pp. 9–10; Gradmann, EWZ, undated, T-81/288/2412150; Skotnicki affidavit, NO-5257, Prosec. Doc. Book VII.

6. Doppler, 20 November 1939, T-81/288/2412177–178; VoMi, 11 December 1939, BA, VoMi R59 36; "Sammellager," T-81/278/2398638–640.

7. Koehler, Doc. Book I, Lorenz; Altena affidavit, no. 58, Doc. Book III, Lorenz, pp. 5–6; Altena, 1 August 1940, T-81/265/2383682–683; photograph and caption, T-81/282/2404492; Bergmann, Doc. no. 17, Doc. Book I, Lorenz, p. 62; Heitz, Doc. Book I, Lorenz, pp. 58–59.

8. Lorenz Final Plea, p. 86; Klingsporn Testimony, p. 2808; Altena, 28 July 1941, T-81/268/2387889.

9. Fidelis, no. 42, Doc. Book I, Lorenz, pp. 95–96; Wolkerstorfer, Doc. Book I, Lorenz, p. 55.

10. Lorenz Testimony, p. 15; Ellermeier Testimony, p. 2784; Klingsporn Testimony, p. 2806; RKFDV, "Tätigkeitsbericht," 1942, T-175/194/2732994–995.

11. Gradmann, "Sammellager," 21 December 1939, BA, R59 24; "Beobachtungslager," T-81/288/2412179–183.

12. Hintze, RKFDV, to HSSPFs, 25 May 1943, T-81/267/2385983–984.

13. "Kriegsgeschichte der EWZ," folder 186, T-81/277/2398375–476.

14. "Abschlussbericht," BA, R69 122; Rüdiger, DAI, 5 March 1940, T-81/273/2373560.

15. "Fliegenden Kommissionen," spring 1940, T-81/274/2394062; Tschierschky, EWZ, April 1940, BA, R69 230.

16. "Anordnung des RFSS," NO-4237, Prosec. Doc. Book IIB; "Fliegenden Kommissionen," T-81/274/2394063–064; RSHA, 24 January 1940, T-81/274/2393967–968.

17. Altena to EWZ Litzmannstadt, 5 February 1941, T-81/265/2383503; Rüdiger, DAI, 21 April 1940, T-81/273/2393585–600; Wirisch Testimony, p. 245; Lorenz Testimony, p. 2626.

18. "Die Durchschleusung," T-81/274/2394103–105; "Plan EWZ," T-74/3/373398–400; "Fliegende Kommissionen," T-81/274/2394063–064; Koehl, *RKFDV*, pp. 105–9.

19. Pancke Testimony, p. 648; EWZ Litzmannstadt, November 1940, BA, R69 178.

20. Kasel Testimony, p. 1125; Dietrich Affidavit, no. 54, Doc. Book III, Lorenz, pp. 21–22.

21. Greifelt to RFSS, 22 September 1941, NO-3097, Prosec. Doc. Book VB; RFSS to Krüger, 11 November 1942, T-175/73/2590456; Krüger to RFSS, 9 November 1942, NO-2400, Prosec. Exhibit 263.

22. "Einsatz," May 1940, T-81/277/2397363.

23. "Die Gesichtspunkte," undated, BA, R69 178.

24. Doppler, 7 April 1941, T-81/268/2387520; "Zum Entwurf," undated, BA,

R69 4; Himmler, 9 May 1940, T-74/15/387123; Altena to all Einsatzführer, 23 January 1941, BA, R59 2.

25. Fähndrich to VoMi, 12 May 1941, T-74/15/387765; RKFDV, 20 February 1942, BA, R49 968.

26. Himmler, 20 March 1941, T-74/15/387757.

27. Greifelt to RKFDV regional officials, 26 March 1941, T-74/15/387761–762; Greifelt to VoMi, 3 May 1941, T-74/15/387759; Greifelt to Reichsarbeits-ministerium, 2 July 1941, T-74/15/387757–758; Greifelt to VoMi, 3 May 1941, T-74/15/387759; Greifelt to VoMi, 22 January 1941, T-74/15/387756.

28. *Das Schwarze Korps*, 8 February 1940, p. 6, pp. 9–10.

29. VoMi, Pommern, to all Einsatzführer, 9 July 1942, T-81/282/2404342; VoMi, München-Oberbayern, 30 October 1940, T-81/279/2400945; VoMi, München-Oberbayern, 19 November 1940, T-81/279/2400884–893.

30. VoMi to all Einsatzführer, 14 December 1942, BA, R59 6; VoMi Schwaben, 6 January 1943, BA, R59 55.

31. Doppler, 19 January 1940, T-81/268/2387226; Stein, no. 76, Doc. Book IV, Lorenz, p. 6; Hagen, Doc. Book I, Lorenz, p. 28.

32. VoMi Schwaben, to all camp commanders, 11 March 1942, BA, R59 55.

33. VoMi to all Einsatzführer, 13 January 1943, BA, R59 6; Bormann, 26 March 1941, T-81/266/2384622; Anordnung A 35/41, 21 August 1941, T-81/8/16646.

34. VoMi Pommern, 14 April 1942, T-81/282/2404257; NSDAP Gau Schwa-ben, 3 January 1941, BA, R59 80.

35. Lorenz Testimony, p. 2674; Stier, in *TWC* 4, Case 8, p. 946; Winger, in *TWC* 4 Case 8, p. 847; Rech, in *TWC* 4, Case 8, p. 848.

36. Greifelt to VoMi, 8 February 1941, T-74/15/387756; VoMi Sachsen, Octo-ber 1942, T-81/283/2405005–008; RKFDV to HSSPFs, 21 May 1942, T-81/267/2385935–938.

37. VoMi Salzburg, 16 October 1940, T-81/283/2405470–475; Hangel, no. 4, Doc. Book I, Lorenz, pp. 38–40; VoMi to all Einsatzführer, May 1941, BA, R59 5; Koehler, Doc. Book I, Lorenz, p. 48; Doppler, 28 May 1941, T-81/268/2387457.

38. RKFDV, 13 June 1940, T-81/266/2384587; Himmler to Greifelt, 3 Decem-ber 1942, T-175/72/2590411–412; RKFDV, 9 December 1942, BDC, Research Division, Notebook 32 RFSS; RKFDV, 12 November 1942, T-175/73/2590407–408. See also Koehl, *RKFDV*, pp. 110–18, 157–58.

39. Koehl, *RKFDV*, p. 115; Himmler, 21 December 1940, T-74/15/287180–183.

40. Himmler, 11 October 1939, NO-4613, in *TWC* 4, Case 8, pp. 854–55.

41. Memo, 30 January 1940, NO-5322, in *TWC* 4, Case 8, pp. 855–59.

42. Greifelt Testimony, p. 1439; Pancke Testimony, pp. 656, 677; Wirisch Testi-mony, pp. 229, 286–90. See also Koehl, *RKFDV*, pp. 110–18, 157–58.

43. Lorenz Testimony, p. 2660.

44. Behrends to Fabritius, 29 November 1941, T-74/6/377747.

45. Gradmann, EWZ, 3 April 1940, T-81/266/2384650–651; Greifelt to VoMi, 8 April 1940, T-74/15/386788–791; Hübner Testimony, p. 2370; Stier Testimony,

pp. 1766–67; Greifelt, 14 December 1940, T-81/266/2384484; "Bericht," undated, T-175/72/2589710–712; Skotnicki Affidavit, NO-5257, Prosec. Doc. Book VII; Krumey Affidavit, NO-5364, Prosec. Doc. Book VIIID; Opinion and Judgment, in *TWC* 5, Case 8, p. 129; "Ansiedlung," 9 April 1940, T-81/266/2384519–520.

46. Altena to all Einsatzführer, 1 August 1940, T-81/265/2383682–683; VoMi Schwaben, 1 April 1942, BA, R59 55.

47. VoMi, 17 February 1940, T-81/288/2412186–188; RKFDV to all Einsatzführer, 5 January 1941, NO-4129, Prosec. Doc. Book VA; Greifelt, 17 July 1941, T-74/16/387795.

48. VoMi to all Einsatzführer, 20 August 1941, BA, R59 5; VoMi to all Einsatzführer, 22 October 1941, BA, R59 5.

49. Gradmann, EWZ, 3 April 1940, T-81/266/2384650–651; "Bericht," undated, T-175/72/2589710–712.

50. Doppler, 21 May 1940, T-81/268/2386956.

51. Hitler, *Table Talk*, 12 May 1942, p. 469.

52. Klingsporn Testimony, p. 2988; Final Plea Lorenz, p. 50; Creutz to Brandt, 1 July 1943, T-175/73/2590309.

53. Himmler, 9 May 1940, T-74/15/387121–122; RKFDV, 15 December 1942, T-74/14/385779–781; Greifelt Final Plea, p. 82.

54. Himmler, "Erlass," 12 September 1940, T-74/14/386017–021; RMI, "Erwerb," 13 March 1941, BA, R49 679; "Stellung und Behandlung," T-74/14/385915; Schwarzenberger Testimony, NO-4713, Prosec. Doc. Book IIB.

55. Schafhäuser Testimony, p. 2760–64; Lorenz Testimony, pp. 2637–38; VoMi to all Einsatzführer, 27 October 1942, BA, R59 6; VoMi Schwaben, to all camp commanders, 1 September 1942, BA, R59 55; Klingsporn to Brückner, 10 February 1943, NO-5201, in *TWC* 4, Case 9, pp. 1057–59.

56. Greifelt to Berkelmann, 9 June 1941, T-81/277/2397415–416; Gradmann to EWZ, 2 March 1943, T-81/307/2435243.

57. Kasel Testimony, pp. 1124–38; VoMi Schwaben to all camp commanders, 29 January 1942, BA, R59 55; VoMi Schwaben to all camp commanders, 15 June 1942, T-81/283/2405786; VoMi Schwaben, 1 April 1942, T-81/283/2405816; VoMi Schwaben, 14 July 1942, T-81/283/2405772.

58. Himmler, 25 June 1942, T-175/53/2567700–701; RKFDV Salzburg to VoMi, 14 September 1942, T-175/53/2567700–701; Ellermeier Testimony, pp. 2772–73; Lorenz Testimony, p. 2657; Klingsporn, in *TWC* 4, Case 8, pp. 907–8.

59. Klingsporn Testimony, pp. 2838–39; Schafhauser Affidavit, NO-5004, Prosec. Doc. Book VIIID; Panzer, NO-5362, Prosec. Doc. Book VIIID.

60. Lorenz Testimony, pp. 2643–44; Radunski Testimony, p. 2892; Rimann Affidavit, Doc. Book I, Lorenz, pp. 21–23; Lorenz to Himmler, 14 February 1944, NO-2746, Prosec. Doc. Book IVD.

61. OKW Torgau to VoMi, 21 January 1944, BDC, Research Division, Notebook 31 RFSS; VDA, 21 January 1944, BDC, Research Division, Notebook 31 RFSS.

62. Pohl to RFSS, 16 December 1944, NO-3990, Prosec. Doc. Book IVD, BDC, Research Division, Notebook 31 RFSS; Lorenz Testimony, p. 2642.

63. Hagen, VoMi, to EWZ, 5 February 1940, T-81/278/2398662; VoMi to all Einsatzführer, 15 July 1941, BA, R59 5; Klingsporn Testimony, p. 2825; Ellermeier Testimony, p. 2775; Kubelke, 15 May 1940, T-81/280/2401178; Altena, 28 March 1941, T-81/268/2387964–970; Altena to RKFDV, 12 September 1941, BDC SSO, Altena; RKFDV to VoMi, Altena, 22 October 1941, BDC SSO, Altena.

64. Altena, VoMi, to all Einsatzführer, 1 July 1942, BA, R59 6; VoMi Schwaben, 14 July 1942, T-81/283/2405772.

65. Lorenz, 25 February 1942, T-81/267/2386322–327; VoMi Niederdonau, 3 March 1942, T-81/280/2401326–328; VoMi Sachsen, 11 June 1942, T-81/283/2405064–065.

66. Kasel Testimony, pp. 1130–31; Schnitzler, no. 68, Doc. Book III, Lorenz, pp. 10–11.

67. "Sammellager," 21 December 1939, T-81/278/2398638–640; "Aktenvermerk," 17 February 1940, T-81/288/2412186–188; Quiring to Csaki, 28 February 1940, T-81/274/2393752.

68. Konekamp, December 1939, T-81/273/2393475–477; Rüdiger, 11 March 1940, T-81/273/2393567; Skotnicki, NO-5257, Prosec. Doc. Book VII; *Das Schwarze Korps*, 8 February 1940, p. 10.

69. Doppler, February and March 1940, T-81/268/2387072–162; Doppler, 1 February 1940, T-81/273/2393411; VoMi, Horse Camp Kattowitz, 6 February 1942, NO-2647, Prosec. Doc. Book XIIIA.

70. Frank to Lublin and Auschwitz camps, 26 September 1942, in *TWC* 13, Case 11, pp. 256–58; Himmler to Pohl, to Lorenz, 24 October 1942, NO-5395, in *TWC* 4, Case 8, pp. 972–73. Pohl, "Bericht," 6 February 1943, NO-1257, Prosec. Doc. Book XIIIB.

71. Lorenz Testimony, pp. 2660–61; Hagen Affidavit, NO-5160, Prosec. Doc. Book XIIIB; Hagen, no. 3, Doc. Book I, Lorenz, pp. 29–30.

72. Himmler, 15 December 1942, T-81/266/2384268; VoMi to Gaubeauftragten, 9 January 1943, T-81/266/2384116.

CHAPTER ELEVEN

1. Albrecht Haushofer to Karl Haushofer, 23 September 1940, T-253/ 56/ 512002–003; A. Haushofer to K. Haushofer, 2 October 1940, T-253/56/ 512004–005; Minke to K. Haushofer, 4 October 1940, T-253/ 52/507368–374; K. Haushofer to Hess, 15 October 1940, T-253/ 56/512014; K. Haushofer to Himmler, 15 October 1940, T-253/ 59/516130–131.

2. Ribbentrop to Lorenz, 18 January 1941, T-175/21/2525725–727.

3. "Anruf," 11 March 1941, T-120/2423/4696H/E226709; Triska, Foreign Ministry, to Ribbentrop, 11 March 1941, T-120/2423/4696H/E226708; Ribbentrop and Himmler, "Vereinbarung," 31 March 1941, PA AA, Inland IIg, 240, Bd. 21.

4. RFSS to Lorenz, 28 July 1942, in Heiber, *Reichsführer!*, p. 168.

5. NSDAP, Ausgabe A, 45/42, 11 November 1942, "Der Führer," 4 November 1942, PA AA, Inland IIg, 293.

6. Himmler and Schwarz, 18 August 1942, T-81/8/16508; Schwarz to Himmler, 30 June 1943, T-175/76/2594262–263; Wolff to Lorenz, 13 July 1943, T-175/76/2594265; Behrends to Brandt, RFSS Pers. Stab, 19 July 1943, T-175/76/2594272.

7. Lohl Affidavit, no. 10, Doc. Book I, Lorenz, p. 33.

8. VoMi, 11 February 1941, PA AA, Inland IIg, 219; VoMi, Lohl, Budget, 9 April 1941, T-120/2424/4699/E227007–008; Lohl to Luther, 4 March 1942, T-120/736/1257/338613–616.

9. Rechnungshof to Foreign Ministry, "Bericht," 29 April 1930, T-120/1178/2168/471081–082; Twardowski to Zech-Burkersroda, the Hague, and to Grosskopf, 28 January 1940, T-120/1178/2168/471060–061; "Beteiligungen," 17 November 1941, T-120/1178/2168/471093.

10. Greifelt, January 1939, T-175/17/2520734–756.

11. "Volksdeutsche in der Waffen SS," 28 December 1943, NO-2015, Prosec. Doc. Book VIA.

12. Sauckel, "Anordnung Nr. 4," 7 May 1942, T-175/71/2588256–265; Brandt to Sauckel and to VoMi, 18 May 1942, T-175/71/2588253–254.

13. Wehofsich, VoMi, "Gedächtnisniederschrift," 3 August 1938, BA, VoMi R59 92.

14. Twardowski, 16 May 1939, T-120/1451/3023H/D599057.

15. Greifelt, 26 January 1940, T-81/288/2411853–857; Legation in Belgrade to Berlin, 13 September 1940, PA AA, Inland IIg, 242, Bd.2

16. Altena, VoMi, to all Einsatzführer, 29 October 1940, BA, R59 2; VoMi Niederdonau, 3 December 1940, T-81/280/2401036; RKFDV, Hintze, 6 May 1941, T-81/280/2401236–237; Doppler, 27 May 1941, T-81/268/2387458; VoMi Oberdonau, 13 October 1941, T-81/280/2401859.

17. Stein, *The Waffen SS*, pp. 94, 168–73; Herzog, *Die Volksdeutsche in der Waffen SS*, pp. 3, 6–7. See also Lumans, "The Military Obligation."

18. Lorenz to RFSS, 7 February 1942, T-175/68/2585179–180; Lorenz to RFSS, 19 February 1942, T-175/125/2650409.

19. Knoblauch, to Pers. Stab, RFSS, 27 May 1943, NO-1650, Prosec. Doc. Book VIA; Max Jamst, "Die Ausschöpfung der Wehrkraft der deutschen Volksgruppen in Südosteuropa durch die SS," 1951, BDC, Research Division, Volkstum-Ausland.

20. SS Richter to Brandt, "Wehrpflicht," 19 February 1945, BDC, Research Division, Volkstum-Ausland.

21. Jamst, "Die Ausschöpfung," BDC, Research Division, Volkstum-Ausland.

22. Radunski, VoMi, to Reichel, Foreign Ministry, 5 May 1943, T-120/3133/6744/E511089–090; Rimann, Doc. Book I, Lorenz, pp. 23–24.

23. SS Hauptamt, Monatsbericht December 1943, 21 January 1944, T-120/1003/1658/393129–133.

24. Stein, *The Waffen SS*, pp. 296–98; Reider, *La Waffen SS*, p. 263.

25. Stein, *The Waffen SS*, p. 192.

26. Eicke to SS Führungshauptamt, 15 November 1941, T-175/108/2632012–013.

27. Stein, *The Waffen SS*, pp. 192–93 n. 66.

28. Berger to RFSS, 3 April 1943, T-175/20/2525234–237; Berger to RFSS, 17 February 1943, T-175/20/2525243.

CHAPTER TWELVE

1. Hoensch, *Die Slowakei*, pp. 181–85; Luig, VoMi, 7 July 1939, PA AA, Dienststelle Ribbentrop, 16/2 VoMi.

2. VoMi, 26 October 1942, NO-3526, Prosec. Doc. Book IIB; Undated Memo on Slovakia, PA AA, Inland IIg, 235, Bd. 16; "Slowakei," 28 December 1943, NO-2015, Prosec. Doc. Book VIA; Stein, *The Waffen SS*, p. 173.

3. Schwarz to Foreign Minister, 31 October 1941, T-120/736/1257/338640.

4. Rüdiger, 13 January 1940, T-81/273/2393543–544; Pancke to Himmler, 18 June 1940, in Král, *Die Deutschen*, no. 308, pp. 405–8.

5. Lorenz to Himmler, 3 February 1942, T-175/75/2593679–680; Lorenz to Himmler, 2 June 1942, T-175/75/2593674–675.

6. Behrends to Himmler, 10 October 1941, National Archives, Washington, D.C., NO-5524; Karmasin to Himmler, 28 July 1942, in Král, *Die Deutschen*, no. 388, pp. 490–91; Lorenz Testimony, p. 2630; "Bericht," 8 September 1943, T-81/285/2408158–172.

7. Berger to Himmler, 21 February 1940, T-175/128/2654378; Series of letters, Berger and Himmler, T-175/75/2593689–723.

8. Karmasin to Himmler, 30 December 1941, in Král, *Die Deutschen*, no. 365, p. 464; Himmler to Karmasin, January 1942, in Král, *Die Deutschen*, no. 365, p. 464; Memo, 5 May 1943, T-120/3133/6744/E511096–099.

9. Undated memo on Slovakia, PA AA, Inland IIg, 235, Bd. 16; "Slowakei," 28 December 1943, NO-2015, Prosec. Doc. Book VIA; Stein, *The Waffen SS*, p. 173.

10. Berger to Himmler, 24 January 1944, T-175/75/2593652–653; Stein, *The Waffen SS*, pp. 173–74; *Expulsion* 4:148–49, 526–27.

11. SS Hauptamt, 21 January 1944, T-120/1003/1658/393129–133; Himmler to Karmasin and VoMi, 15 August 1944, T-175/66/2581924; Karmasin to Himmler, 19 August 1944, T-175/66/2581917–918; Lipták, "Role of the German Minority," p. 175.

12. SS Südostraum, 2 September 1944, T-120/1003/1658/393262; German Military, 3 September 1944, T-120/1003/1658/393264; Sichelschmidt, VoMi, 11 October 1944, T-120/1757/3579/E025412–417; *Expulsion* 4:151–63.

13. Sichelschmidt, to Foreign Ministry, 6 September 1944, T-120/1318/2380/D498416–417; Wrangell, Foreign Ministry, 6 September 1944, T-120/1757/3579/E025198; Sichelschmidt, VoMi, 11 October 1944, T-120/1757/3579/E025412–417; Wagner, 21 October 1944, T-120/1025/1762/405498–500; Lorenz to OKW, 6 November 1944, PA AA, Inland IIg, 266.

14. VoMi, September 1944, T-120/1146/2068/449435–443; Rimann, VoMi, 13

October 1944, T-120/1757/E025424–426; VoMi, October 1944, T-120/1042/1820/416544–575.

15. *Expulsion* 4:163.

16. Protocol, 30 August 1940, PA AA, Inland IIg, 237, Bd. 18; Paikert, *The Danube Swabians*, pp. 120–21; Door, "Zur Vorgeschichte," p. 109.

17. Paikert, *The Danube Swabians*, pp. 114–15, 120–25, 170–76; Arató, "Der 'Volksbund der Deutschen in Ungarn,'" pp. 291–92; VoMi, 26 October 1942, NO-3526, Prosec. Doc. Book IIB.

18. Heger, RMI, to Foreign Ministry, T-120/1306/2363/489039–049.

19. Stuckart to Foreign Minister, 18 April 1941, T-120/2415/E221526; Triska, Foreign Ministry, 21 April 1941, T-120/2415/4670H/E221521–523; Wehler, "Reichsfestung Belgrad," p. 75; Paikert, *The Danube Swabians*, pp. 171–74.

20. Paikert, *The Danube Swabians*, p. 175.

21. Lorenz to OKW, 16 April 1941, PA AA, Inland IIg, 251.

22. OKW report, 8 May 1941, T-120/2415/4670H/E221482–483; Rimann, VoMi, to Foreign Ministry, 16 May 1941, T-120/2415/4670H/E221486–487.

23. Series of Communications, February 1942, T-175/128/2653989–999.

24. VoMi to Luther, Foreign Ministry, 27 February 1942, T-120/736/1257/338610–612; Lohl, VoMi, to Luther, 4 March 1942, T-120/736/1257/338613–616.

25. Rimann, VoMi, to Foreign Ministry, 24 January 1941, T-120/2423/4696H/E226703–705; "Volksdeutsche in der Waffen SS," 28 December 1943, NO-2015, Prosec. Doc. Book VIA; Paikert, *The Danube Swabians*, pp. 144–45 n. 3; *Expulsion* Vol. 2 and 3: 34–35.

26. Jagow, Budapest, to Foreign Minister, 15 January 1942, T-120/2415/4670H/E221630–631; Memo, 5 May 1943, T-120/3133/6744/E511096–099; Paikert, *The Danube Swabians*, p. 146; Herzog, *Die Volksdeutschen in der Waffen SS*, pp. 9–10.

27. Jagow, Budapest, to Foreign Minister, 15 January 1942, T-120/2415/4670H/E221630–631; Memo, 5 May 1943, T-120/3133/6744/E511096–099; Paikert, *The Danube Swabians*, p. 146; Herzog, *Die Volksdeutschen in der Waffen SS*, pp. 9–10.

28. Series of communications, 1942, Foreign Ministry, VoMi, Berger and Himmler, T-175/73/2590613–716.

29. Sichelschmidt, VoMi, to Foreign Ministry, 1 March 1943, T-120/3133/6744/E511086; Kubitz, VoMi, to Brandt, 20 March 1943, T-175/73/2590639; Berger, 20 March 1943, T-175/60/2575927–928; Jagow to Foreign Ministry and Brandt, 20 April 1943, T-175/73/2590595–597.

30. Lorenz to Himmler, 19 August 1943, T-120/1757/3579/024810–821; Germanische Leitstelle, 21 January 1944, T-120/10031658/393129–133; Paikert, *The Danube Swabians*, pp. 146–48; Herzog, *Die Volksdeutschen in der Waffen SS*, pp. 9–10

31. Paikert, *The Danube Swabians*, pp. 147–48; Herzog, *Die Volksdeutschen in der Waffen SS*, pp. 9–10.

32. Paikert, *The Danube Swabians*, pp. 252–53.

33. Twardowski to Wolff and Behrends, 11 January 1940, T-175/128/

2654336–337; Schmidt to VoMi, April 1940, PA AA, Inland IIg, 236, Bd. 17; Twardowski, 20 May 1940, T-120/1451/3023H/D599206–207; Berger to Himmler, 21 May 1940, T-175/128/2654282–283.

34. Ergänzungsamt to Himmler, 2 December 1940, T-175/128/2654206–207; VoMi, 26 October 1942, NO-3526, Prosec. Doc. Book IIB; Schmidt, July 1942– September 1943, T-120/1003/1658/393139–171.

35. Series of documents in PA AA, Inland IIg, 234, Bd. 15.

36. Series of Communications, January–April 1940, T-175/128/2654302–357; Lorenz, Foreign Ministry, to Berger and Henniger, VoMi, 13 June 1940, PA AA, Inland IIg, 236, Bd. 17.

37. Rimann, VoMi, to Foreign Ministry, 24 January 1941, T-120/2423/4696H/ E226703–705; Triska to Bucharest, 1 February 1941, T-120/2423/4696H/ E226707; Triska to Bucharest, 13 February 1941, T-120/1451/3023H/ D599344.

38. Rimann, VoMi, to Foreign Ministry, 1 February 1941, T-120/1306/2363/ 489031–033; Ribbentrop to Killinger, Bucharest, 3 February 1941, T-120/ 1306/2363/489029–030; Killinger, Bucharest, to Foreign Ministry, 20 February 1941, T-120/1451/3023H/D599338–340; Triska to RFSS, 24 March 1941, PA AA, Inland IIg, 240, Bd. 21.

39. Killinger to Foreign Ministry, 28 April 1941, T-120/1451/3023H/D599365; Berger to Foreign Ministry, 9 May 1941, T-120/1306/2363/489069–070; Himmler to Lorenz and Berger, 23 January 1942, T-175/125/2650411.

40. Berger to Himmler, 18 February 1943, T-175/128/2653705–706; Sichelschmidt, VoMi, to Foreign Ministry, 1 March 1943, T-120/3133/ 6744/E511086; "Stand der Werbung," 5 May 1943, T-120/3133/ 6744/E511096–099.

41. Schmidt to Lorenz, 23 September 1943, T-175/128/2653698–699; Berger to Himmler, 28 September 1943, T-175/128/2653691–692.

42. "Volksdeutsche in der Waffen SS," 28 December 1943, NO-2015, Prosec. Doc. Book VIA; Paikert, *The Danube Swabians*, pp. 253–54; Herzog, *Die Volksdeutschen in der Waffen SS*, pp. 4, 14–15.

43. VoMi Report, 17 May 1944, T-120/1005/1659/393459.

44. Police Report, 1 September 1943, T-175/128/2653703; Monatsbericht, December 1943, 21 January 1944, T-120/1003/1658/393129–133; Monatsbericht, January 1944, T-120/1003/1658/393191–201.

45. Report to Berger, Foreign Ministry, Lorenz, 28 August 1944, T-120/1757/ 3579/E025273; Monatsbericht, September 1944, T-120/1146/ 2068/449415– 434; Rimann, VoMi, 13 October 1944, T-120/1757/ 3579/E025424–426.

46. Konnerth, September 1944, T-120/1030/1797/408931–935; Wagner to Foreign Minister, 16 September 1944, T-120/1005/1659/393324–325.

47. "Andreas Schmidt," 19 September 1944, T-120/1146/2068/449323–324; Altenburg to Foreign Minister, 25 September 1944, T-120/1757/3579/E025404; Foreign Ministry, 3 October 1944, T-120/1757/3579/E025339; Wagner to Foreign Minister, 16 November 1944, T-120/2961/6367H/E473958.

48. Paikert, *The Danube Swabians*, p. 173; Wuescht, *Jugoslawien*, pp. 56–58.

49. Stuckart, to Foreign Minister, 18 April 1941, T-120/2415/ 4670H/

E221524–525; Paikert, *The Danube Swabians*, pp. 277–78; Wuescht, *Jugoslawien*, p. 265; Undated memo, T-175/72/2590105.

50. "Serbien und Banat," 26 October 1942, NO-3526, Prosec. Doc. Book IIB; "Restserbien," NO-3526, Prosec. Doc. Book IIB.

51. Janko to Himmler, 3 July 1943, T-175/72/2590037–042.

52. Rimann, VoMi, to Foreign Ministry, 24 January 1941, T-120/2423/4696H/ E226703–705.

53. Series of communications, January 1941, Foreign Ministry and VoMi, T-120/2423/4696H/E226686–705; Paikert, *The Danube Swabians*, p. 276.

54. Paikert, *The Danube Swabians*, p. 277; Stein, *The Waffen SS*, pp. 168–70; Herzog, *Die Volksdeutschen in der Waffen SS*, pp. 12–13; Benzler to Foreign Ministry, 22 July 1941, T-120/2424/4699/E226995–996; Himmler to Lorenz, 24 January 1942, T-175/72/2590101.

55. Lorenz to Himmler, 31 March 1942, T-175/72/2590114; Memo, 12 July 1943, NO-1649, in *TWC* 13, Case 11, pp. 315–16; Himmler to Lorenz, 25 October 1942, T-175/21/2526366; Kubitz Testimony, p. 2861; Wuescht, *Jugoslawien*, pp. 276–77.

56. "Banat und Serbien," 28 December 1943, NO-2015, Prosec. Doc. Book VIA; VoMi, September 1944, T-120/1146/2068/449415–434.

57. Paikert, *The Danube Swabians*, pp. 280–81; Steiner, *Die Freiwilligen*, p. 219.

58. Monatsbericht, January 1944, T-120/1003/1658/393191–201.

59. Wuescht, *Jugoslawien*, pp. 267–68; Hory and Broszat, *Der Kroatische Ustascha-Staat*, pp. 70–71; "Denkschrift," T-120/2424/4699/E226950–972; Triska to Luther, Foreign Ministry, 17 November 1941, T-120/2415/4670H/ E221618–620.

60. Berger to Lorenz, 21 November 1942, T-175/21/2526857–869.

61. VoMi, 26 October 1942, NO-3526, Prosec. Doc. Book IIB; Wuescht, *Jugoslawien*, p. 269; Zagreb, 21 July 1942, PA AA, Inland IIg, 243, Bd. 1.

62. AO to Berger, 21 November 1942, T-175/21/2526857–869.

63. Sundhaussen, "Zur Geschichte der Waffen SS."

64. Ibid., pp. 180–82; "Stand der Werbung," 5 May 1943, T-120/3133/6744/ E511096–099; Luther to Foreign Minister, 17 June 1942, T-120 736/ 1257/ 339914–916; Berger to Himmler, 25 March 1942, T-175/ 72/2590117;

65. "Stand der Werbung," 5 May 1943, T-120/3133/6744/E511096–099; Kasche to Foreign Ministry, 12 November 1942, T-175/21/2526833–834; Berger to Wolff, 5 December 1942, T-175/21/2526825; Lorenz Testimony, pp. 2654–55.

66. Kasche to Foreign Ministry, 12 November 1942, T-175/21/2526833–834; Sundhaussen, "Zur Geschichte der Waffen SS," pp. 188–89.

67. Sundhaussen, "Zur Geschichte der Waffen SS," p. 191; Kammerhofer, Doc. Book I, Lorenz, pp. 91–92; "Volksdeutsche," 28 December 1943, NO-2015, Prosec. Doc. Book VIA; Kasche to Foreign Ministry, 25 June 1943, in *TWC* 13, Case 11, p. 310; Berger to RFSS, 13 July 1943, T-175/119/2645154–156; Kasche, 29 October 1943, T-175/21/2526769–770.

68. VoMi, August 1944, 15 September 1944, T-120/1003/1658/393265–271; Paikert, *The Danube Swabians*, p. 281.

69. Luther to Foreign Minister, 17 June 1942, T-120/1003/1658/393265–271.

70. Kasche, Zagreb, to Foreign Ministry, 19 January 1044, PA AA, Inland IIc, Bd. 5.

71. Paikert, *The Danube Swabians*, p. 284; Ruhrig, 14 April 1944, T-120/3133/6744/E511175.

72. Paikert, *The Danube Swabians*, p. 284–85; VoMi, October 1944, 23 November 1944, T-120/1042/1820/416544–575; VoMi, August 1944, T-120/1003/1658/393265–277; Monatsbericht, September 1944, T-120/1146/2068/449415–434.

73. Foreign Ministry, 27 November 1941, in *DGFP*, D, 13, no. 510, pp. 861–64.

74. Lorenz (not Werner), Foreign Ministry, 9 April 1940, in *DGFP*, D, 9, no. 77, p. 115.

75. Grundherr to Foreign Minister, 4 November 1941, in *DGFP*, D, 13, no. 447, pp. 737–40.

76. Renthe-Fink to Foreign Ministry, 22 June 1940, in *DGFP*, D, 9, no. 532, pp. 685–86; Renthe-Fink to Foreign Ministry, 27 February 1941, in *DGFP*, D, 13, no. 479, pp. 796–98.

77. Rimann, VoMi, to Foreign Ministry, 23 January 1941, T-120/2423/4696H/E226696–699; VoMi, 26 October 1942, NO-3526, Prosec. Doc. Book IIB.

78. Refer to documents in T-120/1372/2634/D526170–220.

79. "Übersicht," 15 January 1942, T-175/109/2633910; also Stein, *The Waffen SS*, pp. 148–57; Memo, 6 May 1940, in *DGFP*, D, 6, no. 199, p. 287; Larsen, Apenrade, to Lorenz, 29 January 1942, T-175/68/2585181–187.

80. "Nordschleswig," 28 December 1943, NO-2015, Prosec. Doc. Book VIA; Stein, *The Waffen SS*, p. 139.

81. Monatsbericht, January 1944, T-120/1003/1658/393191–201.

82. Sichelschmidt, VoMi, to Foreign Ministry, Inland II, 11 Sept. 1944, PA AA, Inland IIg, 258; Wagner, Foreign Ministry, to Copenhagen, 14 Sept. 1944, T-120/3133/6744/E511167; Monatsbericht, September 1944, T-120/1146/2068/449413–434.

83. Riesen, no. 65, Doc. Book III, Lorenz, pp. 43–44; Brückner Testimony, pp. 2723–26.

84. Himmler to Lorenz and Heydrich, 11 July 1941, NO-4274, Prosec. Doc. Book VIIC.

85. Lorenz Testimony, p. 2631; BDC SSO Hoffmeyer; Kubitz Testimony, p. 2854; Koehl, *RKFDV*, p. 148; Luther, Foreign Ministry, 5 November 1941, T-120/2424/4699/E227036; Herzog, *Besatzungsverwaltung*, pp. 18–19; "Vereinbarung," 13 December 1941, T-175/194/2733072–076; "Rumänien" 18 December 1942, T-81/290/2414467.

86. VoMi, 15 March 1942, T-175/68/2585161–167; Dallin, *German Rule in Russia*, p. 289.

87. Hoffmeyer, 15 March 1942, T-175/68/2585155–160; Godzik, no. 9, Doc. Book I, Brückner, p. 39.

88. Hoffmeyer, 15 March 1942, T-175/68/2585155–160; Godzik, no. 9, Doc. Book I, Brückner, p. 39. Also, Ohlendorf, in *TWC* 4, Case 8, p. 854; *TWC* 4, Case

8, p. 669; Behrends to Naumann, 6 July 1942, NO-5095, Prosec. Exhibit No. 741, in *TWC* 4, Case 8, p. 850; Brandt, 20 April 1942, NO-2278, Prosec. Doc. Book VA; Lorenz Testimony, pp. 2632–33; VoMi, 21 May 1944, BDC SSO Siebert.

89. Memo, 17 August 1942, T-175/17/2521076–079; Lorenz Testimony, pp. 2631–32; Lorenz Opening Defense Statement, p. 1270; Wallrabe, no. 6, Doc. Book I, Brückner, p. 32.

90. Lorenz to Himmler, 10 July 1942, T-175/66/2582330–331; Lorenz to Himmler, 18 August 1942, T-175/66/2582329.

91. "Bericht," September 1941, T-175/72/2582321–332; Radunski, VoMi, to Brandt, 25 February 1943, T-175/66/2582335; Brandt to Radunski and Berger, 6 March 1943, T-175/66/2582333.

92. Lorenz to Himmler, 21 January 1942, NO-5317, Prosec. Doc. Book VE; Brandt to Lorenz, 30 January 1942, NO-5318, Prosec. Doc. Book VE; Brückner, VoMi, to Brandt, 10 March 1942, T-175/71/2588909; Pieger Testimony, p. 2794.

93. Berger to Lorenz, 4 February 194, NO-4643, Prosec. Doc. Book VIB; Pers. Stab to Berger, 30 July 1943, T-175/19/2522909–910.

94. Himmler to Berger, to VoMi, 4 February 1943, NO-4643, Prosec. Doc. Book VIB.

95. Himmler, 13 February 1943, T-175/71/2588162.

96. Himmler to Berger, Lorenz, Prützmann, Kruger, 24 February 1943, T-175/128/2653712; Himmler to RKFDV, 9 March 1943, T-175/128/2589203; "Der Grosse Kriegstreck 1944," T-81/294/2419153–158; RKFDV, Stier to Brandt, 17 March 1943, T-175/72/2590344; Wallrabe, Doc. No. 5, Doc. Book I, Brückner, pp. 27–28.

97. "Der Grosse Kriegstreck 1944," T-81/294/2419153–158; Brückner to Einsatzgruppe B, 3 March 1943, NO-5332, in *TWC* 4, Case 8, p. 818; Müller to Rosenberg, 19 November 1943, T-175/119/2645089–100; Pieger Testimony, p. 2794.

98. "Die Grosse Kriegstreck 1944," T-81/294/2419153–158; BDC SSO Siebert, Beurteilung Hoffmeyer, 21 May 1944.

99. Müller to Rosenberg, 19, 20 November 1943, T-175/119/2645089–103.

100. Hoffmeyer to Himmler, 13 March 1944, T-175/72/2589289; Lorenz to Himmler, 16 March 1944, T-175/72/2589284; Himmler to Führer and Lorenz, 23 May 1944, T-175/72/2589230; Wagner, Foreign Ministry to RFSS and VoMi, 20 April 1944, T-175/72/2589240–242; Lorenz to RFSS, 21 April 1944, T-175/72/2589239; Foreign Ministry, 18 April 1944, T-120/3133/6744/E511172–173; Brandt, 19 July 1944, T-175/72/2589229.

CHAPTER THIRTEEN

1. Lorenz to SS Personal Hauptamt, 27 March 1943, BDC SSO Kubitz.

2. Brückner Testimony, pp. 2722, 2730–31; Eilers, Doc. Book I, Brückner, p. 13.

3. Memo, Reichel, Foreign Ministry, 13 September 1944, T-120/1005/1659/393320–323.

4. Goeken to Wrangell, Foreign Ministry, 4 September 1944, T-120/1030/1797/408945.

5. VoMi, September 1944, T-120/1146/2068/449435–443; Lorenz to RFSS, 9 September 1944, T-175/59/2574502; Budapest to Foreign Minister, 12 September 1944, T-120/1757/3579/E025214.

6. Goecken, 8 September 1944, PA AA, Inland IIg, 260; Wagner, Foreign Ministry, to Budapest, 9 September 1944, T-120/1757/3579/E025211.

7. Gassenfeit, Foreign Ministry, 8 September 1944, Inland IIg, 260; Wagner to Budapest, 9 September 1944, T-120/1757/3579/E025211; "Evakuierung," 3 November 1944, T-120/1025/1762/405503–505; VoMi to Reichel, 23 November 1944, T-120/1042/1820/416544–575; VoMi Report No. 21, 11 October 1944, T-120/1757/3579/E025412–417.

8. Bazin to Skoda, 15 September 1944, T-175/31/2538470–472.

9. Veesenmayer to Foreign Ministry, 8 September 1944, T-120/1757/3579/E025239–240; Reichel, 29 September 1944, T-120/1757/ 3579/E025304.

10. "Evakuierung," 3 November 1944, T-120/1025/1762/405503–505; VoMi, Report, 11 October 1944, T-120/1757/3579/E025412–417.

11. "Bericht," 30 September 1944, T-120/1030/1797/408966–968; VoMi, Report, 11 October 1944, T-120/1757/3579/E025412–417; VoMi to Reichel, 23 November 1944, T-120/1042/1820/416544–575.

12. Collection of Documents, Lorenz and Himmler, in T-175/71/2587835–849.

13. Ritter to Foreign Ministry, 14 October 1944, T-120/1757/3579/E025427–428; Wagner to Zagreb, 15 October 1944, PA AA, Inland IIg, 271; Wagner to Foreign Ministry, 19 October 1944, PA AA, Inland IIg, 271.

14. Lorenz to Himmler, 12 October 1944, T-175/31/2538497–498; Himmler to Lorenz, 13 October 1944, T-175/31/2538489.

15. VoMi, October 1944, T-120/1042/1820/416544–575; Memo, 3 November 1944, T-120/1025/1762/405503–505.

16. Lorenz to Foreign Ministry, 25 November 1944, T-120/1025/1762/405518.

17. Lorenz, Budapest, 22 November 1944, T-120/1042/1820/416577–580; VoMi to Foreign Ministry, 23 November 1944, T-120/1042/1820/416544–575.

18. VoMi, 4 December 1944, PA AA, Inland IIg, 271; Memo for Foreign Minister, 9 January 1945, T-120/3133/6744/E511044.

19. Czechoslovak Ministry of Interior to President, 4 July 1946, in Král, *Die Deutschen*, no. 438, p. 535.

20. Foreign Ministry Report, 3 November 1944, T-120/1025/1762/405503–505.

21. Hangel, no. 4, Doc. Book I, Lorenz, pp. 39–40.

22. Lorenz, 1 January 1945, NO-3896, Prosec. Doc. Book VIA.

23. Lorenz Testimony, p. 2613; Wolff Testimony, p. 1926.

24. Lorenz Testimony, pp. 2610–12, 2684–85; Opening Statement Lorenz, p. 1; Lorenz affidavit, NO-4701, Prosec. Doc. Book I.

25. Schechtman, *European Population Transfers*, pp. 94, 209–10.

26. Ibid., pp. 275–84; Schechtman, "The Elimination of German Minorities."

27. Schechtman, *European Population Transfers*, pp. 265–71.

28. Ibid., pp. 271–74.

29. Ibid., pp. 6–15.

30. Král, *Die Deutschen*, p. 528 n. 1; Höhne, *Order of the Death's Head*, pp. 312–13.

B I B L I O G R A P H Y

• •

PRIMARY SOURCES

Archival Collections

Auswärtiges Amt, Politisches Archiv, Bonn
  Abteilung VI Kultur
  Büro des Reichsministers
  Dienststelle Ribbentrop
  Inland I Partei
  Inland II (geheim)
  Inland II A/B
  Inland II C
  Inland II D
  Inland D VI
  Politische Abteilung II
  Politische Abteilung III
  Referat Deutschland
Berlin Document Center, Berlin
  Document Center Research Division Collection
  SS Officer Personnel Files
Bundesarchiv, Koblenz
  NS 2, Rasse und Siedlungshauptamt SS
  NS 19, Reichsführer SS und Chef der Deutschen Polizei
  NS 26, Hauptarchiv der NSDAP
  NS 34, SS Personalhauptamt
  R 35, Deutsche Umsiedlungs-Treuhandsgesellschaft mbH
  R 43, Reichskanzlei
  R 49, RKFDV, Reichskommisar für die Festigung des deutschen Volkstums
  R 57, Deutsche Auslands-Institut
  R 59, Volksdeutsche Mittelstelle
  R 69, Einwandererzentralstelle, Litzmannstadt (Lodz)
  R 75, Umwandererzentralstelle, Litzmannstadt und Posen
Center for Research Libraries, Chicago
  Copies of transcripts of Case 8, United States of America v. Ulrich Greifelt et
    al., United States Tribunal at Nuremberg.
Institut für Zeitgeschichte, Munich
  Collection of pamphlets, rare periodicals, and similar materials from the Nazi
    period.

National Archives, Washington, D.C.
Evidence Division, Documentation Branch. SEA Series, Box 28–36. "NO series" documents.
Transcripts of Case 8, United States of America v. Ulrich Greifelt et al., United States Tribunal at Nuremberg, 1 July 1947–10 March 1948.

Microfilms

National Archives Microfilm, filmed at Alexandria, Va.

T-74 Office of the Reich Commissioner for the Strengthening of Germandom.

T-81 Records of the National Socialist German Labor Party; and Records of the Deutsche Auslands-Institut.

T-82 Records of Nazi Cultural and Research Institutions; Including Records Pertaining to the Deutsche Akademie.

T-84 Miscellaneous German Records Collections.

T-175 Records of the Reichsführer SS and Chief of the German Police.

T-253 Records of Private German Individuals; Including the Papers of Karl Haushofer.

T-454 Records of the Reich Minister for the Occupied Eastern Territories.

T-459 Records of the Office of the Reich Commissioner for the Baltic States.

T-581 NSDAP Hauptarchiv.

Captured German Documents Filmed at Berlin

T-580 Records Filmed at the Berlin Document Center.

Records of the German Foreign Ministry, filmed at Whaddon Hall, England

T-120 Records of the German Foreign Ministry and Reich Chancellery.

Published Documents

Arbeitsgemeinschaft zur Wahrung sudetendeutscher Interessen. *Dokumente zur Austreibung der Sudetendeutschen.* Edited by Wilhelm K. Turnwald. 4th ed. 1951. Reprint. Munich: Arbeitsgemeinschaft zur Wahrung sudetendeutscher Interessen, 1952.

Germany. Bundesministerium für Vertriebene, Flüchtlinge und Kriegsgeschädigte. *Die Vertreibung der deutschen Bevölkerung aus den Gebieten östlich der Oder-Neisse.* Vols. I/1 and I/2 in *Dokumentation der Vertreibung der Deutschen aus Ost-Mitteleuropa.* Edited by Theodor Schieder. Bonn: Bundesministerium für Vertriebene, Flüchtlinge und Kriegsgeschädigte, 1953.

———. *Das Schicksal der Deutschen in Ungarn.* Vol. II in *Dokumentation der Vertreibung der Deutschen aus Ost-Mitteleuropa.* Edited by Theodor Schieder. Düsseldorf: Oskar Lesner-Druck, 1956.

———. *Das Schicksal der Deutschen in Rumänien.* Vol. III in *Dokumentation der Vertreibung der Deutschen aus Ost-Mitteleuropa.* Edited by Theodor Schieder. Berlin: Bernard and Graefe, 1957.

———. *Die Vertreibung der deutschen Bevölkerung aus der Tschechoslowakei.* Vols.

IV/1 and IV/2 in *Dokumentation der Vertreibung der Deutschen aus Ost-Mitteleuropa*. Edited by Theodor Schieder. N.p.: n.d.

———. *Das Schicksal der Deutschen in Jugoslawien*. Vol. V in *Dokumentation der Vertreibung der Deutschen aus Ost-Mitteleuropa*. Edited by Theodor Schieder. Düsseldorf: Oskar Lesner-Druck, 1961.

———. *The Expulsion of the German Population from Hungary and Rumania*. Vol. II/III in *Documents on the Expulsion of the Germans from Eastern-Central Europe*. Edited by Theodor Schieder. Göttingen: Schwartz and Co., 1961.

———. *The Expulsion of the German Population from Czechoslovakia*. Vol. IV in *Documents on the Expulsion of the Germans from Eastern-Central Europe*. Edited by Theodor Schieder. Leer, Ostfriedland: Gerhard Rautenberg, 1960.

Heiber, Helmut. *Reichsführer! Briefe an und von Himmler*. Munich: Deutscher Taschenbuch Verlag, 1970.

International Military Tribunal. *Trial of the Major War Criminals before the International Military Tribunal*. 42 vols. Nuremberg: International Military Tribunal, 1949.

Jacobsen, Hans-Adolf, ed. *Hans Steinacher, Bundesleiter des VDA, 1933–1937: Erinnerungen und Dokumente*. Schriften des Bundesarchivs, no. 19. Boppard am Rhein: Harald Boldt Verlag, 1970.

———. *Karl Haushofer: Leben und Werk*. Vol. I, *Lebensweg: 1869–1946*. Vol. II, *Ausgewählter Schriftwechsel*. Boppard am Rhein: Harald Boldt Verlag, 1979.

Král, Václav. *Die Deutschen in der Tchechoslowakei, 1933–1947: Dokumentsammlung*. Prague: Nakladatelství Československé Akademie VED, 1964.

Král, Václav, and Karel Fremund, eds. *Lessons from History: Documents Concerning Nazi Policies for Germanization and Extermination in Czechoslovakia*. Prague: Orbis, 1961.

Loeber, Dietrich A., ed. *Diktierte Option: Die Umsiedlung der Deutsch-Balten aus Estland und Lettland, 1939–41*. Neumünster: Karl Wachholz Verlag, 1972.

United States, Chief of Counsel for Prosecution of Axis Criminality. *Nazi Conspiracy and Aggression*. 8 vols. Washington, D.C.: Government Printing Office, 1946–48.

United States, Chief of Counsel for War Crimes. *Trial of War Criminals before the Nuremberg Military Tribunals*. 15 vols. Washington, D.C.: Government Printing Office, 1949–53.

United States, Department of State. *Documents on German Foreign Policy, 1918–1945: Series D, 1937–1945*. 13 vols. Washington, D.C.: Government Printing Office, 1949–57.

Contemporary Periodicals

Der Auslanddeutsche	*Nationalsozialistische Monatshefte*
Deutsche Arbeit	*Nation und Staat*
Deutscher Lebensraum	*Neues Volk*
Deutsches Grenzland	*Das Schwarze Korps*
Geist der Zeit	*Die Sonne*

Der Untermensch
Völkischer Beobachter
Volkstum und Heimat
Volk und Boden
Volk und Rasse
Volk und Reich

Volk und Welt
Der Weltkampf
Wille und Macht
Wir Deutsche in der Welt
Zeitschrift für Geopolitik

Memoirs, Diaries, and Other Works

Achterberg, Gerhard. "Der deutsche Osten-Aufgabe und Verpflichtung." *Nationalsozialistische Monatshefte* 12, no. 130 (1941): 16–20.

Auslandsorganisation der NSDAP. *Jahrbuch der Auslandsorganisation der NSDAP, 1941.* Berlin: Gauverlag der AO, 1941.

Best, Werner. "Grundfragen einer deutschen Grossraum-Verwaltung." In *Festgabe für Heinrich Himmler.* Darmstadt: L. C. Wittich Verlag, 1941.

Boehm, Max-Hildebert. *Die deutschen Grenzlande.* Berlin: R. Hobbing, 1930.

Burgdörfer, Friedrich. *Volksdeutsche Zukunft: Eine biologisch-statistische Betrachtung der gesamtdeutschen Bevölkerungsfrage.* Schriften der Hochschule für Politik, no. 34. Berlin: Junker und Dünnhaupt Verlag, 1938.

D'Alquen, Gunther. *Die SS: Geschichte, Aufgabe und Organisation der Schutzstaffel der NSDAP.* Schriften der Hochschule für Politik. Berlin: Junker und Dünnhaupt Verlag, 1939.

Darré, R. Walther. *Das Bauerntum als Lebensquell der Nordische Rasse.* 2d. ed., 1929. Reprint. Munich: J. F. Lehmanns Verlag, 1933.

———. *Neuadel aus Blut und Boden.* 2d ed., 1930. Reprint. Berlin and Munich: J. F. Lehmanns Verlag, 1943.

———. "Der Rassengedanke als Bollwerk gegen die Landflucht." *Nationalsozialistische Monatshefte* 10, no. 106 (1936): 33–39.

Ehrich, Emil. *Die Auslands-Organisation der NSDAP.* Schriften der deutschen Hochschule für Politik. Berlin: Junker und Dünnhaupt Verlag, 1937.

Fabritius, Fritz. "Blut und Boden im Leben der deutschen Volksgruppen." *Zeitschrift für Politik* 29 (1939).

———. "Volkstum und Boden." *Nation und Staat* 10, nos. 2–3 (1936): 124–27.

Fochler-Hauke, Gustav. "Gefahren und Hemmungen für das Deutschtum im Südosten." *Zeitschrift für Geopolitik,* no. 8 (1938): 613–21.

Frick, Wilhelm. "Die Nichtdeutschen Volksgruppen im Deutschen Reich." *Nationalsozialistische Monatshefte* 10, no. 110 (1939): 387–401.

Geisler, Walter. *Der deutsche Osten als Lebensraum für alle Berufsstande.* Berlin, Prague, and Vienna: Volk und Reich Verlag, 1942.

———. *Deutscher! Der Osten ruft Dich!* Berlin: Volk und Reich Verlag, 1942.

Greiser, Arthur. "Die Grossdeutsche Aufgabe im Wartheland." *Nationalsozialistische Monatshefte* 12, no. 130 (1941): 46–50.

Grimm, Hans. *Volk ohne Raum.* Munich: A. Langer, 1926.

Gross, Walter. "Grundfragen nationalsozialistischer Rassen und Bevölkerungspolitik." *Nationalsozialistische Monatshefte* 12, no. 137 (1941): 656–60.

————. "National Socialist Racial Thought." In *Germany Speaks: Twenty-one Leading Members of Party and State*, pp. 66–78. London: Thornton Butterworth, 1938.

————. "Die Rassen- und Bevölkerungspolitik im Kampf um die geschichtliche Selbstbehauptung der Völker." *Nationalsozialistische Monatshefte* 10, no. 115 (1939): 882–88.

Hassell, Ulrich von. *The Von Hassell Diaries, 1938–1944*. Garden City, N.Y.: Doubleday, 1947.

Haushofer, Albrecht. "Ein Volk, ein Staat!" *Zeitschrift für Geopolitik*, no. 4 (1938): 262–66.

Haushofer, Karl. "Geopolitik als Grundlage jeder Raumordnung." *Zeitschrift für Geopolitik*, no. 2 (1936): 128–30.

————. *Der nationalsozialistische Gedanke in der Welt*. Munich: Georg D. W. Callwey Verlag, 1933.

Heimberger, Philipp. "Volksgruppe und Wirtschaft." *Nation und Staat* 15–16, no. 3 (1941): 76–82.

Himmler, Heinrich. "Denkschrift Himmlers über die Behandlung der Fremdvölkischen im Osten, Mai 1940." *Vierteljahrshefte für Zeitgeschichte* 5, no. 2 (1957): 194–98.

————. *Geheimreden 1933 bis 1945 und andere Ansprachen*. Edited by Bradley F. Smith and Agnes F. Peterson. Frankfurt a. M. and Berlin: Propyläen Verlag, 1970.

————. *Rede des Reichsführers SS im Dom zu Quedlinburg am 2. Juli 1936*. Berlin: Norland Verlag, n.d.

Hitler, Adolf. *Hitler's Table Talk, 1941–44: His Private Conversations*. Translated by Norman Cameron and R. H. Stevens. 2d ed., 1953. Reprint. London: Weidenfeld and Nicolson, 1973.

————. *Hitlers zweites Buch: Ein Dokument aus dem Jahr 1928*. Edited by Gerhard L. Weinberg. Stuttgart: Deutsche Verlags-Anstalt, 1961.

————. *Mein Kampf*. Translated by Ralph Manheim. Sentry Edition. Boston: Houghton Mifflin, 1943.

————. *My New Order*. Edited by Raoul de Roussy de Sales. New York: Reynal and Hitchcock, 1941.

————. *Secret Conversations with Hitler: The Two Newly-Discovered 1931 Interviews*. Edited by Edouard Calic. Translated by Richard Barry. 1969. Reprint. New York: John Day Co., 1971.

Hockl, Nikolaus Hans. "Die volkspolitische Stellung der volksdeutschen Jugend." *Nation und Staat* 13, nos. 5–6 (1940): 150–54.

Johst, Hanns. *Ruf des Reiches—Echo des Volkes: Eine Ostfahrt*. 7th ed., 1940. Reprint. Munich: Verlag Franz Eher Nachf., 1944.

Kordt, Erich. *Nicht aus den Akten: Die Wilhelmstrasse in Frieden und Krieg; Erlebnisse, Begegnungen und Eindrücke, 1928–1945*. Stuttgart: Union deutsche Verlagsgesellschaft, 1950.

Maschke, Erich. "Ostsee und Ostseeraum im Geschichtlichen Werden des deutschen Volkes." *Nationalsozialistische Monatshefte* 10, no. 110 (1939): 402–13.

Mohr, Friedrich Wilhelm, and Walter von Hauff. *Deutsche im Ausland.* Breslau: Ferdinand Hirst, 1923.

NSDAP, Der Reichsorganisationsleiter. *Organisationsbuch der NSDAP.* Munich: Zentralverlag der NSDAP, 1936, 1938, 1940, 1943.

Reichsführer SS. *Aufbruch: Briefe germanischer Kriegsfreiwilliger der SS-Division Wiking.* Berlin and Leipzig: Nibelungen-Verlag, 1943.

———. *Dich ruft die SS.* Berlin: Verlag Hermann Hillger, n.d.

———. *Lehrplan für die weltanschauliche Erziehung in der SS und Polizei.* Berlin: SS Hauptamt, n.d.

———. *Der Menscheneinsatz: Grundsätze, Anordnungen und Richtlinien.* N.p.: Hauptabteilung 1 des RKFDV, 1940.

———. *Sicherung Europas.* Berlin: RFSS Hauptamt, n.d.

———. *SS Mann und Blutfrage.* N.p., n.d.

———. *Der Untermensch.* Berlin: SS Hauptamt, 1941.

———. *Der Weg der NSDAP: Entstehung, Kampf und Sieg.* Berlin: RFSS, SS Hauptamt, n.d.

Ribbentrop, Annelies von, ed. *Joachim von Ribbentrop, Zwischen London und Moskau.* Leoni: Druffel, 1954.

Schellenberg, Walter. *The Labyrinth: Memoirs of Walter Schellenberg.* Translated by Louis Hagen. New York: Harper and Brothers, 1956.

Schreiber, Georg. *Das Auslanddeutschtum als Kulturfrage. Deutschtum und Ausland,* nos. 17–18. Münster in Westfalen: Aschendorfsche Verlagsbuchhandlung, 1929.

Schwarz, Maria. *Die Umsiedlung und die Sowjets: Erlebnisse einer deutschen Frau.* Volksdeutsche Heimkehr, nos. 12–13. Berlin and Leipzig: Nibelungen Verlag, 1942.

Strobel, Hans. "Kritik der Zeit: Volkstumsarbeit ohne Wissenschaft?" *Nationalsozialistische Monatshefte* 10, no. 106 (1939): 69–72.

Valters, M. *Mana Sarakste: Ar Kārli Ulmani un Vilhelmu Munteru Latvijas Tragiskajos Gados.* Stockholm: LPC Grāmatnīcu, 1957.

Waldeck, R. G. *Athene Palace.* New York: Robert M. McBride and Co., 1942.

Weizsäcker, Ernst von. *Memoirs of Ernst von Weizsäcker.* Translated by John Andrews. Chicago: Henry Regnery, 1951.

Wrangell, Baron Wilhelm von. "Volkstum und Volkszugehörigkeit." *Nation und Staat* 10, nos. 2–3 (1936): 105–12.

SECONDARY SOURCES

Ackermann, Josef. *Heinrich Himmler als Ideologue.* Göttingen: Musterschmidt, 1970.

Albrich, Gerhard, Hans Christ, and Hans Wolfram Hockl. *Deutsche Jugendbewegung im Südosten.* Bielefeld: Verlag Ernst und Werner Gieseking, 1969.

Arató, Endre. "Der 'Volksbund der Deutschen in Ungarn'—eine Fünfte

Kolonne des Hitlerfaschismus." *Jahrbuch für Geschichte der UdSSR und der Volksdemokratischen Länder Europas* 5 (1961): 289–96.

Arndt, Veronika. "Ständische Ideologie im Henleinfaschismus—das Programm Franz Künzels." *Jahrbuch für Geschichte der sozialistischen Länder Europas* 18, no. 2 (1974): 199–212.

Aronson, Shlomo. *Reinhard Heydrich und die Frühgeschichte von Gestapo und SD.* Stuttgart: Deutsche Verlags-Anstalt, 1971.

Arz, Wilhelm. "Das Deutschtum des Buchenlandes." *Nation und Staat* 14, no. 1 (1940): 16–22.

Azcarate, P. de. *League of Nations and National Minorities.* Translated by Eileen E. Brooke. Washington, D.C.: Carnegie Endowment for International Peace, 1945.

Bahr, Richard. *Deutsches Schicksal im Südosten.* Hamburg: Hanseatische Verlag, 1936.

———. *Volk jenseits der Grenzen: Geschichte und Problematik der deutschen Minderheiten.* Hamburg: Hanseatische Verlagsanstalt, 1933.

Baltenbriefe zur Rückkehr ins Reich. Volksdeutsche Heimkehr, no. 2. Berlin-Leipzig: Nibelungen Verlag, 1940.

Basch, Franz. "Deutscher Aufbruch in Ungarn." *Nation und Staat* 12, no. 4 (1939): 204–11.

Bayle, Francois. *Psychologie et Ethique du Nationalsocialisme: Étude Anthropologique des Dirigents SS.* Paris: Presses Universitaires de France, 1953.

Bell, Karl. *Das Deutschtum im Ausland: Banat; Das Deutschtum im rumänischen Banat.* Dresden: Deutscher Buch- und Kunstverlag, 1926.

Bell, Leland V. "The Failure of Nazism in America: The German-American Bund, 1936–1941." *Political Science Quarterly* 85, no. 4 (1970): 585–99.

"Die Bessarabiendeutschen: Ein volksbiologischer Rückblick." *Neues Volk* 12 (1940): 9–13.

"Die Bevölkerungspolitische Entwicklung Nordschleswigs seit dem Ende des Weltkrieges." *Nation und Staat* 15, no. 1 (1941): 9–16.

Bierschenk, Theodor. *Die Deutsche Volksgruppe in Polen, 1934–39.* Würzburg: Holzner-Verlag, 1954.

———. "Die polnischen Richtlinien zur Behandlung der deutschen Volksgruppe vom 9. Juli 1936." *Zeitschrift für Ostforschung* 17, no. 3 (1968): 534–38.

Bigler, Robert M. "Heil Hitler und Heil Horthy! The Nature of Hungarian Racist Nationalism and Its Impact on German-Hungarian Relations, 1919–1945." *East European Quarterly* 8, no. 3 (1974): 251–72.

Bilek, Bohuslav. *Fifth Column at Work.* London: Trinity Press, 1945.

Birke, Ernst. "Schlesien." In *Die Deutschen Ostgebiete zur Zeit der Weimarer Republik*, pp. 150–86. Studien zum Deutschtum im Osten, no. 3. Cologne-Graz: Böhlau Verlag, 1966.

Bischoff, Ralph F. *Nazi Conquest through German Culture.* Cambridge: Harvard University Press, 1942.

Bistram, Roderich von. "Republik der Wolgadeutschen." *Nation und Staat* 10, no. 4 (1937): 197–203.

Boberach, Heinz. *Meldungen aus dem Reich: Auswahl aus den Geheimen Lage-berichten des Sicherheitsdienstes der SS, 1939–1944.* Neuwied and Berlin: Hermann Luchterhand Verlag, 1965.

"Der Bodenkampf der deutschen Volksgruppe in Posen und Pommerellen." *Nation und Staat* 11, no. 9 (1938): 531–35.

Bodensieck, Heinrich. "Volksgruppenrecht und nationalsozialistische Aussenpolitik nach dem Münchener Abkommen, 1938." *Zeitschrift für Ostforschung* 7, no. 3 (1958): 502–18.

Boehm, Max Hildebert, and Karl von Loesch. *Jahrbuch des Instituts für Grenz-und Auslandsstudien, 1938.* Berlin: Deutsche Buchvertriebstelle Kurt Hofmeier, 1938.

Boehnert, Gunnar C. "An Analysis of the Age and Education of the SS Führerkorps, 1925–1939." *Historische Sozialforschung* 12 (October 1979): 4–17.

Boelitz, Otto. *Das Grenz- und Auslandsdeutschtum: Seine Geschichte und seine Bedeutung.* Munich and Berlin: R. Oldenbourg, 1926.

Bollmus, Reinhard. *Das Amt Rosenberg und seine Gegner: Studien zum Machtkampf im nationalsozialistischen Herrschaftssystem.* Stuttgart: Deutsche Verlags-Anstalt, 1970.

Bonwetsch, Gerhard. *Geschichte der deutschen Kolonien an der Wolga.* Schriften des Deutschen Ausland-Instituts Stuttgart, 2. Stuttgart: Verlag von J. Engelhorns, 1919.

Bosse, Heinrich. *Der Führer ruft: Erlebnisberichte aus den Tagen der grossen Umsiedlung im Osten.* Berlin: Zeitgeschichte-Verlag, 1941.

Botting, Douglas. *From the Ruins of the Reich: Germany, 1945–1949.* New York: Crown, 1985.

Bracher, Karl Dietrich. "Das Anfangsstadium der Hitlerschen Aussenpolitik." *Vierteljahrshefte für Zeitgeschichte* 5, no. 1 (1957): 63–76.

Branig, Hans. "Pommern als Grenzland in der Zeit der Weimarer Republik." In *Die Deutschen Ostgebiete zur Zeit der Weimarer Republik,* pp. 133–49. Studien zum Deutschtum im Osten, no. 3. Cologne-Graz: Böhlau Verlag, 1966.

Braunias, Karl. "Das deutsche Volk und die Völker des Südostens." *Nation und Staat* 12, nos. 6–7 (1939): 344–55.

———. "Die verfassungsrechtliche Stellung der Slowakei." *Nation und Staat* 12, no. 4 (1939): 217–36.

Bräutigam, Otto. *Überblick über die besetzten Ostgebiete während des 2. Weltkrieges.* Studien des Instituts für Besatzungsfragen in Tübingen, zu den deutschen Besetzungen im 2. Weltkrieg, 3. Tübingen: Instituts für Besatzungsfragen in Tübingen, 1954.

Breitman, Richard. *The Architect of Genocide: Himmler and the Final Solution.* New York: Alfred A. Knopf, 1991.

Breyer, Richard. *Das Deutsche Reich und Polen, 1932–1937: Aussenpolitik und Volksgruppenfragen.* Marburger Ostforschungen, 3. Würzburg: Holzner-Verlag, 1955.

Broszat, Martin. "Deutschland-Ungarn-Rumänien. Entwicklung und Grundfak-

toren nationalsozialistischer Hegemonial- und Bündnispolitik, 1938–1941."
Historische Zeitschrift 206, no. 1 (1968): 45–96.

———. "Faschismus und Kollaboration in Ostmitteleuropa zwischen den
Weltkriegen." *Vierteljahrshefte für Zeitgeschichte* 14, no. 3 (1966): 225–51.

———. "Die Memeldeutschen Organisationen und der Nationalsozialismus,
1933–1939." *Vierteljahrshefte für Zeitgeschichte* 5, no. 3 (1957): 273–78.

———. *Nationalsozialistische Polenpolitik, 1939–1945.* Schriftenreihe der Vierteljahrshefte für Zeitgeschichte. Stuttgart: Deutsche Verlags-Anstalt, 1961.

———. "Das Sudetendeutsche Freikorps." *Vierteljahrshefte für Zeitgeschichte* 9, no.
1 (1961): 30–49.

———. "Die völkische Ideologie und der Nationalsozialismus." *Deutsche
Rundschau* 84, no. 1 (1958): 53–68.

———. *200 Jahre deutsche Polenpolitik.* Munich: Franz Ehrenwirth Verlag, 1963.

Brown, MacAlister. "The Third Reich's Mobilization of the German Fifth Column in Eastern Europe." *Journal of Central European Affairs* 19, no. 2 (1959):
128–48.

The Brown Network: The Activities of the Nazis in Foreign Countries. New York:
Knight Publications, 1936.

Brügel, Johann Wolfgang. "Die Aussiedlung der Deutschen aus der Tschechoslowakei." *Vierteljahrshefte für Zeitgeschichte* 8, no. 1 (1960): 134–64.

———. "Deutsche Demokraten in der Tschechoslowakei, 1935–1938." *Deutsche
Rundschau* 86, no. 9 (1960): 804–12.

———. "German Diplomacy and the Sudeten Question before 1938." *International Affairs* 37, no. 3 (1961): 323–31.

———. *Tschechen und Deutsche, 1918–1938.* 2 vols. Munich: Nymphenburger
Verlagsverhandlung, 1967.

Brunner, Heinz. "Biologische und soziologische Streiflichter auf das Südost-
deutschtum." *Nation und Staat* 13, nos. 11–12 (1940): 362–71.

———. "Die Entwicklung der deutschen Volksgruppe in Jugoslawien." *Nation
und Staat* 12, no. 3 (1938): 138–48.

———. "Volksdeutsche Wende im südosteuropäischen Raum." *Nation und Staat*
14, nos. 10–11 (1940–1941): 358–68.

Buchheim, Hans. "Die Höheren SS- und Polizeiführer." *Vierteljahrshefte für
Zeitgeschichte* 11, no. 4 (1963), 362–91.

———. "Die SS in der Verfassung des Dritten Reiches." *Vierteljahrshefte für
Zeitgeschichte* 3, no. 2 (1955): 127–57.

———. *SS und Polizei im NS-Staat.* Duisdorf bei Bonn: Selbstverlag der Stu-
diengesellschaft für Zeitprobleme, 1964.

Calic, Edouard. *Himmler et son Empire.* Paris: Stock, 1966.

Campus, Eliza. "Die Hitlerfaschistische Infiltration Rumäniens, 1939–1940."
Zeitschrift für Geschichtswissenschaft 5 (1957): 213–28.

Cecil, Robert. *The Myth of the Master Race: Alfred Rosenberg and Nazi Ideology.*
New York: Dodd Mead and Co., 1972.

Čelovsky, Boris. *Das Münchener Abkommen von 1938.* Stuttgart: Deutsche
Verlags-Anstalt, 1958.

Cesar, Jaroslav, and Bohumil Černy. "The Nazi Fifth Column in Czechoslo-vakia." *Historica* 4 (1962): 191–255.

———. "Die nazistische Bewegung der Deutschen in der Tschechoslowakei." *Historica* 15 (1967): 183–225.

———. "The Policy of German Activist Parties in Czechoslovakia in 1918–1938." *Historica* 6 (1963): 239–81.

Claude, Inis L. *National Minorities: An International Problem*. Cambridge: Harvard University Press, 1955.

Craig, Gordon A., and Felix Gilbert, eds. *The Diplomats, 1919–1939*. 2 vols. Princeton: Princeton University Press, 1953.

Cronenberg, Allen Thomson. "The Volksbund für das Deutschtum im Ausland: Völkisch Ideology and German Foreign Policy, 1881–1939." Ph.D. dissertation. Stanford University, 1969.

Cyprian, Tadeuss, and Jerzy Sawiski. *Nazi Rule in Poland, 1939–1945*. Warsaw: Polonia Publishing House, 1961.

Czollek, Roswitha. "Nationale Minderheiten im Konzept imperialistischer Expansionsstrategie. Zur Rolle des Deutschen Ausland-Instituts Stuttgart (DAI) in den Jahren der faschistischen Kriegsvorbereitung." *Jahrbuch für Geschichte der sozialistischen Länder Europas* 19, no. 1 (1975): 139–50.

———. "Zur Geschichte der baltendeutschen Minderheit nach der Restaration des Kapitalismus im Baltikum (1920 bis zur Umsiedlung 1939)." *Jahrbuch für Geschichte der sozialistischen Länder Europas* 20, no. 2 (1976): 155–84.

Dallin, Alexander. *German Rule in Russia, 1941–1945: A Study of Occupation Policies*. London: Macmillan and Co., 1957.

Dankelmann, Otfried. "Aus der Praxis auswärtiger Kulturpolitik des deutschen Imperialismus, 1933–1945." *Zeitschrift für Geschichtswissenschaft* 20, no. 6 (1972): 719–37.

Dawidowicz, Lucy S. *The War against the Jews, 1933–1945*. New York: Holt, Rinehart, and Winston, 1975.

De Jong, Louis. *The German Fifth Column in the Second World War*. Translated by C. M. Geyl. Chicago: University of Chicago Press, 1956.

Deschner, Gunther. *Reinhard Heydrich: Statthalter der totalen Macht*. Esslingen: Bechtle, 1977.

"Die deutsche Litauens." *Nation und Staat* 12, no. 9 (1939): 578–88.

"Die deutsche Minderheit in der UdSSR." *Nation und Staat* 8, no. 2 (1934): 79–88.

Die Deutschen Ostgebiete zur Zeit der Weimarer Republik. Studien zum Deutschtum im Osten, no. 3. Cologne-Graz: Böhlau Verlag, 1966.

"Die deutsche Volksgruppe in Polen." *Nation und Staat* 12, nos. 10–11 (1939): 629–41.

"Das Deutschtum in Ungarn." *Nation und Staat* 12, nos. 10–11 (1939): 665–75.

Diamond, Sander A. *The Nazi Movement in the United States, 1924–1941*. Ithaca: Cornell University Press, 1974.

Dierssen, Hanns. "Die deutsche Volksgruppe in Kroatien." *Nation und Staat* 14, no. 12 (1941): 411–14.

Door, Rochus. "Wesen und Besonderheiten des faschistischen deutschen Be-

satzungsregimes in Ungarn." *Jahrbuch für Geschichte der UdSSR und der Volksdemokratischen Länder Europas* 15 (1971): 37–56.

———. "Zur Vorgeschichte der deutschen Besetzung Ungarns am 19. März
1944." *Jahrbuch für Geschichte der UdSSR und der Volksdemokratischen Länder Europas* 10 (1967): 107–32.

Drechsler, Karl. "Europapläne des deutschen Imperialismus im zweiten Weltkrieg." *Zeitschrift für Geschichtswissenschaft* 19, no. 7 (1971): 916–31.

———. "Zwangsaussiedlungen und Germanisierung in den Kriegsziel-
planungen der faschistischen deutschen Monopolbourgeoisie." *Zeitschrift für
Geschichtswissenschaft* 22, no. 2 (1974): 208–18.

Dress, Hans. *Slowakei und faschistische Neuordnung Europas, 1939–1941.* Deutsche
Akademie der Wissenschaften zu Berlin, Schriften des Zentralinstituts für
Geschichte, 37. Berlin: Akademie-Verlag, 1972.

Drobisch, Klaus. "Die Zwangsarbeit ausländischer Arbeitskräfte in Deutschland
während des zweiten Weltkrieges." *Zeitschrift für Geschichtswissenschaft* 18
(1970): 626–40.

"Die Einigung des Sudetendeutschtums vollzogen." *Nation und Staat* 11, no. 6
(1938): 353–59.

Engelhardt-Kyffhäuser, Otto. *Das Buch vom Grossen Treck.* Berlin: Verlag Grenze
und Ausland, 1940.

———. *Der Grosse Treck: Die Heimkehr der deutschen Bauern aus Galizien und Wolhynien.* Berlin: VDA im Auftrag der VoMi, 1940.

Ernst, Robert. "Elsass und Lothringen unter deutscher Flagge." *Nation und Staat*
13, nos. 11–12 (1940): 354–56.

Faltan, Samo. "Partizan war in Slovakia in the Period 1944–1945." Translated
by J. Simo. *Studia Historica Slovaca* 5 (1967): 57–92.

Fenyo, Mario D. *Hitler, Horthy, and Hungary: German-Hungarian Relations, 1941–
1944.* New Haven: Yale University Press, 1972.

Fest, Joachim C. *The Face of the Third Reich: Portraits of the Nazi Leadership.* Translated by Michael Bullock. New York: Ace Books, 1970.

Fink, Carole. "Defender of Minorities: Germany in the League of Nations,
1926–1933." *Central European History* 5, no. 4 (1972): 330–57.

———. "The Weimar Republic as the Defender of Minorities, 1919–1933."
Ph.D. dissertation. Yale University, 1968.

Fittbogen, Gottfried. "Die Lage der Deutschen in Slawonien und Syrmien." *Nation und Staat* 11, no. 6 (1938): 362–70.

———. *Was jeder Deutsche vom Grenz- und Auslanddeutschtum wissen muss.* 8th ed.
Munich and Berlin: Druck und Verlag von R. Oldenbourg, 1937.

Fletcher, Willard Allen. "The German Administration in Luxemburg, 1940–
1942: Toward a 'De Facto' Annexation." *Historical Journal* 13, no. 3 (1970):
533–44.

Forster, Albert. "Der Reichsgau Danzig-Westpreussen." *Nationalsozialistische
Monatshefte* 12, no. 130 (1941): 33–35.

Frensing, Hans Hermann. *Die Umsiedlung der Gottscheer Deutschen: Das Ende einer
südostdeutscher Volksgruppe.* Munich: Verlag R. Oldenbourg, 1970.

Frischauer, Willi. *Himmler, the Evil Genius of the Third Reich*. London: Oldhams Press, 1953.

Frye, Alton. *Nazi Germany and the American Hemisphere, 1933–1941*. New Haven: Yale University Press, 1967.

Garleff, Michael. *Deutschbaltische Politik zwischen den Weltkriegen: Die parlamentarische Tätigkeit der deutschbaltischen Parteien in Lettland und Estland*. Quellen und Studien zur baltischen Geschichte, no. 2. Bonn-Bad Godesberg: Verlag wissenschaftliches Archiv, 1976.

Gauss, Paul. *Das Buch vom deutschen Volkstum: Wesen-Lebensraum-Schicksal*. Leipzig: Brockhaus, 1935.

Gehl, Jürgen. *Austria, Germany, and the Anschluss, 1931–1938*. London: Oxford University Press, 1963.

Geiger, Joseph. "Das Deutschtum in Osteuropa." *Nationalsozialistische Monatshefte* 10, no. 109 (1939): 322–36.

Gentzen, Felix-Heinrich. "Die Rolle der deutschen Regierung beim Aufbau deutscher Minderheitsorganisation in den an Polen abgetretenen Gebieten (1919–1922)." *Jahrbuch für Geschichte der UdSSR und der Volksdemokratischen Länder Europas* 10 (1967): 159–82.

———. "Die Rolle der 'Deutsche Stiftung' bei der Vorbereitung der Annexion des Memelgebietes im März 1939." *Jahrbuch für Geschichte der UdSSR und der Volksdemokratischen Länder Europas* 5 (1961): 71–94.

———. "Zur Geschichte des deutschen Revanchismus in der Periode der Weimarer Republik." *Jahrbuch für Geschichte der UdSSR und der Volksdemokratischen Länder Europas* 4 (1960): 40–76.

Georg, Enno. *Die Wirtschaftlichen Unternehmungen der SS*. Schriftenreihe der Vierteljahrshefte für Zeitgeschichte, no. 7. Stuttgart: Deutsche Verlags-Anstalt, 1963.

Gerlach, Fritz. "Ein neuer Abschnitt deutscher Volksgeschichte." *Zeitschrift für Geopolitik* 18, no. 3 (1941): 146–54.

———. "Die Heimkehr der Gottscheer Deutschen." *Neues Bauerntum* 33, no. 12 (1941): 460–65.

Germany Speaks: Twenty-one Leading Members of Party and State. London: Thornton Butterworth, 1938.

Gilbert, Felix. "Mitteleuropa—The Final Stage." *Journal of Central European Affairs* 7 (1947–48): 58–67.

Goldbach, Kuno. "Die Slowakei als Schutzstatt des Reiches." *Nationalsozialistische Monatshefte* 12, no. 131 (1941): 112–20.

Graber, G. S. *The History of the SS*. New York: David McKay, 1978.

Gradmann, Werner. "Die Erfassung der Umsiedler." *Zeitschrift für Politik* 32, no. 5 (1942): 346–51.

———. "Die umgesiedelten deutschen Volksgruppen." *Zeitschrift für Politik* 31, no. 5 (1941): 277–93.

"Der Grosse Treck." *Neues Volk* 3 (1940): 19–21.

Gruchmann, Lothar. *Nationalsozialistische Grossraumordnung: Die Konstruktion einer "deutschen Monroe-Doktrin."* Schriftenreihe der Vierteljahrshefte für Zeitgeschichte, no. 4. Stuttgart: Deutsche Verlags-Anstalt, 1962.

Grunberger, Richard. *Hitler's SS.* New York: Delacorte Press, 1970.

Grundman, Karl-Heinz. *Deutschtumspolitik zur Zeit der Weimarer Republik: Eine Studie am Beispiel der deutschbaltischen Minderheite in Estland und Lettland.* Beiträge zur Baltischen Geschichte, no. 7. Hannover-Döhren: Harro von Hirschheydt, 1977.

Haas, Gerhart. "Zur Aggressionspolitik des deutschen Imperialismus gegen die Tschechoslowakei und zur Appeasement-Politik der Westmächte, 1933–1939." *Jahrbuch für Geschichte der sozialistischen Länder Europas* 18, no. 2 (1974): 33–52.

Harriman, Helga H. "Slovenia as an Outpost of the Third Reich." *East European Quarterly* 5, no. 2 (1971): 222–31.

Hasbach, Ervin. "Die Lage der deutschen Volksgruppe in Polen vor dem Zweiten Weltkriege." *Zeitschrift für Ostforschung* 1, no. 2 (1952): 262–64.

Hausser, Paul. *Soldaten wie andere auch: Der Weg der Waffen SS.* Osnabrück: Munin Verlag, 1966.

———. *Waffen SS im Einsatz.* Göttingen: Plesse Verlag K. W. Schütz, 1953.

Hegemann, Margot. "Die Deutsche Volksgruppe in Rumänien—eine Fünfte Kolonne des deutschen Imperialismus in Südosteuropa." *Jahrbuch für Geschichte der UdSSR und der Volksdemokratischen Länder Europas* 4 (1960): 371–84.

Hehn, Jürgen von. *Die Baltischen Lande: Geschichte und Schicksal der baltischen Deutschen.* Der Göttingen Arbeitskreis, Schriftenreihe, no. 17. Kitzingen/Main.

———. "Die Entstehung der Staaten Lettland und Estland, der Bolschewismus und die Grossmächte." *Forschungen zur Osteuropäischen Geschichte* 4 (1956): 103–218.

———. *Die Umsiedlung der baltischen Deutschen—das letzte Kapitel baltischedeutscher Geschichte.* Marburg/Lahn: J. G. Herder Institut, 1984.

———. "Zum deutsch-lettischen Verhältnis im Jahr 1939." *Zeitschrift für Ostforschung* 23, no. 4 (1974): 661–75.

Heike, Otto. "Die ersten Opfer des Zweiten Weltkrieges: Fälschung und Wahrheit über den Umfang der Gewaltmassnahmen gegen die Deutschen in Polen im September 1939." *Zeitschrift für Ostforschung* 18, no. 3 (1969): 475–82.

Helmreich, E. C. "The Return of the Baltic Germans." *American Political Science Review* 36, no. 4 (1942): 711–16.

Henri, Ernst. *Hitler over Europe.* New York: Simon and Schuster, 1943.

Herzog, Robert. *Besatzungsverwaltung in den besetzten Ostgebieten—Abteilung Jugend—insbesondere: Heuaktion und SS-Helfer-Aktion.* Studien des Instituts für Besatzungsfragen in Tübingen, no. 19. Tübingen: Instituts für Besatzungsfragen in Tübingen, 1960.

———. *Grundzüge der deutschen Besatzungsverwaltung in den ost- und südosteuropäischen Ländern während des zweiten Weltkrieges.* Studien des Instituts für Besatzungsfragen in Tübingen, no. 4. Tübingen: Instituts für Besatzungsfragen in Tübingen, 1955.

———. *Die Volksdeutsche in der Waffen SS.* Studien des Instituts für Besatzungs-fragen in Tübingen, no. 5. Tübingen: Instituts für Besatzungsfragen in Tübingen, 1955.

Hiden, J. W. "The Baltic Germans and German Policy towards Latvia after 1918." *Historical Journal* 13, no. 2 (1970): 295–317.

Hilberg, Raul. *The Destruction of the European Jews.* 1961. Reprint. New York: Franklin Watts, 1973.

Hill, Leonidas E. "The Wilhelmstrasse in the Nazi Era." *Political Science Quarterly* 82, no. 4 (1967): 546–70.

Hillgruber, Andreas. "Die Endlösung und das deutsche Ostimperium als Kern-stücke des rassenideologischen Programms des Nationalsozialismus." *Viertel-jahrshefte für Zeitgeschichte* 20, no. 2 (1972): 133–53.

———. *Hitler, König Carol, und Marschall Antonescu: Die Deutsch-Rumänischen Beziehungen, 1938–1944.* Wiesbaden: Franz Steiner Verlag, 1954.

Hoensch, Jörg K. *Die Slowakei und Hitlers Ostpolitik: Hlinkas Slowakische Volkspartei zwischen Autonomie und Separation, 1938–1939.* Cologne-Graz: Böhlau Verlag, 1965.

———. *Die ungarische Revisionismus und die Zerschlagung der Tschechoslowakei.* Tübingen: Mohr, 1967.

Hofer, Walter. "Hitler und der Osten." *Deutsche Rundschau* 83 (1957): 798–802.

Hoffman, Emil. "Die Volkerwerdung der Deutschen im Südosten." *Zeitschrift für Politik* 30 (1940): 100–104.

Hoffman, George W. "South Tyrol: Borderland Rights and World Politics." *Journal of Central European Affairs* 7 (1947–48): 285–308.

Höhne, Heinz. *The Order of the Death's Head: The Story of Hitler's SS.* Translated by Richard Barry. 1966. Reprint. New York: Random House, 1971.

Homze, Edward L. *Foreign Labor in Nazi Germany.* Princeton: Princeton Univer-sity Press, 1967.

Hoptner, Jacob B. *Yugoslavia in Crisis, 1934–1941.* New York: Columbia Uni-versity Press, 1962.

Hory, Ladislaus, and Martin Broszat. *Der Kroatische Ustascha-Staat, 1941–1945.* Schriftenreihe der Vierteljahrshefte für Zeitgeschichte, no. 8. Stuttgart: Deutsche Verlags-Anstalt, 1964.

Hubatsch, Walther. "Die deutsche Berufsdiplomatie im Kriege: Um die dänische Souveränität, 1940–1943." *Aussenpolitik* 6 (1955): 170–80.

———. "Das Memelland und das Problem der Minderheiten." In *Die Deutschen Ostgebiete zur Zeit der Weimarer Republik.* Studien zum Deutschen im Osten, no. 3. Cologne-Graz: Böhlau Verlag, 1966.

Hüttenberger, Peter. *Die Gauleiter: Studie zum Wandel des Machtgefüges in der NSDAP.* Schriftenreihe der Vierteljahrshefte für Zeitgeschichte. Stuttgart: Deutsche Verlags-Anstalt, 1969.

Institut für Zeitgeschichte. *Gutachten des Instituts für Zeitgeschichte*, vol. 1. Mu-nich: Selbstverlag, 1958.

————. *Gutachten des Instituts für Zeitgeschichte*, vol. 2. Stuttgart: Deutsche Verlags-Anstalt, 1966.

Jablonowski, Horst. "Die Danziger Frage." In *Die Deutschen Ostgebiete zur Zeit der Weimarer Republik*, pp. 65–87. Studien zum Deutschtum im Osten, no. 3. Cologne-Graz: Böhlau Verlag, 1966.

Jäckel, Eberhard. *Frankreich in Hitlers Europa: Die deutsche Frankreichpolitik im Zweiten Weltkrieg*. Quellen und Darstellungen zur Zeitgeschichte, no. 14. Stuttgart: Deutsche Verlags-Anstalt, 1966.

————. *Hitler's Weltanschauung: A Blueprint for Power*. Translated by Herbert Arnold. Middletown, Conn.: Wesleyan University Press, 1972.

Jacobsen, Hans-Adolf. *Nationalsozialistische Aussenpolitik, 1933–1938*. Berlin and Frankfurt am Main: Alfred Metzner Verlag, 1968.

Jaensch, Erich. "Leben und Sterben der Volksgruppen in Polen." *Nation und Staat* 10, no. 8 (1937): 501–6.

Jahn, Egbert Kurt. *Die Deutschen in der Slowakei in den Jahren 1918 bis 1929: Ein Beitrag zum Nationalitätenproblematik*. Munich and Vienna: Oldenbourg, 1971.

Janowsky, Oscar I. *Nationalities and National Minorities*. New York: Macmillan, 1945.

Jelinek, Yeshayahu. "Bohemia-Moravia, Slovakia, and the Third Reich during the Second World War." *East European Quarterly* 3, no. 3 (1969): 229–38.

————. *The Parish Republic: Hlinka's Slovak People's Party, 1939–1945*. New York: Columbia University Press, 1976.

————. "Slovakia's Internal Policy and the Third Reich, August 1940–February 1941." *Central European History* 4, no. 3 (1971): 242–70.

Jeske, Reinbold. "Die Germanisierungspolitik des deutschen Faschismus gegenüber Polen." *Zeitschrift für Geschichtswissenschaft* 6 (1964): 994–1010.

————. "Die Germanisierungspolitik des Hitlerfaschismus im Polen während des zweiten Weltkrieges als Mittel der Ostexpansions des deutschen Imperialismus." *Jahrbuch für Geschichte der UdSSR und der Volksdemokratischen Länder Europas* 13 (1969): 35–56.

Joesten, Joachim. *Rats in the Larder: The Story of Nazi Influence in Denmark*. New York: G. P. Putnam's Sons, 1939.

Kamenetsky, Ihor. *Secret Nazi Plans for Eastern Europe: A Study of Lebensraum Policies*. New Haven: College and University Press, 1961.

Karmasin, Franz. "Deutsche in der Slowakei und der Karpaten-Ukraine." *Nation und Staat* 12, no. 4 (1939): 212–16.

Kater, Michael H. *Das "Ahnenerbe" der SS, 1935–1945: Ein Beitrag zur Kulturpolitik des Dritten Reiches*. Stuttgart: Deutsche Verlags-Anstalt, 1974.

————. "Die Artamenen—völkische Jugend in der Weimarer Republik." *Historische Zeitschrift* 213, no. 3 (1971): 577–638.

Kempner, Robert M. W. *SS im Kreuzverhör*. Munich: Rütten and Loening Verlag, 1964.

Kertész, Stephen. "The Expulsion of the Germans from Hungary: A Study in Postwar Diplomacy." *Review of Politics* 15, no. 2 (1953): 179–208.

Kettenacker, Lothar. *Nationalsozialistische Volkstumspolitik im Elsass*. Stuttgart: Deutsche Verlags-Anstalt, 1973.

Klein, Richard. "Die Umsiedlung der Gottscheer Deutschen." *Nation und Staat* 15–16, no. 5 (1942): 148–55.

Klietmann, K. G. *Die Waffen SS: Eine Dokumentation*. Osnabrück: Die freiwillige, 1965.

Kluke, Paul. "Nationalsozialistische Europaideologie." *Vierteljahrshefte für Zeitgeschichte* 3, no. 3 (1955): 240–75.

Koch, Fred C. *The Volga Germans: In Russia and the Americas from 1763 to the Present*. University Park: Penn State University Press, 1977.

Koehl, Robert L. *The Black Corps: The Structure and Power Struggles of the Nazi SS*. Madison: University of Wisconsin Press, 1983.

———. "The Character of the Nazi SS." *Journal of Modern History* 34, no. 3 (1962): 275–83.

———. "The Deutsche Volksliste in Poland, 1939–1945." *Journal of Central European Affairs* 15, no. 4 (1956): 354–66.

———. "Feudal Aspects of National Socialism." *American Political Science Review* 54, no. 4 (1960): 921–33.

———. "The Politics of Resettlement." *Western Political Quarterly* 6, no. 2 (1953): 231–42.

———. "A Prelude to Hitler's Greater Germany." *American Historical Review* 59, no. 1 (1953): 43–65.

———. *RKFDV: German Resettlement and Population Policy, 1939–1945; A History of the Reich Commission for the Strengthening of Germandom*. Cambridge: Harvard University Press, 1957.

———. "Toward an SS Typology: Social Engineers." *American Journal of Economics and Sociology* 18, no. 2 (1959): 113–26.

Kogon, Eugen. *Der SS Staat: Das System der deutschen Konzentrationslager*. Munich: Verlag Karl Alber, 1946.

Komjathy, Anthony, and Rebecca Stockwell. *German Minorities and the Third Reich: Ethnic Germans of East Central Europe between the Wars*. New York and London: Holmes and Meier, 1980.

Korzec, Pawel. "Polen und der Minderheitenschutzvertrag (1919–1934)." *Jahrbücher für Geschichte Osteuropas* 22 (1974): 515–55.

Kosinski, L. A. "Population Censuses in East-Central Europe in the Twentieth Century." *East European Quarterly* 5, no. 3 (1971): 279–301.

Kraeter, Dieter, and Hans Georg Schneege. *Die Deutschen in Osteuropa Heute*. Nachbarn in Ostmitteleuropa, no. 1. Bielefeld: Verlag Ernst und Werner Gieseking, 1970.

Král, Vaclav. "The Policy of Germanization Enforced in Bohemia and Moravia by the Fascist Invaders during the Second World War." *Historica* 2 (1960): 273–303.

Kramer, Juraj. "Ausländische Einflüsse auf die Entwicklung den slowakischen autonomischen Bewegung." *Historica* 3 (1961): 159–93.

Krausnick, Helmut. "Hitler und die Morde in Polen: Ein Beitrag zum Konflikt zwischen Heer und SS um die Verwaltung der besetzten Gebiete." *Vierteljahrs-hefte für Zeitgeschichte* 11, no. 2 (1963): 196–209.

———. "Legenden um Hitlers Aussenpolitik." *Vierteljahrshefte für Zeitgeschichte* 2, no. 3 (1954): 217–39.

Krausnick, Helmut, Hans Buchheim, Martin Broszat, and Hans-Adolf Jacobsen. *Anatomy of the SS State*. Translated by Richard Barry et al. 1969. Reprint. New York: Walker and Co., 1972.

Krekeler, Norbert. *Revisionsanspruch und geheime Ostpolitik der Weimarer Republik: Die Subventionierung der deutschen Minderheit in Polen, 1919–1933*. Schriftenreihe die Vierteljahrshefte für Zeitgeschichte. Stuttgart: Deutsche Verlags-Anstalt, 1973.

Krimper, Ronald L. "The Diplomatic Prelude to the Destruction of Yugoslavia." *East European Quarterly* 7, no. 2 (1973): 125–47.

Krofta, Emil. *Die Deutschen im Tschechoslowakischen Staate*. Prague: Orbis-Verlag, 1937.

Krupnyckyi, B. "Die Karpathen-Ukraine." *Nation und Staat* 12, no. 2 (1938): 73–80.

Kruszewski, Charles. "Germany's Lebensraum." *American Political Science Review* 34, no. 5 (1940): 964–75.

Kügelgen, Carlo von. "Kulturleistungen der Deutsch-Balten." *Nationalsozialistische Monatshefte* 10, no. 106 (1939): 3–10.

———. "Die Russlanddeutschen." *Nation und Staat* 12, nos. 6–7 (1939): 3–10.

Kuhn, Axel. *Hitlers aussenpolitisches Program: Entstehung und Entwicklung, 1919–1939*. Stuttgarter Beiträge zur Geschichte und Politik. Stuttgart: Ernst Klett Verlag, 1970.

Kulischer, Eugene M. *The Displacement of Population in Europe*. Montreal: International Labour Office, 1943.

———. *Europe on the Move: War and Population Changes, 1917–1947*. New York: Columbia University Press, 1948.

Lange, Friedrich. *Deutsches Volk in 15 Staaten*. Leipzig: Verlag Philipp Reclam, n.d.

———. *Ostland kehrt Heim*. Volksdeutsche Heimkehr, no. 5. Berlin-Leipzig: Nibelungen Verlag, 1940.

Lange, Karl. "Der Terminus 'Lebensraum' in Hitler's Mein Kampf." *Vierteljahrshefte für Zeitgeschichte* 13, no. 4 (1965): 426–37.

Latour, Conrad F. "Germany, Italy, and South Tyrol, 1938–45." *Historical Journal* 8, no. 1 (1965): 95–111.

———. *Südtirol und die Achse Berlin-Rom, 1938–1945*. Schriftenreihe der Vierteljahrshefte für Zeitgeschichte, no. 5. Stuttgart: Deutsche Verlags-Anstalt, 1962.

Lemberg, Eugen. "Zur Geschichte der deutschen Volksgruppen in Ostmitteleuropa." *Zeitschrift für Ostforschung* 1, no. 2 (1952): 321–45.

Lemkin, Raphael. *Axis Rule in Occupied Europe*. Washington, D.C.: Carnegie Endowment for International Peace, 1944.

Lerner, Daniel. *The Nazi Elite*. Hoover Institute Studies, Series B; Elite Studies, no. 3. Stanford: Stanford University Press, 1951.

Lettrich, Jozef. *History of Modern Slovakia*. New York: Frederick A. Praeger, 1955.

Leuschner, Joachim. *Volk und Raum: Zum Stil der nationalsozialistischen Aussenpolitik*. Göttingen: Vandenhoeck and Ruprecht, 1958.

Levine, Herbert S. *Hitler's Free City: A History of the Nazi Party in Danzig, 1925–39*. 1970. Reprint. Chicago: University of Chicago Press, 1973.

———. "Local Authority and the SS State: The Conflict over Population Policy in Danzig–West Prussia, 1939–1945." *Central European History* 2, no. 4 (1969): 331–55.

Liess, Otto. "Siebenbürgen tausend Jahre deutsche Kulturleistung." *National-sozialistische Monatshefte* 11, no. 127 (1940): 37–65.

Lipták, L'ubomír. "The Role of the German Minority in Slovakia in the Years of the Second World War." *Studia Historica Slovaca* 1 (1963): 150–78.

Loock, Hans-Dietrich. "Zur Grossgermanischern Politik des Dritten Reiches." *Vierteljahrshefte für Zeitgeschichte* 8, no. 1 (1960): 37–65.

Lück, Kurt. *Die Cholmer und Lubliner Deutschen kehren Heim ins Vaterland*. Posen: 1940.

Lumans, Valdis O. "The Ethnic German Minority of Slovakia and the Third Reich, 1938–45." *Central European History* 15, no. 3 (1982): 266–97.

———. "The Military Obligation of the Volksdeutsche of Eastern Europe towards the Third Reich." *East European Quarterly* 23, no. 3 (1989): 305–23.

———. "The Nordic Destiny: The Peculiar Role of the German Minority in North Schleswig in Hitler's Plans and Policies for Denmark." *Scandinavian Journal of History* 15 (1991): 109–23.

Lundin, C. Leonard. "The Nazification of the Baltic German Minorities." *Journal of Central European Affairs* 7 (1947): 1–28.

Luža, Radomir. *The Transfer of the Sudeten Germans: A Study of Czech-German Relations, 1933–1962*. New York: New York University Press, 1937.

Macartney, Carlyle A. *Hungary and Her Successors: The Treaty of Trianon and Its Consequences, 1919–1937*. London: Oxford University Press, 1937.

———. *National States and National Minorities*. London: Oxford University Press, 1934.

———. *October Fifteenth: A History of Modern Hungary, 1929–1945*. 2 vols. 2d ed., 1956. Reprint. Edinburgh: University Press, 1961.

McKale, Donald M. *The Swastika outside Germany*. Kent: Kent State University Press, 1977.

Mamatey, Victor S., and Radomir Luža, eds. *A History of the Czechoslovak Republic, 1918–1948*. Princeton: Princeton University Press, 1973.

Manvell, Roger, and Heinrich Fraenkel. *Heinrich Himmler*. London: Heinemann, 1965.

Markmann, Fritz. "Die Zips." *Zeitschrift für Geopolitik*, no. 11 (1941): 601–11.

Marrotte, Paul Arthur. "Germany at the League of Nations Council: The Defense of German Minority Groups in Poland, Memel, and Yugoslavia." Ph.D. dissertation. University of North Carolina, Chapel Hill, 1953.

Marrus, Michael R. *The Unwanted: European Refugees in the Twentieth Century.* New York: Oxford University Press, 1985.

Mastny, Vojtech. *The Czechs under Nazi Rule: The Failure of National Resistance, 1939–1942.* New York: Columbia University Press, 1971.

Mekarski, Stefan. "Die Südostgebiete polens zur Zeit der deutschen Besatzung (Juni 1941 bis Juni 1943): Verwaltung und Nationalitätprobleme." *Jahrbücher für Geschichte Osteuropas* 16 (1968): 381–428.

Melzer, Roland. "Der Kriegseinsatz der deutschen Volksgruppen." *Nation und Staat* 15–16, nos. 10–11 (1942): 342–51.

Miege, Wolfgang. *Das Dritte Reich und die deutsche Volksgruppe in Rumänien, 1933–38: Ein Beitrag zur nationalsozialistischen Volkstumspolitik.* Frankfurt am Main: Peter Lang, 1972.

Mikuš, Joseph A. "Slovakia between Two World Wars." *Slovak Studies, Historica* 1 (1961): 95–104.

Mollo, Andrew. *A Pictorial History of the SS, 1923–1945.* London: Macdonald's and Jane's, 1975.

Müller, K. V. "Die Bedeutung des deutschen Blutes in Südosteuropa." *Südostdeutsche Forschungen* 3 (1938): 582–623.

Müller, Sepp. *Von der Ansiedlung bis zur Umsiedlung: Das Deutschtum Galiziens, insbesondere Lembergs, 1772–1940.* Johann Gottfried Herder Institut, no. 54. Marburg/Lahn: Ernst Bahr, 1961.

Mulligan, Timothy. *The Politics of Illusion and Empire: German Occupation Policy in the Soviet Union, 1942–1943.* New York: Praeger, 1988.

Nellner, Werner. "Das Schicksal der 'deutschen Minderheite' in Niederschlesien unter polnischer Verwaltung." *Zeitschrift für Ostforschung* 17, no. 2 (1968): 292–96.

Neumann, Rudolf. "Die Lage der Deutschtumsreste in östlichen Mitteleuropa nach 1945." *Zeitschrift für Ostforschung* 1, no. 3 (1952): 427–32.

Neusüss-Hunkel, Ermenhild. *Die SS.* Hannover and Frankfurt am Main: Norddeutsche Verlagsanstalt, 1956.

Niehaus, Heinrich. "Die Osthilfe." In *Die Deutschen Ostgebiete zur Zeit der Weimarer Republik*, pp. 187–211. Studien zum Deutschtum im Osten, no. 3. Cologne-Graz: Böhlau Verlag, 1966.

Norton, Donald H. "The Influence of Karl Haushofer on Nazi Ideology." Ph.D. dissertation. Clark University, 1963.

———. "Karl Haushofer and the German Academy, 1925–1945." *Central European History* 1, no. 1 (1968): 81–99.

Nyomarkay, Joseph. *Charisma and Factionalism in the Nazi Party.* Minneapolis: University of Minnesota Press, 1967.

Orend, Misch. "Deutsches Bauerntum in Rumänien." *Nationalsozialistische Monatshefte* 10, no. 109 (1939): 307–10.

Orlow, Dietrich. *The History of the Nazi Party, 1919–1945.* 2 vols. Pittsburgh: University of Pittsburgh Press, 1973.

———. *The Nazis in the Balkans: A Case Study in Totalitarian Politics.* Pittsburgh: University of Pittsburgh Press, 1968.

Paetel, Karl O. "Die SS: Ein Beitrag zur Soziologie des Nationalsozialismus." *Vierteljahrshefte für Zeitgeschichte* 2, no. 1 (1954): 1–33.

Paikert, Geza C. *The Danube Swabians: German Populations in Hungary. Rumania, and Yugoslavia and Hitler's Impact on Their Patterns.* The Hague: Martinus Nijhoff, 1967.

Perman, Dagmar. *The Shaping of the Czechoslovak State.* Leyden: Brill, 1962.

Peterson, Edward N. *The Limits of Hitler's Power.* Princeton: Princeton University Press, 1969.

Plieg, Ernst-Albrecht. *Das Memelland, 1920–1939.* Würzburg: Holzner Verlag, 1962.

Pohl, Otmar. "Die Slowakei lösst die Judenfrage." *Nation und Staat* 15, no. 2 (1941): 56–58.

Poland, Western Press Agency. *Transfer of the German Population from Poland: Legend and Reality.* Warsaw: Western Press Agency, 1966.

Polish Ministry of Information. *The Quest for German Blood: Policy of Germanization in Poland.* Polish Studies and Sketches, no. 5. London: Polish Ministry of Information, 1943.

Rabius, Wilhelm. "Die Kirche in Volkstumskampf des Ostens." *Zeitschrift für Politik* 29 (1939): 301–15.

Radspieler, Tony. *The Ethnic German Refugee in Austria, 1945 to 1954.* The Hague: Martinus Nijhoff, 1955.

Ramme, Alwin. *Der Sicherheitsdienst der SS: Zu einer Funktion im faschistischen Machtapparat und im Besatzungsregime des sogenannten Generalgouvernements Polen.* Berlin: Deutscher Militärverlag, 1969.

Rauschning, Hermann. *Men of Chaos.* New York: G. P. Putnam's Sons, 1942.

Reider, Frederic. *La Waffen SS: Histoire de la SS par L'Image.* Paris: Editions de la Pensée Moderne, 1975.

Reitlinger, Gerald. *The Final Solution: The Attempt to Exterminate the Jews of Europe, 1939–1945.* New York: Beechhurst Press, 1953.

———. *The House Built on Sand: The Conflicts of German Policy in Russia, 1939–45.* New York: Viking Press, 1960.

———. *The SS: Alibi of a Nation, 1922–1945.* London: Heinemann, 1956.

Rhode, Gotthold. "Die Deutschen im Osten nach 1945." *Zeitschrift für Ostforschung* 2, no. 2 (1953): 371–88.

Rich, Norman. *Hitler's War Aims: Ideology, the Nazi State, and the Course of Expansion.* 2 vols. New York: W. W. Norton, 1973.

Richter, Hans. *Heimkehrer: Bildberichte von der Umsiedlung der Volksdeutschen aus Bessarabien, Rumänien, aus der Süd-Bukowina und aus Litauen.* Berlin: Zentralverlag der NSDAP, 1941.

Rimscha, Hans von. "Paul Schiemann als Minderheitenpolitiker." *Vierteljahrshefte für Zeitgeschichte* 4, no. 1 (1956): 43–61.

———. *Das Staatswerdung Lettlands und das Baltische Deutschtum.* Riga: N.p., 1939.

———. *Die Umsiedlung der Deutschbalten aus Lettland im Jahre 1939.* Baltische Hefte. Hannover-Döhren: N.p., 1958.

————. "Zur Gleichschaltung den deutschen Volksgruppen durch das Dritte Reich." *Historische Zeitschrift* 182, no. 1 (1956): 29–63.

Ritter, Ernst. *Das Deutsche Ausland-Institut in Stuttgart, 1917–1945: Ein Beispiel deutscher Volkstumsarbeit zwischen den Weltkriegen.* Frankfurter Historische Abhandlungen, no. 14. Wiesbaden: Franz Steiner Verlag, 1976.

Röckel, H. "Bessarabien." *Zeitschrift für Politik* 28, no. 9 (1938): 563–73.

Rohrbach, Paul. *Deutschtum in Not! Die Schicksal der Deutschen in Europa ausserhalb des Reiches.* Berlin and Leipzig: Wilhelm Andermann Verlag, 1926.

Ronnenberger, Franz. "Fünf Jahre slowakischer Staat." *Zeitschrift für Politik* 34, nos. 3–4 (1944): 95–100.

————. "Die Kriegsleitung des Volksdeutschtums." *Zeitschrift für Politik* 33, no. 3 (1943): 184–91.

Rossipaul, Lothar. "Die deutsche Volksgruppe in der Slowakei." *Nation und Staat* 12, no. 12 (1939): 741–57.

Roucek, Joseph S. "German Geopolitiks." *Journal of Central European Affairs* 2, no. 2 (1942): 180–89.

Runge, Georg. "Zur Umsiedlung der Volksdeutschen." *Nation und Staat* 13, no. 4 (1940): 114–18.

Schacher, Gerhard. *Germany Pushes South-East.* London: Hurst and Blackett, 1937.

Schechtman, Joseph B. "The Elimination of German Minorities in Southeastern Europe." *Journal of Central European Affairs* 6 (1946–47): 154–66.

————. *European Population Transfers, 1939–1945.* New York: Oxford University Press, 1946.

————. "Resettlement of Transferred Volksdeutsche in Germany." *Journal of Central European Affairs* 7 (1947–48): 262–84.

Schickel, Alfred. "Wehrmacht und SS." *Wehrwissenschaftliche Rundschau* 19, no. 5 (1969): 241–64.

Schieder, Theodor. "Nationalstaat und Nationalitätenproblem." *Zeitschrift für Ostforschung* 1, no. 2 (1952): 161–81.

————. "Die Vertreibung der Deutschen aus dem Osten als wissenschaftliches Problem." *Vierteljahrshefte für Zeitgeschichte* 8, no. 1 (1960): 1–16.

Schnabel, Reimund. *Macht ohne Moral: Eine Dokumentation über die SS.* 2d ed. 1957. Reprint. Frankfurt am Main: Röderberg Verlag, 1958.

Schneefuss, Walter. *Deutschtum in Süd-Ost-Europa.* Leipzig: Wilhelm Goldmann Verlag, 1939.

Schröder, Hans-Jürgen. "Südosteuropa als 'Informal Empire' Deutschlands, 1933–1939: Das Beispiel Jugoslawien." *Jahrbücher für Geschichte Osteuropas* 23 (1975): 70–96.

Schubert, Günter. *Anfänge nationalsozialistischer Aussenpolitik.* Cologne: Verlag Wissenschaft und Politik, 1963.

Schubert, H. H. "Errichtung einer Volkstumsgrenze." *Volk und Rasse* 17, no. 4 (1942): 63–67.

Schuller, Franz. "Das deutsche Genossenschaftswesen Rumäniens in der Wende." *Nation und Staat* 12, nos. 6–7 (1939): 427–38.

Seabury, Paul. *The Wilhelmstrasse: A Study of German Diplomats under the Nazi Regime*. Berkeley: University of California Press, 1954.

Seeber, Eva. "Der Anteil der Minderheitsorganisation 'Selbstschutz' an den faschistischen Vernichtungsaktionen im Herbst und Winter 1939 in Polen." *Jahrbuch für Geschichte der sozialistischen Länder Europas* 13, no. 2 (1969): 3–34.

Sereni, Angelo P. "The Status of Croatia under International Law." *American Political Science Review* 35, no. 6 (1941): 1144–51.

Smelser, Ronald M. "The Betrayal of a Myth: National Socialism and the Financing of Middle Class Socialism in the Sudetenland." *Central European History* 5, no. 3 (1972): 256–77.

———. "Reich National Socialist and Sudeten German Party Elites: A Collective Biographical Approach." *Zeitschrift für Ostforschung* 23, no. 4 (1974): 639–60.

———. *The Sudeten Problem, 1933–1938: Volkstumspolitik and the Formulation of Nazi Foreign Policy*. Middletown: Wesleyan University Press, 1975.

Smith, Arthur L. *The Deutschtum of Nazi Germany and the United States*. The Hague: Martinus Nijhoff, 1965.

Smith, Bradley F. *Heinrich Himmler: A Nazi in the Making, 1900–1926*. Stanford: Hoover Institution Press, 1971.

Šnejdárek, Antonin. "The Beginning of the Sudeten Organizations in Western Germany after 1945." *Historica* 8 (1966): 235–52.

———. "The Participation of the Sudet-German Nazis in the Munich Tragedy." *Historica* 1 (1959): 241–65.

Sodeikat, Ernst. "Der Nationalsozialismus und die Danziger Opposition." *Vierteljahrshefte für Zeitgeschichte* 14, no. 2 (1966): 139–74.

Sohl, Klaus. "Die Kriegsvorbereitungen des deutschen Imperialismus in Bulgarien am Vorabend des zweiten Weltkrieges." *Jahrbuch für Geschichte der UdSSR und der Volksdemokratischen Länder Europas* 3 (1959): 91–119.

Sommer, Hellmut. *135,000 gewannen das Vaterland: Die Heimkehr der Deutschen aus Wolhynien, Galizien und dem Narewgebiet*. Volksdeutsche Heimkehr, no. 4. Berlin-Leipzig: Nibelungen Verlag, 1940.

Spira, Thomas. *German-Hungarian Relations and the Swabian Problem: From Karolyi to Gömbos, 1919–1936*. New York: Columbia University Press, 1977.

Stamati, Constantin. "Die Entwicklung des Wolgadeutschtums in 178 Jahren." *Nation und Staat* 15, no. 1 (1941): 3–9.

———. "Probleme des Memellandes." *Nation und Staat* 12, no. 2 (1938): 64–72.

Stein, George H. *The Waffen SS: Hitler's Elite Guard at War, 1939–1945*. Ithaca: Cornell University Press, 1966.

Steiner, Felix. *Die Freiwilligen: Idee und Opfergang*. Göttingen: Plesse Verlag, 1958.

Stelzer, Herbert. "Der Stand der deutschen Arbeit in Ungarn." *Nation und Staat* 14, nos. 7–8 (1941): 226–33.

Steyer, Stephan. "Das Deutschtum in Ungarn." *Nationalsozialistische Monatshefte* 10, no. 113 (1939): 692–97.

Stökl, Günther. *Osteuropa und die Deutschen: Geschichte und Gegenwart einer span-nungsreichen Nachbarschaft*. Oldenburg and Hamburg: Gerhard Stalling Verlag, 1967.

Stone, Julius. *International Guarantee of Minority Rights*. London: Oxford University Press, 1932.

Strassner, Peter. *Europäische Freiwillige: 5. SS-Panzer division Wiking*. Osnabrück: Munin Verlag, 1968.

Sundhaussen, Holm. "Zur Geschichte der Waffen SS in Kroatien, 1941–1945." *Südost-Forschungen* 30 (1971): 176–96.

Suško, Ladislav. "German Policy towards Slovakia and Carpatho-Ukraine in the Period from the September Crisis in 1938 up to the Splitting of Czechoslovakia in March 1939." *Historica Slovaca* 8 (1975): 111–55.

Svatosch, Franz. "Zum Untergang der böhmisch-deutschen Bourgeoisie." *Jahrbuch für Geschichte der sozialistischen Länder Europas* 15, no. 2 (1971): 83–98.

Sydnor, Charles W. "The History of the SS 'Totenkopfdivision' and the Postwar Mythology of the Waffen SS." *Central European History* 6, no. 4 (1973): 339–62.

———. *Soldiers of Destruction: The SS Death's Head Division, 1933–1945*. Princeton: Princeton University Press, 1977.

Tägil, Sven. *Deutschland und die deutsche Minderheit in Nordschleswig: Eine Studie zur deutschen Grenzpolitik, 1933–1939*. Stockholm: Svenska Bokförlaget, 1970.

Tenenbaum, Joseph. *Race and Reich: The Story of an Epoch*. New York: Twayne Publishers, 1956.

Thompson, Larry. "Lebensborn and the Eugenics Policy of the Reichsführer SS." *Central European History* 4, no. 1 (1971): 54–77.

Thoss, Alfred. "Das Deutschtum in Bessarabien und dem nördlichen Buchenland." *Nationalsozialistische Monatshefte* 11, no. 127 (1940): 626–30.

———. *Heimkehr der Volksdeutschen*. Berlin: Zentralverlag der NSDAP, 1942.

———. "Die Umsiedlung der Volksdeutschen aus Bessarabien, der Bukowina und der Dobrudscha." *Zeitschrift für Geopolitik*, no. 3 (1941): 164–67.

———. "Die Umsiedlung und Optionen im Rahmen der Neuordnung Europas." *Zeitschrift für Geopolitik*, no. 3 (1941): 125–36.

Tilkovsky, Lorant. "Die deutsche Minderheit in Ungarn in der Zeit des Faschismus vor dem zweiten Weltkrieg." *Jahrbuch für Geschichte der sozialistischen Länder Europas* 15, no. 2 (1971): 57–82.

Tönnesen, Johannes. "Aus dem deutsch-dänischen Grenzland." *Deutsche Rundschau* 81, no. 1 (1955): 11–15.

Der Treck der Volksdeutschen aus Wolhynien, Galizien und dem Narew-Gebiet. Büchen der Heimkehr, in commission of the Reichsführer SS. Berlin: Volk und Reich Verlag, 1941.

Uexküll-Güldenband, Ferdinand. "Der Todesweg der Deutschen in der Sowjetunion." *Nation und Staat* 8, no. 10 (1935): 628–33.

Verband Deutscher vereine im Ausland. *Wir Deutsche in der Welt*. Berlin: Verband Deutscher vereine im Ausland, 1939.

"Der Verwaltungsaufbau des Reichskommissariats Ostland und seine Voraussetzungen." *Nation und Staat* 15–16, no. 8 (1942): 262–69.

Viererbl, Karl. "Auslandsdeutsche Rundschau." *Nationalsozialistische Monatshefte* 10, no. 106 (1939): 80–84.

———. "Auslandsdeutsche Rundschau: Heimkehr der Baltendeutschen," *Nationalsozialistische Monatshefte* 10, no. 117 (1939): 1038–39.

Vnuk, František. "Slovakia's Six Eventful Months (October 1938-March 1939)." *Slovak Studies IV, Historica* 2 (1964): 7–16.

Vogelsang, Reinhard. *Der Freundeskreis Himmler.* Zürich and Frankfurt: Musterschmidt Göttingen, 1972.

Wachtsmuth, Wolfgang. *Von deutscher Arbeit in Lettland, 1918–1934.* 3 vols. Cologne: Comel Verlag, 1951–53.

Wagner, Gustav. *Die Deutsche in Litauen: Ihre kulturellen und wirtschaftlichen Gemeinschaft zwischen beiden Weltkriegen.* Marburg-Lahn: Herder Institut, 1959.

Waite, Robert G. L. *Vanguard of Nazism: The Free Corps Movement in Postwar Germany, 1918–1923.* 1952. Reprint. New York: W. W. Norton, 1969.

Wegner, Bernd. "Das Führerkorps der Waffen SS im Kriege." In *Das Deutsche Offizierkorps, 1860–1960,* edited by Hans Hubert Hofman. Boppard am Rhein: Harald Boldt, 1981.

Wehler, Hans-Ulrich. "Reichsfestung Belgrad: Nationalsozialistische 'Raumordnung' in Südosteuropa." *Vierteljahrshefte für Zeitgeschichte* 11, no. 1 (1963): 72–84.

Weinberg, Gerhard L. *The Foreign Policy of Hitler's Germany: Diplomatic Revolution in Europe, 1933–1936.* Chicago: University of Chicago Press, 1970.

———. *The Foreign Policy of Hitler's Germany: Starting World War II, 1937–1939.* Chicago: University of Chicago Press, 1980.

———. *Germany and the Soviet Union, 1939–1941.* Leyden: Brill, 1954.

Weingartner, James J. *Hitler's Guard: The Story of the Leibstandarte SS Adolf Hitler, 1933–1945.* Carbondale: Southern Illinois University Press, 1974.

———. "Sepp Dietrich, Heinrich Himmler, and the Leibstandarte SS Adolf Hitler, 1933–1938." *Central European History* 1, no. 3 (1968): 264–84.

Weiss, Hellmuth. "Das Volksgruppenrecht in Estland vor dem Zweiten Weltkriege." *Zeitschrift für Ostforschung* 1, no. 2 (1952): 253–56.

Weise, Hans Richard. *Auslanddeutsche Erneuerung.* Berlin: Volk und Reich Verlag, 1936.

Winkler, Wilhelm. *Deutschtum in aller Welt: Bevölkerungsstatistische Tabellen.* Vienna: Verlag Franz Deuticke, 1938.

———. *Statistisches Handbuch der europäischen Nationalitäten.* Vienna and Leipzig: Wilhelm Braumüller, 1931.

Winter, Eduard. *Die Deutschen in der Slowakei und in Karpathorussland.* Münster in Westfalen: Aschendorff, 1926.

Wiskemann, Elizabeth. *Czechs and Germans: A Study of the Struggle in the Historic Provinces of Bohemia and Moravia.* Oxford: Oxford University Press, 1938.

Wolfe, Henry C. *The German Octopus: Hitler Bids for World Power.* Garden City, N.Y.: Doubleday and Doran, 1938.

Wolfgramm, Eberhard. "Grenzlandkämpfer: Zur Ideologie, den historischen Wurzeln und den Hintergründen des sudetendeutschen Revanchismus."

Jahrbuch für Geschichte der UdSSR und der Volksdemokratischen Länder Europas 4 (1960): 9–39.

Wolter, Helmut. "Zur Volksbiologie der deutsche Volksgruppen: Bevölkerungs- und Volkstumsfragen in Ost- und Südosteuropa." *Nation und Staat* 13, no. 3 (1939): 82–96.

Wuescht, Johann. *Jugoslawien und das Dritte Reich: Eine dokumentierte Geschichte der deutsch-jugoslawischen Beziehungen von 1933 bis 1945.* Stuttgart: Seewald Verlag, 1969.

Zachar, L'udo. *Die jahrhundertalte Freundschaft zwischen Deutschen und Slowaken.* Schriftenreihe der Slowakisch-Deutschen Gesellschaft, no. 2. Bratislava: Slowakisch-Deutschen Gesellschaft, 1940.

Zantke, S. "Die Heimkehr der Wolhyniendeutschen." *Nationalsozialistische Monatshefte* 11, no. 120 (1940): 169–71.

Zipfel, Friedrich. "Schicksal und Vertreibung der Deutschen aus Ungarn, Rumänien und der Tschechoslowakei." *Jahrbuch für die Geschichte Mittel- und Ostdeutschland* 7 (1958): 379–93.

———. "Vernichtung und Austreibung der Deutschen aus den Gebieten östlich der Oder-Neisse-Linie." *Jahrbuch für die Geschichte Mittel- und Ostdeutschland* 3 (1954): 145–79.

Der Zug der Volksdeutschen aus Bessarabien und dem Nord-Buchenland. Bücher der Heimkehr, in commission of Reichsführer SS. Berlin: Volk und Reich Verlag, 1942.

INDEX

• • • • • • • • • • • • • • • • • • • •

Non-Aggression, 12, 19, 104, 112, 132, 158, 161, 171, 172
Nedić, Milovan, 232
Netherlands, 58, 123, 210
Neumann, Ernst, 91, 92
Neurath, Konstantin von, 41, 63
North Schleswig, 23; VoMi's prewar activities in, 124–27; VoMi's wartime activities in, 239–43; postwar situation, 260, 261

Oberlander, Theodor, 63, 64
Ossa. *See* Vereinigte Finanzkontore

Pancke, Gunther, 218–19
Panzer, Arnulf, 145–46
Pavelić, Ante, 239
Perthen, Karl-Heinrich, 147
Phleps, Arthur, 235
Pohl, Oswald, 200, 203
Poland, 10, 18, 19, 21, 22, 23, 26, 29, 55, 58, 61, 68, 71, 86, 87, 121, 131, 132; VoMi's prewar activities in, 93–100, 127; resettlement in, 116, 161, 165, 169, 171, 185, 187, 188, 195; RKFDV program in, 141, 144, 147, 151, 152, 154, 157, 158, 234, 245; evacuation of, 248, 249; expulsion of *Volksdeutsche* from, 257, 258, 259
Posen (Poznan), 23, 56, 94, 140, 154, 161, 186, 188, 189
Prinz Eugen Division, 216, 235, 238, 260
Protectorate of Bohemia-Moravia, 87, 195, 217, 255
Przemysl, 17, 18, 19, 20, 21, 30, 31, 39, 162, 163, 262
Puls, Adolf, 54, 143, 149

Radunski, Konrad, 140, 142, 170
Rasse und Siedlungshauptamt (RuSHA), 137, 189, 218, 246
Rauschning, Hermann, 46, 47
Reichardt, Oskar von, 93

Reichsführer SS. *See* Himmler, Heinrich
Reichssicherheitshauptamt (RSHA), 137
Reichskommissar für die Festigung deutschen Volkstums (RKFDV), 12, 13, 14; Himmler as RKFDV, 18, 66, 133–34; RKFDV office, 134–35; ties to VoMi, 135–37, 138, 142, 145, 146, 205, 206, 207, 213; SS influence, 149–50; resettlement program, 154, 155, 157, 158, 161, 163, 167, 169, 192, 196, 202, 203, 246; role in resettlements, 172, 173, 174, 175, 177, 180, 198; and Germanization, 185; and evacuation, 250, 253, 254, 255
Reinhardt (Fräulein), 141
Renthe-Fink, Cecil von, 240, 242
Ribbentrop, Joachim von: as Hitler's foreign policy expert, 35–36; friendship with Himmler, 36; enters *Volkstum* fight, 36–37, 38; role in founding VoMi, 41, 42, 43, 45, 54, 57, 66; relations with SS, 49, 53, 54, 65, 66; activities within minorities, 70, 78, 83, 87, 92, 97, 98; involved in resettlement, 158, 162, 166, 168, 172, 176; differences with Himmler, 207–8; paving way for Waffen SS recruitment, 215, 224, 229, 234, 238
Rimann, Waldemar, 139, 143, 200
Röhm purge, 48, 51
Rosenberg, Alfred, 30, 35, 36, 39, 162, 244
Roth, Hans Otto, 231, 232
Rüdiger, Wilhelm von, 105, 106, 140
Rumania, 10, 22, 29, 55, 58, 71, 226, 239, 256; VoMi's prewar activities in, 107–12, 116, 119, 120, 121; resettlement from, 171–75, 179, 188, 189, 196, 205; VoMi's wartime involvement in, 209, 220, 222, 227–32, 245; recruitment of Waffen SS, 216–17, 228–30, 234, 235, 237; evacuation of, 248, 251, 252, 253; postwar treatment of *Volksdeutsche*, 259

and Luxemburg, 179–82; activities in Soviet Union, 182–83, 243–49; RKFDV duties, 184; role in Germanization, 185–86; camp system, 186–88, 192–95, 200–202; role in processing, 189–92; settlement of resettlers, 195–98; dealings with non-Germans, 198–200; role in final solution, 202–4; activities in Serbia-Banat, 232–36; activities in Croatia, 236–39; performs evacuation, 250–55; final demise, 255–57; in overall perspective, 261–62. *See also* Waffen SS
Volksdeutscher Rat, 34, 35, 37

Waffen SS, 11, 13, 15, 188; serves Himmler's purposes, 18, 39; membership of VoMi personnel, 52, 55, 57, 138, 139, 149; recruitment in Estonia, 104; recruitment of *Volksdeutsche*, 206, 207, 208, 211–16; recruitment in Slovakia, 219–20; recruitment in Hungary, 224–26; recruitment in Rumania, 228–30; recruitment in Serbia-Banat, 234–35; recruitment in Croatia, 236–39; recruitment in Denmark, 241–42;

activities in Soviet Union, 246, 247, 248; Lorenz assumes command, 256
Wagner, Robert, 180, 181
Waldeck (Countess), 46, 47, 173
Warthegau, 48, 147, 161, 165, 172, 185, 186, 195, 196, 248, 249, 255
Wehofsich, Franz, 41, 54, 55, 63, 77
Wehrmacht, 39, 188, 212, 213, 214, 225, 235, 237, 244, 247, 248
Weibgen, Hans, 251, 252
Weidhaus, Anton, 147
Weimar Republic, 24, 25, 95
Wiesner, Rudolf, 96, 99
Wilhelmstrasse. *See* Foreign Ministry
Wolff, Karl, 40, 41, 49, 155, 164
Wrangell, Wilhelm von, 103

Yugoslavia, 10, 22, 23, 29, 55, 58, 71, 77, 172, 174, 195, 222, 223, 256; VoMi's prewar involvement, 117–22; resettlement from Croatia and Slovenia, 175–78, 179, 205; recruitment for Waffen SS, 215, 216, 234–38; VoMi's wartime activities in, 232–39; evacuation from, 253; expulsions from, 259, 260

Printed in Great Britain
by Amazon